WITHDRAWN

D1715525

# SAXOPHONE SOLOISTS
# AND THEIR MUSIC
# 1844–1985

# SAXOPHONE SOLOISTS
## AND THEIR MUSIC
## 1844–1985

*An Annotated Bibliography*

## HARRY R. GEE

INDIANA UNIVERSITY PRESS
*Bloomington*

Manufactured in the United States of America

Library of Congress Cataloging in Publication Data

Gee, Harry R.
Saxophone soloists and their music, 1844–1985.
Bibliography: p.
Includes index.
1. Saxophone music—Bibliography.   2. Saxophonists—Biography.
3. Music—Bio-bibliography.   I. Title.
ML128.S247G4   1986        016.788′66        85-45537
ISBN 0-253-35091-3
1   2   3   4   5   90   89   88   87   86

# CONTENTS

# PREFACE

In the last fifteen years, the saxophone has enjoyed a rebirth of interest. This can be seen in the many artists' activities in recitals and concerts and the growth of specialized organizations for saxophonists. The first organization, the World Saxophone Congress, began in Chicago in December, 1969, and national affiliated groups elsewhere soon followed. These have become known as the North American Saxophone Alliance, the Association des Saxophonistes de France, the Clarinet and Saxophone Society of Great Britain, and the Arbeitsgruppe Saxophon. The last organization was established during the Seventh World Saxophone Congress (July, 1982) in Nuremberg, Germany.

Student interest in learning the saxophone has been generated by hearing more recordings of saxophonists, seeing more use of the instrument in various entertainment media, and encouragement of jazz styles by high school bands and other entertainment groups. All of these activities have led to an ever-increasing number of students who wish to learn and perform on the saxophone. Many universities now have full-time saxophone specialists to teach and guide the growing number of music students. A historical reference about past and present American and European saxophone soloists and their music will be of value in these times of growing awareness of our youngest instrument.

Adolphe Sax (1814-1894), one of the greatest original geniuses in the history of wind-instrument making, patented many of his creations in Paris in the nineteenth century; the saxophone is the last major contribution to our modern group of wind instruments. After 1846, the year of the patent for the saxophone family, tutors, compositions, and arrangements for the instruments (in solo

and in ensemble) quickly followed.  Additionally, the saxophone began to be utilized in opera and in French military
bands.  This early creativity began in France, and publications for the saxophone took another large step after
1919 in the United States.  Although much of this early
literature is out of print, I have sought information
about titles, composers, dates of compositions, and later
reprints in addition to contemporary compositions dedicated to living performers.

In recent years, numerous books on the saxophone by
Léon Kochnitzky, Marcel Perrin, Larry Teal, Jaap Kool,
Jean-Marie Londeix, Wally Horwood, and Eugene Rousseau,
and the important dissertation by Frederich Hemke--to say
nothing of other dissertations, pamphlets, and articles
by other writers--indicate that saxophonists, both professional and amateur, along with other performers and
teachers, have had a consistent curiosity for more knowledge about the instrument.  These writings have usually
yielded much information about the construction of the
saxophone, its early acceptance, the many lawsuits and
tribulation of its inventor, and its rebirth in the United
States.  The books, 125 Ans de Musique pour Saxophone and
Musique pour Saxophone, Volume II by J. M. Londeix give
much valuable information about literature for the instrument.  Rousseau's book Marcel Mule:  His Life and the
Saxophone, gives interesting data about the development of
saxophone playing and literature in France.  However,
there has not yet been a book published about saxophone
soloists and music written for them.

A study of saxophone literature should also include
information about saxophone soloists.  Although some performers wrote for the instrument, many instrumentalists
inspired composers to contribute major works, ensembles,
and smaller solos to the repertoire.  In addition to the
research about early saxophonists in Europe and the United
States, a second part of my investigation has been to contact living saxophone soloists and specialized teachers.
I sent about six hundred questionnaires to American, Canadian, European, and Asian artists and solicited the
following information:

    Date and place of birth
    Principal teachers, influence, and education
    Debut or beginning of concert career
    Published compositions and arrangements by the soloist
    Compositions dedicated to the artists by composers
        (with dates of premieres, if known)
    Solo or ensemble recordings which are currently
        available.

Many saxophonists are aware of the rich legacy of
soloists such as E. A. Lefèbre, H. Benne Henton, Rudy
Wiedoeft, Jascha Gurewich, and Elise Hall.  These saxo-

phonists, along with many performers on other instruments, have been unsung heroes, and information about their lives and careers has not been included in the standard musical encyclopedias.  I hope that readers will find information in this book about important saxophonists and composers which will assist in future research.  It is certain that many composers have made important contributions to musical literature as a result of their contacts with the great saxophonists of this century who are still living--Sigurd Rascher, Marcel Mule, Cecil Leeson--and many young emerging artists who continue to defend and claim an equal place for recognition of the saxophone in serious musical expression.

# ACKNOWLEDGMENTS

Completion of this book was made possible by the assistance and cooperation of a number of individuals. Some financial aid from Indiana State University was received in the form of two faculty research grants during the summers of 1982 and 1983. Securing much information on twentieth-century saxophonists and composers was made possible with the help of the Reference Department and the Department of Inter-library loans of the university library.

Recent and specialized information, not in books of musical literature, was obtained directly from the publication of the North American Saxophone Alliance and the Association des Saxophonistes de France. The following libraries generously provided information: Edwin A. Fleisher Collection of Orchestral Music of the Free Library of Philadelphia and the Curtis Institute of Music Library (early saxophone soloists with the Philadelphia and Boston Orchestras). I am also grateful for the cooperation and materials received about contemporary saxophone music written in the United States and various countries from the following national music centers: Gerald Deakin, American Society of Composers, Authors and Publishers, American Music Center, Belgian Centre for Music Documentation, Canadian Music Center, Centre de Documentation de la Musique Contemporaire (in France), and the Music Information Centers from Holland, Finland, Norway, Sweden, and Poland.

I should also like to acknowledge the assistance and the sharing of information by the following individuals: Irving Levin, Rego Park, New York, about early saxophone recordings; Dr. Larry Teal, Professor Emeritus, University of Michigan, about the early days of his teaching career; and Lee Patrick, for information about Sigurd and Carina

Rascher.  Other details about early saxophone playing in
America have been made available by Dr. Cecil Leeson and
his Archival Saxophone Collection in the Bracken Library
at Ball State University; Bert Gould, from San Francisco
and a long-time friend of Clyde Doerr; Don Diogena, American Federation of Musicians, Local 77, Philadelphia;
Stephen Trier, former student and friend of Michael Krein;
Paul Bierley, a Sousa historian, for dates about saxophonists with the Sousa Band; Daniel Deffayet, Professor at
the Conservatoire National Supérieur de Musique, for
recent information about Solos de Concours; François
Daneels, Professor, Conservatoire Royal de Musique, for
information and recordings from Belgium; Jean-Marie
Londeix, Professor at the National Conservatory in Bordeaux, France, for his enthusiastic support and information
about dates and addresses of saxophonists in Europe and
Japan; Jean-Marie Paul, at the University of Strasbourg,
for his valuable research at the Bibliothèque Nationale de
Musique, for dates and titles of early saxophone solos in
France; and Michael Jacobson, past Membership Director,
North American Saxophone Alliance, for the complete 1982-83
membership list.

As editor of "Clarinet and Saxophone Topics" for The
School Musician, I have been fortunate to receive many
saxophone publications for review from the Theodore Presser Company, sole agent for many European publications,
and additional saxophone scores and catalogs from other
publishers.  Many of these releases have yielded information about new titles and contemporary composers for the
saxophone.

Last, but not least, should be mentioned the assistance given me by my wife, Marie Louise Gee, who, in addition to typing the final draft, did the correspondence
in French.  Valuable and professional help in proofreading
and editing was provided by Thomas L. Liley, editor of
The Saxophone Symposium, and Mary Ellen Gee, Division of
the General College of the University of Minnesota.
Thanks are due to all the saxophonists and composers who
supplied additional information in the form of brochures,
recordings, press notices, and lists of music dedicated to
and premiered by them along with their questionnaires.

# ABBREVIATIONS

| | |
|---|---|
| A | $E^b$ alto saxophone (when used in an ensemble) |
| AATB | saxophone quartet (two altos, tenor, and baritone) |
| ATB | saxophone trio (alto, tenor, and baritone) |
| ABC | American Broadcasting Corporation |
| acc. | accompaniment; accompanist |
| adv. | advanced (level) |
| alto | alto (voice) |
| app. | appearance; appeared |
| arr. | arranger; arrangement |
| ASCAP | American Society of Composers, Authors, and Publishers |
| AsSaFra | Association des Saxophonistes de France |
| ass'n | association |
| assoc. | associate; associated |
| asst. | assistant |
| avail. | available |
| | |
| B | $E^b$ baritone saxophone (when used in an ensemble) |
| b | flat (musical symbol) |
| b. | born |
| B.A. | Bachelor of Arts |
| bar. | baritone (voice) |
| BBC | British Broadcasting Corporation |
| bcl. | bass clarinet |
| beg. | beginning (level) |
| B.M.Ed. | Bachelor of Music Education |
| B.M. | Bachelor of Music |
| bn. | bassoon |
| br. | brass instrument(s) |
| B.S. | Bachelor of Science |
| Bs. | $B^b$ bass saxophone (when used in an ensemble) |

BSO                         Boston Symphony Orchestra

c.                          circa
c.a.                        cor anglais
Cb                          E$^b$ contra bass saxophone (when used in an
                               ensemble)
cb. cl.                     contra bass clarinet
cbn.                        contrabassoon
CBC                         Canadian Broadcasting Corporation
CBS                         Columbia Broadcasting System
cel.                        celeste
ch.                         chamber (ensemble)
chor.                       chorus
cl.                         clarinet (B$^b$ unless otherwise specified)
CNRM                        Conservatoire National Régional de Musique
CNSM                        Conservatoire National Supérieur de
                               Musique (Paris)
comm.                       commissioned
comp.                       composer; composed
cond.                       conductor; conducted
corp.                       corporate; corporation
cym.                        cymbal

d.                          died; deceased
db.                         double bass
DC                          District of Columbia
ded.                        dedicated
dept.                       department
D.Hum.                      Doctor of Humane Letters
dipl.                       diploma
dir.                        director; directed
div.                        division
D.M.A.                      Doctor of Musical Arts
D.Mus.                      Doctor of Music

ed.                         editor; edited
Ed.D.                       Doctor of Education
Ed.M.                       Master of Education
educ.                       education; educated; educational
elem.                       elementary (level)
ens.                        ensemble
euph.                       euphonium; baritone horn

fac.                        faculty
fl.                         flute
fl-a.                       alto flute

gen.                        general
govt.                       government
grad.                       graduate; graduated
guit.                       guitar

hn.                         horn
hon.                        honor; honorary
hp.                         harp

| | |
|---|---|
| inc. | incorporate; incorporated |
| incl. | including; included |
| interm. | intermediate (level) |
| instr. | instrument; instrumental |
| intro. | introduction |
| | |
| Ltd. | Limited |
| | |
| M.A. | Master of Arts |
| mar. | marimba |
| M.Ed. | Master of Education |
| MENC | Music Educators National Conference |
| mgr. | manager |
| M.M. | Master of Music |
| M.M.Ed. | Master of Music Education |
| mov't | movement |
| ms. | manuscript(s) |
| MTNA | Music Teachers National Association |
| | |
| NACWPI | National Association of College Wind and Percussion Instructors |
| NAJE | National Jazz Education Association |
| nar. | narrator; narrated |
| NASA | North American Saxophone Alliance |
| NBC | National Broadcasting Corporation |
| N.Y. | New York State |
| N.Y.C. | New York City |
| | |
| ob. | oboe |
| OP | out of print |
| orch. | orchestra(s) |
| org. | organ |
| | |
| per. | percussion |
| perf. | performer; performed |
| pf. | piano |
| Ph.D. | Doctor of Philosophy |
| Phil. | Philharmonic |
| pic. | piccolo |
| prem. | premiere; premiered |
| prin. | principal |
| prof. | professor |
| pts. | parts (from a musical score) |
| publ. | publication(s); publish(ed) |
| | |
| quar. | quartet |
| quin. | quintet |
| q.v. | which see |
| | |
| RCA | Radio Corporation of America |
| rec'd | received |
| rev. | revision; revised |
| | |
| S | B$^b$ soprano saxophone (when used in an ensemble) |

| | |
|---|---|
| SACEM | Société des Auteurs, Compositeurs, et Editeurs |
| SATB | saxophone quartet (soprano, alto, tenor and baritone) |
| sax | saxophone (alto, unless otherwise specified) |
| sax-b. | baritone saxophone |
| sax-bs. | bass saxophone |
| sax-cb. | $E^b$ contra bass saxophone |
| saxes | saxophones |
| sax-s. | soprano saxophone |
| sax-sp. | sopranino saxophone |
| sax-t. | tenor saxophone |
| sm. | small (chamber orchestra) |
| soc. | society |
| sop. | soprano (voice) |
| Sp. | Sopranino saxophone (when used in an ensemble) |
| str. | string |
| strs. | strings; string orchestra |
| SUNY | State University of New York |
| symph. | symphony; orchestra |
| synth. | synthesizer |
| T | $B^b$ tenor saxophone (when used in an ensemble) |
| ten. | tenor (voice) |
| tim. | timpani |
| tpt. | trumpet |
| tran. | transcribe(d); transcription |
| trans. | translated; translation |
| trb. | trombone |
| TV | television |
| U. | University; universities |
| U.S.A. | United States of America |
| USSR | Union of Soviet Socialist Republics |
| vcl. | violoncello |
| vib. | vibraphone |
| vla. | viola |
| vn. | violin |
| w. | wind |
| WSC | World Saxophone Congress |
| ww. | woodwind(s) |
| xyl. | xylophone |

Note: Major keys are given in capital letters ($B^b$ = B-flat major); minor keys are given in lower-case letters ($b^b$ = B-flat minor).

# SAXOPHONE SOLOISTS
# AND THEIR MUSIC
# 1844–1985

# 1.
# A Brief Historical Background

Antoine-Joseph Sax, who became known as Adolphe Sax, was born 6 November 1814 in the picturesque city of Dinant on the Meuse river, under French rule.  This southern part of today's Belgium had been part of France for 17 years as a result of the Treaty of Campoformio, signed in October, 1797.  (This peace treaty between France and Austria ceded to France all the latter's claims in the Low Countries.)

Charles-Joseph Sax (Adolphe's father) studied architecture.  At the age of 15, he began work as an apprentice cabinet maker; he also performed as an amateur musician with a local music society, playing the serpent.  Annoyed at having to use a borrowed instrument, he studied the serpent's construction and felt he could make a fair replica; this was an exercise to be well remembered in later years. With the defeat of Napoleon and the First Empire (at the Battle of Waterloo in 1815), the factory where Charles Sax worked was closed, and he moved his family to Brussels. During the years from 1815 to 1820, he turned his combined skills of draftsman, craftsman, and engineer to good account, first with the making of serpents and flutes, and then by additionally making clarinets, bassoons, and brass instruments.  When he was 27, a great honor was conferred upon Charles by King William I:  he was appointed the official instrument maker to the court of the Netherlands-- a position that carried with it considerable financial assistance.  He soon became known as a maker of instruments comparable to the best of Germany and France.

As a child, Adolphe was able to make toys from odd bits of metal in his father's workshop.  A wise father, Charles Sax encouraged his son to become familiar with the shape and structure of brass and woodwind instruments, and before his early teens, the boy was able to drill pieces of a clarinet to perfection as well to perform other

tasks connected with the making of keys and parts of instruments.  At 14, after completing a good formal education, Adolphe became a music student, but not at the Royal
Conservatory, as many contemporary biographers state,
since this institution was not founded until 1832; its
forerunner was called the Royal School of Singing.[1]  Apart
from instruction in the vocal arts, he studied the flute
with Professor Labou, and later took up the clarinet with
Valentine Bender (1801-1873), a German-born clarinetist
who was the Belgian Guides bandmaster.  Bender was an excellent teacher and Sax soon showed potential virtuosity.
(Another famous pupil was Henri Wuille, 1822-1871, who
was born in Antwerp; I will speak of him later, because
he became an international artist performing on the clarinet and the bass clarinet, as well as the saxophone.)
There is little doubt that Sax could have made a successful career as a clarinet virtuoso and achieved a life of
relative tranquility.  However, his manual skills and in-
ventiveness won out.

As an advanced player, he could appreciate the many
flaws inherent in the clarinets and bass clarinets of the
day; it was natural that he should address himself to experiments and modifications to improve their tone quality
and solve their acoustical problems.  When he was 16, his
first entries were displayed at the Brussels Exhibition
of 1830, and his two flutes and a clarinet, all made of
ivory, received favorable comment.  Later, at the 1835 Exhibition, his 24-key clarinet received honorable mention.
The original specifications of his bass clarinet were dated
19 June 1838 (his father deserves much credit for Adolphe's
early work on boring techniques and study of proportions);
the bore of the new instrument was far superior to that of
any other bass clarinet and has remained unrivaled to this
day.

In 1839, when still only 25, Sax read in the newspaper
that Franco Dacosta (1778-1866), a well-known clarinetist
in Paris, proposed to exhibit and play in various countries
a bass clarinet which he had helped perfect with Louis-
Auguste Buffet.  This caused the young man much agitation,
because he was convinced that his own was vastly superior.
He packed his bass clarinet and some other instruments and
set off for the French capital.  In addition to winning
over Dacosta (who gave up the projected tour and eventually
acquired a Sax instrument himself), his charm, good looks,
and sincerity opened the door to many important contacts
and such life-long friends as Meyerbeer, Berlioz, Halévy,
Kastner, and others.  Reluctantly returning to Brussels,
Sax, like many before and since, carried Paris in his
heart.  The encouragement given him by the famous composers
and people interested in the improvement of military band
instruments must have made Brussels seem dull by compari-
son.  It was soon time for the 1841 Belgian Exhibition,
and he entered several of his woodwind and brass creations,

including the clarinets of advanced design and his bass
clarinet.

Hardly had Sax achieved the acoustical reform of these
instruments when he saw the possibility of applying some
of the same principles of sound production to another form:
a conical-shaped reed instrument made of brass.  Prelimi-
nary work on the saxophone was completed, and it would
also have been exhibited had it not been damaged at the
last moment.  Although the examining committee was de-
lighted with his instruments and recommended Adolphe for
the highest award, the Central Jury refused to grant him
the First Gold Medal on the grounds that he was too young.
Disgusted, Sax said, "If I am too young for the gold medal,
I am too old for the silver," and he was resolved not to
spend another year in Brussels.  A few months later, in
the spring of 1842, he arrived in Paris (his father finally joined him there in 1853).  Although on his arrival he
had very little money and great ambitions, his reputation
among musicians was already solidly established and his
influential friends provided him with funds to begin a
factory on rue St. Georges.  About his life in Paris, one
of his biographers, Albert Remy, summarizes:

> . . . a strange life began for Sax; a prodigious, tormented
> existence, darkened by dire experiences, and upheld with cou-
> rage and fortitude.  The young inventor--he was not twenty-
> eight--had to pay the ransom for his genial creativeness; he
> had to face the envy and jealousy, the wrath and hatred of his
> rivals and colleagues; he underwent all kinds of misery, suf-
> fering and affliction.  Glory was to be his reward, later, much
> later, in the course of his long career.[2]

There is no doubt that Adolphe Sax took his early saxophone to Paris; conceived in Belgium, it was perfected in
Paris and the family of saxophones was patented on 28 June
1846.  Even before the French Patent of the saxophone
family, contemporary composers and friends of Adolphe Sax
were impressed by the original tone quality and blending
possibilities of the instrument.  Among these early ad-
mirers, in 1844, were Berlioz (who transcribed his Chant
Sacré to demonstrate six of Sax's instruments, including
a bass saxophone in C) and Georges Kastner (1810-1867),
who included a part for the bass saxophone in his oratorio
Le dernier Roi de Juda.  A little later, other nineteenth-
century composers began, cautiously, to include the saxophone in their lyric scores.  Some of these outstanding
French composers were J. F. Halévy (Le Juif Errant, 1852),
Ambroise Thomas (Hamlet, 1868), Georges Bizet (L'Arlésienne
Suites, No. 1, 1872, and No. 2, 1879), Jules Massenet
(Hérodiade, 1881, and Werther, 1892), and Vincent d'Indy
(Fervaal, 1895).

According to Fridorich, "There were twenty-seven
symphonic and operatic compositions with saxophone parts

written by European composers from 1844 to 1919."[3]  This
is a conservative count, as Hemke lists no fewer than 55
compositions which included the saxophone by European composers during the same period.[4]  Kastner, more musicologist
than composer, was secretary to the commissioner of French
military music and wrote a method for saxophone during the
years 1844-1845 for instructional use in the regiments.
Included in this first tutor were two original works entitled Variations faciles et brillantes and Sextuor.  They
represent the earliest solo and ensemble works for the
saxophone and were dedicated to Sax; the Variations were
published in 1851 by Branous et Cie., and Sextuor was published by Ethos Publications in 1982.  Sigurd Rascher
realized the score of the sextet from the original instrumentation of two soprani in C, an alto in F, two bassi in
C, and one contrabasso in F, and changed it to present-day
instrumentation for B-flat and E-flat saxophones as follows:  two soprani, alto, tenor, baritone, and bass.
Hemke gives the identity of the first composition for alto
saxophone solo with band (based on Adolphe Sax's instrumentation) as Les Souvenirs de Paris by J. Garrouste.  He
states, "It was not profound, but the concept was unique."[5]

## Early Saxophone Instruction

     The sonorous saxophone, more suitable for out-of-
doors performance than the bassoon, was eagerly accepted
to play an increasing role in French military and civilian
bands.  By 1867, saxophones had become a regular part of
infantry and cavalry bands as well as civilian fanfares.
According to Hemke,

>     Saxophone instruction was not confined to Paris alone and it
> was undoubtedly taught at the Geneva Conservatory prior to the
> 1850s. . . .  Bernard Bellax, who won a "Prix de Virtuosité"
> on saxophone in 1850 at the Geneva Conservatory, produced a
> good saxophone trill chart.[6]

     Before the older style Gymnase Musical Militaire was
suppressed in 1855 in favor of the Conservatoire's training
of military musicians, Klosé and Cokken (a clarinetist and
a former bassoonist, respectively) taught saxophone as
early as 1846.  Student concours, or final competitions,
typify the educational system of France even to this day,
and prizes for saxophone students were awarded as early
as 1847.  Upon the death of Luigi Cherubini in 1842, King
Louis-Philippe appointed Daniel Auber as Director of the
Conservatoire.  The latter knew Adolphe Sax and his work;
under his guidance, the Minister of State created special
classes for military instruments at the Paris Conservatory
in 1857.  Sax was immediately named professor of saxophone
and served brilliantly in this capacity for the next 13
years, teaching more than 150 pupils. After the defeat of
the French in the Franco-Prussian War of 1870, the special

military classes were abolished for financial reasons.
This was a great disappointment for Sax and a disaster for
students of the saxophone.  Despite the lack of encouragement in Paris, saxophone instruction was carried on by
clarinetists in regional conservatories.  One of the oldest,
at Lille (created as early as 1803), continued to offer instruction in saxophone.  Eugène Gaubert, an 1858 graduate
in clarinet at Lille, became a saxophone soloist and began
teaching the saxophone at that conservatory in 1879.  Gaubert retired in 1900 and the class continued under Professor Lequy's direction.  Hemke says, "At the yearly final
examination each saxophone class performed an original
composition written for the instrument, many of which remain currently in print."[7]

Between 1832 and 1844, Nazaire Beeckman served as
Professor of Clarinet at the Brussels Conservatory, and
at the creation of the saxophone class in 1867, became
Professor of Saxophone.  He composed three clarinet solos,
two for saxophone, and a saxophone method; only two of
his original compositions remain in print: Deuxième Morceau de Concert, opus 17 (1888, dedicated to P. Ségouin)
and Concerto Militaire, opus 23 (1891, dedicated to C.
Bender); they are available from Billaudot.

Another clarinetist, C. Gustav Poncelet (1844-1903),
was well known throughout Belgium as a brilliant soloist.
A fine teacher of both clarinet and saxophone, he served
at the Conservatory from 1871.  When he officially retired in 1901, he continued to teach the saxophone until
1903, when that course was terminated for financial reasons.  Two of his many outstanding pupils, Joseph Schreurs
(1863-1921) and Gustav Langenus (1883-1951), became well-
known performers with symphony orchestras in Chicago and
New York, respectively.  Edward Mills (1865-1944), one of
his English students, carried the Belgian tradition back
to England.

## Early Saxophone Literature

Nineteenth-century woodwind solos reflected the popular interests and styles of the day; they consisted of
fantasias and variations or air variés (usually on opera
themes).  Most of the composers were conductors of military bands and they composed, arranged, and adapted many
of the early saxophone pieces from existing clarinet and
oboe solos or from string literature.  Adolphe Sax arranged works for his students at the Conservatoire and
also promoted the publication of solos and ensembles dedicated to him by various composers.  These publications
were advertised along with his woodwind and brass instruments; a few of the compositions were later published by
other editors.

Klosé and Mayeur

Many of the skilled soloists and teachers of the day
also composed and arranged music for publication, as well
as examination pieces for their classes.  Hyacinthe Klosé
(1808-1880), who enjoyed a long tenure as professor of
clarinet at the Paris Conservatory from 1838 to 1868, was
a prolific composer of clarinet solos, tutors, and studies.
He also took an interest in saxophone performance and
teaching and wrote two original solos, a few transcriptions, and methods for the latter instrument.  Some of
the material from Klosé's and Mayeur's methods can still
be found in the 1908 Carl Fischer edition of Paul de
Ville's Universal Method.  On pages 282-285, there is a
solo entitled "Morceau Caractéristique," attributed to
Klosé; however, research at the Bibliothèque Nationale in
Paris indicates that this work is not one of his original
saxophone solos.  He wrote two solos in 1858 and 1859 which
were published by A. Sax; both were entitled "Solo."  The
first work, dedicated to Sax, was edited in 1926 by the
bandmaster G. Corroyez for Leduc.  The second piece, written for soprano or alto saxophone, bears the dedication
"à Monsieur Escudie"; a string quartet accompaniment was
also written for this solo.  H. L. Escudie (1816-1881) was
a writer and musician who composed numerous pieces.  His
Third Fantasia (Theme and Variations), opus 46, was arranged for saxophone and piano or band by H. Prendiville
and published in the United States by Cundy-Bettoney in
1887.  Both the third and fourth Fantasies (for either
B-flat or E-flat saxophone and piano) are still available
from Molenaar in Holland.

Klosé's early fantaisies on melodies by Depas and
Schubert, dating from 1869 to 1880, were also revised by
Corroyez and published by Leduc.  Although these solos are
all out of print, his Méthode Complète des Saxophones
(written in 1877) was revised and enlarged by Eugène Gay,
a prominent clarinet professor at the Conservatory of Lyon,
for Leduc in 1950.  Molenaar's catalog also lists Klosé's
Méthode (in two volumes) edited by Buijzer.  Klosé wrote a
beginning method for each of the saxophones entitled Méthode Elémentaire; all were published by Leduc in 1886.
They were composed in this order:  alto and tenor in 1877,
baritone in 1879, and soprano in 1881.  He also adapted
some of his clarinet studies for the saxophone; these collections of studies have gone through several revisions
(see H. Klosé in the saxophonists' bibliography).

An 1860 first-prize winner of clarinet at the Paris
Conservatory, Louis-Adolphe Mayeur (1837-1894), studied
saxophone with both Klosé and Sax.  Mayeur soon became the
most accomplished master of the saxophone of his time and
was soloist at the Paris Opera from October, 1871 on.  He
performed first as a clarinetist with the Musique de l'Ar-
tillerie of the Garde Impériale, a forerunner of the Garde

Républicaine Band.  He played bass clarinet and saxophone
at the Paris Opera and also conducted concerts at the Jardin d'Acclimatation and the Jardin Mabille.  He wrote his
Grande Méthode for saxophone in 1867; it was first published by Evette and Schaeffer in 1896.  E. Gallet republished the method in 1907 and identified Mayeur as the
saxophone soloist at the Brussels Opera.  The last edition
of his method was revised and expanded by Marcel Perrin
for Leduc in 1963; it is advertised as the Nouvelle Grande
Méthode.  Mayeur is credited with seven solos composed for
the clarinet and as many for the saxophone.  In addition,
he wrote many transcriptions of solos for flute, clarinet,
and saxophone from the works of Chopin, Beethoven, Rossini,
and Donizetti.  (His compositions are listed in chapter 7.)

# 2.
# Paris Conservatoire and Other Nineteenth-Century Solos

Copyrights were nonexistent in France until after World War II, so music written before 1860 cannot be precisely dated. Unfortunately, composers rarely included dates on their compositions, and only a few dates have been found in press reviews of concerts of the time. The Conservatoire in Paris does not list the saxophone solos chosen for the examinations during Sax's tenure as professor because the music had not been published by the time of the end-of-the-year examinations. However, the Bibliothèque Nationale printed a date on the music received and it also marked most of the years in which various pieces were used as solos de concours. After these examinations, Sax usually published solos used by or dedicated to him, and although most of this literature is out of print, a few compositions from his catalog were eventually reprinted by other editors. The following solos were used as morceaux de concours at the Conservatoire from 1858 to 1867:

| Year | Composer | Title | Instrument |
|------|----------|-------|------------|
| 1858 | J. B. Singelée (1812–1875) | Concerto, opus 57 | S/T |
| | J. B. Singelée | Fantaisie, opus 60 | B |
| 1859 | (unknown) | | |
| 1860 | J. B. Singelée | Souvenir de la Savoie, opus 73 | S |
| | J. B. Singelée | Solo de Concert, opus 74 | T |
| | J. B. Singelée | Fantaisie, opus 75 | S/T |
| 1861 | J. B. Singelée | Adagio et rondo, opus 63 | T |
| | J. B. Singelée | Solo de Concert, opus 77 | B |
| | J. B. Singelée | Concertino, opus 78 | A |
| 1862 | J. B. Singelée | Caprice, opus 80 | S |
| | J. B. Singelée | 3rd Solo de Concert, opus 83 | B |
| | J. B. Singelée | 4th Solo de Concert, opus 84 | T |
| | J. B. Singelée | Fantaisie brillante sur un thème original, opus 86 | A |

| Year | Composer | Title | Instrument |
|------|----------|-------|------------|
| 1863 | J. B. Singelée | Fantaisie Pastorale, opus 89 | S/A |
|      | J. B. Singelée | 5th Solo de Concert, opus 91 | A |
|      | J. B. Singelée | 6th Solo de Concert, opus 92 | T |
|      | J. B. Singelée | 7th Solo de Concert, opus 93 | B |
| 1864 | J. B. Singelée | Fantaisie, opus 102 | S |
| 1865 | J. Demerssemann (1833-1866) | Premier Solo, Allegro et Allegretto, (ded. to M. Staps) | A |
| 1866 | J. Demerssemann | Premier Solo, Andante et Bolero (ded. to C. Panne) | T |
|      | J. Demerssemann | Deuxième Solo, Cavatine | B |
| 1867 | J. Demerssemann | Deuxième Solo | S |

It can be seen from the above list that Singelée and Demerssemann composed most of the music used for the Conservatory's solos de concours from 1858 to 1867. Jean-Baptiste Singelée was born in Brussels on 25 September 1812, and died in Ostend on 29 September 1875. He was a violinist and composed much music for his instrument; his 144 works included two violin concertos and many solos and fantasias on operatic airs. He also became a prolific composer for the saxophone, writing solos for four principal instruments; he composed the first original quartets for saxophones. In addition to the above works, many other of his compositions were published by Sax, and a few of these works were later reprinted by other editors.

The following reprints may still be available:

Quatuor en 4 Parties, opus 53, 1857 (reconstitution by J. M. Londeix). Molenaar, 1977.
Allegro de Concert (from the same work, ed. by E. A. Lefèbre, SATB or AATB). Carl Fischer, 1912.
Fantaisie sur "La Somnambule," opus 49 (sax-s.). Carl Fischer (One of the favorite solos by early saxophonists).
Concerto, opus 57 (S/T, 1858, reprinted as Concerto No. 1). Alfred.
Concerto No. 2 (1858). Alfred.
Solo de Concert, opus 74 (1860, sax-t.). Rubank, 1941.
4th Solo de Concert, opus 84 (1862, sax-t.). Molenaar.
Fantaisie Pastorale, opus 89 (1863, S/A). Molenaar (ed. by Arbeel).

Jules Demerssemann, flutist and composer, was born in Belgium on 9 January 1833, and died in Paris on 1 December 1866. He studied counterpoint and fugue at the Paris Conservatory and wrote a number of fine solos for woodwind instruments in the short 33 years of his life. The 1882 concours for clarinet featured his Solo in B-flat written in 1862. About the same time, he dedicated his Fantaisie sur un thème original to his friend, the brilliant clarinetist and saxophonist, Henri Wuille.  Hemke reminds us:

> This charming composition for alto saxophone and piano, so typ-
> ical of many other mid-nineteenth-century solo wind pieces,
> exhibits sweeping lyricism and demanding technical lines.
> Wuille's great performance ability becomes fully appreciated
> when the mechanical limitations of those early saxophones are
> taken into account.[1]

While Demerssemann's works published by Sax have long been
out of print, two compositions are still available:  Solo,
opus 46, was published by Rubank (1933) and the solo In
Arcadie, for B-flat saxophone or clarinet, is still available from Molenaar in Holland.

     An advertisement for Sax's music and instruments
(dated 14 February 1864) listed numerous published works
for saxophone and piano, as well as for saxophone ensembles
of four, five, six, seven, and eight instruments.  Among
the many listed works were La Chanson du Printemps (voice
and saxophone) by J. Cressannois, Arban's Caprice et Variations, and two original fantasies by Savari.  Jean-Nicolas
Savari was a military bandmaster; Londeix lists eleven of
his publications from Sax's catalog.[2]  Another bandmaster,
Sylvain Petit (called Alexandre), was born in Paris in
1864; in addition to being a trumpet player with the Garde
Républicaine Band and at the Opera, he wrote Première
Etude de Concours and dedicated it to Gabriel Parès.  It
is still available from Billaudot and Carl Fischer.

     Paul Agricol Génin (1832-1904), born in Avignon,
France, was a first-prize winner in flute at the Paris
Conservatory in 1861.  He dedicated his Solo de Concours,
opus 13, to Sax, but the published edition by Costallat
gave no date of composition.  Since the date of the composer's Fantaisie variée sur "Le Carnaval de Venise,"
opus 14, has been established as 1872, it is most likely
that the Solo de Concours was written and used for Sax's
classes at the Conservatoire between 1868 and 1870.  The
Carnaval de Venise Variations was revised by Mule in 1937.
The above compositions and the following were published
by Costallat; most of these solos are still available from
Billaudot (Presser, in the United States):

> Fantaisie sur un air Napolitain (from Six morceaux,
>      opus 15, 1879).
> Air Florentin (from Trois morceaux, opus 65, clarinet
>      or saxophone, ded. to Victor Lelièvre, 1892).

Other composers in the nineteenth century writing for
the saxophone were Pierre Signard (1829-1901), who composed five solos and airs with variations (the works were
published by Millereau in Paris), and Charles Colin (1832-
1881), who won a first prize on the oboe in 1852 and a
first prize on the organ two years later.  After winning

the "Second Prix de Rome" in 1858, he became Professor of
Oboe at the Conservatoire in 1868.  He wrote his <u>Premier
Solo de Concours</u> for saxophone in 1884, and Londeix lists
four additional <u>solos de concours</u>, the <u>Airs Italiens Fan-
taisie</u>, and <u>Mélodie</u>--all published by Millereau.[3]

Two conductors of the Garde Républicaine Band, Gustave Wettge (1844-1909) and Gabriel Parès (1860-1934),
wrote solos for the saxophone.  The former wrote <u>Fantaisie
Variée</u> in 1886 and 2<u>e Fantaisie de Concert</u> a year later.
Gabriel Pares was born on 28 November 1860, and won a
first prize on the cornet at the Conservatoire in 1879; he
followed Wettge as conductor of the Garde in 1893.  He died
on 2 January 1934, and is well known today through the use
of his <u>Foundation Studies</u>, which appear in the Rubank methods for all wind instruments and as a separate publication
for the saxophone, edited by Whistler.  His compositions
for the saxophone are as follows:

<u>1er Solo de Concert</u> (1897).  Billaudot (Presser).
<u>Crépuscule</u> (1907).  Billaudot (published for alto,
  tenor, or baritone by Rubank, 1945).
<u>Fantaisie Caprice</u> (1911).  Billaudot (Presser).

The Garde Républicaine band featured a section of outstanding saxophone virtuosi:  Ségouin, Fasquelle, Patteyn,
Thiels, Dupaquier, Lalaude, Meyer.  Paul Ségouin wrote
several transcriptions for the saxophone from 1891 to 1896
for the publishers Millereau and Evette-Schaeffer.  His <u>25
Etudes artistiques</u> (in two volumes) was written in 1893 and
is available from Billaudot.  Another member of the saxophone
section, Dupaquier, became a featured soloist with the band
in the early years of this century.  On a saxophone made to
his own design by the Couesnon Company, he could play over
a chromatic compass of three octaves.  A third member of
the above organization was Victor Thiels (1867-1925), who
became, in the early twentieth century, the assistant conductor of the Paris Opera stage orchestra; he also performed
with the orchestra when a saxophone was required.  In the
1920s, he wrote a saxophone method (published by Lemoine)
and <u>15 Etudes mélodiques</u>.  His article "Le Saxophone" appeared in the <u>Encyclopédie de la Musique et Dictionaire
du Conservatoire</u>.[4]  Thiels and the son of Adolphe Sax were
the teachers of Gustav Bumcke (1876-1963), credited as the
first German musician to pay due attention to the saxophone.
Bumcke came to Paris in 1902 to study and brought eight
saxophones back to Berlin for performance and instruction.
Over 14 of this composer's works for saxophone have been
published (a list of his compositions and transcriptions
will be found in the section of saxophonists).


## End of an Era

With the death of Adolphe Sax in 1894, the saxophone

fell into desuetude.  Although several French composers
and friends of Sax made sporadic efforts on behalf of the
saxophone and used it as a color instrument for an occa-
sional solo, the majority of orchestral composers relapsed
into their earlier traditional techniques of orchestration.
The old woodwinds and brasses had their roots in a more
leisurely time, some of them having existed in rudimentary
forms for centuries.  The saxophone continued to exist
primarily in military and civilian bands, where it was
taught and played like a clarinet--without vibrato.  In
the twentieth century, the saxophone became known in England and then in the United States.  In closing, a quo-
tation from Cecil Leeson is appropriate:

> The saxophone, denied this chance [of having a permanent place
> in the orchestra] by reason of its late arrival, was forced to
> make its bid for recognition unprepared--being asked, in effect,
> to disregard its newness and to compete on equal footing with
> experience.  Faced with impossible odds, the saxophone subsided
> to lick its wounds and to wait a more favorable opportunity for
> development; an opportunity, which, in its largest sense was
> not to come for many years, and then under conditions which
> would have surprised its inventor, to say the least.[5]

# 3.

# Early Saxophonists in England and the United States

Louis Antoine Jullien (1812-1860) showed enterprising talents as a conductor who strived to bring music, in a palatable form, to the general public. His colorful life as a conductor and impresario took him on concert tours to England and the United States in the mid-nineteenth century. A student of Halévy at the Paris Conservatory, he left before graduation in 1836. During his tours to London and the United States, he featured, for the first time, two clarinetists as saxophone soloists. These early artists were Henri Wuille, born in 1822 at Antwerp, Belgium, and Souallé, a Frenchman, born in the department of Pas-de-Calais. Souallé first appeared in London with Jullien in 1850; and the next year, in Paris, he received a critical notice with much praise from Berlioz. In succeeding years, he traveled extensively to give concerts in Europe and places as far away as India and Australia. He was very successful in these tours and often featured his compositions entitled "Souvenirs of Ireland," "Souvenirs of Java," and "Souvenirs of Shanghai." In 1861, he published, independently, his "Caprice for Saxophone and Piano." While Souallé had the honor of the first solo appearance in London, Wuille played there in 1852 in a subsequent tour. His talent brought him notice and the patronage of Mr. Anderson, chapel master to the Queen of England; Hemke says, "Because of this association, Wuille was able to sign an excellent engagement [for a tour of the United States] with Jullien."[1]

Grove's Dictionary of Music (1940) states that William B. Wooton (1832-1912) was the "Earliest [saxophone] player in England." Henry Farmer states:

I can show for a list of the Royal Artillery Band in 1848 . . . that Henry Rigby was playing the saxophone in the band in that same year. I possess two programmes of the Band performing at

Newcastle in September, 1855, which feature Rigby as a saxophone soloist, whilst the Band Fund Accounts, R.A., for the 1856-57 season prove that the band was in possession of two Alto and two Tenor Saxophones.[2]

During the extended tour in the United States, from 1853 to 1854, Wuille served as first clarinetist and was additionally featured as a saxophone soloist. He is credited with the first saxophone solo performance in the United States in a concert presented by Louis Jullien in New York on 19 December 1853.

## E. A. Lefèbre

Edouard A. Lefèbre, another clarinetist, born about 1834 of French parents in Holland, became entranced with the saxophone. After meeting the inventor in Paris, he promised to devote himself to the study of the instrument and to promote its use. During his tours to London and Leipzig in 1871, he received high and unsolicited praise from such composers as Gounod and Wagner. After further concertizing that year in Hanover, Berlin, Hamburg, Dresden, Wiesbaden, Stockholm, and Denmark, he came to the United States to accompany the famous vocalist Madame Euphrosyne Parepa-Rosa. It was at this time that he met Patrick Stephen Gilmore (1829-1892), who later featured him as saxophone soloist with the Twenty-second Regiment Band in New York City on 18 November 1873. Sections of saxophones were soon to be a normal feature of American bands during the latter part of the nineteenth century. Gilmore's band, organized for an European tour in 1878, carried three saxophones; in a series of winter concerts given in the same year at the Grand Opera House in New York, the band featured a quartet composed of Messrs. Lefèbre, Walrabe, Steckelberg, and Schultz. About some of the featured music for saxophone, Hemke says:

A typical Gilmore program, found in Goldman's "The Wind Band," listed E. A. Lefèbre performing Variations on "Casta Diva" of Bellini on a program of Dec. 9, 1876.[3]

A program of May 25, 1890, from Albaugh's Grand Opera House included a solo for saxophone--The Image of the Rose by Reichardt with E. A. Lefèbre accompanied by a horn quartet [with a background by the whole band].[4]

Lefèbre was not, however, the only performing American saxophonist toward the end of the century. Thomas Ryan, a founding member of the Boston Mendelssohn Quintet Club, was a versatile musician who performed as a clarinetist and a violist. He also taught a number of other instruments and appeared on 29 November and 6 December 1862, as a saxophonist, performing musical arrangements of works by Rode and Schubert. The "new instrument" must have gained popular appeal, for Ryan was heard on three more concerts, on 13 and 27 December and in May, 1863.  Hemke also remarks:

> . . . an unknown saxophonist performed the solos in the Bizet
> L'Arlésienne Suite in the Boston Philharmonic concerts of April,
> 1881 and a Mr. E. Timmons, a regular member of the Exposition
> orchestra under the direction of Theodore Thomas, performed the
> same solo at the Chicago Columbia Exposition of 1893.[5]

In 1887, Frederick Innes, a trombonist in Gilmore's band,
formed his own concert group and featured Fagotti, Conway,
Williams, Klosé, and Trount in a saxophone quintet.  A few
years later he formed the Innes Festival Band, in which the
saxophonists were H. Morrin (alto), E. Shaap (tenor), and
Vincent Ragone (baritone).  Horwood reminds us:

> Other notable saxophonists before the turn of the century were
> J. Paul Waite (Thomas Preston Brooke's Band), F. A. Maginol
> (Liberati's Band), R. E. Trognitz (City Guard Band of San Diego).
> . . . It was mainly due to these and the many excellent bands
> then playing--not to forget vaudeville acts such as "The Five
> Nosses"--that the saxophone began to become both familiar and
> popular with American audiences.[6]

It should be mentioned that there were some early saxophonists involved with recording before the turn of the
century.  Probably the first saxophonist--and certainly
one of the first to record--was a female performer.  Allen
Koenisberg's book Edison Cylinder Records, 1889-1912
reveals that on 23 April 1892--more than a quarter of a
century before Rudy Wiedoeft made his first record--Miss
Bessie Meeklens produced twelve Edison cylinders of saxophone solos with piano accompaniment.  The solos were mostly slow-paced and comparatively simple pieces.  Later, in
November, 1911, a less-known player, Henry S. Barbour, was
represented by a solo entitled "Tyrolienne Serenade."  A
year before, in March, H. Benne Henton made a two-minute
cylinder, playing his own composition "Laverne--Waltz Caprice."

The earliest Columbia saxophone recordings are played
by Eugene Coffin; they are listed in the August, 1896 cylinder catalog, which says:

> The saxophone is an instrument unrivaled in sweetness of tone,
> and Mr. Coffin's work on it is of an extremely high order.
> These records are among the most pleasing novelties we have
> ever presented.

The titles of his selections were "Rocked in the Cradle of
the Deep"--with variations, "Sea Flower Polka" ("with Mar-
velous Triple-Tongue Execution"), "The Palms," "Polonaise,"
"Fantasie for Saxophone," "Culver Polka," "Say Au Revoir,
but Not Good-Bye," and "Tramp, Tramp, Tramp."  Columbia
saxophone recording before the twentieth century began and
for some years afterward must have left a good deal to be

desired, for no Coffin records were in the 1898 catalog.
(Coffin had the honor of playing a saxophone solo entitled
Sea Flower Polka on the tenor saxophone at the inauguration
of President McKinley in 1896.)   The saxophone made its
first appearance on Columbia double-faced discs in Decem-
ber, 1908, when "Morceau d'Elévation," a solo by Steve
Porpora, was coupled with a cornet version of Gounod's
"Berceuse," played by Vincent Buono.

Saxophonists with the Sousa Band

     John Philip Sousa (1854-1932), a professional violin-
ist-conductor in Philadelphia, was selected in 1880 (because of his encompassing knowledge of wind instruments)
to become the leader of the United States Marine Band.
On 1 August 1892, he resigned to form his own concert organization.   Rudolph Becker, a baritone saxophonist with
the Philadelphia Wanamaker Band, and Stanley Lawton were
the saxophonists who performed in Sousa's first concert in
Plainfield, New Jersey, on 26 September 1892.   After Gilmore's sudden death in 1892, a number of his musicians
eventually joined the Sousa Band.   E. A. Lefèbre (who had
been a soloist with Gilmore for 19 years), Maxwell Davidson, and T. F. Shannon joined the saxophone section of
Sousa's Band in 1893.   Known as the "Saxophone King,"
Lefèbre was unquestionably the outstanding soloist in the
1870s and the 1880s, enjoying popularity with audiences
for both the novelty of the instrument and his impressive
technique.   He remained in the United States and became an
American citizen in 1884.   By 1905, Lefèbre had formed a
saxophone quartet, playing transcriptions of classical
music and touring the United States and Europe; by 1907,
it traveled to such frontiers as Alaska and the Philippines.   Lefèbre made many transcriptions and arrangements
for Carl Fischer; a publication dated 1900 lists no fewer
than 25 solos, including J. B. Singelée's Fantaisie Pastorale and Somnambule.   Several of his fantasy-variations
on operatic themes were added to Paul de Ville's Universal
Method of 1908.

     As an employee of the C. G. Conn Corporation, Gus
Buescher built the first saxophone in the United States in
1885; it was designed for E. A. Lefèbre and based on his
model from Adolphe Sax.   In 1895, Lefèbre was employed by
Conn to supervise the manufacture of American saxophones.
He died in his Brooklyn home on 22 February 1911; "leaving
behind a legacy of musical integrity, technical competence
and a rich heritage for the historical saxophone."[7]

     Jean H. B. Moeremans, born in Belgium, was one of the
most popular saxophonists of his day; he was the saxophone
soloist with the United States Marine Band in the 1890s
and early 1900s.   Before the turn of the century, he began
making disk records for Emile Berliner's Records and did
Victor recording for a number of years after the 1890s.

By 1899, the National Gram-o-phone took over Berliner's
business and its catalog, which contained 15 solos by Moeremans.  In addition, there were three saxophone and flute
duets by Moeremans and Frank Badollet, flutist; two saxophone and clarinet duets by Moeremans and another Marine
bandsman named Vompoucke (or Van Poucke) playing the clarinet.  Victor labels were issued later with the following
comment:  "Note--The above records are the most pleasing
and musical instrumental duets ever made."  By 1906, the
list of Moeremans' solos numbered five and they were available in both seven- and ten-inch sizes; the 1911 Victor
catalog (of two-sided discs) contained the full listing of
his solos.

Moeremans' name appeared on a program as early as 16
October 1897 and was listed in a program by the St. Louis
Post Dispatch of 25 September 1898.  As a soloist, he appeared at the Pittsburgh Exposition in the summer of 1898
and in Sousa's Willow Grove programs of 1902, 1903, and
1905.  He evidently was associated with Sousa for at least
ten years, according to Bierley,[8] who has a photo taken of
Sousa's men dated 1894; the last program with Moeremans as
a soloist, was dated 7 April 1904.  It is not known how long
Moeremans played with the Marine Band, but Vompoucke (mentioned earlier) was the next saxophone soloist in the band;
he was followed by Frank Wilbitzhouser.  The latter was a
fine euphonium, trumpet, and cello player.  A Victor catalog published in 1900 credited Moeremans with renditions
of Carnaval de Venise, Fantasy on "Old Folks at Home," Gounod's Serenade, Arthur Pryor's Little Nell, and other recordings made while he was still a member of the Marine Band.

The Sousa World Tour Band of 1910 featured 66 bandsmen, two women soloists (a soprano and a violinist), and
the band's physician.  Many of Sousa's regular musicians
begged off from this long tour; however the band was still
excellent.  Its ranks included such old timers as Edmund
Wall, clarinetist and mailman; Stanley Lawton, baritone
saxophonist (member of the band from 1892-1911); and Albert Knecht, tenor saxophonist and historian (1905-1920).
Among the newer members for that tour were two important
soloists--the cornetist Herbert L. Clarke and the saxophonist Benjamin Vereecken.  The latter had been soloist
with Arthur Pryor, and he stayed with Sousa until 1915.
An advertisement dated 23 October 1915 listed him in the
Pan-American Pacific Exposition in San Francisco.  Vereecken's tutor The Foundation to Saxophone Playing, published in 1917 by Carl Fischer, became a standard method
during the first half of the twentieth century.  In addition to this and other tutors, he wrote over 25 arrangements and fantasy variations which were published by
Fischer in 1922.  Many of these solos were for E-flat, or
C melody saxophones.  About 1924, he became a member of
the Long Beach Municipal Band and played there for at least
four or five years.

## H. Benne Henton

H. Benne Henton was born in Shelbyville, Illinois about 1867. Beginning at the age of ten, Benne Henton played clarinet in the local band and it was not long before he became a local celebrity; his services were sought after for miles around. After leaving home with a circus band, he toured with the Hi Henry and the Vogel and Deming Minstrels as an Eb clarinetist. Henton soon discovered there was more to music than vaudeville shows and decided to go to Chicago and study. It is not known who his teacher was, but he became greatly interested in developing correct phrasing and style. Attending count- less concerts by the Theodore Thomas Orchestra, he began to think about a future as a soloist. When he heard Knox Wilson play a saxophone, he made up his mind to become a saxophone soloist. At that time there was only one other saxophone player in Chicago, and Henton began to map out a course of study, using singers and violinists as guides. He even studied voice to help with expression and phrasing. As a member of the Lulu Tyler Gates Company for two years, he played a clarinet solo and a saxophone solo on each program. By 1906, he was performing with the Bohumir Kryl Band and was advertised as one of its ten soloists.

Already nationally well known, Henton was considered by many to be the greatest living saxophonist because of his brilliant execution and seductive tone quality. Richard Strauss appointed him to lead and personally select the saxophone quartet for the first American performance of the composer's Symphonia Domestica, in Carnegie Hall, New York, on 21 March 1904. In New York City, he was engaged by the Edison Company to make cylinder records; a catalog indicated that he recorded his own composition, "Laverne," in March, 1910. A 1918 Victor catalog lists the same solo and "When You and I Were Young, Maggie"--this time with the Patrick Conway Band. Conway assembled "pickup" bands of top performers to fill his summer engagements. This cautious course enabled him to escape the competitive pro- blems of other bands, which had to keep a roster of musi- cians employed throughout the year.

From 1909 to 1920, Henton was featured regularly with the Conway Band, and he also followed Ben Vereecken as so- loist with the Sousa Band. A 1920 photo in a publication by the Conn Company shows Henton and Albert Knecht, alto saxophones; Andrew Jacobson, tenor saxophone; Arthur Ro- sander, baritone saxophone; and Charles Weber, Jr., bass saxophone, as a section in the uniforms of the Sousa Band. In the early 1920s, Henton established the Henton-Knecht Company in Philadelphia with his friend Albert Knecht, former saxophonist and historian with the Sousa band; Hen- ton still continued to break away in the summers to perform with Conway's bands.  Schwartz relates:

> On Conway's programs Henton was often called on to play a solo
> entitled "Eleven O'Clock."  One of the features of the rendition
> of this solo was an almost impossible cadenza which Henton
> created [in 1911].  The cadenza soars away above the conven-
> tional range of the instrument.[9]

This cadenza incorporated a written range of small A# to
c4 and gave Henton the distinction of being the first American to play solo performances with altissimo notes.  H.
Benne Henton died in 1938.

## Jascha Gurewich

Gurewich (1896-1938), born in Russia, was the composer
of a saxophone concerto, a sonata, and numerous lighter
works.  During Gurewich's year as soloist with Sousa's band
(from 1920 to 1921), the famous conductor regarded the soloist's abilities as exceptional.  Gurewich's Concerto,
opus 102 (written about 1925), was dedicated to Sousa; it
is still available from the Rubank Company.  One of the
earliest saxophonists to perform with different symphony
orchestras, he was the first to give a recital of serious
literature in New York City's Aeolian Hall, on 31 January
1926.  Hemke says, "Gurewich was an exceptional artist and
an American pioneer in concert saxophone performance."[10]

## Harold B. Stephens

Stephens (1897-1983) was engaged as saxophone soloist
with the Long Beach Municipal Band on 15 November 1923.
Upon recommendation from the band's conductor, Herbert L.
Clarke, Harold became a member of the Sousa Band and was a
soloist from 1925 to 1926.  This was the last long season
of the band, which terminated on 6 March 1926 at Richmond,
Virginia.  He returned to the Long Beach Band, where he
remained until retirement after 38 years, in 1962.  Stephens was a soloist and conductor in a Sousa memorial concert on 28 January 1967 at Gahanna, Ohio.  He performed the
Carnival of Venice, arranged by de Luca.

As early as 1910, Sousa was apprehensive about the
future of the concert band.  Schwartz says:

> Trouping along the various vaudeville circuits were an increas-
> ing number of saxophone ensembles. . . . The most successful
> and famous were the Five Nosses and the Six Brown Brothers.
> Also, bands of six, eight, or ten players on assorted instru-
> ments were becoming popular as purveyors of ragtime, a type of
> music best played by small groups of musicians.  While these
> small musical acts probably did not take a single engagement
> away from Sousa, he could see that tastes were changing, and
> that the traveling band was no longer the great and unique
> attraction it had been.[11]

Sousa's popularity lasted for over a third of a century, and in 1922 he set a mark in the size of his band, which carried 100 members.  Like Gilmore before him, Sousa contributed greatly to the popularity of the saxophone as a solo instrument in the United States.  These and other band conductors did much to establish the basic band instrumentation.  By 1924, the Sousa Band comprised 75 men, and it carried eight saxophones--four altos, two tenors, a baritone, and a bass.  Feeling the ground swell of popular jazz, Sousa included in his programs mediums such as the coon song, cake-walk, and ragtime, along with classical and semi-classical music.  Calling it "syncopated music" to avoid controversy, he presented to the public only a lame sort of jazz.

In addition to the soloists mentioned above, there were countless other members of saxophone sections who traveled with concert bands during the latter part of the nineteenth and early twentieth centuries.  Detailed study of the rosters of Sousa's and other bands would reveal a long list of names.

Elise Hall

No history of early saxophone soloists in the United States would be complete without mentionning the enthusiastic and diligent activity of Elise Boyer Hall.  She was born in Paris, France on 15 April 1853, married a well-known Boston surgeon, Richard J. Hall, and became a prominent society woman.  While visiting California, she contracted typhoid fever, which left her hearing deficient.  Her husband advised her to take up a wind instrument to improve the condition, and the saxophone was her choice.  Although she was 47 years of age at that time, she worked hard and studied with Georges Longy, director of the Boston Orchestra Club and Principal Oboist with the Boston Symphony Orchestra from 1898 to 1925.  As the first Frenchman imported for Boston's all-German orchestra, conducted by Karl Muck, Longy, along with Mrs. Hall, promoted French music and a cosmopolitan appreciation of new compositions, and they both contributed much to the musical life in Boston in the early part of this century.

By 1900, Elise Hall associated herself with the Boston Orchestra Club, became its president in 1902, and by 1904, was its chief benefactor.  Longy coached her often (even in France during their summer vacations) and advised her about available composers to write orchestral works featuring the saxophone.  Her activities with the amateur group included the commissioning of over 20 works and the performances of nearly that many.  Her dedication to the instrument was unique, and she must be recognized as the first American person to have encouraged major composers to write for the instrument.

Probably the most famous composer to be engaged by Mrs. Hall was Claude Debussy, whose Rapsodie was commissioned in 1901. Due to much delay by the composer, she received only a three-to-four line score in 1911. Debussy died on 25 March 1918, and his student Roger Ducasse, a well-known orchestrator, completed the full orchestration and changed the title from Rhapsodie mauresque to Rapsodie. This work was finally premiered on 11 May 1919 by François Combelle with the Société Nationale under the direction of André Caplet.

Research indicates some interesting facts about early performances of Debussy's Rapsodie in the United States.[12] The earliest date I found was 22 April 1927, featuring Frédéric Parme as soloist with the Philadelphia Orchestra. Parme, a French bass clarinetist and saxophonist, had been engaged by Leopold Stokowski to double the string bass part on the contrabass clarinet with the Philadelphia Orchestra from 1925 to 1927. Although the program notes do not say whether this was the first performance of the work in the United States, it was certainly one of the earliest performances on the saxophone in North America. Frédéric Parme is also remembered for his work in the development of saxophone mouthpieces and for a composition for saxophone and piano published by Carl Fischer. On 26 April 1934, Lucien Cailliet was the soloist for a second performance of the Rapsodie in Philadelphia. In Boston, the Symphony Orchestra programmed Debussy's work on 13 February 1932, with Louis Speyer on the English horn. In an article published in 1942, Sigurd Rascher states:

> It was not until the year 1939 that the "Rhapsodie" was given a performance in its original form—that is, on the saxophone—when the writer played it with the Boston Symphony Orchestra.[13]

Thus, Parme's 1927 performance in Philadelphia predates Rascher's 1939 performance in Boston.

Most of the works dedicated to Mrs. Hall, in manuscript form, reside at the music library of the New England Conservatory. This saxophone literature by fine composers is not available for public performance, and the manuscripts may be viewed by request only on the premises of the Conservatory. (See chapter 6 for the list of works commissioned by and dedicated to Mrs. Hall.) In summing up the situation, Hemke says:

> Mrs. Hall may indeed have appeared unusual performing in her pink frock of 1904, but her true significance will certainly become realized when the New England Conservatory of Music decides or is allowed to make her extraordinary compositions available to saxophone performers.[14]

# 4.

# Vaudeville and Popular
# Awareness

Military and touring bands, long the purveyors of
popular music, featured from time to time a number of saxophonists playing theme and variation-type solos or groups
playing ragtime selections; the public began to notice and
like what it heard. The fact that the saxophone was both
a novelty and not difficult to learn on an elementary level
of performance added to the impact of public awareness.
Resurrected from the streets and parks, the instrument became phenomenally popular from 1918 onwards, causing a far
greater furor than the electric guitar of the 1960s.

Probably the earliest activities to generate a strong
public image were the vaudeville acts which became aware
of the entertainment possibilities of saxophone groups.
As early as 1911, the average person began to identify the
saxophone with pieces like "Bullfrog Blues," "Chicken
Walk," "That Moanin' Saxophone Rag," and many other friv-
olous arrangements, which more often than not stressed vul-
gar effects and the trivial side of the instrument's possibilities. Circus and vaudeville acts welcomed the new
instrument, and groups of saxophone players in clown cos-
tumes and blackened faces were seen on minstrel shows and
tours in the Lyceum and Chautauqua circuits. The most
popular group to feature saxophones in all sizes was led
by Tom Brown, who was received with great popularity before 1914. The Brown Brothers Saxophone Sextet brought
the awareness of the instrument to millions well into the
mid-1920s. One of the highest-paid acts on the circuits,
the Brown Brothers attracted, fortunately or unfortunately
for the saxophone's reputation, many imitators--both male
and female. About the saxophone's reputation in those
years, Horwood says:

> The legitimate world of music was, in varying degrees, shocked,
> disgusted and outraged by this commercial cacophony. With what,

in hindsight, seems to have been a queer lack of perception, most of its wrath and sarcasm was directed at the saxophone as though the instrument itself, and not the way it was played, was responsible for the offense. The other instruments of the dance band--trumpet, trombone, clarinet and others--did no come in for anything like the same criticism although their treatment in the bands of jazz and dance musicians was every bit as unorthodox as was the saxophone's. Perhaps this was because those instruments had a "respectable" existence in the symphony orchestra and elsewhere; the saxophone had no such noble connections and was thus the obvious scapegoat.[1]

From the armistice of World War I through the "Roaring Twenties," the newly found prosperity produced a veritable epidemic of saxophone mania. In addition to an extremely large production of instruments from constantly expanded factory facilities, Conn, Buescher, King, and later Selmer published trade journals with countless photos of performers and groups who endorsed their saxophones. Music publishers were also alert to the good times and released a wide variety of flexible ensembles written and arranged for groups of two to eight saxophones. Two important publishers in Chicago were Will Rositer and Finder & Urbanek. The latter was principally a saxophone shop and is now a publisher known as Rubank, Inc., based in Miami, Florida. In addition to the many arrangements of classical compositions and popular songs, the period saw the publication of the following instruction books by early teachers:

> David J. Bolduc. Complete Course of Twelve Lessons in the Art of Playing High Notes. Cleveland, 1922.
> Beach J. Cragun. The Business Saxophonist. Finder & Urbanek, 1923.
> _____. Cragun Conservatory Method. Finder & Urbanek.
> Walter Eby. Scientific Method for Saxophone. New York: Walter Jacobs, Inc., 1922.
> Ernst. The Ernst Modern Graded Studies for Saxophone. Irving Berlin Standard Music Corp., 1929.
> Art Horn. Modern Method for Saxophone. Nicomede Music Co., 1925.
> L. L. Lyon. How to Play Tones Above the Regular Saxophone Register. Sterling, Kansas, 1922.
> L. B. McNeal. McNeal's Modern Preparatory Studies. Finder & Urbanek, 1925.
> Charles Nicholls. How to Conduct Saxophone Bands. Libertyville, Ill., 1921
> Giuseppe Pettine. Modern Method for the Saxophone. Rhode Island Music Co., 1928.
> Winn's How to Rag and Jazz on the Saxophone. New York, 1925.

Would-be saxophonists were enticed by advertisements such as the following by the Conn and Buescher companies:

It you can whistle a tune, you can master the saxophone.

3 free lessons give you a quick start. Play scales in an
hour, tunes in a week.

Anybody can soon learn to play popular airs on a saxophone.

Popularity, pleasure, profit--all are yours when you play a
Conn saxophone. Entertain your friends; play professionally
all or part time.[2]

Hemke relates:

Between the years 1919 and 1925, the United States underwent a
saxophone "craze" during which time over one half million saxophones were sold. . . . The early saxophone patents displayed
an amazing awareness of the needs of the artist performer, but
a market had been created which enabled not only the artist,
but virtually an entire population, to share in the joy of
music making. The mass-produced saxophone provided answers to
a society which enjoyed and fervently demanded popular music.[3]

The swan-like tenor saxophone in C, re-christened "C
melody," was especially popular with amateur players, who
were able to read the voice line directly from popular
sheet music. Along with the piano, the sweet and mellow-
voiced saxophone became a standard home and party instrument. In band music, there was no place for the C saxophone, and it was often assigned the oboe part; but it
was a dubious substitute because the C tenor sax sounded
an octave too low. A large number of published solos were
usually written for the alto as well as the C melody. Saxophone ensembles and bands, which became increasingly popular in the 1920s, included arrangements from two to eight
parts for all sizes of Bb, C, and Eb instruments. Saxophone bands, sponsored by enterprising teachers and frater-
nal organizations, included from six to 100 players, and
were often augmented by piano, percussion, accordion, etc.

The F mezzo-soprano saxophone, also from the orchestral group of F and C instruments, was reintroduced in the
1920s by the Conn Company. Well-known performers like
Arnold Johnson recorded solos with the F saxophone for the
Brunswick Company; and other prominent soloists, such as
Chet Hazlett of the Paul Whiteman Orchestra, and Duke Rehl,
a saxophonist and composer in Chicago, endorsed it. The
C and F instruments were not adaptable to modern orchestration, and the survivors in the saxophone family have
been the Bb soprano, tenor, and bass, along with the Eb
alto, baritone, and contrabass. In spite of snide remarks
and derogatory writing from informed and uninformed observ-
ers, it is amazing that the saxophone craze continued well
into the 1930s.

## Rudy Wiedoeft

At the time when the saxophone was becoming part of

the everyday experience of Americans, both young and old,
a man named Rudy Wiedoeft achieved a high level of performance and gained some respectability for the saxophone.
(See chapter 6.)  After World War I, his flair for show-
manship, artistry, and brilliant technique spread (mostly
through his recordings); and his playing incorporated all
the possibilities of the saxophone, which caught the mood
of the post-war years.  He became a renowned virtuoso of
his time and, in his unfortunately short career, drew lit-
erally thousands of people in every theater where he was
booked.  In an interview with Mike Guerra, Ted Hegvik
relates an opinion of one professional musician of the
era:

> He's the man who made the saxophone!  Wherever he played they
> would pack the house. . . .  He used to come over to Camden
> and make solo recordings for the Victor Talking Machine Company
> when I was playing in the orchestra. . . .  The man was fan-
> tastic.  He had such a beautiful style and tone for that day
> (although it was more open sound than, for example, we would
> use today).  Very good intonation, and a fabulous technique--
> clean as a whistle!  The speed of his tongue was beyond belief.
> He claimed that it was a single stroke, not a double-tongue, but
> I don't know--I still have to question that. . . .  The saxophone
> was just coming in and he's the one who put it over.  In fact,
> he inspired many clarinet players to go to sax.  He's the "Papa
> of the Saxophone" as far as I'm concerned.[4]

Through his many recordings, Wiedoeft inspired people to
realize the great expressive and technical potential of his
instrument.  Among his pupils was Rudy Vallee, who says:

> Rudy Wiedoeft was one of God's kindlier creatures, a man of charm
> and personality, and I don't think he ever knew anything but
> friendship from those around him. . . .  As I watched him record,
> kidding with the rest of the band that he had gathered for the
> recording date, I realized he was not only a great artist but a
> lighthearted, warm individual who perhaps never realized how
> great was his genius, never knew the impression he had made upon
> the world for the saxophone and music in general.  The loss of
> two of his three brothers in tragic accidents was probably the
> beginning of the end for this charming and capable man who cov-
> ered his own personal feeling with a quip and a joke and a
> superb command of the instrument which he had mastered so
> thoroughly.[5]

Wiedoeft, no doubt, found a paucity of suitable solo
material for his talents, and with the collaboration of
various arrangers, wrote a number of novelty solos which
were featured in his many popular recordings from 1916 to
1931.  Other early recording artists were Wheeler Wadsworth
(1916 and 1923), Bennie Krueger (1923), Clyde Doerr (1921
and 1924), Nathan Glantz (from 1919 to 1924), Duane Sawyer
(1924), various groups with the above men, and other organized ensembles.

Saxophones in Dance Orchestras

With the saxophone's immense popularity and commercial force, dance orchestras began to add the new instrument.  Many people attribute this popularity solely to the
appeal of jazz.  This impression is definitely false, for,
in spite of the interest among the paying public, very few
professional jazz musicians played the saxophone before
1920.  In New Orleans, the cradle of Dixieland music, the
saxophone was used very little and was not a featured solo
instrument like the clarinet, cornet, or trombone.  When
used in the dance halls and on the streets, it was in a
more rhythmic or contrapuntal fashion and not a frontline
solo instrument.

Art Hickman, who started his San Francisco orchestra
in 1915, did not at first use saxophones, but by 1920, he
had a section of three during his residency in New York
for the Ziegfield Follies.  Another well-known leader,
Isham Jones (1894-1956), started as a tenor saxophonist in
an instrumental trio before 1915 in Chicago.  In the 1920s,
he organized a large orchestra and was often featured at
the Sherman House.  Jones was a leader in the "Chicago
Style," which used three saxophones consisting of two altos
and a tenor with players doubling on sopranos and clarinets, and his smooth, relaxed style became very popular.
The violin, mainstay of the dance orchestra for many years,
struggled to maintain its place.  Russell says:

> In 1924, Vincent Lopez required all members of his violin section
> to start doubling on alto saxophone.  Jess Stone and Alphonse
> Trent, whose later recordings reveal fully mature and trained
> reed sections, may have been using saxophones at an even earlier
> date.  In the case of both jazz and society dance orchestras,
> the objectives appear to have been the same:  to augment the
> overall sonority of the ensemble, which was the idea behind the
> saxophone when it was invented by Adolphe Sax. . . .  Their pop-
> ularity would follow experiments on the part of dance and jazz
> band leaders.  Solo work by individual musicians would come
> later.[6]

Paul Whiteman (1890-1967) began the violin in 1906,
played the viola in the Denver Symphony Orchestra, and
moved to California to join the San Francisco People's Orchestra in 1917-18.  During World War I, he conducted a 40-
piece Navy Band, then a hotel orchestra.  Wishing to bring
a symphonic approach to dance music, he gained much fame
at his concert at Aeolian Hall on 12 February 1924, when
he premiered George Gershwin's Rhapsody in Blue.  The work,
dedicated to him, was included during his tour to Europe
in 1926.  "The King of Swing," as he was called, gave up
his band in 1940 after many years of success--according to
George Simon, he never really had a "true" jazz band.
Whiteman was a great showman and a great salesman, who
featured top jazz people.  His saxophonists were Alvy West

and Frank Trumbauer, alto sax; Chester Hazlett and John
Cordaro, tenor sax.  In 1938, Simon lists Al Gallodoro,
Art Dollinger, Sal Franzella, and Frank Gallodoro in his
saxophone section.[7]

## Saxophones in Jazz

By the mid-1920s, the use of the saxophone began to be
acknowledged as one of the important new developments in
commercial and jazz mediums and led to its popularity with
professional musicians.  Russell sums up the fall of New
Orleans as the jazz capital:

> One day in November, 1917, the employment boom for jazz musicians
> in New Orleans ended.  The good times to be had in the red light
> district were looked upon as not in the best national interest
> during World War I.  An order, originating with the secretary of
> the navy, put a stop to the fun, the music, and the jobs, where-
> upon New Orleans jazz began its decline.[8]

When musicians left New Orleans for better-paying jobs,
mostly in Chicago, jazz spread to other cities, such as
Memphis, St. Louis, Oklahoma City, and Kansas City.  Russell says:

> Evidence favors Kansas City's claim to being a saxophonist's
> town and Kansas City style as peculiarly oriented to those
> hybrid reed-brass instruments.[9]

Also Ostransky states:

> The ten years of important jazz activity in Kansas City fall
> within what is called pre-swing (principal figures besides
> Basie, Moten, and others from Kansas City were Armstrong,
> Fletcher Henderson, and Duke Ellington) and the early years
> (1924 to 1936) of the swing era. . . . Starting in the 1920s
> with New Orleans' idea of three individual voices (cornet, clar-
> inet, and trombone) and rhythm sections, the Kansas City bands
> grew slowly and steadily toward the big band idea that included
> groups of like instruments—in short, the idea of a brass section
> (trumpets and trombones), a reed section (saxophones and a clar-
> inet or two), and a rhythm section. . . . Of the individual jazz
> band instruments to come into their own in Kansas City in the
> '20s the saxophone is by far the most important.[10]

In the small bands of the Southwest, the art of improvisation, practiced through jam sessions, developed the saxophone as an instrument unsurpassed for jazz soloists and
became, in their hands, an extension of the performer.  Kansas City's political boss, Tom Pendergast, permitted an open
city with many saloons and an atmosphere similar to that of
New Orleans, which provided a renaissance for jazz.  Isola-
tion on the American prairies favored Kansas City, and it
escaped certain disturbing commercial pressures which began
to nag at jazz in Chicago and New York City.  Russell says:

The provincial capital was far removed from New York and the
complex of music-publishing houses and recording companies,
with their shock troops of song pluggers, artists and repertoire
men, talent scouts, and band bookers, who controlled the music
industry.[11]

Kansas City jazz produced many great soloists, such
as Lester Young, Charlie Parker, Coleman Hawkins, Buster
Smith, and others, who will be discussed in the next chapter.  Influenced by Rudy Wiedoeft, who concertized and
toured vaudeville performing on the C melody saxophone,
Coleman Hawkins was the first great soloist on the bigger
tenor saxophone, which became, in his hands, the most important reed instrument of the jazz band.  Another great
player was Lester Young, who developed a lighter sound on
the tenor saxophone as a result of studying the recordings
of Frank Trumbauer, another C melody saxophone soloist.
About the use of saxophones and clarinets, Russell says:

> The soprano and C melody saxophones were not widely used in
> southwestern bands and after the early twenties, the clarinet
> fell into disuse, being used mainly for novelty effects, clari-
> net trios, and other arranged parts. . . . The abandonment of
> the clarinet by the southwestern reed men is another character-
> istic of regional style and suggests an almost obsessional con-
> cern with saxophones.[12]

The jam session was a Kansas City specialty, and in
its long history of informal playing, there was no city
where the jam session was so popular.  The fiercely competitive spirit was so widespread that it became necessary
to divide the sessions into contests of various classes--
almost like sporting events.  For musicians like Lester
Young and Charlie Parker, the after-hours activity of the
jam session was more important than the dance job.  Serving
jazz in many useful ways, the improvising brought about the
interchange of ideas among local and visiting musicians.
The high standard of performance of the jam sessions served
to bring unknown talents to the public eye and to the attention of band leaders.  According to Russell:

> The spirit of Kansas City jam sessions went to New York with
> Charlie Parker, Charlie Christian, Lester Young, and other jazz-
> men who turned up in Harlem after the end of the Pendergast re-
> gime.  Jam sessions at Minton's Playhouse and Monroe's Uptown
> House were features of the years from 1940 to 1947 and had a
> great deal to do with the formation of the bebop style.[13]

The small jazz bands of the 1920s, with their personal
and intimate style, depended on the individual performer's
intuition and could not endure the weight of more complicated harmony and the addition of more soloists.  As bands
became larger in the 1930s, a fourth saxophone was added
with additional brass, and the arranger became more important.  The more ambitious harmony of added notes gave each

saxophone an independent line, and without the arranger-
composer, none of the big bands would have had individua-
ity.  As competition became keener in the 1940s, the style
and distintive sounds of the larger bands were increasingly
important.

## The Big Bands

After the 1929 stock-market crash, the high living
and prosperity of the roaring twenties came to an end and
the mood of the country began to slow down.  A search for
security, sweetness, and reassurance was reflected in musical tastes.  A decided preference for dance music, which
encouraged romantic, sentimental, and mood-provoking ballads, became an escape.  The 1930s saw an era that nurtured several outstanding sweet bands; some of them remained nostalgically popular, especially for the older
audience, well after the decline of the big bands.  A few
of these groups should be mentionned because they were led
by saxophonists.  An important band led by Glen Gray
(1906-1963), also known as "Spike" Knoblaugh, began to at-
tract attention after its recordings in 1929.  About this
orchestra which helped usher in the swing era, Simon says:

> Soon not only musicians were listening to Glen Gray and the Casa
> Loma Orchestra.  Kids, especially those in colleges, flocked to
> hear the handsome-looking band that produced such mellow, musical
> moods; they stood around in awe as it let loose with an exciting,
> different-sounding big band barrage.  More than any other group,
> the Casa Loma Orchestra set the stage for the emergence of the
> swing bands and eventually the blossoming of the entire big band
> era.[14]

Other bands were the Lombardo Brothers, Hal Kempe (with his
tenor saxophonist, Saxey Dowell, who wrote and sang novelty
songs), Isham Jones, Wayne King, and Freddie Martin.

In addition to making many recordings, Isham Jones and
Wayne King wrote numerous songs.  Jones had a well-disci-
plined and melodic ensemble which included three violins,
three saxophones, two trumpets, two trombones, piano,
string bass, and rhythm.  Outstanding saxophonists in the
Isham Jones Orchestra were Milt Yaner, first alto and hot
clarinet; Saxie Mansfield, tenor sax who often doubled the
trumpet melody an octave lower; and the young Woody Herman,
who also sang and played clarinet.  After the Jones Orchestra's 1924 appearance in London, its fame grew and
reached its peak in 1932-34.  In 1931, one of its earliest
recording featured "Star Dust," by the Indiana composer
Hoagey Carmichael.  Between 1919 and 1951, Jones wrote over
45 songs.  In 1942, he disbanded the orchestra, afterward
leading bands at intervals in California; he died in Hollywood in 1956.

Wayne King (1901-85) was born in Savannah, Illinois and

attended Valparaiso University in Indiana.  In Chicago, he
joined the Benson Orchestra, and later he was the first
clarinetist and assistant conductor of the Tivoli Theatre
Orchestra.  When the Aragon Ballroom opened in 1927, King
became an orchestra leader.  Like many of the big bands,
his group was very popular on radio shows and was awarded
the Radio Guide Trophy as the most popular dance orchestra
for seven consecutive years.  Known as the "Waltz King," he
was composer or co-composer of the following popular songs:
"That Little Boy of Mine" (1931), "The Waltz you saved for
Me" (1931), "Goofus" (1932), "Blue Hours" (1933), "Josephine" (1937), and lesser compositions.  From the 1950s into
the 1970s, King's dreamy style was still popular, and he
occasionally toured and presented stage entertainment.

The largest saxophone section of any of the big bands
was led by Shep Fields, born 12 September 1910, in Brooklyn.  He first led a band while attending St. John's University in Brooklyn; in 1934 he had important professional
engagements in Miami and New York with his own band, known
for its "rippling rhythm."  After his first big break in
1936, he made many tours and broadcasts, and the band was
known as the Veloz and Yolanda Dance Orchestra.  From 1940
to 1941, Fields and his "new music" pioneered another style:
nine reeds, with good arrangements, which cleverly dis-
guised the absence of brass.  The men doubled on 25 to 35
reed instruments, and the arrangers were Glenn Osser, Lew
Harris, and Freddy Noble.  During World War II, musicians
capable of handling the arrangements were few, and, in
1947, Fields returned to "rippling rhythm."  Still a music-
ally pleasing organization, the band did not retain its
1930 popularity into the 1950s.

In December, 1946, the big bands' popularity came to
an end.  According to Simon:

> Inside of just a few weeks, eight of the nation's top bands
> broke up--Benny Goodman's, Woody Herman's, Harry James', Tommy
> Dorsey's, Les Brown's, Jack Teagarden's, Benny Carter's, and
> Ina Ray Hutton's.[15]

The reasons for this were the higher cost of salaries for
musicians, transportation, the continuing 20 percent amuse-
ment tax, and the complicated band arrangements, which made
the music more difficult to dance to.  A number of players,
spoiled by the unusually high wartime wages, became apa-
thetic about the hardship of travel; other more progressive
jazz soloists were attracted by bop and smaller groups; and
Americans in general showed more appreciation for home life
and were soon engrossed in the greatest of all home enter-
tainment--television.

## Development of Classical Interest

As the popularity of the saxophone grew during the

1920s, the number of international symphonic and operatic
compositions for this instrument increased from 36 to 65
by the end of the 1930s.  The beautiful saxophone solo
(inspired by jazz themes) in Darius Milhaud's La Création
du Monde, written in 1923, pre-dates by one year Gershwin's
sparse use of three saxophones in the Rhapsody in Blue.
Other composers in the following decade to use the instrument in their scores were Berg, Britten, Cowell, Gould,
Grainger, Honegger, Ibert, Kodaly, Prokofieff, Schönberg,
Shostakovich, Walter, Weill, and Vaughan-Williams.  But in
the 1940s, according to Fridorich, the number of saxophone
parts for symphonic and operatic compositions decreased
from 65 to 52.

> Interestingly, the decline paralleled a decline in the popularity
> of the "big bands" in the United States, in which the instrumen-
> tation always included a section of five saxophones—two altos,
> two tenors, and a baritone.[16]

Although composers in the United States contributed the
largest number of compositions which included saxophone,
with ten works in the 1920s and 14 in the 1930s, it is in
France, the instrument's birthplace, where we must look
for its most-important classical revival.  In 1928, Marcel
Mule, solo saxophonist in the Garde Républicaine Band,
established a quartet with his colleagues.  Although the
early repertoire consisted of arranged music, original
quartets by Glazunov (1932), Pierné (1936), Schmitt (1943),
and others followed.  In 1942, Claude Delvincourt, director
of the Paris Conservatory, appointed Mule as professor, and
the saxophone class was re-established after a gap of 72
years since the closing of Adolphe Sax's section in 1870.

In the 1930s, Sigurd Rascher became known in Germany
and premiered the Concerto by Edmund von Borck on 3 October
1932.  After a second performance of this work with the
Berlin Philharmonic, he left Germany because of the Nazis'
prejudice against the saxophone and was appointed professor
at the Royal Academy of Music in Copenhagen.  During Rascher's numerous guest appearances on the European, American,
and Australian continents, many composers were inspired to
write for him.  Since his arrival in the United States in
1939, he has taught the saxophone to an ever-increasing
circle of disciples.  Renewed interest in the classic saxophone during this time was still a rarity.

After the first saxophone recitals in 1926 in Aeolian Hall by Jasha Gurewich 31 January, and Rudy Wiedoeft
17 April, Cecil Leeson was the first soloist to debut in
Town Hall, on 5 February 1937.  Most of the serious compositions for the saxophone before 1950 were written for
Rascher, Mule, or Leeson.  The work of these three pioneers
has borne fruit, for the saxophone is now accepted as a
principal instrument worthy of study at most higher insti-
tutions of learning and is now on the curriculum of several

major university schools of music for doctoral study.

The idea of a rallying point for dedicated saxophonists on an international scale was due to the interest and
promotional efforts of Paul Brodie and Eugene Rousseau,
who organized the first meeting of the World Saxophone Congress.  This meeting occurred in Chicago in December, 1969,
and 500 enthusiasts attended.  Since that time, national
and international meetings among saxophonists, friends, and
composers have made a considerable step toward fostering an
improved image and the acceptance of the saxophone as a
serious concert instrument.

# 5.
# Annotated Bibliography of Selected Jazz Saxophonists

Although this book does not pretend to encompass a history of jazz or give a complete survey of jazz saxophone specialists, every effort has been made through research, questionnaires, and personal letters to include some of the outstanding jazz soloists. These specialists are mentioned because of their contributions through performing (both live and on record), composing, arranging, and teaching. To be included in this bibliography, a saxophonist must have been an innovator or made some lasting or continuing contribution to the art of saxophone performance. It is particularly interesting to see how the saxophone became so highly developed and widely used, especially in the earlier days, when there were few opportunities for serious study of the instrument.

A great amount of detail is contained in this book; information about deceased performers has been researched as completely as possible. Some performers' activities have not been reported or publicized, and other saxophonists are not sufficiently known in musical circles to be included. If living performers did not give complete information or answer questionnaires (or letters), the writer could only record known information, and he apologizes to those saxophonists or composers who, for one reason or another, were not included or completely represented in this book.

N.B.: The bibliography is arranged alphabetically by performer, and after a brief summary of his career, information is classified as follows: compositions by the saxophonist, solos or concertos dedicated to or commissioned by him (with dates of composers and of premieres when known), and recordings (sources of solos, combos, and bands). Unless otherwise indicated, all compositions are for alto saxophone with piano, orchestra, or jazz band.

The dates of compositions (or dates of publications) are
listed when known.  The information is given in the following order:  date of composition, instrumentation, premiere date, and duration (if known).

The listings include known publishers.  When compositions are no longer available, they are marked with "OP"
(out of print), and compositions republished from earlier
literature are identified with the current editors and
known copyright dates.  Abbreviations of publishers are
used;  the addresses and agents of foreign publishers are
included in the "Key to Publishers" listed in the Appendix.  Only recent selected LP recordings are listed.


AEBERSOLD, JAMEY
b. New Albany, Indiana
   21 July 1939

     A graduate of Indiana University, Aebersold performed
in a graduate recital in 1962 for the M.M.  He also studied
jazz with Roger Pemberton.  Aebersold has published many
books with his own company and has contributed to the
study of jazz performance through many clinics in the U.S.,
Canada, and W. Germany.  In 1984, he was elected Jazz
Coordinator for The Saxophone Symposium, the journal of the
North American Saxophone Alliance.

## Compositions/Publications:

     A New Approach to Jazz Improvisation (16 vols.) CPP.

## Selected Recording:

     Wichhunt (Freddleish-Aebersold, JA 1975, 1974).

     (See Aebersold Publications in Appendix.)


BECHET, SIDNEY
b. New Orleans, Louisiana        d. Garches, France
   14 May 1897                      14 May 1959

     Bechet was the youngest child in a musical Creole
family.  His older brothers had a band, but little Sidney
was too young and had no place in the group.  Leonard
Bechet, twenty years older than Sidney, was a trombonist
and was learning the clarinet.  Although the instrument
was locked up in a dresser drawer, Sidney found the key and
began teaching himself the clarinet at six years of age.
He later received tuition from some of the great jazz clarinetists nurtured in New Orleans--Lorenzo Tio, "Big-eye"
Louis Nelson, and George Buquet.  Bechet became a great
attraction in the family band and, as a young player, ma-
tured with an almost frightening rapidity.  Desiring to

play with more experienced bands, he finally broke away at
13 and did not return to New Orleans until 1940.  Like most
of the jazz clarinetists of the time, he played the Albert
System and never changed to the Boehm.

About 1917, many black musicians left New Orleans for
the North, mostly Chicago, as word came back that work
there was plentiful and well paid.  Bechet joined the
Bruce Stock Company for a tour through Georgia, Alabama,
Ohio, and Indiana, and left the company in Chicago.  Years
before, Sidney had heard a soprano saxophone when an Orpheum act called the "Six Brown Brothers" came to New Orleans.  This ragtime reed sextet utilized all six members
of the saxophone family.  Blesh relates:

> The Brown Brothers' showcase number was "The Bullfrog Blues."
> When the soprano soared into its high, silvery little song
> with the bass sax croaking way below, the boy clarinetist was
> thrilled.[1]

While in Chicago Bechet bought a soprano sax (curved model),
but his first experience with the difficult instrument was
not successful and he abandoned it a few weeks later.  He
was playing at the South Side's De Luxe Cabaret one evening
in 1918 when Will Marion Cook, a composer of many beautiful
songs and a leader of a noted black orchestra, heard him.
He lost no time inviting Bechet to join the Southern Syncopated Orchestra and took him to New York.  Cook insisted
that all of his sidemen be able to read music, but soon
discovered that young Sidney could not read or memorize
parts.  For the first time Cook relaxed his rule; the 21-
year-old Creole was just too good to let escape.  He allowed Sidney to fake at will, smoothed the ruffled feathers
of his jealous bandsmen, and prepared special arrangements
for the orchestra to back up the young New Orleans artist
in featured solos.  In June, 1919, they sailed for London
and opened at the Royal Philharmonic Hall.  In the audience was the musician-critic and well-known Swiss conductor Ernest Ansermet, who did not have the immovable mental
blocks of most classical musicians; he found the black
music startling and profoundly impressive.  In what was
possibly the first critique on jazz ever written, Ansermet
wrote "Sur un orchestre nègre" in Revue Romande (5 October
1919), a glowing account of Bechet's playing.  The conductor also brought examples of this New Orleans jazz to Igor
Stravinsky, who was living in Paris.  Evidently jazz made
a deep impression on the composer, for ragtime and dance
are ingeniously incorporated into the scores of L'Histoire
du Soldat, Piano Rag Music, and Three Pieces for Clarinet
Solo.  The last work, probably the most famous work for
unaccompanied clarinet, explores some of the virtuoso qua-
lities of that instrument.  Although the Three Pieces were
written for and dedicated to Werner Reinhart, a wealthy
amateur clarinetist whose generosity made it possible to
stage L'Histoire du Soldat, it is very possible that the

composer was influenced in some way by Bechet's playing.
The last piece of the little suite bears a close resem-
blance to the composer's concept of ragtime.  Blesh says:

> Sidney was a wonder on the clarinet--all that Ansermet said he
> was--but not unique.  There were other clarinet wonders in New
> Orleans.  And, apart from solos, there were ones who were
> better than he in ensembles.  Sidney, who would become an im-
> perious man, was already an imperious player who often let
> his clarinet part expand until . . . it threatened the primacy
> of the trumpet.  He seemed most at home in his solos.  No
> doubt, temperamentally, Sidney was a trumpeter without a
> trumpet.[2]

Although the soprano saxophone was shunned by musicians
as an unpredictable horn of unreliable response, particularly in pitch, Sidney resolved (this time in London) to
conquer the instrument by agreeing with it.  Blesh says:

> He developed a style in which one tone slides into the next.
> The melody became a series of long, sinuous, weaving lines, in
> which individual notes were simply parts of the continuous
> line. . . .  However, solving one problem created another one;
> how to play swing when you can't punch the off-beat and between-
> beat notes?  . . .  Sidney solved this new problem too; first,
> he did punch the safe notes, and, second, he put whiplike
> stresses into the flowing line, so that the Bechet melodic line
> writhes and lashes like a snake. . . .  As Sidney developed his
> style, he added another unorthodoxy; a vibrato, or tremolo, so
> wide that it seems to oscillate. . . .  He emphasized the tre-
> molo even more and made it into a positive thing in itself.
> So it came to express soul like the vox humana on the organ,
> which is the one with a tremolo.  That, at the same time, it
> further covered up errant pitch was Sidney's bonus.[3]

Bechet remained to play in small breakaway groups in
Paris and London until his return in 1921 to New York to
play with and lead many groups.  In September, 1925, he
left again for Europe with the "Revue Nègre," featuring
Josephine Baker.  He continued an active career as leader
and featured performer in many residencies in both the U.S.
and Europe.  From the summer of 1951, Bechet made his permanent home in southern France and had various tours and
guest star bookings in 1953.  In 1956-58, he returned to
the U.S. and Britain; he also performed in Argentina,
Chile, and Belgium.  Bechet's most incredible ability was
the spontaneity of his improvisations--creating new melodies on the spot.  Wilber says:

> His unrivaled supremacy on the soprano saxophone has tended to
> obscure his pre-eminent place in the history of jazz clarinet.[4]

During the last ten years of his life, Bechet was the
spiritual father of young French jazz men and the most
popular figure on the European jazz scene.  His eminence

was rivaled only by Louis Armstrong's.  He remained musi-
cally active until shortly before succumbing to cancer,
and he died on his 62nd birthday.  His bronze bust now
stands in a public place in Antibes, France.

Autobiography:

> Treat It Gentle.  New York:  Hill and Wang, Inc.,
> n.d. (c. 1960) and London:  Cassell and Company,
> Ltd., n.d., reprinted by Da Capo Press, 1976.

Compositions:  Over 300 popular songs have been written
    by Bechet; some of the most popular are the fol-
    lowing:

> Nouvelle Orleans; Petite Fleur (a number one hit
> record, 1959); The Night is a Witch; Waste No Tears;
> Without a Home.

Films:

> Série Noire (France, 1955); Ah! Quelle équipe!
> (France, 1956).

Selected Recordings:

> Bechet (Riverside 149); L. Armstrong & S. Bechet,
> 1923-1925 (Smithsonian Collection, CBS, 1981); Bechet
> of New Orleans (Victor LPV 510); Bechet with Bunk
> Johnston (Blue Note 81201/2); Bechet Story (Bruns-
> wick B1 54048); Blue Bechet (Victor LPV 535); Ce Mos-
> sieu qui parle, Les Oignons, Marchand de Poisson
> (Vocalion E EPV 1020); Immortal Bechet (Reprise
> 96076); In Memoriam (Riverside 138/9); New Orleans
> Jazz (with Armstrong, 1940, Decca DL 8233); Noble
> Sissle's Orchestra (1937, reissue, French CBS 13
> 63093).

(For additional titles, see Roger Kinkle, The Complete Encyclopedia of Popular Music and Jazz, vol. 2,
pp. 561-62.)


BEECHLER, ELMER
b. Springfield, Illinois
   5 September 1904

    After his high school years, Beechler started his
career in 1923, playing vaudeville with Chaucey Gray's
orchestra.  By 1938, he played with the Tommy Dorsey Band
(at the Lincoln Hotel) and later he worked with Paul Whiteman, Glen Gray-Casa Loma, and Joe Venuti.  Since 1979, he
has been making sax mouthpieces with Arnold Brilhart, and
with the retirement of Brilhart, Beechler became President
of Remle Musical Products, Inc.

BONACIO, SEBASTIANO (BENNY)
b. Sicily, 1904                    d. United States
                                      10 January 1974

     Bonacio began his musical education at the age of
nine with a teacher in Nineo.  After coming to the U.S.
when he was 17, his first professional engagement was
with the Ortona Band in Newburgh, N.Y.  Later he performed
with a number of bands in the Hudson River Valley and many
top orchestras of that time, including those of Paul Whiteman, Percy Faith, Vincent Lopez, and Rudy Vallee, as well
as with Morton Gould, André Kostelanetz, and the New York
Philharmonic.  He also worked with many theatre orchestras
and was active in TV.  He played saxophone, clarinet, and
flute and was a studio teacher, conductor, and composer.

Compositions:

          Daily Warm-up Exercises for Clarinet and Saxophone;
          Te Ame (song, recorded by Ezio Pinza); The Wishing
          Well; My Search for You Is Ended; My Love for You;
          Melodica (sax, pf.); Dance of the Pelicans; Admi-
          ration; Saxette (Alfred, OP).


BRILHART, ARNOLD
b. Southington, Connecticut
   30 September 1904

     Brilhart started his professional career in 1918 and
was one of the few musicians who studied and recorded with
Rudy Wiedoeft.  He began as lead sax with the Flotilla Orchestra in 1922.  From 1928 to 1952, he was very active in
New York, playing an average of 30 radio shows a week, and
was equally busy in the recording field.  He performed with
the Artie Shaw, Jimmy Dorsey, Benny Goodman, Glenn Miller,
Red Nichols, and other bands.  In 1939, he became disen-
chanted with the quality and performance of available reed
instrument mouthpieces and decided to design and produce
his own line.  The first precision mouthpiece of hard rub-
ber was made in August, 1934.  Twenty-eight patents in this
field were issued for plastic and stainless steel products
as well as synthetic reeds.  In 1966, he sold out to Selmer
and, in 1978, decided to reenter the mouthpiece and reed
business to produce a series of tools, molds, and machines
to manufacture an entirely new line of precision products;
his new trade name became ARB.


CARNEY, HARRY HOWELL
b. Boston, Massachussetts          d. New York, New York
   1 April 1910                       8 October 1974

     Beginning on the piano, then on the clarinet before
taking up saxophone, Carney went to New York and free-

lanced. By the last of June, 1927, he became a member of the Duke Ellington Band and soon specialized on the baritone sax. He was to the baritone what Coleman Hawkins had been to the tenor, and, perhaps more than any other individual, made Ellington's band instantly recognizable.

Recordings:

(See Feather and Gitler, The Encyclopedia of Jazz in the Seventies, pp. 128 and 177.)


CARTER, BENNETT LESTER (BENNY)
b. New York, New York
   8 August 1907

An all-time great alto sax soloist, versatile musician on many instruments, composer and arranger for many stars and films scores, Carter was known for his great facility on alto sax, beautiful tone, and tasteful solo style. He was essentially from the mainstream jazz school and absorbed some of its elements into his style in later years. He began as a teenager, playing jobs in small clubs. In 1924, he intended to enroll at Wilberforce College (as a theology major), but left to play with Horace Henderson and the college band in New York City. He worked with Fletcher Henderson for brief periods, with Charlie Johnson in 1927-28, toured with his own band the next year, and began arranging in 1930. He also wrote scores for McKinney's band, Duke Ellington, Teddy Hill, and Benny Goodman. Late in 1935, Carter went to Europe and played with Willie Lewis in Paris (1936-38), was also an arranger for Henry Hall's BBC band, toured Scandinavia, played with Freddy Johnson in Amsterdam, and led the band at Boeuf sur le Toit in Paris before returning to the U.S. After many tours and residencies on the east and west coasts, he moved permanently to Los Angeles in 1945. In the 1950s and 1960s, he led numerous bands and made additional European tours. Feather says:

> Despite the infrequency of his playing [in later years], he remained possibly the most eloquent and melodically appealing saxophonist in jazz.[5]

His overseas tours included Australia and Japan (in the 1960s), Cologne (late 1961), and Copenhagen (June, 1971). His musical scores were heard on national TV series and included M Squad, Alfred Hitchcock, and the Chrysler Theater programs.

During the 1970s, Carter aligned himself with the world of jazz education and has been artist in residence at Baldwin-Wallace University (1970), University of Colorado (1972), Princeton (1973), and Cornell (1974). In 1973, he was awarded an honorary D.Hum. from Princeton.

Compositions:  A few of Carter's jazz tunes are the fol-
    lowing:

    Blues in My Heart (1931); Blue Interlude (1933);
    Melancholy Lullaby (1939); Hurry, Hurry (1943); Deep
    South Mood.

Film Scores:  During the past 25 years, Carter arranged
    and composed dozens of important musical scores for
    films; these include:

    As Thousands Cheer (1943); Stormy Weather (1943);
    The Snows of Kilimanjaro (1952); Clash by Night
    (1952); The View from Pompey's Head (1955); A Man
    Called Adam (1966); Buck and the Preacher (1972);
    Louis Armstrong, Chicago Style (TV movie, 1975).

Selected Recordings:

    Further Definitions; Additions to Further Definitions
    (Imp.); Waitress in a Donut Shop (Repr.); With Love,
    Carmen (Temponic); Greatest Concert in the World
    (Pablo).

    (For further titles of songs, films, or recordings,
see Roger Kinkle, The Complete Encyclopedia of Popular
Music and Jazz, pp. 686-88.)


COLTRANE, JOHN WILLIAM (TRANE)
b. Hamlet, North Carolina     d. Huntington, New York
   23 September 1926             17 July 1967

    At 19, Coltrane joined the U.S. Navy Band and, upon
his discharge, spent the next seven years as a relatively
unknown professional jazz musician.  In 1955, his first
established recognition came as a sideman with Miles
Davis's band; and in 1957-58, he began producing his own
recordings as a leader.  His preeminence in bebop was particularly striking with his biting, hard-edged tone, harmonic concept, superimposed chords, and rhythms (which
featured the 16th note instead of the 8th as a basic metri-
cal division coupled with uneven rhythmic groupings of 4,
7, 9, etc.).

    In the early 1960s, he presented a wide variety of
recordings under the auspices of Atlantic Records.  He
used various combinations of musicians, and the best known
album was Giant Steps.  In 1962, he began a long relationship with producer Bob Thiele, and the next three years
saw an amazing variety of recorded material ranging from
live performances at New York's Village Vanguard and Birdland to an album each with singer John Harman and Duke
Ellington

   The year 1965 marked a drastic change in the direction
of Coltrane's style.  There was a tribalistic, almost
ritual atmosphere to his music, and this period seemingly
defies analysis.  In his later years it was the avant-
garde which influenced Coltrane and the musicians in his
quartets.  The most important aspect was that Coltrane
represented the zenith in acoustic post-bebop jazz.  The
prevalent use nowadays of modal music can probably be
traced directly to the material in Coltrane's group.  He
is considered one of the major innovators in the history
of jazz and the spiritual aspect of his music, a source of
inspiration, is unrivalled.  (See "Perspectives of John
Coltrane," NAJE Educator, vol. X, 4.)

Compositions:

   The Artistry of John Coltrane (Dorn); Naima; Cousin
   Mary; Spiral; Countdown; Giant Steps; Mr. P. C.;
   Syeeda's Song Flute; Alabama; Ogunde; Moment's Notice;
   Blue Train; A Love Supreme; Trane's Blues; Crescent;
   Manifestation; Reverend King; Lord Help Me to Be; The
   Sun; Expression; Father, Son and Holy Ghost.

Selected Recordings:

   My Favorite Things (Atlantic 1361, 1960); Impressions
   (Impulse AS 42, 1961-63); Live at Birdland (Impulse
   AS 5, 1963); Ascension (Impulse AS 95, 1965).

   (For additional titles, see Feather and Gitler The
Encyclopedia of Jazz in the Seventies, p. 98.)


DESMOND, PAUL (PAUL EMIL BREITENFELD)
b. San Francisco, Califor-    d. New York, New York
   nia, 25 November 1924          30 May 1977

   Gaining the rudiments of music from his father, an
organist for silent movies, Desmond played the clarinet in
high school before switching to saxophone.  He attended
San Francisco State College, did military service in the
late 1940s, freelanced on the west coast, and worked with
Jack Fina and Jack Sheedy (1950), and Alvino Rey (1951).
In mid-1951, he rose to fame as the most popular alto saxophonist of cool jazz.  With his cool dry tone, unhurried
sense of swing, and fluent solos, he formed a perfectly
integrated team with pianist Dave Brubeck; he remained in
the quartet until it was finally disbanded in 1967.  After
1974, he returned at intervals to play some club dates, and
made recordings before the final reunion for the anniver-
sary tour with Brubeck.

   He wrote several tasteful and inventive ballads for
the Brubeck Quartet, and the 1951 composition "Take Five"

(in 5/4 meter), sold over a million records; it was adop-
ted as their signature song.

Selected Recordings:

> In addition to many recordings with Dave Brubeck
> (some of which have been reissued on Atlantic and
> Columbia), Desmond made the following:
>
> Desmond (Fan, 10", 3-21); Desmond Blue (Vi LPM 2438);
> Glad to Be Unhappy (Vi LSP 3407); Paul Desmond and
> Friends (WB 1356); Summertime (A&L 3015); Bridge Over
> Troubled Waters (A&L 3032); Two of a Mind (Vi LPM 2624,
> with Gerry Mulligan); Paul Desmond-Don Elliott (Fan
> 3235); Time Out (PC 8192).

DE VOL, FRANK
b. Moundsville, West Virginia
   20 September 1911

A talented musician and composer, De Vol grew up in
Ohio and attended Miami University.  He began playing
violin in his father's orchestra, and by the 1930s he was
playing saxophone, eventually becoming lead sax and arranger for radio broadcasts in Los Angeles, where he led
background bands for singers on recordings and networks
shows.  In addition to leading bands for early TV, De Vol
also appeared as a bit actor.  He composed and arranged
for many TV shows and movies.

Songs:

> Friendly Tavern Polka; I and Claudie; My Chinese
> Fair Lady; The Chaperone.

Films Scores:

> The Big Knife (1955); Pillow Talk (1959); The Bramble
> Bush (1960); Boys' Night Out; What ever happened to
> Baby Jane? (1962); Under the Yum Yum Tree (1963);
> Good Neighbor Sam; Send Me No Flowers (1964); Hush,
> Hush, Sweet Charlotte; Cat Ballou (1965); The Glass
> Bottom Boat (1966); The Dirty Dozen; Guess who's
> Coming to Dinner (1967).

Selected Recording (as lead sax with Horace Heidt):

> Sweet as a Song/Half Moon on the Hudson (Br. 8043);
> History of Sweet Swing/Toy Trumpet (Br. 8048); I Fall
> in Love With You Every Day/How'dja Like to Love Me?
> (Br. 8073); Shadows on the Moon/Who Are We to Say
> (Br. 8096); Lovelight in the Starlight/Where Have We
> Met Before? (Br. 8110).

(For additional titles and recordings as conductor/ arranger, see Roger Kinkle, The Complete Encyclopedia of Popular Music and Jazz, p. 810.)


DOERR, CLYDE CHARLES
b. Kinderhook (near Cold-        d. San Mateo, California
water), Michigan                    3 August 1973
24 June 1894

Doerr's father, an accomplished violinist, trombonist, and pianist, guided Clyde to study the violin, which he played during his school years at the local opera house and in a dance orchestra. Clyde became interested in the saxophone and studied it seriously with Homer Dickenson, who had returned to Coldwater after touring as a sax soloist with Sousa's band. When his father died, his mother took him west to San Jose to visit her parents, and Clyde enrolled as a student at the King Conservatory, where he concentrated on violin, became concertmaster with the San Jose Orchestra, and graduated in December, 1915 with a B.M.

Doerr's career began at the Techau Tavern (on Powell Street) in San Francisco--not as a violinist but as a saxophonist. In February, 1919, he joined Art Hickman's orchestra at the St. Francis Hotel and was featured in a sax duet with Bert Ralton. Hickman, who began his orchestra in 1915, was one of the first leaders to add saxophones, in 1919. The reputation of this group spread, and the Columbia Recording Company invited Hickman to New York to make a recording debut of several songs, including Hickman's famous "Rose Room." Doerr also recorded some of his solos and duets with Ralton. In 1920, Ziegfield engaged them to play on the roof of his new theater at New Amsterdam. If they were a success, the new music with saxophones was a double success. The next year Doerr chose not to go to Europe with Hickman but joined Paul Whiteman at the café de Paris in August, followed by another engagement, directed by Doerr, at the Club Royale. They were an immediate hit and took New York by storm. Their recording, "The Sheik of Araby," (November, 1931) sold over a million and a half copies.

Remaining in New York, Doerr formed his own orchestra in 1922, and in September, he opened at the Congress Hotel in Chicago, where he was the director of music until 1924. In the summers of 1923 and 1924, his orchestra toured the Orpheum circuit. Back in New York in 1925, he organized his sax orchestra (six saxes with three men doubling on clarinet, piano, and banjo). The saxophonists with Doerr were Andy Sannella, Joe Dublin, Gus Sharp, Maurice Pierce, and Keith Pitman. The first program of the David Baking Company, on 6 October, featured the sax ensemble; it was also heard on radio and recordings until

1934. During this time, Doerr also made many recordings and broadcasts as a sax soloist. During 1926, his sax group appeared on the White Rock Show, in two films, and for programs sponsored by Elgin Watches, Everready, Eastman Kodak, Cities Service, General Motors, and others.

In 1928, music became an added attraction for the new talkies, which were made in Hollywood but recorded in New York on large 16-inch discs; Clyde scored or played backgrounds for over 20 motion pictures. His sax solo carried the love story theme throughout Joan Crawford's first sound movie, Our Dancing Daughters. He wrote many marches; the best known were "March in Time" (for the Century of Progress in Chicago) and "The Vermont Academy March." Doerr remained in New York until 1934, when he returned to San Francisco to become musical director of KPO, the NBC network outlet.

In 1935, while Doerr and his wife were returning from a weekend in Yosemite, they were struck by another auto; from that time on, Clyde suffered from back trouble and it marked the end of his active performing career on the violin, piano, and saxophones (soprano, alto, and baritone). He returned to New York to work the Major Bowes and Cities Service programs and did other freelance work (with Andy Sannella, Chet Hazlett, and others) while going to chiropractic school, where he graduated with top honors.

He returned to San Francisco for the last time in 1940. During World War II, he entered the war effort as a tool and die maker; he remained in this field for over 20 years before going to work for the Apollo project. In 1967, he began his last career and was a successful real estate salesman until his death.

Compositions (the following pieces for saxophone, published by Carl Fischer and Robbins, are all out of print):

Jeunesse; Saxonola; Saxorient; Valse Hilda; Saxophone Classique; Valse Brilliante (1922); Ma Favourite (1924); Valse Impromptu (1927); Technicalities (Valse Chromatique, 1929); Saxophonist's Dream (1932); Versatility; Going Places; Saxanette (1936); Saxophone Moods (1938).


DORSEY, JAMES (JIMMY)
b. Shenandoah, Pennsylvania   d. New York, New York
   29 February 1904              12 June 1957

Beginning on the slide trumpet and the cornet in early childhood, Dorsey played in his father's band from the age of seven. He switched to the saxophone in 1915. He and his brother, Tommy, a trombonist, formed various groups called the "Dorseys' Novelty Six" and the "Dorseys'

Wild Canaries," played during a long residency in Baltimore, and became one of the first jazz groups to broadcast. About 1924, they joined the California Ramblers and did freelance work regularly with Jean Goldkette, Harry Thies, Ray Miller, Vincent Lopez, Paul Whiteman, Red Nichols, and others.  Following a 1930 engagement with Ted Lewis, which included a tour of Europe, they played with numerous groups and subsequently organized their own 11-piece band on a full-time basis in the spring of 1934.

During their residency at Glen Island Casino in May, 1935, the brothers had a violent disagreement, resulting in Tommy's leaving to form his own band.  Jimmy continued to form and re-form his big band, and in 1943, it reached its zenith.  He achieved widespread success with several best-selling records and continued to be featured on both clarinet and sax, but his alto playing was superior.  In the spring of 1953, the brothers were reunited and the partnership lasted two years, until Tommy's sudden death.

Compositions (most of the following are out of print):

Oodles of Noodles (later entitled Contrasts, Big 3, 1933); Metodo per sassofono (Curci); Jimmy Dorsey's 100 Hot Breaks for Eb Alto Saxophone (Robbins); Just Lately (1937); It's the Dreamer in Me (1938); Beebe (Robbins); So Many Times (1939); Talkin' to My Heart (1940); Isles of Pines; One for All (1941); I'm Glad There Is You (1942); Two Again (1944); John Silver; Dixieland Detour (Robbins); Hollywood Pastime (Robbins); Tailspin (Robbins); Tap Dancer's Nightmare (Robbins); What Makes Sammy Run (Robbins); Finger Bustin' (Robbins).

Films:

That Girl from Paris (1936); Shall We Dance? (1937); The Fleet's In (1942); I Dood It (1943); Lost in a Harem (1944); Four Jills in a Jeep (1944); Hollywood Canteen (1944); The Fabulous Dorseys (1947).

Selected Recording:

The Best of Jimmy Dorsey (MCA 4073E).

(For additional titles, see Roger Kinkle, The Complete Encyclopedia of Popular Music and Jazz, pp. 828-830.)


FREEMAN, LAWRENCE (BUD)
b. Chicago, Illinois
   13 April 1906

One of the all-time jazz tenor saxophonists, Freeman played with a gutty bouncing style, easily identifiable.

He was the brother of Arnie Freeman, a movie star.  Start-
ing in 1923 on the C melody sax, Freeman took a few lessons with Jimmy McPartland's father; later, he studied
with the well-known Chicago saxophonist Duke Rehl.  From
April, 1926, he played the tenor, jobbing around Chicago,
touring, and leading a recording band.  After joining the
Ben Pollack band, he went to New York in February, 1928,
where he worked with many bands.  He returned to Chicago
in 1933.  After playing with Ray Noble, he joined Tommy
Dorsey (April, 1936), then Benny Goodman (March-November,
1938), and led bands of his own until his military service
in 1943-45.  After the war, he continued recording and performing activities.  He made several solo visits to England,
toured Europe in 1967, and spent a good part of the 1970s
working in Europe.

Book:

> You Don't Look Like a Musician.  Detroit:  Balamp
> Publishers, 1974.

Compositions:

> Bud Freeman's 50 Swing Phrases; Bud Freeman's Daily
> Exercises for Saxophone; Bud Freeman's Studies & Im-
> provisations for Saxophone (Robbins, OP); That D Minor
> Thing; Song of the Dove; Out of My Road, Mr. Toad;
> Uncle Haggart's Blues; Crazeology; Inside the South-
> side; Atomic Era; A Study in Augmented Intervals; The
> Barracuda; The Eel; The Octopus; The Sailfish.

Recordings:

> (See Roger Kinkle, The Complete Encyclopedia of Pop-
> ular Music and Jazz, pp. 932-33.)


GETZ, STANLEY (STAN)
b. Philadelphia, Pennsylvania
   2 February 1927

Getz moved to New York as a youngster of 15 and
began working with Dick Rogers (1944-45) and Stan Kenton
(mid-1945), led a trio in Hollywood, then joined Benny
Goodman (1945-46).  After working with Woody Herman's
Second Herd (1947-49), he formed his own quartet and has
been a leader ever since.  During the 1950s, the great popularity he had enjoyed as an innovator began to wane; however, his career was revived when he became the first American musician closely identified with the bossa nova movement.  He had much success in Europe in the 1960s and
1970s and maintained a second residence near Marbella,
Spain, working frequently throughout the Continent.  Late
in 1971, Getz met Chick Corea in London and commissioned
him to write a series of original compositions; this combo

made its debut in January, 1972, at the Rainbow Grill in
New York.  A continuing participant in the Newport Jazz
Festival, Getz toured Europe again in late 1974.  Feather
says:

> Getz managed to establish a broad base of support among younger
> fans and appeared successfully at Rock Clubs.  His style re-
> mained basically unaltered; in the view of most critics and
> fellow musicians, he was still one of the most melodic and
> creative innovators in the history of the tenor sax.[6]

Composition:

> Book (sax solo, Colin).

Compositions dedicated to S. Getz, available from Margun:

> Alec Wilder (1907-1980):  Suite No. 1 (sax-t., strs.,
>      1965).
> _____:  Suite No. 2 (sax-t., strs., 1966).
> _____:  Small suite (3 Ballads for Stan, sax-t.,
>      orch., 1966).
> _____:  Concerto for Tenor Saxophone (1966).

Selected Recordings:

> Captain Marvel (Col.); Classics, Stan Getz (Prest.);
> Dynasty, History, Communications (cond. by M. Legrand);
> Stan Getz and Bill Evans (Verve); Change of Scene
> (Euro. Verve); Newport in New York '72; Jam Sessions,
> Vols. 1 & 2 (Cobble); Pure Jazz (CJ 188).


GORMAN, ROSS
b. United States            d. New York, New York
   c. 1890-91                  28 February 1953

     As a youngster, Gorman performed with his father in
vaudeville.  In the 1920s, he was the leader of a hot-style
band and played with Vincent Lopez before 1920 and with
Paul Whiteman in 1921-25.  Gorman is credited as the first
clarinetist to use the glissando in the opening cadenza
in Gershwin's Rhapsody in Blue, written for Whiteman, who
featured it in his 1926 European tour.  The premiere took
place on 12 February 1924 in Aeolian Hall in New York.
Gorman was an unusually versatile artist, who could play
many woodwind instruments and saxes.  He recorded with many
orchestras, including Red Nichols and Miff Mole; he led
other groups for engagements and recording into 1927.  A
staff musician on NBC radio, he played many top shows; and
as a contrabass clarinetist, he was a valued member of the
Band of America.

Composition:

> Rose of the Rio Grande (which became a standard, 1922).

HAWKINS, COLEMAN (HAWK)
b. St. Joseph, Missouri       d. New York, New York
   24 October 1904               19 May 1969

Hawkins is generally considered to be the father of
jazz tenor sax playing.  In 1923, he began his career as a
sideman with Mamie Smith's Jazz Hounds; he also made his
first recording that year.  Soon after, he joined Fletcher
Henderson's band and was one of its finest soloists until
he left in 1934.  He freelanced in Europe in 1934-39 (touring Britain and France).  At the outbreak of World War II
he returned to the U.S. and in October, 1938, he recorded
the famous song "Body and Soul."  This began the decade of
his most consistent playing.  In 1944, with Dizzy Gillespie,
Hawkins hired the pianist Thelonious Monk and worked with
him at the 52nd Street Club in New York.  He also made many
tours with Norman Glanz; the last one was in Europe in 1968.

Although considered to be a swing player, Hawkins was
prominent in the jazz scene of the 1940s.  His ability to
comprehend difficult chord progressions helped him adjust
to newer styles.

Compositions:

Lamentation, White Hat and Red Hair; What is the
Name?; Devotion (Peter Maurice Ltd., London, OP);
Disorder at the Border; Feeling Zero; I'll Never be
the Same; Without a Song (Robbins, OP).

Compositions dedicated to C. Hawkins:

William Karlins (b. 1932): Sonata (sax-t., pf.).
SMC, 1969.  (Although dedicated to F. Hemke, the
2nd movement bears the inscription, "In Memory of
Coleman Hawkins.")
Donald Erb (b. 1927): The Hawk (Concertino for 5
saxes, br., per.).  Highgate Press, 1982 (pts.
rental from Galaxy Music Corp.).

Selected Recordings:

Feather says, "The number of albums in which Hawkins
is heard as leader, co-leader, or sideman seems almost limitless."[7]  (See Feather and Gitler, The Encyclopedia of Jazz in the Seventies, pp. 170-71, for a
list of important recordings, many of which are still
available.)

HAZLETT, CHESTER G. (CHET)
b. Indiana, 1892          d. 11 April 1974

The career of this clarinet and saxophone player
spanned one of the most colorful and exciting eras in the

history of music.  Hazlett began playing in his native
Indiana at 17, when vaudeville and dance bands captured the
hearts of the people during the 1920s, and he eventually
performed in theatres across the country.  In 1924, while
Hazlett was playing in San Francisco, Paul Whiteman heard
him and offered him a job with his orchestra.  In 1926,
they began a whirlwind tour of Europe, making appearances
in London, Paris, Holland, Hamburg, and Berlin.  During
the period with Whiteman, Hazlett developed close asso-
ciations with Bing Crosby, Al Rinker, Tommy and Jimmy Dorsey, Henri Busse, Ferde Grofé, and George M. Cohan, among
others.  He returned to Hollywood with Whiteman for the
movie King of Jazz.

Hazlett had a sweet tone and was also credited with
the development of the "sub-tone" style of clarinet playing.  Merle Johnston, a fine saxophonist and teacher, ex-
plained that Hazlett's sub-tone clarinet effect was achieved
by actually placing the tongue against the reed to deaden
the sound.  This lowered the pitch, so he had a special
short barrel made for playing sub-tone only.  Most people
thought he merely played the lower register softly against
a microphone.

Around 1933, Hazlett began to feel the pressure of
continuous traveling and decided to remain in New York
as a member of the Whiteman Orchestra for all its engagements there.  At this time he also broke into radio work
with the Eddie Cantor Show, the Firestone Hour, and the
Bell Telephone Hour.  His last tour of the country was in
1950 as a member of the NBC Orchestra under Arturo Tosca-
nini.  Retiring from professional playing in 1958, Hazlett
kept active as a teacher of woodwind instruments in the
schools of Orange, Massachussetts.

Composition:

Valse Inspiration (Fox, 1924).

Selected Recordings (demonstrating his "sub-tone" effect):

Valse Inspiration (with Roy Bargy, pf.)/To a Wild
Rose (MacDowell, arr. F. Grofé, Columbia 1844 D and
English Columbia DB 664, 10" 78 rpm).


HEATH, JAMES EDWARD (JIMMY)
b. Philadelphia, Pennsylvania
  25 October 1926

At the end of World War II, Heath was touring but,
anxious to learn the new Bebop style, he returned to his
home city and formed his own band, which included John Coltrane, Benny Golson, and others.  In late 1947, he and his
brother Percy (a string bass player) toured with Howard

McGhee; this tour included the First International Jazz
Festival in Paris (1948).  Jimmy, known for his earthy,
driving tenor saxophone and for his composing, became
equally proficient on the flute and the soprano sax.   In
his early career, he became closely identified with Parker's alto sax style and was called "Little Bird."   The
Heath brothers joined Dizzy Gillespie's band, the undis-
puted mecca of bebop at the time, and after working with
Art Farmer (1965-68), they played in New York for more
than ten years.  Jimmy also taught with the Jazzmobile and
at the City College of New York (1973).   In 1974, he received the New York State Council of the Arts Grant; in
the same year, Percy and Jim joined forces with their
brother Albert (a percussionist) and Stanley Cowell (a
pianist) to form the Heath Brothers.  1980 found them on
an exhaustive but fruitful touring schedule; their itiner-
aries included Senegal, Mexico, and Canada.  Their appearance at the 1981 Montreux Jazz Festival was one of the
highlights.

Composition:

   Afro-American Suite of Evolution. (CAPS, Grant, 1975).

Selected Recordings:

      Picture of Heath (Xanadu); The Gap Sealer (Cobble);
      Love and Understanding (Music); Olinga (CTI); Kwanza;
      These are Soulful Days (Muse); The Quota (MPS);
      Kawaida (Trip.); Hot House (Montreux Fest., 1981);
      The New York/Montreux Connection (1981); Expressions
      of Life; Dreamin'; Brotherly Love (1982); Jimmy (MR 138).


HODGES, JOHN CORNELIUS (JOHNNY OR RABBIT)
b. Cambridge, Massachusetts  d. New York, New York
   25 July 1906                11 May 1970

   With Benny Carter, Hodges shares the honor of being
one of the definitive alto sax pioneers in the great for-
mative years of jazz.  Feather says, "He occasionally
doubles on soprano, modeling his style after that of his
idol, Sidney Bechet."[8]  Hodges was featured with the
Ellington band and splinter groups from 1928 to 1951 and
again after 1955.

Compositions (Hodges is credited for, or is co-composer
      with Ellington, of the following songs):

      Jeep's Blues; I'm Beginning to See the Light; Hodge,
      Podge; Wanderlust; It Shouldn't Happen to a Dream;
      Squatty Roo; Good Queen Bess; The Jeep is Jumpin';
      Mama Knows; Bustin' with Buster; Away from You; Blues
      A-Plenty; Juice A-Plenty; Sir John (and many more
      titles).

## Selected Recordings:

Ellingtonial! (Onyx); Johnny Hodges; Hodges & Hines--
Swing's Our Thing; Mess of Blues (Hodges-Wild Bill
Davis); Rippin' & Runnin'; The Eleventh Hour (Hodges
with Billy Strayhorn Orch.); Don't Sleep in the Sub-
way; Blue Hodge; Blues Summit (Hodges-Ellington, Verve);
Triple Play; Things Ain't What They Used to Be (Hod-
ges-Rex Steward, RCA); Lawrence Welk & Johnny Hodges
(Dot); Hodge, Podge (featured with Ellington, Epic);
Esquire's All-American Hot Jazz (RCA).


JOHNSON, ALBERT J. (BUDD)
b. Dallas, Texas              d. New York, New York
   14 December 1910          20 October 1984

     Before arriving in Kansas City to join George E. Lee
in 1927, Johnson barnstormed throughout the Southwest,
first as a boy drummer and later as a tenor saxophonist.
He worked with Teddy Wilson (1932), Louis Armstrong (1933),
Earl Hines (1934), Billy Eckstine (1944), Woody Herman
(1945), and Dizzy Gillespie (1946). A versatile musician,
he was also a good soloist on alto, section leader, musical
director, arranger, and organizer of recording sessions.
His arranging for Eckstine, Herman, Boyd Raeburn, and Gillespie were among the best of the 1940s. He survived the
bebop period, and his later career included long tours of
America and France with Count Basie, Benny Goodman, Cab
Calloway, and Snub Mosely. In 1957, he went to Asia with
Goodman. His forceful solos were a prominent feature of
the Earl Hines Band reunion at the 1968 Monterey Jazz Festival.

     Johnson's willingness to listen to musical trends and
innovations kept him a working musician for more than 60
years; he was the oldest working Kansas City jazz man. He
lived in New York, where he was in much demand as a teacher
of improvisation, giving workshop at SUNY (Stony Brook),
Queens College, and N.Y.U. He was director of Atlantic
Records.

## Songs:

Tag Along; You Dirty Old Man; Mr. Bechet; Blues for
Sale; Tribulations; Southern Exposure; Montreux (1971).

## Selected Recordings:

Budd Johnson and the Four Brass Giants (Riverside,
RLP 343); Air Mail Special (with Billy Eckstine,
AFRS Broadcasts, 1945, Spotlite 100); Blues à la Mode,
Montreux '71 (Master Jazz, English RCA); New Communi-
cations in Jazz; Black & Blue (Bluebird); Newport in
New York (1972); The Jam Sessions, vols. 3, 4 (Cobble);

Colorado Jazz Party (MPS/BASF).

(For additional titles, see Roger Kinkle, The Complete Encyclopedia of Popular Music and Jazz, pp. 1178-79.)


KRUEGER, BENNIE
b. Newark, New Jersey          d. United States
   1899                          30 April 1967

An outstanding and versatile saxophonist, Krueger had moderate success in leading the Brunswick Orchestra in the 1920s and other sweet style groups in the 1930s. Along with Rudy Wiedoeft, he was an idol of Rudy Vallee, who said:

> Krueger was in his usual fine form as he played the then popular "Somebody's Wrong." First, he played the melody straight as written, beautifully, cleanly, followed by a series of stunning variations. He would then play it in a style representing a drunken man hiccoughing and stumbling home from a party. He would make the melody sound like a Hawaiian guitar and, in a comic way, would practically talk the lyrics on his horn. I watched with my mouth agape as I realized I was hearing an exhibition such as I had never heard before and probably would never hear again.[9]

Krueger made appearances and music store demonstrations with Wiedoeft to stir enthusiasm for the saxophone when he was in the Chicago area. He recorded in the 1930s and performed on the Pick & Pat radio show from 1936 to 1938. He also led bands at various times for Rudy Vallee's Fleischmann Hour and other shows in 1946-47. Acknowledged as one of the era's leading saxophonists, Krueger earned mention in Who's Who in American Musicians.

Recordings:

(See Roger Kinkle, The Complete Encyclopedia of Popular Music and Jazz, pp. 1261-62.)


LA PORTA, JOHN D.
b. Philadelphia, Pennsylvania
   13 April 1920

After early study of clarinet with Joseph Gigliotti, La Porta attended the Manhattan School and completed the B.M. in 1957. He studied clarinet with Leon Russianoff, flute with Robert Morris, jazz improvisation with Lennie Tristano, and composition with Ernst Toch and Alexei Haeiff. Under Leopold Stokowski, he played in the All-American Youth Orchestra and performed in concerts and on recordings with Walter Hendl, Igor Stravinsky, Alexei Haeiff, Gunther Schuller, Leonard Bernstein, and others.

A founder of the Eastern Region of the National Association of Jazz Educators, La Porta has taught clarinet, flute, sax, and improvisation at national conventions for the Music Educators National Conference since 1960. He has performed and arranged for the Herb Pomeroy Orchestra since 1976, and played with Charlie Parker, Dizzy Gillespie, Fats Navarro, and Max Roach. La Porta has taught at the Berklee School since 1962 and is presently the Director of Instrumental Performance.

Compositions (published by Berklee, unless otherwise indicated):

> Miniature (sax-b., pf., 1955, Palgin); Concertino (1956, Palgin); Mid-Century Event (1961); Developing the School Jazz Ensemble (22 vols., 1965); A Guide to Improvisation (incl. records & instr. manual, 1968); Ear Training Phase I (1970); Developing Sight Reading Skills in the Jazz Idiom (1971); A Guide to Jazz Phrasing and Interpretation (with record, 1973); Tonal Organization of Improvisational Techniques (Kendor, 1976); Essay for Clarinet Alone (Kendor, 1977); Jazz Ear Training (Kendor, 1980); 14 Jazz-Rock Duets (Kendor, 1981); Rock Bands Arrangements; Spanish Rhapsody (SATB).

Selected Recordings:

> John La Porta: Three Moods (Debut DEB 122, 1954); Jazz Composer's Workshop (Nos. 1 & 2 with Chas. Mingus, Savoy, 1956); South American Brothers (Fantasy 3237, 1956); Igor Stravinsky: Ebony Concerto (Everest LPBR 8009, 1957); Jazz Compositions of the 20th Century (Columbia, 1957); Manhattan Monodrama (Debut 125, 1957); What's New? (Columbia CL 842, 1957); The Most Minor (La Porta Quartet, Everest LPBR 5037, 1959); Spanish Rhapsody (Berklee Faculty SATB, Berklee BLP 102, 1972); The Clarinet Artistry of John La Porta (Fantasy 3248); A Jazz Journey (with Rusty Dedrick, Nonmouth-Evergreen).


LEONARD, HARLAN QUENTIN (MIKE)
b. Butler, Missouri
   2 July 1905

After moving to Kansas City, Leonard played clarinet at Lincoln High School, where he was taught by Major N. Clark Smith. He studied the saxophone with Eric "Paul" Tremaine and was one of the better-trained young musicians in Kansas City at the time of his graduation in 1923. (Tremaine was a fine musician and one of the first important alto saxophonists in the country; he was the son of Prof. Tremaine, leader of the Kansas City Municipal Band.)

Leonard's first important engagement was with Bennie Moten
in late 1923, for whom he led one of the first sax sections
of the orchestra until 1931.  He eventually became director of the Kansas City Rockets, played residencies in Kansas City, and went to New York for engagements at the
Savoy and Golden Gate ballrooms during 1940.  In the spring
of 1943, he took the band for a residency at the Hollywood
Club, Los Angeles, and continued to front bands until the
mid-1940s.  Faced with family responsabilities, he left
the band business and became a cashier in the Los Angeles
Office of the Department of Internal Revenue.

Selected Recording:

    Harlan Leonard and His Rockets (FCA LPV 531).


MARTIN, FREDDY
b. Cleveland, Ohio              d. Newport Beach, California
   9 December 1906                 30 September 1983


    A side man in the early 1930s with several bands in
various locales, Martin formed his own orchestra in 1932.
His style of playing the tenor sax won him a sizable jazz
following, and his bands established the "sweet jazz sound."
Johnny Hodges called him "Mr. Silvertone," and Chu Berry
once said that Martin was his favorite musician on the instrument.  His band was one of the dozens that played in
New York's top hotel ballrooms in the 1930s and 1940s.  In
1938, they began performing at the Coconut Grove in Los
Angeles for a long run, returned often, and eventually
made it their base in later years.  Martin's career sky-
rocketed in 1947 when he recorded "Tonight We Love," which
had been adapted by Ray Austin from Tchaikovsky's Piano
Concerto in Bb minor.  The song was a huge hit, and adap-
tations followed of other classical melodies from Grieg,
Rachmaninoff, and Rimsky-Korsakoff.  Through the 1950s
and 1960s, Martin appeared at charity balls and conventions
around the country.  He performed nostalgia shows into the
1970s, honoring the big bands, and worked until June of the
last year of his life.  Martin's band was featured in the
following movies:

    The Mayor of 44th Street (1942); Seven Days' Leave
    (1942); Stage Door Canteen (1942); What's Buzzin!
    Cousin? (1943); Melody Time (1948).


Often recording under the pseudonyms of Bob Causer, Albert
Taylor, Hotel Bossert Orchestra, Ed Loyd, and Allen Burns,
Martin had a prolific output of excellent recordings (see
Roger Kinkle, The Complete Encyclopedia of Popular Music
and Jazz, pp. 1383-84).

MULLIGAN, GERALD JOSEPH (GERRY)
b. New York, New York
   6 April 1927

        An important jazz artist from the late 1940s into the
1970s, Mulligan is a top performer on baritone sax, leader,
arranger, and composer.  He grew up in Philadelphia, where
he gained early experience in both playing and arranging
before moving to New York.  He played with Gene Krupa
(1944), Miles Davis (1948), Eliot Lawrence (1950), and
Claude Thornhill (1952), and organized a quartet on the
West Coast which became well known into the mid-1950s.  In
1968, he made a series of tours as a guest with Dave Brubeck.  In 1956-57 and 1974, Mulligan also took a large
band to France and Italy.  Feather quotes Brubeck:

> With Gerry, you feel as if you're listening to the past, pres-
> ent, and future of Jazz all at one time, and it's with such
> taste and respect that you're not quite aware of the changes in
> idiom. . . . You feel not that tradition is broken, but rather
> that it's being pushed forwards.[10]

## Compositions:

        Disco Jockey Jump (for G. Krupa); Jeru, Boplicity;
        Venus de Milo; Godchild (for M. Davis); Elevation
        (for E. Lawrence); K-4 Pacific; Golden Notebooks;
        Maytag; Country Beaver; It's Sandy at the Beach;
        A Weed in Disneyland; Grand Tour; Song for an Un-
        finished Woman; Song for Strayhorn; By Your Grace;
        The Sounds of Gerry (sax solo book, Colin); Great
        Jazz Tunes of Gerry Mulligan (tran., ed. R. Ricker,
        vol. 6, Black Swan).

## Compositions dedicated to G. Mulligan:

        Alec Wilder (1907-1980): Suite No. 1 (sax-b., ww.
           quin., 1965).  Margun.
        _____ : Suite No. 2 (sax-b., ww. quin., per., 1971).
        Frank Proto: Concerto (sax-b., orch.).
        Harry Freedman: Celebration (sax-b., orch.).

## Recordings:

        Age of Stream (A&M); Carnegie Hall Concerts (CTI);
        Astor Piazzoli; Summit (Carosello, Italy); Compadres;
        Blue Roots (Berlin Phil. Collection); Revelation
        (with Lee Konitz, reissue, B.N.); Thelonious Monk/
        Gerry Mulligan (Milestone M 47067).


NASH, TED
b. Sommerville, Massachusetts
   31 October 1922

Nash left high school at 17 to travel with a band.
In the early 1940s, he worked with bands of Dick Rogers,
Johnny Long, Clyde Lucas, and Van Alexander.  During World
War II, he joined the Maritime Service and was a member of
the Catalina Base Band.  After playing with Horace Heidt
and Phil Harris in 1942-43, he became a featured tenor
player with the Les Brown Band in 1943-47, and worked with
Jerry Gray (later 1940s into 1950s).  He was a studio mu-
sician in radio, movies, and recording, was active with
Mort Lindsay in the 1960s, and played on the Merv Griffin
TV show late in the 1960s and 1970s.

## Publication for Saxophone:

Ted Nash's Studies in High Harmonics (Leeds, 1946).

## Selected Recordings:

Star Eyes (Co CL 989 and Starlight 6001); The Brothers Nash (Lib 6011); Combo! (with H. Mancini, Vi
LPM 2258); Like Someone in Love (with E. Fitzgerald,
Verve MGV 4004); Movie and TV Themes (with E. Bernstein, Choreo A 11); Hollywood Jazz Stars (with J.
Beau, Cor CRL 57247); Battle of the Saxes (EmArcy MG
36023).

(For additional titles with Les Brown, Jimmy Jones,
Joe Thomas, Harry Carney, Dave Tough, and Billy May, see
Roger Kinkle, The Complete Encyclopedia of Popular Music
and Jazz, p. 1500.)


NEWSOM, THOMAS PENN (TOMMY)
b. Portsmouth, Virginia
   23 February 1929

Newsom graduated from Peabody Conservatory, where
he studied piano and saxophone.  After three years in the
Air Force Band, he completed the M.A. at Columbia University.  He played with the bands of Benny Goodman, Les Elgart, and Skitch Henderson, and also arranged for Byrd,
Goodman, Herman, and Kostelanetz.  Joining NBC as a staff
musician in 1962, he became the lead sax and assistant
conductor of the Tonite Show Orchestra in 1968.  Newsom
is considered one of the finest musicians in his field
and appears with jazz combos and symphony orchestras
throughout the U.S.

## Compositions:

La Boheme; Titterpipes (for B. Goodman); Puddintane
(for Ed Shaughnessy); Suite for trumpet (for Doc Sev-
erinsen); Tommy Newsom's Standard & Popular Solos
(Armstrong); Air and Rondo (sax, band).

Selected Recordings:

> LP's (with Severinsen, RCA); LP's (with C. and B.
> Byrd, Columbia).

NIEHAUS, LEONARD (LENNIE)
b. St. Louis, Missouri
   29 June 1929

   Active in commercial playing and arranging for night
club artists and for TV shows, Niehaus was a featured alto
sax soloist and arranger for the Stan Kenton Orchestra.
His early publications for basic jazz conception were endorsed by Kenton.

Compositions/Publications:

> Jazz Conception (4 vols.); Jazz Conception Duets;
> Jazz Conception for Sax Section; Jazz Improvisation
> (Try); A Dozen and One (2 saxes, WIM, 1966); Of Days
> Remembered (WIM); Palo Alto (sax, band, WIM); Waltzin'
> the Blues Away (WIM); Fugue; Mosaics (SATB, Leonard);
> Halloween Fantasy; Romantic Sketch; Summer Nocturne;
> The Storm; Symphonette (all SATB, Highland); Ron-
> dolette; Swing Shift (all SATB or AATB, Kendor, 1983);
> 10 Jazz Inventions (2 saxes, Kendor, 1983); Cleanin'
> up (AATB, Kendor, 1983); One For All (AATB, Kendor,
> 1984); Small Fry (AATB, Kendor, 1984).

   He has recorded six albums of his own compositions
with Mel Lewis, Shelly Manne, Jimmy Giuffre, and others.

PARKER, CHARLES CHRISTOPHER
(CHARLIE, YARDBIRD, BIRD)
b. Kansas City, Missouri        d. New York, New York
   29 August 1920                  12 March 1955

   Too young to be admitted into the saloons for the
famous jam sessions in Kansas City, Parker spent almost his
entire youth drifting from one club to the other listening
outside to the famous players.  The jam session became a
way of life, and this after-hours activity was more important to musicians than their jobs.  Like Lester Young,
Parker was a professional at 16.  First viewed, with some
justification, as a disciple of Young, he expanded Young's
rhythmic, melodic, and harmonic concepts to a point that
would have been unimaginable in the 1930s.

   Parker's first appearance was a disaster, as he had
learned the scale of G on his alto saxophone and only two
tunes in a single key.  He was laughed off the stand when
the fellows played "Body and Soul," and he had to leave

the club.  Later he received some excellent and needed
training on a job he held for several months with Tommy
Douglas' band.  Douglas (1911-1969) was a hard-luck musician, who had little success as a sideman, leader, or recording artist.  But he had studied at the Boston Conservatory (1924-28) and had toured with Jelly Roll Morton and
Jap Allen (c. 1931).  Douglas, in 1935, was using passing
tones, added chords, and double-time experiments that
would be used by the beboppers ten years later; he also
helped Parker become proficient in soloing on the clarinet.
Another intensive woodshedding period was to follow for
Parker, as Russell relates:

> Charlie joined a George Lee unit booked to work the summer at
> Eldon, a town in the Ozark lake region and a favorite vacation
> spot for people from Kansas City.  Two men in the band inter-
> ested Charlie:  Efferge Ware, the guitarist . . . and Carrie
> Powell, the band's pianist.  Both were known for their musician-
> ship and knowledge of harmony.  He worked the dance job by night,
> snatched a few hours sleep, and rose early to study harmony. .
> . . Additional time was devoted to scales, arpeggios, and sax-
> ophone drills. . . .  When Charlie Parker returned to Kansas
> City in the fall of 1937, the bullies, pranksters, and estab-
> lished professional musicians who had poked fun at him were in
> for a rude shock.[11]

After his first major recording in the middle 1940s,
it became impossible for any alto saxophonist not to be
affected to some degree by Parker's music; the first of
the new players to grasp the elements of Parker's style
were Sonny Stitt, James Moody, and Sonny Criss.  Parker's
playing, according to Heckman,

> developed in more than one direction and was many things to many
> people.  Some heard only piercing edges of sometimes strident
> tone; others heard the warm, intimate intensity of his ballad
> style.[12]

Parker's influence eventually divided into two general
areas:  the first, a reflection of his driving, up-tempo
style (produced in the 1940s) and the later endless stream
and quiet lyricism of his ballads in the 1950s.  Except for
bouts of ill health brought on by his need for drugs, Parker remained an intensely creative musician until a few
months before his death.  Russell says:

> There was one style of jazz before Charlie Parker and quite an-
> other after Charlie Parker.  He took the new musical language
> that emanated from his native Kansas City, shaped it to his
> personal use and gave it to the world.[13]

Compositions.  The following were published by Colin:

> Charlie Parker Originals (Eb or Bb sax solo); Big
> Foot; Bird's Feather; Bird's Nest; Bongo Beep; Bongo

Bird; Bongo Bop; Dexterity; Gerry Bird; Hot Blues;
Relaxin' at Camarillo; Tail Feathers; The Hymn; Yardbird Originals; Famous Yardbird Transcriptions; Bebop
for Alto Sax; 14 Recorded Solos.

Between 1940 and 1954, about 20 different recordings were
issued, chiefly on Dial and Savoy-Mercury-Clef labels.
Every year previously unknown recordings appear, and about
700 different ones have been reissued on LPs.


PEPPER, ARTHUR EDWARD (ART)
b. Gardena, California          d. Los Angeles, California
   1 September 1925                15 June 1982

Pepper was a top alto saxophonist with Stan Kenton in
1943-44 and on and off until 1952.  He waged a war against
his drug habit and was released from San Quentin Prison in
1956.  For several months in 1968, he played lead alto
with Buddy Rich and was featured in the ballad "Alfie."
During one 16-month period, he marked more time in prison
and hospitals than on bandstands.  He gave a detailed account of his fight with narcotics in his 1979 autobiography. Miraculously though, his style grew into a distinctive,
fiery lyricism.  Pepper felt that his most powerful in-
fluences were Lester Young, Zoot Sims, and John Coltrane.


Autobiography:

Straight Life:  The Story of Art Pepper (New York:
Schirmer Books, 1979).

Selected Recordings:

Gettin' Together; Art Pepper plus Eleven; The Way It
Was (Contemporary); Omega Man (Onyx).


POLO, DANNY
b. Clinton, Indiana             d. Chicago, Illinois
   1901                            July 1949

In the early 1920s, Polo began playing in Chicago
with the Arnold Johnson Band (c. 1925).  In 1926-27, he
worked with Ben Bernie and Jean Goldkette and then went to
Europe until 1938.  It was there that he made his reputation in a swing style band in London led by Bert Ambrose.
Polo did much recording, and it was said that he was a
clarinetist who matched Benny Goodman; he also played multiple saxophones.  By the first winter of World War II, he
returned to the U.S. and joined Jack Teagarden for two
years.  He performed with Claude Thornhill from late 1939
until the group was disbanded (when Thornhill enlisted in
the Navy on 26 October 1942).  He and other members of
the sax section returned to the band in 1947 and again in

1948-1949. The other members of the section were Buddy
Dean, George Paulsen, Conn Humphreys, Jack Ferrier, and
Ted Goodhard.

Recordings:

(See Roger Kinkle, The Complete Encyclopedia of Popular Music and Jazz, p. 1577).


RICKER, RAMON L.
b. Camp Forrest, Tennessee
   16 September 1943

   After finishing the M.M. at Michigan State University
in 1967, Ricker completed the D.M.A. at Eastman in 1973.
He presently performs with the Rochester Philharmonic on
bass clarinet and sax and teaches at Eastman. His saxophone teachers have been Al Regni and J. M. Londeix. He
is a fine jazz improvisation performer and has toured with
his combo. He gave a recital at Alice Tully Hall in January, 1976 and was jazz editor for The Saxophone Symposium.

Compositions/Publications:

   Electra-sax in Blue (1979); Solar Chariots (sax-s.,
   pf., Dorn); Ramon Ricker Improvisation Method (5
   vols.); Jazz Technique Books (4 vols., with cassettes,
   Black Swan); Ramon Ricker Improvisation Series (4
   vols., CPP); Variations on a Theme by Sweelinck (SATB,
   Kendor, 1982).

Compositions dedicated to R. Ricker:

   Verne Reynolds (b. 1926): Capriccio (c. 1979).
   James Wiley (b. 1939): To Wake the Dad (c. 1972).


ROLLINI, ADRIAN
b. New York, New York         d. Homestead, Florida
   28 June 1904                  15 May 1956

   A talented and versatile musician important in the
1920s and 1930s, Rollini was a pioneer in the use of the
bass sax as a solo instrument. He was the older brother
of Arthur Rollini (an underrated tenor player) and was a
child prodigy on the piano. At 14 he led a band in New
York, and he worked with the California Ramblers from 1924
to 1927. He performed in London with Fred Elizalde in
1928-29 and with Bert Lown in 1930-31, followed by engagements with Leo Risman and Richard Himer. He did much
free-lance recording, mostly leading studio groups of top
jazzmen such as Benny Goodman, Pee Wee Russell, Joe Venuti,
Manny Klein, Jack Teagarden, and the Dorsey Brothers.
About 1936, he began concentrating on the vibraphone and

did radio work in the band on <u>Your Hit Parade</u>. He did much
work with a trio into the 1950s and then settled in Florida;
his last job was at a Miami hotel in September, 1955.

Compositions:

> Vibrollini; Vibraphonia Number 2; Gliding Ghost;
> Preparation; Au Revoir; Stuff, Etc.; Nothing but
> Notes; Mellow as a Cello; Tap Room Blues.

Recordings:

> (See Roger Kinkle, <u>The Complete Encyclopedia of Pop-</u>
> <u>ular Music and Jazz</u>, p. 1666.)

ROLLINS, THEODOR WALTER (SONNY)
b. New York, New York
  7 September 1929

Rollins started on the alto sax as a child, but
changed to the tenor in high school; upon his graduation
in the late 1940s, he jumped into the thick of New York's
bebop era. Working with the established masters--Davis,
Coltrane, Thelonious Monk, and others--he soon developed
his own burly tone and became a brilliant improviser, following the Parker tradition. From the mid-1950s on, he
led his own small groups, a role which won him international renown. He became prominent in 1957, when he won
the Down Beat Critics Poll as a new star. He made retreats
to Japan and India to study yoga and Eastern philosophies
in 1959-61 and 1968-71. In June, 1971, he toured Europe,
giving college concerts; and in 1972 he composed a concerto
with the help of a Guggenheim Fellowship. Rollins has been
featured in festivals in Newport (1973-75), Chateauvallon
(1973), Montreux, Antibes, Konisberg (1974), and in a film
--<u>Live at Ronnie Scott's Club</u> (BBC, London, 1974).

In addition to the intensity and scope of his live
performances, Rollins has produced many recordings with
his wife/manager/co-producer, Lucille. Albums recorded in
the 1960s concentrated on avant-garde concepts and open-
ended compositional forms. In the 1970s his eclecticism
started to emerge, and he surprised his fans by adding,
among other things, modern harmony and blues to his playing and compositional styles.

Compositions:

> Alfie's Theme (movie <u>Alfie</u>); Sonnymoon for Two; The
> Cutting Edge; St. Thomas (adaptation of a West Indian
> melody).

Selected Recordings (fantasy reissues and other notable
      releases):

Vintage Sessions (Prestige P 24096, 1951-54); Saxo-
phone Colossus and More (Prestige P 24050, 1951-56);
Taking Care of Business (Prestige P 24082, 1955-56);
Sonny Rollins Plus (Milestone M 47007, 1957-58); Sonny
Rollins with the Modern Jazz Quintet (Original Jazz
Classics OJC 011, 1953); Jazz Classics (Prestige
P 7433, 1954); Worktime (Original Jazz Classics OJC
007, 1955); Sonny Plays for Bird (Prestige P 7553,
1956); Tenor Madness (Prestige P 7657, with J. Coltrane); Three Giants (Prestige P 7821); Sound of Sonny;
Blues for Tomorrow (Original Jazz Classics OJC 029/
030, 1957); Sonny Rollins, Vols. 1 & 2 (RCA 741074/
075); A Night at the Village Vanguard (Blue Note BST
81581, 1958); The Standard Sonny Rollins (RCA LPS
3355, 1965); Next Album; Horn Culture; The Cutting
Edge; Nucleus; The Way I Feel; Easy Living; Don't
Stop the Carnival; Don't Ask; Love at First Sight; No
Problem; Reed Life (all current releases from Milestone).


STABILE, DICK
b. Newark, New Jersey
   29 May 1909

An underrated virtuoso on alto sax, Stabile played
with a beautiful tone, clean execution, and was one of the
early jazz artists to perform in the altissimo register.
As a teenager he was playing in pit orchestras for Broadway shows.  He was lead sax with Ben Bernie (1928-36) and
formed his own band in late 1936.  His sax section was mellow in tone due to his leadership; his theme, "Blue Nocturne," featured him.  He had important midday radio cover-
age from New York and was featured at the New York World's
Fair in 1940.  During his military service, his wife,
Gracie Barrie, fronted the band.

In 1949, Stabile led a band at Ciro's in Hollywood
behind Dean Martin and Jerry Lewis and stayed with the
team during the 1950s for movies, radio, and TV.  His band
boasted a superb, crisp sound with fine arrangements, and
his sax solos remained effective.  He continued performing
into the 1950s, usually backing name entertainers.

Publications:

Saxophone studies (Republics, 1941, OP).

Recordings:

(See Roger Kinkle, The Complete Encyclopedia of Popular Music and Jazz, pp. 1797-98).

TRUMBAUER, FRANK (TRAM)
b. Carbondale, Illinois          d. Kansas City, Missouri
   30 May 1901                      June 1956

Growing up in St. Louis, Trumbauer studied piano, violin, flute, and trombone before concentrating on C melody saxophone. He later played cornet, alto sax, and bassoon. After World War I and military service, and working with the bands of Max Goldman, Earl Fuller, Gene Rodemich, Joe Kayser, and others, he joined the Benson Orchestra (1923) in Chicago. Rust says:

> At the time when dance music was usually clipped and staccato in its phrasing . . . which had characterized it since pre-Dixieland days--Trumbauer's smooth legato playing and advanced musical phraseology made him the most emulated saxophonist in the U.S.A. and his records became known everywhere.[14]

While Trumbauer was leading a small band at the Arcadia Ballroom in St. Louis (1925), Bix Beiderbecke joined his group and they became great friends. After playing a summer job at Hudson Lake, Indiana, they were engaged with Jean Goldkette's band, where they were prominently featured until they joined Paul Whiteman in late 1927. Trumbauer remained with Whiteman until the spring of 1932 and rejoined the band late 1933 through most of 1936. The sax section consisted of Alvy West and Trumbauer (altos), and Chester Hazlett and John Cordaro (tenors). Lester Young (q.v.) acknowledged Trumbauer as a great influence in his developing years. Late in 1937, Trumbauer co-led a big band with Manny Klein, and he led his own band (sometimes billed as the Frank Trumbauer Band) in 1938. The famous song "Singing the Blues" was used as their theme song.

In the 1930s, he became a pilot; he was a test pilot during World War II and eventually a flying instructor as the big band era drew to a close. He led bands briefly in 1940 and 1945 in New York.

Compositions (many of the following pieces composed or co-authored by Trumbauer were recorded; they were published by Robbins and are all OP):

Frank Trumbauer's Saxophone Studies; Trumbology; F Blues; Wildcat; Tailspin; Krazy Kat; Sun Spots; Loved One; G Blues; Three Blind Mice; Eclipse; The Bouncing Ball; Bass Drum Dan; Red Hot Barb Wire Blues; Wringin' and Twistin'; I'm Glad; Meteor.

Trumbauer recorded five discs with Jean Goldkette, 18 with Paul Whiteman, one with Joe Venuti, and 18 under his own name. (For titles, see Roger Kinkle, The Complete Encyclopedia of Popular Music and Jazz, vol. 3, pp. 1874-75.)

VIOLA, JOSEPH E.
b. Malden, Massachusetts
    25 June 1920

In addition to his gifts as a soloist, Viola is a
master of eight woodwind instruments.  His teachers have
been Ferdinand Gillet, Joseph Allard, and Marcel Mule.
Having chosen to devote his talents to the educational
aspect of the saxophone, he focuses his teaching approach
on a full, vibrant sound, which has attracted students from
all over the world to the Berklee School.  Since 1947, he
had been Supervisor of Woodwind Instruction, and over 500
of his former students are currently active professionally
in jazz groups, studio orchestras, and name bands.

Compositions/Publications (all released by Berklee):

        Technique of the Saxophone: Vol. 1 (Scale Studies,
        1963); Vol. 2 (Chord Studies, 1965); Vol. 3 (Rhythm
        Studies, 1971); Creative Reading Studies (1982).

Compositions dedicated to J. Viola:

        Manny Albam:  Six Pieces for Eight Winds.  Berklee,
        1961.
        Thomas Oboe Lee (b. 1945):  A Piece for Viola.  Dorn,
        1979.
        David Tanner:  Improvisation (1973).

Recordings:

        Joe Viola Plays Manny Albam (Berklee, 1961); Berklee
        Saxophone Quartet (Berklee BLP 102, 1972, Bavicchi,
        La Porta, Kacinskas, Mozart).


WOODS, PHILIP WELLS (PHIL)
b. Springfield, Massachusetts
    2 November 1931

Established as one of the top alto saxophone performers with Dizzy Gillespie, Thad Jones, Benny Goodman, and
his own groups in the 1950s and 1960s, Woods led a busy
life in New York.  He also taught jazz at Ramblery (New
Hope, Pennsylvania, 1966-67).  He lived in Europe from
March, 1968 until 1972, when he moved to California.  He
returned to the East Coast in October, 1973, to write and
teach.

Compositions:

        Round Trip; Rights of Swing; Saxophone Method (CJC);
        Sonata (Kendor, 1980); Three Improvisations (SATB,
        Kendor, 1980); Peace (a ballet for French TV); Phil
        Woods Series (comp. and arr. for jazz ens., Kendor);

Phil Woods Solos (tran., ed. Kynaston, CPP, 1980);
11 Sax Solos (tran. from recent LP's, Aebersold).

Selected Recordings:

Musique du Bois (Muse); New Music (Testament); Round
Trip (Verve); Rights of Swing (Barnaby); Early Quin-
tets (Prestige); At the Frankfurt Jazz Festival (Em-
bryo); At the Montreux Jazz Festival (MGM); You've Got
It Bad Girl (A&M); Images (with M. Legrand, RCA); Live
at Jimmy's (RCA); Double Exposure (with J. Roccisano
and Victor Morosco, Protone PR 153); Saxes Inc. (Warner Bros. W 1336); Phil Woods/Lew Tabackin (Omni N
1033); Phil talks with Quill (Columbia LN 3521).


YOUNG, LESTER WILLIS (PREZ)
b. Woodville, Mississippi      d. New York, New York
   27 August 1907                 15 March 1959

One of the great all-time jazz tenor saxophonists,
Young was particularly outstanding from the mid-1930s to
the mid-1940s. His father, Billy, who had studied at Tus-
kegee Institute, could play nearly every instrument, was a
carnival musician, and gave music lessons to ten-year-old
Lester. At 15, Lester discovered Bix Beiderbecke and also
the C melody saxophonist, Frankie Trumbauer. He became
entranced with the latter's recordings, tried to produce
the same sound on the tenor sax, and eventually developed
a soft, light tone with little vibrato and swung in a
light, clean style. His tone quality and ideas laid the
groundwork for bop and the modern cool sound. This influence by Trumbauer is the first case of a white musician
influencing a black jazz player. Playing both the tenor
and the alto sax, Lester toured with bands in the Midwest
in 1928-30. He was a member of the original Blue Devils
(Oklahoma City, 1932-33), played with Bennie Moten (Kansas
City, 1933-34), Clarence Love, King Oliver, and Fletcher
Henderson (1934), and joined Count Basie at the Reno Club,
Kansas City, early in 1936. He remained with Basie until
late 1940, and his innovative solos won acclaim. In 1941-
43, he co-led a combo with his brother Lee on the West
Coast and in New York. In 1943, he worked with Dizzy Gillespie and Al Sears before rejoining Basie late in 1944.
He was featured on Jazz at the Philharmonic, toured abroad,
and led various groups in the 1940s and 1950s. His last
work was early in 1959, in Paris, and he died shortly after
his return to the U.S.

Compositions (Young was composer or co-composer of the
         following jazz pieces, many of which were recorded):

Jumpin' with Symphony Sid; Tickle Toe; Lester Leaps In
(c. 1939); Dickie's Dream; Taxi War Dance (with Basie);
Rock-a-Bye Basie (with Shad Collins); Nobody knows;

Don't Tell on Me; Sometimes I'm Happy (Young's quartet, 1943).

Film:

Jammin' the Blues (by J. Mili, France, 1943).

Selected Recordings:

At His Very Best (EmArcy 66010); Best of Count Basie
(Decca DXS 7170); Blue Lester (Savoy 12068); Essen-
tial Lester Young (Verve V 68398); Giant of Jazz (Sun
5181); Immortal Lester Young (Savoy 12155); Lester
Leaps In (Epic 3107); Lester Young-Buddy Rich Trio
(Verve V 8164, 1945); Master's Touch (Savoy 12071);
Memorial Album (Epic 3576); Spiritual to Swing Concert
(Vanguard 8523/4).

Young recorded many discs with Basie, the Kansas City
Seven, Glenn Hardman, Billie Holiday, and Teddy Wilson, as
well as under his own name. (See Roger Kinkle, The Complete
Encyclopedia of Popular Music and Jazz, pp. 1989-90 for
additional titles.)

# 6.

# Annotated Bibliography of Saxophone Soloists in the American Hemisphere

Every effort was made to include all known, serious saxophone soloists through research, questionnaires, and personal letters and contacts, including interviews and telephone conversations.

A great amount of detail is contained in chapters 6, 7, and 8; information about deceased performers has been researched as completely as possible. Some performers' activities have not been reported or publicized, and other saxophonists are not yet well known in musical circles. If living performers did not give complete information or answer questionnaires (or letters), the writer could only record known information. The author apologizes to those saxophonists or composers who, for one reason or another, are not included or completely represented in these chapters.

N.B.: The bibliography is arranged alphabetically by performer. After a brief summary of his or her career, information is classified as follows: compositions or publications by the saxophonist, solos or chamber music dedicated to or commissioned by the soloist (with dates of premieres when known), and recordings of solo or ensemble performances. Unless otherwise indicated, all compositions are for alto saxophone and piano or orchestra. The composers' birth dates, dates of compositions (or date of publication), their duration and premiere dates are listed when known. Some compositions have not been published, but many are available in manuscript copies from the composers. In these instances, the word "Composer" after the title will refer the reader to the composers' addresses listed in the appendix. [Information in parentheses uses the following order: date of composition, combination of instruments, and premiere date (if known).]

ABATO, VINCENT
b. Willmerding, Pennsylvania
  c. 1920

     After studying at Peabody and Juilliard, Abato spe-
cialized on the clarinet, bass clarinet, and saxophone.
Highlights of his busy career include performances under
Artur Rodzinski and Leopold Stokowski and appearances with
the Los Angeles Philharmonic, Boston Pops, New York Phil-
harmonic, and other orchestras.  No stranger to the re-
cording field, he has performed with Percy Faith, Morton
Gould, André Kostelanetz, and others.  He premiered the
Creston Saxophone Concerto with the New York Philharmonic
in 1944 and also played it with the Baltimore Orchestra.
Abato has taught at Columbia Teachers College, Hofstra
University, and Juilliard, and is currently professor at
Brooklyn College.  He is the bass clarinetist and saxo-
phonist with the Metropolitan Opera Orchestra.


Music dedicated to V. Abato:

     Rex Mitchell:  Song of the City (1967, sax, band or
        pf.).  Colin
     Alfred Reed (b. 1921):  Ballade (sax, pf./band).
        SMC, 1956


Recordings:

     Glazunov/Ibert (Nonesuch H 71030); Music for Alto
     Saxophone (Music Minus One, MMO Nos. 8022, 8024, 8026,
     8028); Creston: Sonata (Columbia ML 4989, P. Creston,
     pf.).


ADIRONDACK SAXOPHONE QUARTET
founded 1976

     Highlights in the quartet's history have been a full-
length concert taped for WMHT-PBS TV and performances as
featured soloists with the Northeast Symphonic Band, a
professional band based in Albany, New York.  Active in
concerts and clinics, the ASQ includes in its repertoire
many transcriptions done by members of the quartet as well
as the standard literature.  Nathaniel Fossner (soprano
sax) received degrees from Eastman and Columbia University
Teachers College.  He teaches in the South Colonie Central
School District in Albany, performs on the English horn
with the Albany Symphony Orchestra, and plays first oboe
with the Northeast Symphonic Band.  James Corigliano (alto
sax) earned degrees at SUNY and Fredonia, and was a student
of Laurence Wyman.  He teaches in the Guilderland Central
School District and at the College of Saint Rose in Albany.

Other members of the ASQ are Thomas Gerbino (tenor sax) and George Smith (baritone sax).

Compositions dedicated to the Adirondack Saxophone Quartet:

> David Deason (b. 1945): Quartet (1983). Prem. 23
> September 1984, Potsdam (2nd and 3rd mov'ts., see
> Steven Mauk).
> Emil Kaled: Isomorphica.


ALDUINO, ANTHONY C.
b. Rockville Center, New York
   20 December 1950

A student of Laurence Wyman and Sigurd Rascher, Alduino earned his B.Ed. and M.Ed. in 1972 and 1976, respectively, at SUNY, Fredonia. He has been soloist on the soprano and alto sax at Region Eight meetings of NASA and the sixth WSC in 1979. He plays soprano sax with the Saxophone Sinfonia. In addition to teaching in the Susquehanna Valley Schools (Conklin, N.Y.), he was an instructor at Onondaga Community College and saxophonist with the Syracuse Symphony Orchestra from 1977 to 1982.

Recordings:

> The Fredonia Saxophone Ensemble (Mark MES 37575, 1972);
> The Rascher Saxophone Ensemble (vols. 1 & 2 Coronet
> LPS 3022, 1974 and LPS 3031, 1975); The Saxophone
> Sinfonia (Golden Crest CRSDG 4221, 1982).


ALLARD, JOSEPH A.
b. Lowell, Massachusetts
   30 December 1910

After studying clarinet at the New England Conservatory, Allard began to play in various bands. He took some instruction from Gaston Hamelin on clarinet and Rudy Wiedoeft on saxophone. While playing first sax with the Red Nichols band, he decided to settle in New York. He played first clarinet on the Bell Telephone Hour for 18 years and the Dupont Radio Show for 19 years. He also played sax with the New York Philharmonic and performed for the RCA Victor recording of Bizet's L'Arlésienne Suite, conducted by Stokowski, in the 1940s. He is a highly respected teacher at Juilliard, New York University, and Mannes College.

Published works:

> Three Octave Scales (1947); Advanced Rhythms; Jazz
> Progressive Studies.  Composer.

Composition dedicated to J. Allard:

>    Gunther Schuller (b. 1925):  Concerto (sax, orch.,
>    comm. by pupils of Mr. Allard, it was completed
>    for Allard's 70th birthday).  AMP.  Prem. 17 Jan.
>    1984, Pittsburgh, Pa., by K. Radnofsky.


AMATURO, MATTHEW
b. Salerno, Italy              d. Chicago, Illinois
   10 December 1887               14 January 1965

    As a former member of the Six Brown Brothers, Amaturo
appeared with them in Jack O'Lantern, a musical comedy.
In 1916, he moved to Chicago from Seattle and became identified with Benson, the well-known musical producer, performed before thousands in saxophone solos, and was regarded as one of Benson's greatest attractions.  He recorded with the Benson Orchestra for the Victor Talking
Machine Co.  In addition to his performances, he was a
highly respected sax teacher in Chicago.


ATOR, JAMES D.
b. Kansas City, Kansas
   15 October 1938

    A saxophonist, clarinetist, and composer, Ator began
his studies at Drake University, where he worked with
Nathan Jones.  From 1960 to 1963, he served in the U.S.
Military Academy Band; in 1964 he earned a master's degree
at Wichita University (as a student of Vance Jennings); and
he has completed the DMA in composition with William Latham,
Merrill Ellis, and Samuel Adler.  Since 1973, he has been
an Associate Professor teaching Composition and Woodwinds
at Indiana University-Purdue University (Fort Wayne).
Earlier teaching assignments were at Millikin University
and Wichita State University.

Compositions:

>    Woodwind Quartet (fl., cl., sax, bn., Seesaw, 1969);
>    Three Pieces for Saxophone and Piano (Seesaw, 1970);
>    Enuffispluntee (sax, per., Seesaw, 1972); Life Cycle
>    (ob., sax, vcl., mezzo sop., Seesaw, 1974); Duo for
>    Saxophone and Tuba (Dorn, 1981); Adagio for Saxophone
>    Quartet (Dorn, 1981); Duo for Saxophones (Dorn, prem.
>    March, 1984, Ft. Wayne).


AYSCUE, BRIAN T.
b. Camden, New Jersey
   25 April 1948

    A graduate of Glassboro State College (New Jersey) in

1970, Ayscue studied clarinet and saxophone with Anthony Ciccarelli. He also studied saxophone with Sigurd Rascher and composition with Joel Thome. Ayscue is a contributing editor in charge of reviews of recordings for The Saxophone Symposium, the quarterly journal of NASA.

Compositions:

> Three Pieces for Alto Saxophone Solo (1969, Artisan, 1970); Mourning Piece for Alto Saxophone and Piano (1970, to G. J. Webber, Sr.); The Place of Peace (sax-t., pf., 1972, to Bruce Weinberger); Permutations I (fl., ob., cl., tpt., sax-t., 1972, to J. Thome); Quartet for Saxophones (1982).

BAMBER, DENNIS R.
b. South Bend, Indiana
   7 December 1947

A pupil of Eugene Rousseau and Daniel Deffayet, Bamber earned the B.M. (1970) and the M.M. (1972) at Indiana University, has taught at Notre Dame University, and currently has a private studio and music store in South Bend.

Recordings:

> Music for Saxophone, Vols. I and II (Etoile DB 1, 1974); American Saxophone Quartet (Etoile DB 2, 1976); Duo Saxophonists (Crystal Records, with E. Rousseau, S 156, 1981); Yamaha Suite (Golden Crest 4224, with Rousseau Quartet, music by Carisi, Heiden, Linn, and Paich).

BANGS, LINDA
b. United States
   unknown

A graduate of SUNY, Fredonia, Linda Bangs was a student of Laurence Wyman, studied additionally with Sigurd Rascher, and is an original member of the Rascher Quartet. She specializes in the baritone saxophone and continues to play in the quartet led by Carina Rascher. Bangs teaches at the Waldorf Schule in Mannheim, Germany.

Music dedicated to L. Bangs:

> Werner Glaser (b. 1910): Tale for Baritone and Percussion (1977, 4 per.).
> Walter Hartley (b. 1927): Little Suite (1974, sax-b., pf., 5'30). Dorn, 1976.
> Lukas Zdenek (b. 1928): Raccontino. Prem. 9 July 1982, Nuremberg.

Recordings:

   (See Sigurd Rascher.)


BECKENSTEIN, RAYMOND
b. Brooklyn, New York
   14 August 1923

     Originally a student of the violin, Beckenstein became
interested in the clarinet and the saxophone.  His teachers
were Joseph Allard (saxophone), Leon Russianoff (clarinet),
and Harold Bennett and Julius Baker (flute).  A professional musician since 1941, he is among the top studio
musicians currently active in New York.  His vast experience includes recordings, motion pictures, jazz bands,
and symphony work.  He has appeared with Frank Sinatra,
Nat "King" Cole, Paul McCartney, Miles Davis, Benny Goodman, Artie Shaw, and the New York Philharmonic (under
Bernstein, Leopold Stowkowski, and André Kostelanetz).

     In 1959, he began to play the soprano saxophone with
the New York Saxophone Quartet shortly after the original
four (Danny Bank, Al Cohn, Stan Getz, and Hal McKasick)
began the group.  He is the oldest member of the current
ensemble; earlier performers were Albert Regni, David
Tofani, Ed Caine, Al Epstein, and Harvey Estrin.  The present quartet, led by Beckenstein, consists also of Dennis
Anderson (alto), William Kerr (tenor), and Walter Kane
(baritone).  Their first recital was in Town Hall in 1965,
and their many appearances have included meetings in Bordeaux (1974) and Nuremberg (1982).  Under conductor R. Davies
the quartet premiered Calvin Hampton's Concerto for quartet,
strings, and percussion in 1975; it was also performed in
Minneapolis and New Hampshire.  In addition to classical
compositions, the quartet excells in works in the jazz
idiom, including improvisation.

Compositions dedicated to the New York Saxophone Quartet:

        Manny Albam (b. 1922):  Quartet No. 1 (1964).
        John Carisi:  Quartet No. 1 (1964).
        Rusty Dedrick (b. 1918):  Modern Jazz Suite.
           Kendor.
        Eugene DiNovi:  La Blues (1964).
        Don Hammond:  Ballad and Scherzo (1964).
        Calvin Hampton (b. 1938):  Concerto (strs., per.).
           Prem. 1975, New York.
        George Handy (b. 1920):  Quartets Nos. 1, 2, 3 (1964).
        Chico O'Farrell:  Three Pieces.
        Don Stratton:  Nocturne.
        _____ :  Small Symphony No. 2.
        Phil Woods (b. 1931):  Three Improvisations. Kendor,
           1981.

Recordings:

> N.Y.S.Q. (20th Century Records TEM 3150, 1964);
> N.Y.S.Q. (Stash Records ST 210, 1980, music by Albe-
> niz, Hampton, Kaderavek, Kerr, Matthews, Sauter); An
> American Experience (Stash Records ST 220, 1982, Music
> by Carisi, Dodgion, Dunbar, Gershwin, Rood, Strayhorn).

BECKER, RUDOLPH
b. United States                d. 1952
   Unknown

    Becker is the last survivor of the original Sousa
band.  He played in the first concert with Sousa in Plainfield, New Jersey on 26 September 1892.  He was a baritone
saxophonist with the Wanamaker Band in Philadelphia when
he was signed by Sousa; the salary was $35.00 per week for
nine weeks.  According to Schwartz, "It has been estimated
that twelve to fifteen hundred different musicians played
in the Sousa Band during its existence."[1]

BESTMAN, JAMES F.
b. Chicago, Illinois
   8 February 1935

    A professional musician in Chicago, Bestman attended
Northwestern University and earned the B.M. and the B.M.Ed.
(1958) and the M.M. (1959).  His saxophone teachers were
Santy Runyon, D. V. O'Neil, and Cecil Leeson.  He has composed two sonatas and a concerto, which are unpublished.

Compositions dedicated to J. Bestman:

> Willis Charkovsky: Fantasy Sonata.  Prem. May, 1959.
> Lawson Lunde (b. 1935): Sonata No. 1 (1958-1963).
>     SMC, 1967.  Prem. May 1959 (first mov't only; see
>     Brian Minor).

BILGER, DAVID
b. Reading, Pennsylvania
   16 April 1945

    A pupil of Donald Sinta, Sigurd Rascher, and Joseph
Allard, Bilger completed the B.M. at Ithaca College in
1967 and did graduate study at the Hartt School of Music.
The Bilger Duo (with wife Dorinne) has performed in many
recitals in the U.S., at various regional meets of NASA,
and at the 5th WSC in London (1976).  A New York recital
was given in Carnegie Hall, 20 April 1983.  Bilger has
played bass saxophone for Rascher's Saxophone Ensemble and
is the conductor of the 18-piece Saxophone Sinfonia, which
appeared in Alice Tully Hall in New York on 11 June 1982.

He teaches at his own music studio in Shillington, Pa. and
at Lebanon Valley College.

## Compositions dedicated to D. Bilger:

Henk Badings (b. 1907): <u>Largo Cantabile</u> (1983, 6').
Don.

Sy Brandon (b. 1945): <u>Bachburg Concerto No. 2</u> (sax,
pf. or orch). Prem. Nov. 1980.

_____: <u>Conversations</u> (1977). Tenuto, 1981. Prem.
12 May 1978. Composer.

_____: <u>Introduction and Dance</u>. Prem. 29 April
1969. Composer.

Erwin Chandler (b. 1944): <u>Sinfonia</u> (2S,4A,2T,B,Bs.).
Prem. 11 June 1982, N.Y.C.

_____: <u>Sonata</u>, opus 25 (1969). Prem. 30 April 1973.
Composer.

_____: <u>Suite</u>. Prem. 22 Sep. 1985, Annville, Pa.
Composer.

_____: <u>Three Pieces for Alto Saxophone and Piano</u>.
(1982). Composer.

Harry Gee (b. 1924): <u>Intrada</u>. Prem. 12 May 1978,
Muncie, Indiana. Composer.

## Recordings:

The Bilger Duo (5 Studios Inc., 6123 N6, music by
Badings, Bozza, Chandler, Cowell, Fiocco, Handel,
Hartley); The Bilger Duo Plays Recital Favorites
(Trutone Records 520458, music by Benson, Brandon,
Koechlin, Martini, Milhaud, Mondonville, Wiedoeft);
The Rascher Saxophone Ensemble (vols. 1 & 2, Coronet
LPS 3022, 1974; LPS 3031, 1975); The Saxophone Sin-
fonia (Crest 4221, 1982, music by Bach, Caravan,
Chandler, Grieg).


BLACK, ROBERT
b. Sentinel, Oklahoma
   21 October 1951

In 1969 Black graduated from Interlochen Arts Academy,
where he had been a pupil of Jack Kripl. He continued his
studies and earned a B.M. at Northwestern University with
Frederick Hemke as his teacher. In 1971, after winning
several Chicago-area competitions, Black received a grant
from the M. H. Berlin Foundation to spend his junior year
abroad studying with Jean-Marie Londeix. During this year
in France, he made several appearances on French National
Radio, was soloist twice with the Bordeaux Symphony Orchestra, and was awarded an unanimous first prize from the
CNRM, Bordeaux. His first appearance in England was at
Wigmore Hall in 1972; he also performed in London at the
WSC in 1976. He has been soloist with the Chicago Civic
Orchestra (1972) and the St. Louis Symphony (1976). Black

is the soprano saxophonist with the Chicago Saxophone
Quartet and a professor at Roosevelt University since 1977.

Compositions dedicated to R. Black:

> H. William Karlins (b. 1932): Concerto (1981-82).
> ACA. Prem. 8 July 1982, Nuremberg.
> _____: Quartet No. II. CF, 1975.

Recordings:

> Concert Repertoire for Saxophone (Brewster 1216, 1976,
> music by Cowell, Husa, Ibert); Chicago Saxophone Quar-
> tet (Brewster, music by Albeniz, Bach, Duckworth,
> Lantier, Pierné).


BOITOS, JAMES A.
b. Detroit, Michigan
  1 July 1946

A student of Phil Urso, Fez Bryant, and Frederick
Hemke, Boitos received the M.M. at Northwestern University
in 1971. He was a soloist at the fifth, sixth, and seventh
WSC and participated in the first and second International
Saxophone Symposiums with the U.S. Navy Band in 1978 and
1979. Appointed in 1971, he is an associate professor at
Illinois State University (Normal).

Compositions dedicated to J. Boitos:

> Roque Corero (b. 1917): Soliloquios No. 2 (sax solo).
> SMPC, 1976.
> Wolfgang Hofmann: Concertino (sax, strs., orch.).
> Prem. 1982.


BONGIORNO, FRANK J.
b. Brooklyn, New York
  2 March 1958

A pupil of James Riggs and Steven Mauk, Bongiorno
graduated from Ithaca College (B.M., 1980) and North Texas
State University (M.M., 1982). He played a solo recital
at the seventh WSC in Nuremberg and teaches at the University of North Carolina, Wilmington. He is a doctoral
candidate at Indiana University.

Compositions dedicated to F. Bongiorno:

> Antonia Dukas (b. 1960): Fantasia. Prem. 13 Feb. 1982.
> David Kechley (b. 1947): Concerto (sax, ch. orch.).
> prem. 13 May 1984.
> Roar Schad (b. 1941): Study (1972, sax, tape, 8'30).

BOURQUE, PIERRE
b. Plessisville, Québec, Canada
   27 January 1938

From 1954 to 1958, Bourque studied at the Conservatoire de Québec with Maurice DeCelles.  When the French
artist Georges Gourdet made a concert tour of Canada in
1957, Bourque took some lessons with him and was encouraged
to continue his education with Marcel Mule in Paris.  From
1958 to 1961, he was a member of Mule's class at the CNSM,
where he graduated with a first prize.  In 1963, Bourque
established the Quatuor de Saxophones Pierre Bourque,
which gave many concerts in Canada, the U.S., and France.
The other members of the quartet have also received first
prizes from the CNSM; they are Claude Brisson (1970),
Jacques Larocque (1969), and Jean Bouchard (1972).  Bourque
is Professor of Saxophone and Chamber Music at the Conservatoire de Musique in Québec.

Compositions dedicated to the Pierre Bourque Saxophone
Quartet:

> Denis Bédard (b. 1952): Suite (1983).
> Alexander Brott (b. 1915): Saxi-Fonie-Saties (1972,
>    16').
> Marc Fortier: Tempo I (1968).
> Marc Gagné (b. 1938): Le Petit Chaperon Rouge (1982).
> Pierre Genest (b. 1945): Phonie-Ma (1976, comm. by
>    the Conseil des Arts du Canada).
> _____ : Saxologie (1971).
> Piérick Houdy (b. 1929): Chemins (1977).  Bil., 1979.
> Jean-Clément Isabelle: Quintette, opus 4 (1982).
> Claude Vivier: Pulau Dewata.  CMC.  Prem. 29 June
>    1979, WSC, Evanston.

Recording:

> Quatuor de Saxophones Pierre Bourque (RCA LSC 3141,
> 1969, music by Absil, Dubois, Fiala, Françaix).


BRIGHTMAN, NICHOLAS
b. Anderson, Indiana
   19 November 1948

A student of Cecil Leeson, Brightman completed graduate studies in 1972, was a graduate assistant and an ad-
junct faculty member at Ball State University, and later
opened a private studio in Indianapolis.  In addition to
solo appearances, he performs with the Indianapolis Symphony Orchestra when a saxophonist is required.  He played
Husa's Concerto with the Butler University Band (1973) and
with the Cleveland Philharmonic (1975).  He was also soloist in Ibert's Concertino da Camera with the Nebraska
Chamber Orchestra in Lincoln.

Compositions dedicated to N. Brightman:

> Garland Anderson (b. 1933): Sonata for Baritone
> Saxophone and Piano. SMC, 1976.
> Robert Jager (b. 1939): Concerto No. 2 (sax, band).
> CPP, 1979. Prem. 19 April 1978, Indianapolis.

Compositions premiered by N. Brightman:

> Garland Anderson (b. 1933): Sonata for Tenor Saxo-
> phone and Piano. SMC, 1968 (ded. to C. Leeson).
> Prem. May, 1971.
> William Presser (b. 1916): Concerto for Tenor Saxo-
> phone (1965, ded. to C. Lesson). Prem. 5 May
> 1969, Muncie, Indiana.
> Leon Stein (b. 1910): Sonata (sax-t., pf.). SMC,
> 1967. Prem. 1968, Muncie, Indiana.
> Burnet Tuthill (1888-1982): Concerto, opus 56 (sax-t.,
> orch./band or pf., 1965). SMC, 1965. Prem. April,
> 1967, Muncie, Indiana.

Recording:

> The Compositions of Robert Jager (Crest ATH 5068).


BRISCUSO, JOSEPH J.
b. St. Louis, Missouri
   17 August 1939

Studying with J. Roger Miller and Carlos Camacho,
Briscuso earned degrees from the St. Louis Institute of
Music (B.M.Ed., 1961), Millikin University (M.M., 1963),
and the University of Iowa (Ph.D., 1972). Since 1972, he
has been the Professor of Saxophone at Towson State University. A director of the American Single Reed Workshop,
he also served as a clinician at the Iowa Music Educators
Association and various summer music camps in 1972 and
1973.

Recordings:

> Towson Chamber Players (Crest RE 7086, music by T.
> Myers); Johnny Rinaldo Band (J & D Records, 1964 and
> 1965).


BRISSON, CLAUDE
b. Chicoutimi, Québec, Canada
   20 March 1943

From 1963 to 1967, Brisson studied with Pierre Bourque
at the Conservatoire de Québec, and from 1967 to 1970, was
a member of the saxophone classes of Marcel Mule and Daniel
Deffayet at the CNSM, Paris. Winning a first prize in 1970,

he was appointed Professor of Saxophone at the Conservatoire de Québec in 1972. Brisson has been soloist in Canada, England, Germany, and the U.S. for meetings of the
WSC. He also won the Silver medal at the Concours International de Genève in 1970. He has been a member of the
Quatuor Pierre Bourque since 1963.

## Compositions dedicated to C. Brisson:

Denis Bédard (b. 1952): Sonate (1981). Prem. 9
July 1982.
M. Gagné (b. 1938): Quatuor (1981).
Pierre Genest (b. 1945): Saxolo (1972).
Piérick Houdy (b. 1929): Kastchentamoun (1974).

## Recordings:

Houdy: Hommage à Teilhard de Chardin (Disque Radio
Canada, 1983). (Also, see P. Bourque.)


BRODIE, PAUL
b. Montréal, Québec, Canada
   11 April 1934

Brodie's studies with Larry Teal at the University of
Michigan led to degrees in B.M.Ed. (1956) and a Masters in
Woodwinds (1958). He was also a pupil of Marcel Mule and,
in 1969, in Chicago, was one of the founders of the WSC,
of which he is a past president. Brodie has performed
over 2,000 concerts in Canada, the U.S., Australia, Mexico,
and Europe as soloist and with his saxophone quartet. He
has also appeared with several Canadian orchestras in Toronto, Vancouver, Winnipeg, Regina, and Halifax, and with
many community orchestras. He was featured on the sound-
track for the Academy Award film Heaven Can Wait and appeared in the film A Circle of Two with his saxophone
quartet.

## Publication by P. Brodie:

Students' Guide to the Saxophone, 3 vols. (Harris,
1983).

## Compositions dedicated to P. Brodie (many of the following
composers were contacted by Brodie and their works,
in manuscript form, are available from the Canadian
Music Centre):

André Ameller (b. 1912): Pic (from Belle Province,
Bb or Eb sax, pf.). Leduc, 1973.
Violet Archer (b. 1913): Sonata (1972, 17'10).
Berandol, 1974.
Robert Bauer (b. 1950): A Sincere and Earnest Appeal
(SATB, 1974, 8'). CMC.

_____: Sakosodic (SATB, 1974). CMC.
_____: 3 Pieces (1975, sax-s., guit.). CMC.
_____: Willy Rag (SATB, 1972, 1'10). CMC.
Lorne Betts (b. 1918): Concertino (1972, sax-s.,
    strs., 9'). CMC.
Keith Bissell (b. 1912): 3 Etudes (1972). CMC.
Wolfgang Bottenberg (b. 1930): Fa, Sol, La, Ti, Do
    (1972, sax-s., str. quar.). CMC.
Charles Camilleri (b. 1931): Fantaisie Concertante
    (1974, sax solo, 11'). CMC.
_____: Suite (1960).
Don Cowan: Impressions (3'). B.H., 1968.
_____: Morceau de Genre (4'). B.H., 1968.
_____: Reflections (4'). B.H., 1969.
Clifford Crawley: Boutade (1977). CMC.
Anne Eggleston: Quartet (1972, SATB). CMC.
George Fiala (b. 1922): Quartet No. 2 (10'15).
    Berandol, 1970.
_____: Sonata (20'). Dorn, 1970.
_____: Sonata for Two (1971, sax-s., accordion). CMC.
Robert Fleming (1926-1976): Threo (1972, sax-s.,
    pf.). CMC.
Clifford Ford (b. 1947): 5 Short Pieces in Circular
    Motion (1971, sax-s., pf., 6'). CMC.
James Gayfer (b. 1916): Quintet Concertante (1972,
    SAATB, 4'). CMC.
Graham George (b. 1912): Quartet (1972, SATB). CMC.
Gary Hulesha: Concertante (1980, sax ww. quin.).
    CMC.
Lothar Klein (b. 1932): 6 Exchanges (1972, sax solo,
    5'55). Tenuto.
_____: Vaudeville (1979, sax-s., ww. quin. 12'). CMC.
Thomas Legrady (b. 1920): Concertino Grossino
    (1977, SATB, band). CMC.
Arthur Lewis (b. 1935): Sonata (1982, sax solo). CMC.
Bruce Mather (b. 1939): Elegy (1959). Wa.
Tibor Polgar (b. 1907): Iona's Four Faces (1970,
    S & A saxes, 12'30). CMC.
Ben Steinberg: Suite Sephardic (1982, sax-s., vn.,
    vla., vcl.). CMC.
Robert Turner (b. 1920): Nostalgia (1972, sax-s.,
    pf.). CMC.
Rudi Van Dijk (b. 1932): Sonata Mouvement (1960). CMC.
William Wallace (b. 1933): Free Soliloquy (1975, sax
    solo, 7'05). CMC.
_____: Introduction and Chaconne (1977, SATB, 9').
    CMC.
John Weinzweig (b. 1913): Divertimento No. 6 (1972,
    sax, strs., 13'10). CMC.
Gerhard Wuensch (b. 1925): Sonata, opus 59 (1971,
    sax-s., pf., 20'35). CMC.
Leon Zuckert (b. 1904): Doina (1967, rev. 1970,
    sax-s., pf., 5'). CMC.
_____: Indian Lullaby (1970, sax-s., pf., 4'). CMC.
_____: Sur le lac Baptiste-Ontario (1972, 9'). CMC.

Recordings:

> Paul Brodie and George Brough (Crest 7028); Paul
> Brodie and Myriam Shechter (Crest 7037); Paul Brodie
> and Antonin Kubalek (Crest 7041, 7056); Paul Brodie
> Plays Sopranino and Soprano Saxophone (Crest 7049);
> Duets for Saxophone (with J. M. Londeix, Crest 7062);
> Unaccompanied Saxophone (Crest 7071); Paul Brodie
> Saxophone Solos (Crest 7090); Paul Brodie Saxophone
> Quartet Albums (Crest 4164, 4131, 4154, 4143); Paul
> Brodie Clinician (Crest 1010); Encores (Crest 7102);
> More Encores (Crest 7103); Music for Alto Saxophone
> (Music Minus One, Beginning Solos, MMO 8021, 8023;
> Intermediate Solos, MMO 8025; Advanced Solos, MMO
> 8027); Koechlin Etudes (Classic 16); Clyde Gilmour's
> Favourites (Umbrella Records); The Golden Age of the
> Saxophone (Crest); Mr. Saxophone and the Three Bears
> (Crest); The Saxophone in Concert (Capitol W 6066).


BROWN BROTHERS:

BROWN, ALEXANDER (ALEX)
b. Chicago (unknown)          d. (unknown)
BROWN, FREDERICK (FRED)
b. Chicago, 1894              d. Chicago, 9 February 1949
BROWN, THOMAS (TOM)
b. Chicago, 1882              d. Chicago, 29 August 1950
BROWN, VERNE
b. Chicago (unknown)          d. (unknown)
BROWN, WILLIAM (BILL)
b. Chicago, 1880              d. Chicago, 25 June 1946

A very popular saxophone ensemble appeared in the
Columbia monthly list of October, 1911. Led by Tom Brown,
it was called the Brown Brothers Saxophone Quintet; their
first recordings were "American Patrol" and "The Bullfrog
and the Coon Medley." The latter was a "coon song" which
Ada Jones had made popular on records, but it had long
passed its popularity when the Brown Brothers' Columbia
recording was made. According to Jim Walsh,

> They apparently liked to play it because it gave the bass sax
> an opportunity to produce humorous "Bullfrog Grunts," and it
> was one of the numbers they recorded when, as the Six Brown
> Brothers, they began playing for Victor in 1915. In 1919, they
> went to Emerson, but returned to Victor a couple years later.[2]

The sixth member was Harry Finkelstein, and he often appeared in blackface and a clown costume. Another saxophonist who later joined the group was the well-known
Chicago soloist and teacher Matthew Amaturo, who appeared
for one season in the musical comedy Jack O'Lantern.

After their resounding "hit" in the Broadway review

called Chin Chin in 1914, the sextet appeared in the Ziegfield Follies and the Orpheum Circuit.  Although all sizes
of saxophones were used, most of the photos show the group
consisting of two altos, tenor, two baritones, and bass
saxophone.  The Brown Brothers enjoyed a remarkably long
career and was one of the highest paid vaudeville acts of
its kind.  In 1920, it made its last recording for a major
label (Victor), and by 1922 Tom Brown had expanded his
routine into a complete musical show featuring other groups
as well as his own.  The sextet was still touring with much
acclaim until 1925; it was disbanded after the Chicago
World's Fair in 1933.

Compositions:

> Chicken Walk (c. 1914, arr. by Arthur Wells, AATB,
> Will Rossiter, Chicago, OP); Tom Brown's Saxophone
> Waltz (c. 1918, arr. by G. E. Holmes, SATB, AATB,
> AATTBB, AATBBBs, Will Rossiter, Chicago, OP); Bull
> Frog Blues (c. 1919, arr. by Lester Brockton, S/A,A,
> C mel.,T,B,Bs, CF, OP).


CAILLIET, LUCIEN
b. Dampière-sur-Moivre,          d. Redondo Beach, California
   France, May, 1891               3 January 1985

Studying clarinet under Defosé at the CNRM, Dijon,
Cailliet received the first prize in 1913.  Later, in
Paris, he studied harmony and counterpoint with P. Fauchet
and G. Caussade; orchestration, arranging, and conducting
with Parès; and composition with Vincent d'Indy.  He was
engaged by Gabriel Parès for a series of concerts by the
Garde Républicaine Band, which was commissioned to play at
San Francisco's Panama-Pacific Exposition in 1915.

Cailliet returned to the U.S. in 1916 and became a
U.S. citizen in 1923.  He was heard as solo clarinetist at
the Roxy Theater, and performed with the chamber music ensemble directed by the French flutist, Georges Barrère.
Stokowski engaged Cailliet as second clarinetist, and it
was not long before Cailliet's talents as an orchestrator
became recognized and he was appointed the official arranger for the Philadelphia Orchestra.  He wrote all the famous transcriptions of Bach and Wagner, which were performed and recorded by the Philadelphia Orchestra.  During
his many years under Stokowski and Ormandy, he played clarinet, Eb clarinet, and saxophone from 1916 to 1930, and
bass clarinet from 1930 to 1937.  He performed the Rapsodie
for Saxophone by Debussy with the orchestra on 26 April
1934.

Cailliet was a guest conductor for many major U.S.
orchestras and composer-conductor in the Hollywood studios,
principally Paramount.  He composed 25 motion picture

scores and also did many orchestrations.  His more than
100 published compositions and arrangements include solos
as well as works for orchestra, band, and small ensembles.

Compositions for Saxophone:

> Method for Alto and Tenor Saxophones (2 vols., Bel.,
> 1941); Eighth Solo (arr. from Colin, SMC); Carnaval
> (SATB, SMC, 1963); Fantasy and Fugue (on "Oh, Susanna,"
> AATB, Bel.); Quartet for Saxophones (AATB, Bel., 1942);
> Canzonetta (2nd mov't arr. from Tschaikovsky Violin
> Concerto, sax, clar. choir, SMC); Flight of the Bum-
> blebee (arr. from Rimsky-Korsakov, sax, clar. choir,
> SMC).

CARAVAN, RONALD L.
b. Pottsville, Pennsylvania
   20 November 1946

Educated as a clarinetist with degrees from SUNY,
Fredonia (B.S., 1968) and the Eastman School (M.A., 1972
and D.M.A., 1974), Caravan later studied sax with William
Willett and Sigurd Rascher.  He was the editor of The
Saxophone Symposium (Journal of NASA) and is an instructor
of saxophone at Syracuse University.  A soprano saxophonist
with the Aeolian Saxophone Quartet and the Saxophone Sinfonia, he has also appeared in many solo performances and
lecture recitals in eastern U.S.  He has made many transcriptions and has published articles on clarinet, saxophone, and contemporary performance techniques.

Compositions:

> Sketch for Alto Saxophone (1973, Seesaw, 1974); Excur-
> sions for A Clarinet (1974, Seesaw, 1974); Monologue
> (1975, sax solo, Ethos, 1979); Five Duets for One Clar-
> inetist (Seesaw, 1976); Paradigms I (sax solo, Dorn,
> 1976); Canzona for Four Saxophones (AATB, Ethos, 1979);
> Three Modal Dances (cl. or sax-s., sax-b., Ethos,
> 1979); Lament for an Unknown Infant Victim of War
> (SATB, pf., Ethos, 1979, prem. 29 June 1979); Prelim-
> inary Exercises and Etudes in Contemporary Techniques
> (cl., Ethos, 1979); Polychromatic Diversions for Clar-
> inet (Ethos, 1979); Preliminary Exercises and Etudes in
> Contemporary Techniques for Saxophone (Dorn, 1980);
> Quiet Time (S/T, pf., Ethos, 1980); Improvisation Ro-
> mani (sax-t., solo, Ethos, 1980); Jubilate! (Concert
> Prelude, SpSAATTBBs, Ethos, 1982); Declamation: A Rhe-
> torical Fanfare for Saxophones (SAATBBs, Ethos, 1982);
> Sonata (sax-s., pf., prem. 22 Sep. 1984, Potsdam).

Compositions dedicated to R. Caravan:

> Paul Goldstaub: Graphic IV (1973).  Dorn.

Walter S. Hartley (b. 1927):  Diversions (sax-s.,
    pf.).  Ethos, 1979.

Recording:

The Saxophone Sinfonia (Crest 4221, 1982).


COGGINS, WILLIS R.
b. Winston-Salem, North Carolina
    20 August 1926

Coggins was educated at Davidson College (B.S., 1949)
and the University of Illinois (M.M., 1957).  He was Professor of Saxophone at the University of Illinois from
1953 to 1984.  His solo appearances include the Brevard
Music Center (1957) and the Winston-Salem Symphony (1965).
From 1969 to 1971, he composed 25 original pieces and arranged and edited 23 music educational publications for
Belwin-Mills; the grade levels are elementary, intermediate,
and advanced.


COHEN, PAUL
b. Teaneck, New Jersey
    29 July 1951

A student of Galan Kral and Joseph Allard, Cohen holds
degrees from Baldwin-Wallace College (B.M., 1973) and the
Manhattan School (M.M., 1975).  Some of his important solo
presentations have been the first performance of Ingolf
Dahl's Concerto (in the original 1949 version) on 7 November 1978, Charles Loeffler's Divertissement Espagnol (first
modern performance since the early 1900s) on 2 February
1981, and the same composer's Ballade Carnavalesque (first
performance since 1905) on 22 April 1978.  He has also
played with the Cleveland Orchestra, the Santa Fe Opera,
the American Philharmonic, and the Chamber Orchestra of
New England.  Cohen has given lectures demonstrating rare
instruments and manuscripts from his private collection
and has contributed thirteen scholarly articles for The
Saxophone Symphosium.

Publications:

The Renaissance Book (Galaxy, 1979); Ossia passages
on Ross Lee Finney's Concerto, third mov't. (Peters).

Compositions dedicated to P. Cohen:

Steven Cohen:  Saxophone Quartet.
Katherine Hoover:  Suite for Saxophones.  Prem. 1982,
    NYC.
Peter Lurye:  Elegy.
Steven Mason:  Chamber Music for 5 Players.

David McBride:  Inner Voices (sax, trp.).
Jim Theobald:  Three Rapsodies (sax, per., orch.).
    Prem. April, 1980, NYC.
Deniz Alben:  Concertino.  Prem. May, 1983, NYC.

Recordings:

The Saxophone Sinfonia (see Bilger); Cleveland Symphonic Winds (Vol. I and III).

CRAGUN, J. BEACH
b. and d. unknown

A graduate of Oberlin College, Cragun studied additionally at the New England Conservatory and the Stern
Conservatory in Berlin.  He did graduate study at the
University of Chicago, where he also taught saxophone for
nine years.  A professional saxophonist, he became well
known nationally as a teacher, and his methods, studies,
and other material were published by Finder & Urbanek, a
saxophone supply store in Chicago, predecessor of Rubank.
At the publication of The Business Saxophonist, the publisher stated:

> The course consists of twenty practical lessons by J. Beach
> Cragun.  Included in separate lessons are the following: One,
> your value as a business player.  "Talking."  "Jazz 'em up"
> effects.  Waltzes, One Steps, Two Steps, Fox Trots, "Breaks,"
> The Laugh, Flutter Tongueing, Slap Tongueing, Rhythm.  Contras-
> ting styles, Improvising, Transposition, Faking.  Double and
> Triple Tongueing.  Vibrato, High Tones (beyond range of instru-
> ment).  Together with introductory matter, legitimate study and
> the plainest of plain DIRECTIONS you can understand, how to DO
> all the things mentioned.  Material for practice is provided in
> handy form.  It is wonderfully complete, remarkably simple,
> strikingly practical, tremendously valuable.[3]

Compositions.  The following were published by Rubank:

The Business Saxophonist (1923, OP); The Cragun Con-
servatory Method (4 vols., OP); Concerto, opus 21
(1925); Ninety-five Duets and Trios for Saxophones;
Fifty-two Progressive Etudes for Saxophone; Eleven
Cadenzas and Twenty-six Etudes for Saxophone; Twenty
Etudes for the Development of Technic Difficulty for
Saxophone; Thirty Melodic Caprices in all Major and
Minor Keys for the Saxophone; Eight Concert Duets for
Two Saxophones (1926); Finishing Routine Studies for
Daily Practice for the Saxophone (1926).

CUNNINGHAM, JAMES
b. Big Spring, Texas
   11 January 1952

After attending Sam Houston University, where he was
a student of Harley E. Rex, Cunningham performed Creston's
Concerto for Saxophone and Orchestra, led by the composer,
at the 1970 annual New Music Festival in Houston, Texas.
Accepted as a member of the U.S. Marine Band, Cunningham
toured as a soloist for four years and performed additionally with the White House Orchestra and Jazz Band.  In
1976, he completed the M.M. at Catholic University and
began a career in radio broadcasting.  He currently hosts
a weekly program, The Contemporary Music Hour on WCVT in
Baltimore, which reflects his dedication to the promotion
of American Music.  In 1978, he studied with Vito Cuscuna
at the Peabody Conservatory and was the first saxophonist
in the history of the school to be awarded the Artist Diploma.  Larry Teal was also one of his teachers.  After
winning the Fifth Annual World Competition for wind instruments in Ancona, Italy, he was nominated for the distinguished alumni award at the Peabody Conservatory.

With his wife, Li-Ly Chang, a pianist-composer, he
formed the Cunningham Duo and made a highly successful Carnegie Hall debut on 29 March 1983.  Their first Asian tour
included concerts and seminars at seven universities and
appearances on radio and TV in Taiwan; these were the first
saxophone recitals given in that country.

Compositions dedicated to and premiered by J. Cunningham:

    Li-Ly Chang (b. 1952):  Impromptu (1979, 5'). Composer.
    Jerry Crawford (b. 1947):  Music for Saxophone and
       Piano (1969, 7').  Composer.  Prem. Spring, 1970,
       Huntsville, Texas.
    James Griffiths (b. 1948):  Dialogue on a Tone Row
       (1969, sax, per., 4').  Composer.  Prem. Fall,
       1969, Huntsville, Texas.
    Irwin Heilner (b. 1908):  The Old Moonshiner.  Compo-
       ser.  Prem. 6 Oct. 1984, Towson, Md.
    Jean Eichelberger Ivey (b. 1923):  Triton's Horn
       (sax-t., 9').  Dorn.  Prem. 29 March 1983, NYC.
    Robert Hall Lewis (b. 1926):  Monophony V (sax solo,
       8').  Peters.  Prem. 29 March 1983, NYC.
    James Marra (b. 1949):  Legacy of the Four Winds (S/T,
       7').  Dorn.  Prem. 20 Feb. 1979.
    William Moylan (b. 1951):  Sonata for Solo Alto Saxo-
       phone (15').  Dorn.  Prem. Fall, 1978, Baltimore.
       : Suite for Baritone or Alto Saxophone and Nar-
       rated Tape (1979, 13').  Dorn.
    Ronald V. Reaser (b. 1954):  Liberare Sonare (sax, per.
       in pf., 20').  SMPC.  Prem. Spring, 1979, Baltimore.
    Harley E. Rex (b. 1930):  Washington Sonata (sax, band/
       pf., 12').  Dorn.  Prem. April, 1974, Washington.
    Newton Strandberg (b. 1922):  Fragments for Alto Saxo-
       phone and Piano (10').  Composer.  Prem. 27 Nov.
       1975, Rockville, Md.

Recording:

> Sam Houston State University (Crest 1973, Rex: Pre-
> ludio et Movendo).

DAILEY, DWIGHT M.
b. Coldwater, Michigan
   22 June 1923

Studying the clarinet with Albert Luconi and William
Stubbins, Dailey completed the B.M.E. and the M.M. at the
University of Michigan in 1945 and 1946 respectively.  He
also studied saxophone with Sigurd Rascher, oboe with Russ
Howland, and conducting with William Revelli.  He taught
clarinet and saxophone at the University of Michigan from
1947 to 1952, and served as Director of Bands at the University of Tulsa from 1952 to 1969.  He was Principal Clarinetist with the Tulsa Philharmonic and Civic Ballet Orchestras, and was a featured soloist in 1964 and 1967.  In
addition, he has appeared in various Oklahoma communities
and teaches clarinet, sax, and theory at the University of
Tulsa.

Composition and Publication:

> Reflections in Gold, Silver and Ebony (sax, fl-a,
> cl., pf., prem. 12 Feb. 1983); Concert Pieces for
> the Tenor Saxophone (Wahr, 1983).

Compositions dedicated to D. Dailey:

> Ted Hansen:  Elegy (1978).
> _____ :  Contrasts (1983, orig. c.a., strs.).  Seesaw.

DAWSON, JAMES
b. United States
   20 May 1944

A student of Larry Teal, Dawson completed the D.M.A.
at the University of Michigan in 1974.  He has performed in
several different states and more than 25 foreign countries
as lecturer and soloist.  He is an associate Professor at
Oakland University (Rochester, Michigan) and has appeared
with the Detroit Symphony Orchestra.  Recognized as an in-
terpreter of "new music," he has had more than 40 works
written for him.

Book:

> Music for Saxophone by British Composers.  Dorn,
> 1981.

Compositions dedicated to J. Dawson (a selective list):

Denis Apivor (b. 1927):  The Protest (sax-s., vcl.,
    pf., 1981).
Charles Dakin (b. 1930): Ragamala (sax-s., vcl.,
    1980, 2'30).
Gregory Kosteck (b. 1937):  Chromatic Fantasy (sax-s.
    solo, 1979, 6'45).  Dorn.
_____ : Serious Developments (SATB).  Prem. 29 June
    1979, WSC, Evanston.
Joseph Schwantner (b. 1943):  Entropy (1967, sax-s.,
    bcl., vcl., 6'43).


Recordings:

Soprano Saxophone (Crystal S 158, music by Benson,
Caravan, Dakin, Hartley, Kosteck, Schwantner); James
Dawson (cassette, Roncorp EMS 013, 1983, music of
Chas. Dakin).


DEANS, KENNETH N. (Buddy)
b. Norfolk, Virginia            d. Hattiesburg, Mississippi
  12 July 1947                    10 January 1984

     A student of James Houlik at East Carolina University,
Deans completed the B.M.Ed. (1969), then studied at the
University of Michigan, where he was awarded the M.M.
(1971).  Additional instruction from Larry Teal and Sigurd
Rascher led to the completion of the D.M.F. in 1980 at the
University of Iowa.  Deans was an active lecturer-recital-
ist for the MTNA, gave recitals for NASA, and performed
at the WSC meeting in London in 1976, and with the Rascher
Saxophone Ensemble.  He taught at the University of Geor-
gia, and in 1978, was appointed Associate Professor at the
University of Southern Mississippi.

Compositions dedicated to K. Deans:

John Corina (b. 1928):  Partita.  Prem. 20 March 1974.
Michael Cunningham (b. 1937):  Piano Trio No. 3, opus
    59 (1974, S, A, pf.).  Etoile, 1976
Robert Donahue (b. 1931):  Sonata (1972).
John David Lamb (b. 1935):  Madrigal (1972, SAT).
    AMP, 1977.
William Presser (b. 1916):  Sonatina (1979, 7'43).
    Tenuto, 1981.
Mark Alan Taggart (b. 1956):  Lament and Credo (1984,
    11 saxes).  Prem. 24 June 1984.
Fisher Tull (b. 1934):  Sarabande and Gigue (1976,
    5'30).  B.H., 1979.
_____ : Threnody (1984, sax solo).
Luigi Zaninelli (b. 1932):  Misterioso. Zalo, 1978.

Recordings:

>Rascher Saxophone Ensemble (Vols. 1 & 2, Coronet LPS
>3022, 1974 and LPS 3031, 1975).

DELIBERO, PHILIP
b. United States
   11 October 1948

A Professor of Saxophone at Westfield State College,
Westfield (Massachusetts) and Western Connecticut State
College, Danbury, DeLibero is an active performer and
teacher.

Publication:

>Contemporary Saxophone Studies (Dorn).

Compositions dedicated to DeLibero:

>Timothy Broege (b. 1947): Nine Arias. Dorn. Prem.
>1 July 1979, Evanston.
>Leo Kraft (b. 1922): Three Pieces (1977). Dorn,
>1979.
>Peter Nagy-Farkas (b. 1933): Sonatine. Dorn.

Recording:

>Phil DeLibero and Mary Smellie (Open Loop, Dorn,
>music by Adler, Bassett, Blank, Denisov).

DEMSEY, DAVID
b. Winchester, Maine
   7 April 1955

A graduate of the University of Maine at Orono (1977),
where he studied with Louis Hall and Joseph Viola, Demsey
completed the M.M. at Juilliard (1980) and received additional instruction from Joseph Allard. He is an Assistant
Professor at the University of Maine, Augusta.

Compositions dedicated to D. Demsey:

>David Deason (b. 1945): Doubletake (sax, tpt.).
>Presser. Prem. 3 March 1980.
>_____ : Five Diversions (sax-s., fl.). Dorn.
>Prem. March, 1981.
>_____ : Jazz Partita (sax solo). Prem. 2 March 1984,
>Orono, Maine.

Recording:

>The Tom Hoffman Sextet (Redwood ES 19, Dec., 1981).

DI PASQUALE, JAMES A.
b. Chicago, Illinois
   4 July 1941

A saxophone student of Frederick Hemke and Sigurd
Rascher, Di Pasquale majored in Composition and received
the B.M. at Northwestern University (1964) and the M.M.
at the Manhattan School (1966).  As a saxophonist he played
with the Chicago Symphony Orchestra and such jazz/dance
bands as those of Paul Winter, Les Elgart, and Jimmy Dorsey.  He is a composer in Los Angeles and won an award for
his score of The Way Back at the American Film Festival in
1965.

Compositions:

> Sonata (sax-t., pf., Southern, 1967, 13'30); Quartet
> (1964, sax-t., tpt., vla., vcl., 10', Composer).

DIRLAM, RICHARD J.
b. Milwaukee, Wisconsin
   22 May 1954

A student of Ruben Haugen at the University of Minnesota, Dirlam went to France to study with Jean-Marie Londeix at the CNRM in Bordeaux, and after two years, won the
First Prize and the Medal of Honor.  On 9 July 1982, he
made his international debut with the Munich Radio Orchestra performing the Ballade by Martin.  Iwan Roth, scheduled
to appear, became ill, and with only two weeks' preparation,
Dirlam performed the work brilliantly.  While at the WSC
meeting in Nuremberg, he was also heard in a recital and
with the Ensemble International de Saxophones de Bordeaux.
He returned to the University of Minnesota to complete the
B.M., and in 1984, served as a graduate assistant at North
Texas University.  He also studied conducting with Serge
Zehnacker.

Compositions dedicated to R. Dirlam:

> Michael Aubart (b. 1952):  Deadly Sins. Prem. Spring,
> 1983.
> _____: Duo.  Prem. 8 July 1982, WSC, Nuremberg.
> _____: Hanblecheyapi: Crying for a Vision.  Prem.
> 21 April 1982.
> Eric Stokes (b. 1930):  Tag (sax, tape, 5'35).  HMC.
> Prem. 9 July 1982.
> _____: Untitled (sax solo).  HMC.  Prem. 8 July
> 1982, WSC, Nuremberg.

Recording:

> Stokes: Tag (New Music Minnesota, MCF-001).

DOUSE, KENNETH
b. Tunbridge Wells, Kent, England
   30 April 1906

     In 1910, Douse's parents came to America, and his
first instruction was on the violin.  At the Washington
College of Music from 1921 to 1925, he became a fine violinist and entered the Marine Corps as a violinist with
the Marine Symphony in 1926.  He began the study of saxophone at the age of 17 with A. Hilton, the only saxophone
teacher in the Washington area; it may be said that Douse
was largely self-taught on this instrument, but he developed a high standard of performance.  He was the solo saxophonist with the Marine Band until 1950 and played solos
for hundreds of concerts and radio broadcasts, chiefly in
the Washington area.  In the 1930s and 1940s, he played
the Saxo-Rhapsody by Coates, Saverino's Concerto Petite,
and many other solos.  From 1951 to 1958, he was violinist and saxophonist with the National Symphony.  Possibly
studying the violin before the saxophone had a great influence on his approach to the saxophone sound, which was
often compared to that of the violin.  He wrote several
marches for band and solos for saxophone and band which
are unpublished.

Compositions:

     Cynthia (CF, 1939); How to Double and Triple Staccato
     (Baron, 1947, OP).

Composition dedicated to K. Douse:

     Louis Saverino:  Concerto Petite (c. 1946).  Mills.


ECKROTH, MARVIN G.
b. Mandan, North Dakota
   1 October 1940

     After graduation from Dickinson State College (North
Dakota), Eckroth became a pupil of Frederic Hemke at
Northwestern University and completed the M.M.  In addition to post-graduate study at that institution, he also
studied with Laurence Teal.  In 1967, he was appointed to
the Music Faculty at Millikin University; and he taught at
the University of Alberta in Edmonton in 1976.  In 1980,
he was appointed to the faculty of the University of Sas-
katchewan where he founded and became the soprano saxophonist with the Saskatoon Quartet in 1981.

Compositions dedicated to the Saskatoon Quartet:

     Violet Archer (b. 1913):  Divertissement for Saxophone
        Quartet (1979).  Prem. on C.B.C. Television.
     Duane Hendricks:  The MacKenzie River Suite (SATB, 1979).

Monte Keene Pishny-Floyd (b. 1941): <u>Five Canadian</u>
   <u>Soundscapes</u>. Prem. 10 July 1982, WSC, Nuremberg.
   _____ : <u>Prelude, Aria, Fantasia</u>. Prem. 27 June 1985,
   WSC, U. of Maryland.

Recording:

Saskatoon Saxophone Quartet (cassette, Roncorp EMS
019, 1983, music by Absil, Arnold, Bach, Byrd, Debussy,
Farmer, Farnaby, Frescobaldi, Gibbons, Glazunov,
Marshall, Pierné, Sweelick).


ERVIN, ELIZABETH ZINN (LIBBY)
b. Detroit, Michigan
   22 September 1941

A student of Larry Teal, Ervin graduated from the
University of Michigan in 1965, won a Fulbright Award to
study saxophone in Paris with Daniel Deffayet for the following year, and completed the M.M. at Arizona State University in 1967. She was a winner of the NACWPI Award for
her performance of George Heussenstamm's <u>Playphony</u> in 1976
and premiered Leslie Bassett's <u>Music for Saxophone and</u>
<u>Piano</u> in Tempe, Arizona, in 1968. She performed at the
1976 WSC in London; has given recitals in Canberra, Australia and the U.S.; and since 1973, has been Professor of
Saxophone at the University of Arizona.

Compositions dedicated to E. Ervin:

Richard Faith (b. 1926): <u>Phantasies</u> (sax, per., 1966).
George Heussenstamm (b. 1926): <u>Playphony</u>, opus 56
   (sax, per., 12'). Price, 1975. Prem. 29 July
   1976, London.
Russell Howland (b. 1908): <u>Quartet No. 4</u>. Prem. 1976.


ESTRIN, HARVEY
b. Burlington, Vermont
   5 July 1929

Estrin is one of New York's busiest and most versatile
musicians. His first saxophone teachers were Gerardo
Iasilli and Lewis Arfine. He began his professional career
at 17, playing with such bands as those of Boyd Raeburn,
Tommy Dorsey, and Sauter-Finegan. He was the saxophone
soloist in the world premiere performance and recording of
Rolf Liebermann's <u>Concerto for Jazz Band and Symphony Or-</u>
<u>chestra</u> with the Chicago Symphony. In 1967, he joined the
ABC Staff Orchestra and played on many TV programs. As a
free-lance musician, he has worked for every major recording company and can be heard on countless TV commercials
and motion pictures. He has played saxophone with all the
major American ballet companies and performed and recorded

Der Wein by Alban Berg with the New York Philharmonic under
Pierre Boulez.

## Compositions dedicated to H. Estrin:

> Irvin Bazelon (b. 1922): Churchill Downs Concerto
> (1972). B.H. Prem. 8 June 1984, N.Y.C.
> Harold Farberman (b. 1929): Concerto (sax, str.
> orch., 1965, 10'20). General, 1966.
> Meyer Kupferman: Jazz Infinities Trio (1961).

## Recordings:

> The Music of H. Farberman: Concerto (SRS 12016);
> Bazelon: Churchill Downs Concerto (CRI SD 287, 1972).


FISCHER, KENNETH M.
b. Clemens, Michigan
   17 September 1951

A pupil of Jack Kripl, Larry Teal, and Eugene Rousseau,
Fischer completed the B.M. at Michigan State University
(1973) and the M.M. at Indiana University (1975). He has
been soloist at WSC meetings in Toronto, Evanston, and
Nuremberg. Since 1979, he has been the Professor of Saxophone at the University of Georgia. In 1984, he was elected
President of the North American Saxophone Alliance.

## Compositions dedicated to K. Fischer:

> Bruno Amato: Sonatella (1979).
> Tommy Joe Anderson (b. 1947): Impromptu, opus 29
> (sax solo). Dorn, 1982.
> Lewis Nielsen: Ain't Misbehavin' (Duo for sax-s.,
> per.). ACA, 1981.
> _____: Dialectical Fantasy (fl., ob., cl., sax-t.,
> hn.). ACA, 1981
> _____: Fantasies for Soprano Saxophone and Tape
> (1983). Prem. 27 February 1984.
> Jerry Sieg: Fantasy. Prem. 26 Jan. 1985, Washington,
> D.C.
> Greg Steincke (b. 1942): Episodes (sax solo). Sea-
> saw, 1973.
> Roger C. Vogel (b. 1947): Quartet for Saxophones.
> Dorn, 1980.
> _____: Temporal Landscape Number 5. Dorn, 1981.
> Michael Zinn (b. 1947): Suspensions (sax, bn., vib.).
> Seasaw, 1973.

## Recordings:

> Indiana Saxophone Quartet (with David Branter, James
> Carroll, Michael Clemente, Coronet 3028, 1975, music
> by Bach, Haydn, Smith, Zajac); Kenneth Fischer (cas-

sette, Roncorp EMS 012, music by Amato, Anderson,
C.P.E. Bach, Robert).


FOLEY, BRAD
b. Indianapolis, Indiana
   30 January 1953

Trained in the Midwest, Foley graduated from Ball
State University in 1975, where he studied with Cecil
Leeson. He completed the M.M. and the D.M.A. at the Uni-
versity of Michigan in 1977 and 1983, respectively, as a
student of Donald Sinta. In 1979, he was appointed as
Assistant Professor of Music at East Carolina University
(Greenville, N.C.), where he specializes in saxophone. He
is the Region Seven Director for NASA.

Compositions dedicated to B. Foley:

Karl Baelter: Three Affections. Prem. 3 Dec. 1983.
Otto Henry (b. 1933): New Adventures (ob., sax,
   tape). Prem. 3 Dec. 1983.

Recording:

Brad Foley (cassette, Roncorp EMS 030, 1984, music
by Bach, Denisov, Noda, Poulenc, Schumann/Hemke,
Villa-Lobos).


FORD, CHRISTOPHER
b. Rockledge, Florida
   9 July 1956

A pupil of Michael Nascimben, John Sampen, and J. M.
Londeix, Ford completed the M.M. in 1979 at Bowling Green
State University. Under the auspices of a Fulbright-Hayes
Fellowship, he won a first prize at the CNRM, Bordeaux, in
1980. He also won awards from the Charleston Symphony,
the Baltimore Music Club, and the Dorn Competition in Boston. In 1981, he was appointed to the faculty of Towson
State University. He also teaches at the Peabody Institute
and the Baltimore School of the Arts. His debut recitals
in New York and Washington, D.C., were at Carnegie Hall
(6 March 1983) and the Renwick Gallery (10 April 1983). He
was heard in the Debussy Rapsodie on tour with the Baltimore Symphony Orchestra (13-30 March 1983) and is active
in performing new music.

Compositions dedicated to C. Ford:

Michael Maloney (b. 1958): Music for Flute, Saxophone
   and Tape. Prem. 11 July 1982.
Charles Wuorinen (b. 1938): Divertimento. Peters.
   Prem. 13 March 1983, NYC.

FORGER, JAMES B.
b. Bronxville, New York
   15 December 1951

   A protégé of Larry Teal and Donald Sinta, Forger
received the B.M. (1974) and the M.M. (1975) at the University of Michigan.  He has been guest lecturer at Ithaca
College and an instructor at the Interlochen Arts Academy
and Olivet College.  He is a former member of the Detroit
Saxophone Quartet and concertized in Belgium during the
summer of 1981.  Since 1979, he has been Assistant Professor at Michigan State University.

Compositions dedicated to J. Forger:

        John Anthony Lennon (b. 1950):  Distances Within Me.
            Dorn.  Prem. 28 June 1979, Evanston.
        David Liptak (b. 1949):  Fantasy.  Dorn.  Prem. Nov.,
            1980.
        Charles Ruggiero (b. 1947):  Three Blues for Saxophone
            Quartet.  Dorn.  Prem. Nov., 1981.

Recordings:

        Compositions of Karel Husa (Crest ATH 5066, Feb.,
        1980):  American Composers Alliance Recording Award.
        (CRI SD 459, 1982, Lennon:  Distances Within Me).


GALLODORO, ALFRED
b. United States
   unknown

        Picking up the saxophone at the age of 12, Gallodoro
was first saxophonist in New Orleans' largest theatre at
15 and was barely out of his teens when he was soloist with
the leading bands of that era, including those of Rudy Vallee, Nat Shilkert, and Isham Jones, an honor accorded to
musicians twice his age.  He joined Paul Whiteman (c. 1937)
for four years and was featured in the "Sax Soctette."
In 1950, he led swing combos in New York and played with
the Seuffert Band (a Sousa type) until 1973.  He did much
studio work for ABC in New York, and his performances on
clarinet, bass clarinet, and sax ranged from the Metropolitan Opera Auditions of the Air to many shows of a lighter
vein.

Pamphlet:

        Saxophone/Clarinet Notebook (Selmer, 1956).

Composition dedicated to A. Gallodoro:

        Ferde Grofé (1892-1972): Gallodoro's Serenade (1959).
            Robbins.

Recordings:

> Gallodoro (Merri 5901, 11 solos acc. by the Gabe Bar-
> told Band); Saxophone Contrasts (Columbia, CL 6188,
> music by Dinicu-Heifetz, Gade, Gershwin, Godowsky,
> Herbert, Monti); Academy Award Favorites (with J.
> Shaindlin). (Also see Roger Kinkle, The Complete
> Encyclopedia of Popular Music and Jazz, for 12 re-
> cordings with Whiteman and one with Bernie Green,
> with Gallodoro on lead sax.)

GARI, RALPH A. (GAROFOLO)
b. New Castle, Pennsylvania
   1927

> Gari studied clarinet, saxophone, flute, and oboe
with Max Adkins, Joseph Allard, Victor Goldring, Henri De-
Busscher, and Daniel Bonade. Versatility has been a great
boon to his career, enabling him to find work in dance
bands and theatre orchestras. In 1954, after playing with
Vincent Lopez, Frankie Carle, and Paul Whiteman, he organized his own chamber-jazz quartet and, a year later, began making recordings on the EmArcy label. The quartet
was contracted to appear as a lounge attraction in Las
Vegas, and, in 1958, he joined the house orchestra of the
Sands Hotel as its principal saxophonist and woodwind performer. The following year he was hired by NBC for its
TV orchestra in Los Angeles, which permitted performances
with symphony orchestras in southern California. In 1960,
he became the saxophone soloist with the Disneyland Band,
where he played many of the film scoring sessions in Hollywood. In 1967, he began teaching at Long Beach State
College. A year later, he was offered a contract as first
saxophonist with the Nat Brandwynne Orchestra at Caesar's
Palace in Las Vegas. Gari combined his performance with
teaching and recitals at the University of Nevada and,
in 1974, was a soloist at the WSC in Bordeaux, France.

Compositions dedicated to R. Gari:

> Jack Hayes:   Concertino for Saxophone.
> Paul Powell:  Nocturne (fl., str. trio).   SMC, 1975.
> John Rarig:   Dance Episode.   WIM, 1976.
> Bill Reddie:  Gypsy Fantasy.

Recordings:

> Ralph Gari in Recital (Young Records 006, music by
> Hayes, and Bozza: Concertino); The Art of the Saxo-
> phone (Citadel CT 6012, music by Bonneau, Bozza,
> Glazunov, Hayes, Rarig, Vellones); Classic Film
> Themes; Ralph Gari Saxophone Quartet (Orion).

GEE, HARRY R.
b. Minneapolis, Minnesota
   20 February 1924

Early clarinet study in Minneapolis with Earl Handlon, of that city's famous orchestra, led Gee, at 17, to positions with the St. Paul Pops and Duluth Symphony Orchestras. A graduate of the Curtis Institute of Music, where he studied with Bernard Portnoy and Ralph McLane, he went to Paris in 1949 and became a pupil of the celebrated French clarinetist, Gaston Hamelin. His professional orchestral background, from 1951 to 1959, includes membership in the Denver Symphony and Opera Orchestras, and four seasons as soloist and member of the Minneapolis Summer Pops Orchestra. After receiving the B.A. from the University of Northern Colorado and the M.M. from the University of Denver, Gee studied composition with Paul Fetler at the University of Minnesota.

Appointed in 1960 to the faculty at Indiana State University, Gee has been active in solo, chamber music, and orchestral performances and now specializes in saxophone. He has studied with Eugene Rousseau and Daniel Deffayet and has been a soloist at the WSC in Bordeaux in 1974 and various regional meetings in the United States. He has served as a faculty member and soloist at the National Music Camp (Interlochen, Michigan), the British Woodwind Workshop, and the American Single Reed Workshop (Towson University). As an adjudicator, he has served on juries at the CNRM, Nancy (France), the Fédération des Harmonies du Québec, and many state music contests in the U.S.

Gee has been editor of "Clarinet and Saxophone Topics" for The School Musician since 1971. He has written over 100 articles and reviews, which have been published in the U.S., England, France, and Australia; and he has composed and arranged over 60 works for saxophone, woodwinds, and band, released by national publishers.

Books:

Clarinet Solos de Concours, 1897-1980: An Annotated Bibliography (Indiana University Press, Bloomington, 1981); Saxophone Soloists and Their Music, 1844-1985: An Annotated Bibliography (Indiana University Press, Bloomington, 1986).

Compositions:

Ballade (A, T or fl., Bel., 1962); 12 Saxophone Trios (AAA/AAT, Bel., 1970); Fugue in Baroque Style (AAT, Bel., 1976); Intrada (1978); Passacaglia (1979, cl. choir, CPP, 1983); Progressive and Varied Etudes (SMC, 1981); Second Ballade (A, or fl., pf., Kendor, 1981).

Compositions dedicated to H. Gee:

Thomas Brosh (b. 1946): Aeolian Suite (1985, sax-t.,
    tape). Composer.
David Deason (b. 1945): Tenor Ventions (1980, sax-t.,
    pf.). Prem. 22 Sep. 1981, Terre Haute, Indiana.
Yolande Uytenhove (b. 1925): Le cygne d'or, opus 109,
    (1984). Adagio-Belgica. Prem. 14 Aug. 1985,
    Terre Haute, Indiana.
    _____ : Sonata, opus 119 (1985). Adagio-Belgica.
John Verrall (b. 1908): Eusebius Remembered, Fantasy
    Sonata (1976, rev. 1982, for sax-t., pf.). ACA.
    Prem. 20 March 1984, Terre Haute, Indiana.
Donald White (b. 1921): Concertino (1971, cl., AATB,
    ww. ens., per.). Lud. 1975. Prem. 13 April 1972,
    Terre Haute, Indiana.

Recordings:

Harry Gee Plays Saxophone (cassette, Roncorp EMS 003,
1983, music by Bernard, Chopin, Duckworth, Stein,
Tomasi, Vaughan-Williams); Harry Gee Plays Saxophone,
Volume Two (cassette, Roncorp EMS 028, 1984, music
by Casals, Charpentier, Deason, Hindemith, d'Indy,
Persichetti, Verrall, Whitney).


GLANVILLE, RUTH
b. and d. unknown

A charming soloist, Glanville was engaged by Innes'
Concert Band for the season of 1919 and Kryl's Band in
1920. When she appeared in Elkhart, the Elkhart Press
stated:

Miss Glanville gave them one of the rarest of treats ever enjoyed in this city. She chose for her first number Herbert
Clarke's solo "Showers of Gold," a most difficult cornet solo
which is peculiarly adaptable for a saxophone solo except that
it is unusually difficult for the latter instrument. Miss
Glanville gave this solo with perfect ease and her phrasing was
beyond any possible adverse criticism. She is a master of the
saxophone. Two encores were not sufficient to satisfy the
audience.


GORNSTON, DAVID
b. Brooklyn, New York          d. Unknown

A saxophonist and woodwind studio teacher, Gornston
first became known during the 1930s directing a saxophone
band. He later collaborated with Ben Paisner, Harry Huffnagel, and Santy Runyon and formed his own publishing company. His method and study book were addressed to the
practical side of saxophone performance. After his death

his publications were taken over by Sam Fox and other publishers. Although many of his publications are out of
print, a few of the following can still be found at music
stores:

> Weird Etudes (Fox, 1936); Progressive Swing Readings
> (May Fair Music Corp., 1944); Saxophone Mechanisms
> (method, compilations, instructions, MCA, 1945); Cho-
> pin Studies (Gornston, 1944); Saxophone Velocity
> (Gornston, 1947); Fun with Scales (Leeds, 1947); All
> Chords (Gornston, 1948); 40 Rhythm Etudes (Gornston,
> 1949); Fun with Swing (Gates Music, 1964); Dailies
> (Kjos, 1965); Brahms Studies (Gornston, 1962); Stream-
> lined Etudes (Gornston, 1968).

GRAINGER, PERCY ALDRIDGE
b. Melbourne, Australia         d. White Plains, New York
   8 July 1882                     20 February 1961

Receiving his early training from his mother, Grainger
appeared as a pianist at several concerts at the age of ten.
In 1894, he went to Germany to study with Kwast in Frankfurt and also took a few lessons from Busoni. In 1900, he
began his career in England and toured South Africa and
Australia. His first contact with the saxophone dated from
1904-1905, when he borrowed wind instruments from Boosey of
London to familiarize himself with their strengths and li-
mitations. A champion of the saxophone from the early years
of the century, he could not understand its early neglect;
he felt strongly that saxophones should be used in complete
and balanced choirs in both bands and orchestras.

He settled in the U.S. in 1914 and made a sensational
debut in New York on 11 February 1915. In 1917, the world
famous composer/pianist enlisted in the U.S. Army as a
musician, and it is reported that he carried a saxophone
with him at the time of his enlistment. He played saxophone and oboe in the band at Fort Totter, N.Y. until he
was given the post of music arranger. Grainger not only
arranged ten Bach and pre-Bach works for saxophone choir,
but also highlighted the use of the saxophone, particularly the soprano, in his compositions Lincolnshire Posey,
Children's March, and other works. His relationship with
the saxophone seems to have been intensely personal, and
he wrote about the possibilities of the instrument in the
orchestra. Cohen says,

> No one could ask for a more committed champion for the saxophone
> . . . . His writings elevate the saxophone to a level equal to
> the most traditional of orchestral instruments.[4]

Compositions for Saxophone:

> Molly on the Shore (1914, unpublished); Ye Banks and
> O'Bonnie Doon (SAATTBBs, c. 1932, Schott, 1936;

Schirmer, 1939); The Immovable Do (choir and sax
choir, 1934, Schirmer, 1941); The Lonely Desert-Man
Sees the Tents of the Happy Tribes (1949, sax, pf. or
ch. orch., ms.).

In viewing Grainger's output for saxophone, one should
take into account the following chamber and orchestral
works, which are elastically scored and can have saxophone
parts:

The Power of Love; The Nightingale and the Two Sis-
ters; Spoon River (1922); Green Bushes; Hill Song
No. 1 and No. 2 (1923, 1929).

His arrangements for saxophone choir exist in manuscript
form at the British Museum, Upsala College Library (E. Orange, N.J.), and Percy Grainger Collection, 7 Cromwell
Place, White Plains, N.Y.


GREENBERG, ROGER D.
b. Pottsville, Pennsylvania
   7 April 1944

A student of Joseph Allard, Harvey Pittel, and Michael
Guerra, Greenberg graduated from Juilliard (B.M.) in 1970
and the University of Southern California (M.M.) in 1973.
A member of the Harvey Pittel Saxophone Quartet, he specializes on the tenor saxophone and has participated at WSC
meetings in Bordeaux and Evanston. He has done free-lance
studio work in Los Angeles, and in 1980 he was appointed to
the faculty of the University of Northern Colorado (Greeley).
In 1981, he made three transcriptions which have been published by Western International Music.

Compositions dedicated to R. Greenberg:

Andrew Charlton: Diversions (fl., sax). Prem. 5
   March 1980.
Keith Clark: Different Callings (sax, pf., per.,
   electronics). Prem. 29 April 1978.
Evan Copley (b. 1930): Trio (sax, hn., pf.). Prem.
   15 May 1982.
George Heussenstamm (b. 1926): Four Miniatures (1975,
   vn., fl., sax-t.). Dorn. Prem. 27 May 1976.
William Schmidt (b. 1926): Concerto for Tenor Saxo-
   phone and Symphonic Winds (14'). WIM. Prem. 10
   April 1981.
   ____ : Sonata for Baritone Saxophone and Piano. WIM.
   Prem. 5 March 1980.
Bruce Yorko: Night Dances (SATB, one perf.). Prem.
   15 May 1982.

Recordings:

Harvey Pittel Saxophone Quartet (Crystal Records S 155,

1980); Don't You Remember the Time (H. Pittel Quartet, 1982); The Art of the Saxophone (vol. 1, WIMR 18, 1980, with James Rotter); Wm. Schmidt: Concerto for Tenor Saxophone (U. of Northern Colorado Wind Ens., avail. UNC Bands, Greeley, Colo.); Westwood Wind Quintet (Crystal S 812, music by Chavez, Cortes, Ginastera, Reuveltas); Orchestra recordings (with 20th Century Fox, Warner Bros., and the Los Angeles Phil.).


GREGORY, EARLE
b. Endicott, New York
   11 May 1949

Gregory was a student of James Stoltie. He completed the B.M. at SUNY, Potsdam (1971), studying with Donald Sinta; earned the M.M. at the University of Hartford; and took additional study with Larry Teal while completing the Ed.D. at the University of Illinois (1982). Gregory has been Assistant Professor of Music at Viterbo College (La Crosse, Wis.) since 1981.

Compositions dedicated to and premiered by E. Gregory:

> Ronald P. Citron (b. 1944): Suite Harlequin. Prem. August, 1976.
> Dan Locklair (b. 1949): Cavatine. Prem. 20 Nov. 1975.
>     : Concerto (sax, wind ens.). Prem. 13 April 1977.
> Duncan Long: Weep Dark Flame (sax, tape). Prem. 25 Feb. 1977.
> Samuel Pellman (b. 1953): Pentacle (sax, quadraphonic tape). Prem. 1976, Ithaca.

Recording:

> Maurice Whitney: Introduction and Samba (U. of Illinois Band, No. 83, 1977).


GREGORY, M. KENT
b. Fairfield, Illinois
   1 July 1957

After graduation from Millikin University in 1978 (B.M., cum laude) as a student of David Jacobsen, Kent completed the M.M. in Saxophone at the University of Southern California in 1980, while studying with Douglas Masek and James Rotter. He has been an instructor of saxophone at Cerritos College (Norwalk) since 1980, and since 1982, at the Colleges of Chapman (Orange) and Santa Ana, California.

Compositions dedicated to K. Gregory:

> Matthew Eichler: Beach Dance (sax, vn., 1982).

_____: Colloquy (sax, tape, 1980).
Roger Olson: Cobwebs (sax, vn., guit., poet, 1983).
D. N. Price: Augury (vn., sax, pf., 1980).  Culver
   Crest.

Recording:

   Chamber Music for Saxophone and Violin (Creative
   S 101, 1983, by Eichler, Eychenne, Olson, Price,
   Telemann).


GUERRA, MICHAEL (MIKE)
b. Philadelphia, Pennsyl-      d. Oaklyn, New Jersey
   vania                          6 June 1976
   25 November 1888

      Guerra grew up hearing bands in the streets and parks
of Philadelphia and knew what he wanted to become.  When he
was ten, his father took him to Pilade Michetti, the Italian-
born clarinetist with whom Guerra studied for three years.
In 1901, at the age of 13, he was hired to play in Lombar-
di's band, and the following season, he worked with Libe-
rati's band.  He then spent three years studying with
Fritz Dieterichs, a member of the newly formed Philadelphia
Orchestra.  Later he went to New York and studied with a
man named Degrigorio, first clarinetist with the Metropolitan Opera, and for nine months with Alexandre Selmer.  He
played occasionally with the Philadelphia Orchestra, which
at the time had only a 22-week season, but the real money
was in vaudeville shows.  Through the depression years,
Guerra worked at the Earl Theater, and, in 1936, he became
a member of the house orchestra at the Forrest Theater.

      When saxophones began to replace second violins and
violas, Guerra, reluctantly, picked up the saxophone as a
part of the first clarinet chair.  His many years of clarinet study made the adjustment hard, and the artist was not
pleased with the results.  Finally, a show with several
musicians came to the Forrest Theatre for six weeks, and a
tenor saxophonist named Eddie Copland helped Guerra produce the proper tone.

      Probably the greatest tribute to Guerra's saxophone
playing was in January, 1941, when the Philadelphia Orchestra premiered Rachmaninoff's Symphonic Dances.  The composer was extremely pleased with the Philadelphia and Carnegie Hall performances of his work and the incidental
saxophone solos played by Guerra.  Guerra became a very
successful teacher; he taught at a studio in the old Presser Building until about 1952 and later at his home in
Oaklyn, New Jersey.  During the 1930s, he had a very successful sax choir, and, through his many years of teaching,
numerous professional clarinetists and saxophonists passed
through his studio.  Some of his outstanding students were

Joseph Gigliotti, Vincent Abato, Gerry Mulligan, Stan Getz,
and John Coltrane. All the young players and professional
colleagues who knew him said that Guerra was a great human-
itarian; he enjoyed teaching and died at 88 years of age
while giving a lesson.

Mike Guerra had three bright children. The youngest,
named Selma, showed a genius for music, and nothing seems
to have been too difficult for her. She had perfect pitch
and a photographic memory. She soloed with the Philadelphia Orchestra on 14 April 1943 in Ibert's Concertino da
Camera. Arthur Hegvik, author of four articles entitled
"The Years of Mike Guerra," says:

> Selma Guerra began the saxophone at twelve. Ten years later,
> to the profound bafflement of every musician who knew her, she
> gave it up, never to play again. Her brilliant career--appear-
> ances with the Philadelphia Orchestra, the New York Philharmonic,
> solos (many on national broadcasts), recitals, recording under
> numerous conductors--all had lasted one decade.[5]

## Compositions premiered by Selma Guerra:

Charles Haubiel (1892-1978): Jungle Tale (sax, vocal
    chorus).
Clair Leonard: Recitative and Abracadabra. Bourne,
    1962 (ded. to S. Rascher).


GUREWICH, JASCHA
b. 1896, Russia              d. 1938, United States

After training as a violinist, Gurewich became a fine
saxophonist and was a soloist with the Sousa Band for the
1920-21 season. On the back cover of the Aeolian Series
of Saxophone Solos (George Sanders Co., 1926), Sousa is
quoted:

> I have heard all of the finest saxophone players of the last
> thirty years and the majority have played for me, but I have
> never heard anyone to equal you.[6]

Known as the Heifetz of the alto saxophone, Gurewich was
one of the first saxophonists to perform with eastern symphony orchestras and the first to give a saxophone recital
of serious music. On 31 January 1926, Gurewich presented
a concert at Aeolian Hall in New York featuring his Concerto, opus 102. The Concerto and his Sonata, opus 130,
were the first large saxophone works published in America.
He also composed and arranged numerous solos of lighter
musical quality for George F. Sanders and other companies;
many were published for alto, tenor, or C melody saxophones.

Compositions:

Kathryne (valse caprice), Passion (Mexican concert tango), The Coo-coo Clock (Rossiter, 1923); Love's Sorrow, Schön Rosmarin, Caprice Viennois, Liebesfreud, Liebeslied, The Old Refrain (all by F. Kreisler, CF, 1924); Fantasy in f (Bel., 1924); Seguidilla (Fox, 1924); Concerto in e, opus 102 (Rubank, 1925, ded. to J. P. Sousa); Capriccio, opus 120 (Schirmer, c. 1925, ded. to Emil Stock); Mélodie d'Amour (Schirmer, 1926); Staccatos and Legatos, Juliana (valse caprice), Jazzima, One Minuet (valse petite), Twilight Romance (Fox, 1927); Italian Serenade, Ilona (Hungarian Dance); Carmelita, Spinning (valse), (Fox, 1928); Sonata, opus 130 (Fox, 1928); Passing Thought (CF); Souvenir de Chamonix (Fox); Saxophonist's Daily Dozen (12 short exercises), 17 Classic Duets (CF); 16 Artistic Etudes (Mills).

GWOZDZ, LAWRENCE S.
b. Niagara Falls, New York
1 April 1953

Gwozdz completed a master's degree in 1976 at the University of Nebraska and the D.M.A. in 1984 at the University of Iowa. His saxophone teachers have been Sigurd Rascher, Ronald Tyree, Laurence Wyman, and Robert Fought. He is a member of the Saxophone Sinfonia and has performed as a recitalist and band soloist in many states. He has served on the music faculties of colleges and universities in the central and southern United States for ten years, and has been heard in solo and chamber performances in several important music centers. In 1984, Gwozdz was appointed to the faculty of the University of Southern Mississippi.

Compositions dedicated to L. Gwozdz:

Arthur Kreutz (b. 1906): Fantasy. Prem. 30 Oct. 1983, Oshkosh, Wis.
_____: Saxonata (1979). Prem. 27 Aug. 1982, Ladysmith, Wis.
Armand Russell (b. 1932): Transfluent Forms (1980, vn., sax, pf.). Prem. 29 March 1981, Kansas City.
Ronald Shroyer: Reflections (sax, wind ens., 1980). Prem. 9 Feb. 1985, Hattiesburg, Miss.
Roger C. Vogel (b. 1947): Divertimento for Saxophone Ensemble. Seesaw. Prem. 2 May 1977, Athens, Ga.
_____: Partita. Tritone. Prem. 1 July 1977, Athens, Ga.
John Worley (b. 1919): Trio (vn., sax, pf.). Prem. 6 July 1983, Eau Claire, Wis.

Recordings:

(See Rasher Saxophone Ensemble and Bilger Saxophone Sinfonia.)

HALL, ELISE BOYER (Mrs. Richard J.)
b. Paris, France            d. Boston, Massachusetts
   15 April 1853               1924

(See chapter 3 for information about Hall.)

Compositions commissioned and/or premiered by E. Hall (the
   following compositions are located in the Hall Collection at the New England Conservatory; published
   works are indicated by an asterisk):

André Caplet (1878-1925):  Impression d'Automne
   (c. 1905).  Prem. 17 April 1906.
_____:  Légende (2 fl., ob., cl., sax, db., Dec.,
   1903).  Prem. 19 Jan. 1905.
*Claude Debussy (1862-1918):  Rapsodie (1903, comm.
   in 1901, but not orchestrated until 1919 by R.
   Ducasse; he changed the name from Rhapsodie).
   Durand.  Prem. 11 May 1919, Paris.  Etoile (rev.
   by E. Rousseau for sax, pf.).
Paul Dupin (pseudonym, Louis Lothar, 1865-1949):
   Chant pour saxophone (Oct., 1910, never performed).
Philippe Gaubert (1879-1941):  Poème élégiaque (Aug.,
   1911).  Prem. 11 March 1912.
*Paul Gilson (1853-1942):  Premier Concerto.  Gervan,
   1902.
Gabriel Grovlez (1879-1941):  Suite (Sep., 1915,
   never performed).
Jean Huré (1877-1930):  Andante (1915).  Prem. 7 Nov.
   1917.
_____:  Concerstück (after 1915, never performed).
*Vincent d'Indy (1851-1931):  Choral Varié, opus 55.
   Durand, 1903.  Prem. 5 Jan. 1904, Boston, 17 May
   1904, Paris.
Charles Martin Loeffler (1861-1935):  Ballade Carna-
   valesque (fl., ob., sax, bn., pf., 1903).  Prem.
   25 Jan. 1904.
_____:  Divertissement espagnol (1900).  Prem. 29
   Jan. 1901.
_____:  Rapsodie (date unknown).
Georges Longy (1868-1930):  Impression (1902).  Prem.
   7 Jan. 1903.
*_____:  Rapsodie (2 cl., hp., db., bn., tim., sax).
   Hürstel, 1904.  Prem. 19 Jan. 1905.
*Léon Moreau (1870-1946):  Pastorale (1903).  Leduc,
   1951.  Prem. 19 April 1910.
Jules Mouquet (1867-1946):  Rhapsodie, opus 26
   (1907).  Prem. 11 Dec. 1908.
*Georges Sporck (1870-1943):  Légende, opus 54 (July
   1905).  Andrieu/Bil.  Prem. 2 Jan. 1906.
Henri Woolett (1864-1936):  Danses Paiennes (date un-
   known).
_____:  Octuor No. 1 (1909).  Prem. 1 Jan. 1912.
_____:  Sibéria, Poème Symphonique (1909-10).  Prem.
   25 Jan. 1911.

Compositions dedicated to E. Hall (not in the Hall Collection):

>   François Combelle (1880-1953): Fantaisie mauresque.
>       Selmer, 1920; Rubank, 1959 (Ed. Voxman).
>   Florent Schmitt (1870-1958): Légende, opus 66 (Aug.,
>       1918) Durand. Prem. on viola by M. Vieux, 25 May
>       1919, Paris; on sax by M. Mule, 13 May 1933.


HAMME, ALBERT P.
b. York, Pennsylvania
   5 January 1939

Hamme majored in clarinet at Ithaca College (B.S.,
1961). He completed the M.M.Ed. at SUNY, Binghamton (1967),
where, since 1968, he has taught saxophone and served as
Chairman of the Department of Music.

Compositions dedicated to A. Hamme:

>   Edith Borroff (b. 1925): Trio (sax-t., pf., per.).
>       Prem. 1982.
>   Paul Jordan (b. 1939): Rhapsody and Waltz (sax-t.,
>       pf.). Prem. 1979.
>   Karl Korte (b. 1928): Dialogue for Saxophone and
>       Tape. Dorn, 1972. Prem. 1969.
>   Jack Morton: Rondo for Saxophone and Rhythm. Prem.
>       1969.

Recording:

>   New York Woodwind Quintet (CRI S 249, 1971, Korte:
>   Matrix).


HASTINGS, DAVID M.
b. Greenwich, Connecticut
   15 July 1956

After study with James Hill at Hartt College, Hastings
went to Northwestern University and completed the B.M. and
M.M. with Frederick Hemke as his teacher. He has also
studied with Ryo Noda. Since his appointment in 1980 to
the faculty of Baylor University, he has been active as a
soloist. In 1984 he began teaching at West Virginia University.

Compositions for percussion and saxophone dedicated to
D. Hastings (premiered 9 July 1982 at the WSC, Nuremberg, Germany):

>   William Kraft (b. 1923): Encounters IX.
>   Verne Reynolds (b. 1926): Five Duos (1981).
>   Fischer Tull (b. 1934): Colloquy.
>   Richard Willis (b. 1929): Colloquy III.

HEGVIK, ARTHUR (TED)
b. Valley City, North Dakota
   16 July 1932

Beginning with a family orchestra in the eighth grade, Ted Hegvik played professionally in every musical idiom from touring bands to the Philadelphia Orchestra. A graduate of the University of Michigan, he obtained a B.M. in saxophone performance in 1958, studied with Larry Teal, and received an M.M. in clarinet in 1959. From 1959 to 1966, he was Principal Clarinetist with the Tampa Philharmonic. He is now Professor at West Chester University (Pennsylvania).

Hegvik has spent many years collecting information on pioneer saxophonists; this has led to a series of concert programs of Rudy Wiedoeft's music. Because of a commitment to perform Wiedoeft's solos as faithfully as possible, he searched everywhere, including many pawn shops, before finding a good C melody saxophone. In 1977, he was working with Lloyd Shorter, a media producer in Philadelphia, and together they produced The Magical Twenties Revisited. In the spring of 1978, Mrs. Wiedoeft's sister, and only surviving heir, invited Hegvik to visit her. She presented him with Rudy's personal scrapbook, blackened from the hotel fire that had killed Wiedoeft's wife in 1963.

Hegvik premiered Gunther Schuller's Tribute to Rudy Wiedoeft (for saxophone and wind ensemble) on 4 December 1978 at the College Band Directors' National Association meeting in Milwaukee.

Publications:

Modern Course for the Saxophone (5 vols., Elkan); Scales and Arpeggios (Elkan).

Compositions dedicated to Ted Hegvik:

Richard Boerlin: Elegy. Shawnee.
Walter S. Hartley (b. 1927): Saxophrenia (sax, pf. or band, 2'20). Dorn, 1976.

Recordings:

The Legacy of Rudy Wiedoeft (Crest CRS 4155); Ted Hegvik, Saxophone Nostalgia of the '20s (Crest CRS 4183, music by Doerr, Hazlett, Sannella, Wiedoeft) Saxophobia/Saxarella (45 rpm, single, Crest GC 455). Ted Hegvik Choral Concert (Crest CRDG 4218, music by Albinoni, Bach, Benson, Bizet, Dill, Vaughan-Williams.

HEMKE, FREDERICK
b. Milwaukee, Wisconsin
   11 July 1935

     Before completing the B.S. at the University of Wis-
consin in 1957, Hemke was accepted as a pupil of Marcel
Mule at the CNSM.  In 1956, he was the first American to
win a Premier Prix de Saxophone.  Further study at Eastman
from 1960 to 1962 brought him the M.M., and in 1975, he was
awarded the D.M.A. at the University of Wisconsin.  He has
been soloist in more than 400 concerts with civic, university, and high school organizations as well as in several
Chicago musical groups.  He has appeared with the Rochester
Civic Orchestra, the New Zealand Broadcasting Symphony, and
the Seoul (Korea) Philharmonic.  Since 1957, he has been a
clinician for the Selmer Company.

     Hemke has been on the faculty of Northwestern Univer-
sity since 1963 and serves as Chairman of the Department of
Wind and Percussion Instruments.  President of NASA from
1976 to 1978, he was the host for the sixth WSC at Evanston
in July, 1979.  His many activities include adjudicator at
the Conservatoire de Musique, Québec; Concours International
de Saxophone, Gap, France; and the Concours International
in Geneva, Switzerland.  In the field of publications, he
is the editor for the Fred Hemke Series of saxophone solos
and quartets for Southern Music Company, author of various
pamphlets released by the Selmer Company, and contributing
editor to the Instrumentalist (since 1977), the Bandwagon,
NACWPI Journal, and The Saxophone Symposium.

Compositions dedicated to F. Hemke:

     Tommy Joe Anderson (b. 1947):  Nemesis (sax, ww.
          quin.).  Prem. 1975.
     Louis Angelini (b. 1935):  Sextet (sax, ww. quin.).
     Terry Applebaum:  Quartet (SATB).
     Ted Ashford:  American Folksong Suite (SATB).
     John Austin:  In Memoria.  Prem. 28 June 1979,
          Evanston.
     Warren Benson (b. 1924):  Dream Net (sax, str. quar.).
          1980-81.
          : Wind Rose (SATB, 7').  1966.
     Rudolph Bubalo (b. 1927):  Organic Concretion (sax,
          org., tape, per.).
     Randolph Coleman (b. 1937):  Divertimento (SATB).
     Anthony Cooke:  Pictures at Hemke's Exhibition (sax,
          band).
     Anthony Donato (b. 1909):  Discourse II.
     Jack Goode (b. 1921):  Dance of Joy (sax, org.).
     Daniel Harris:  Sop with Hemke (SATB).
     Walter S. Hartley (b. 1927):  Petite Suite (1961, sax
          solo).  FEMA.
     Charles Hawes:  Crossover (sax, band).
     Robert Hebble:  Dance.

Robert Jager  (b. 1939):  Concerto (sax, br., per.,
    1967, 20').
M. Williams Karlins (b. 1932):  Music for Tenor Saxo-
    phone and Piano.  SMC, 1969
    _____: Quintet (sax, str. quar.).  Seesaw, 1973-74.
Gerald Kemner (b. 1932):  Quiet Music (sax-s., orch.).
Raphael Kianovsky:  Quintet (1972, sax, str. quar.).
Homer Lambrecht (b. 1943):  Metaphrases (A/S, bcl.,
    cb.cl.).  Prem. June, 1973, Reykjavik, Iceland.
Ryo Noda (b. 1948):  Murasaki No Fuchi 1 (2 saxes,
    10').  Leduc, 1981.
    _____: Quartet, opus 1 (SATB).
Allan Pettersson (1911-1980):  Symphony No. 16 (1979,
    sax, orch., 30').  STIM.  Prem. 24 Feb. 1983,
    Stockholm.
Shulamit Ran (b. 1949):  Encounter.  Prem. 28 June
    1979, Evanston.
Joseph C. Schwantner (b. 1943):  Entropy (sax-s.,
    bcl., vcl., 1968).
Randall Snyder (b. 1944):  Quartet (SATB).
    _____: Quintet (sax, str. quar.).  Dorn.
    _____: Seven Epigrams.  SMC, 1973.
Jared Spears (b. 1936):  Episode (SATB).
Stephen Syverud:  Apotheosis (sax, tape).  1972-74.
Hidenori Tokunaga (b. 1944):  Columnation.
    _____: Eidos (SATB, tape).
    _____: Quartet (SATB).  SMC, 1973.
James Walker (b. 1937):  Recitative in Transition
    (SATB, 1966).
David Ward:  Quartet (SATB).

Recordings:

Contest Music for Saxophone (Lapider Records); The
American Saxophone (Brewster Records BR 1203, music
by Benson, Dahl, Husa); Music for Tenor Saxophone
(Brewster Records BR 1204, music by DiPasquale, Duck-
worth, Hartley, Karlins); Music by Warren Benson
(Composers Recordings CRI SD 433, Benson: The Dream
Net, 1980-81); Winds of Change (New World Records,
NW 211, Finney: Concerto); Recordings of the Chicago
Symph. orch. with Hemke playing incidental solos in
works by Bizet, Del Tredici, Mussorgsky-Ravel, Ravel,
Shostakovich; Pettersson: Symphony No. 16 (Swedish
Heritage Discophile); Shapey: Incantations for
Soprano and Ten Instruments (1961, CRI S-232).


HENTON, H. BENNE
b. Shelbyville, Illinois      d. place unknown
   c. 1867                       1938

(See chapter 3 for information about Henton.)

Compositions:

> Laverne, valse caprice (CF, OP); Nadine, valse caprice
> (CF, OP).

Composition dedicated to H. B. Henton:

> Carl Busch (1862-1943): Valse élégiaque (1933).
> Witmark (OP).

Recordings:

> Lanette (Victor 18117-A, 1916); Laverne (Victor
> 18149-B, with Conway's Band).

HILL, JAMES S.
b. Columbus, Georgia
   26 May 1949

Hill graduated from Northwestern University in 1971
as a pupil of Frederick Hemke. He completed the M.M. in
1974 at Ohio State University, where he studied with Bur-
dette Green. Before his appointment there in 1978, he
taught at the Hartt College of Music. He is the former
Review Editor for The Saxophone Symposium.

Compositions dedicated to J. S. Hill:

> Richard Schenk: Sometimes. Prem. 10 April 1983.
> Tom Wells: Commedia (sax, fl., tpt., vcl.). Prem.
>    15 Jan. 1979.
> _____: Nocturne (1985, sax, computer-generated sound).
>    Prem. 29 June 1985, WSC, U. of Maryland.
> _____: Recitative and Aria. Prem. 10 Oct. 1979.

HOLMES, G. E.
b. Baraboo, Wisconsin          d. Chicago, Illinois
   14 February 1873               10 February 1945

Holmes studied with G. Mitchell, W. F. Heath, Vandercook, Lattimer, and Weldon. He conducted and arranged for
the John Vogel Minstrels and was a teacher at Prior's Conservatory in Danville, Illinois, and at the Vandercook
School in Chicago. He toured with the Smith-Spring-Holmes
Saxophone Quintet and produced numerous arrangements for
Barnhouse, Rubank, and others, many of which are still
published and available.

Compositions:

> Ariel, valse caprice (CF); Ben Bolt (CF); Cosette,
> valse caprice (A, C melody, pf., Barn., 1929);

Tyrolean Fantasia (A or T, pf., CF); Zayda, valse
caprice (A, C melody, pf., Barn, 1929); Night Comes
and the Day Is Done (song); The Prospector, Southland,
Heroic, March Courageous (marches); Colorado; Victory
and Fame; War Correspondent; Safari; Trojan Prince;
Cavalcade, Diane (ouvertures).


HOULIK, JAMES
b. Bay Shore, New York
   4 December 1942


   Studying with William Willett, Sigurd Rascher, and
Willis Coggins, Houlik graduated from SUNY, Fredonia, in
1961. He completed the M.M. at the University of Illinois
a year later. After serving as Assistant Professor of
Music at East Carolina University, he became saxophone
professor and Coordinator of Special Programs in Music at
the North Carolina School of the Arts (Winston-Salem).
Houlik has been a leader in establishing the tenor saxophone as an accepted solo voice for the performance of
serious music. He has appeared as soloist and lecturer in
Chicago, Toronto, London, and New York (recitals in Carnegie Hall in 1978 and Alice Tully Hall in 1981).

Tenor Saxophone Compositions dedicated to J. Houlik:

   Carey Blyton (b. 1932):  Mock Joplin, opus 69 (2').
      Chester, 1979.
   _____:  Saxe Blue, opus 65.  Chester, 1979.
   Sy Brandon:  Concerto (with band).  Composer.
   _____:  Micro Pieces (sax solo).  Composer.
   David Cope (b. 1941):  Clone (7'20).  Seesaw, 1976.
   _____:  Concerto.
   Michael Cunningham (b. 1937):  French Fantasy (1985).
   _____:  Trigon (1969).  Etoile, 1972.
   William Duckworth (b. 1943):  Ballad in Time and Space.
      Seesaw, 1968.
   _____:  Fragments (with band, 1967).
   _____:  Pitt County Excursions (1972).  Seesaw, 1976.
   Walter S. Hartley (b. 1927):  Concertino (with band or
      pf., 1977-78, 9').  Dorn, 1979.
   _____:  Poem (1967, 3'30).  Tenuto, 1968.
   _____:  Rhapsody (1979, sax-t., strs.).  Dorn.
   _____:  Sonata (10'30).  Dorn, 1974.
   Paul Harvey (b. 1935):  Concertino.  Maurer, 1976.
   _____:  Trio (sax-t., ob., cl.).
   Gregory Kosteck (b. 1937):  Concerto.
   _____:  Mini-Variations (1968).
   _____:  Music.
   _____:  Summer Music (sax-t., ob., cl.).
   _____:  Two Songs.
   Marvin Lamb (b. 1946):  Concerto.
   _____:  Serenade (sax-t., ob., cl., pf.).
   Richard Lane (b. 1933):  Suite (1970, with band).  B&H.

_____ : Trio (sax-t., ob., cl., 1973).
David Ott (b. 1947): Essay (sax-t., band, c. 13').
   Prem. 1983, Washington D.C.
Russell Peck: Concerto (1985-86, sax-t., orch.).
William Schmidt (b. 1936): Sonata. WIM, 1985. Prem.
   16 Oct. 1984, Eau Claire, Wisconsin.
_____ : Sonatina. WIM, 1967.
Thomas Turner (b. 1937): Fantasy.
Robert Ward (b. 1917): Concerto (c. 20'). Prem. 15
   Feb. 1984, Charlotte, N.C.
Clifton Williams (b. 1923): Pandean Fable (with band).

Recordings:

   James Houlik Plays the Tenor Saxophone (Crest RE 7060,
   music by Boni, Chopin, Debussy, Duckworth, Hartley,
   Kosteck, Schmidt); A Tenor Saxophone recital (Crest
   RE 7088, music by Cunningham, Glick, Karlins, Ozi,
   Schmidt, Wiedoeft).


HOWLAND, RUSSELL S.
b. Novinger, Missouri
   19 July 1908


   After completion of his high school education in
Kirksville, Missouri, Howland plunged immediately into
the professional music world, performing woodwinds with
a traveling dance band.  In 1927, he studied clarinet
with Gustave Langenus in New York.  He earned the B.A.
(1933) and the M.A. (1948) at the University of Illinois.
After teaching at the University of Michigan from 1941 to
1948, for reasons of health he moved to California, where
he taught woodwinds, harp, and conducting at California
State University.  He attained the rank of Professor,
received the Distinguished Lectureship award, and retired
in 1975.  An early pioneer in the clarinet choir movement,
he published many arrangements for that ensemble.  The
Fresno Saxophone Quartet, which he founded, has been in
existence for 26 years and is still active.  Howland has
arranged Glazunov's Concerto for the University of Illinois Band and composed nine quartets for saxophones.


Compositions:

   Quartet No. 1 (Ybarra Music Co., 1961); Quartet No.2
   (G. Schirmer, 1973); *Quartet No. 3 (1976);
   *Quartet No. 4 (1976); *Quartet No. 5 (1977);
   *Quartet No. 6 (1978); *Quartet No. 7 (1979);
   *Quartet No. 8 (1981); *Quartet No. 9 (1982).

   (*Available on onionskin paper; see William Hill
   in Appendix.)

HUNTER, LAURA E.
b. Ann Arbor, Michigan
   13 June 1956

     A student of Donald Sinta, Jean-Marie Londeix, and
Jack Kripl, Hunter completed the B.M. in 1979 and the M.M.
in 1980, both at the University of Michigan.  A Concert
Artists Guild winner, she presented a Carnegie Hall recital
on 10 March 1980, and in Houston, Texas, won the Ima Hogg
Award and performed with the Houston Symphony Orchestra on
23 June 1982.  She held teaching appointments in Houston
at Texas Southern University and Rice University; she is
currently teaching at the University of California, San
Diego and the University of Redlands.  Among her other solo
appearances, she played Arthur Gottschalk's Jeu de Chat at
the World's Fair in Knoxville, Tennessee on 7 June 1982.
In 1984, she was awarded a $12,000 Consortium Commissioning
Grant from the National Endowment for the Arts; she has
premiered compositions by W. Albright, W. Bolcom, and D.
Diamond.

Transcriptions/Edited Works:

     Ross Lee Finney (b. 1906):  Sonata (tran. for sax,
     Peters) and Two Studies for Saxophone and Piano
     (Peters).

Compositions dedicated to L. Hunter:

     William Albright (b. 1944):  Sonata (1984).  Prem. 5
        May 1985, NYC.
     William Bolcomb (b. 1938):  Lilith (1984).  Marks.
        Prem. 30 Oct. 1984, Houston.
     Laura Clayton (b. 1943):  Simichi-ya (1976, sax, tape).
        Prem. 20 Feb. 1984, NYC.
     Paul Cooper (1926):  Four Impromptus (1983).  Prem.
        30 Oct. 1984, Houston.
     David Diamond (b. 1915):  Duo Concertante (1984).
        _____ :  Sonata.  Prem. 5 May 1985, NYC.
     Ross Lee Finney (b. 1906):  Two Studies for Saxophone
        and piano.  Prem. 10 March 1981, NYC.
     Laura Karpman:  Capriccio.  Dorn, 1983.  Prem. 14
        March 1982.
     Scott Reich:  Trio for Duo.


JACKSON, REGINALD B.
b. Tyler, Texas
   7 November 1945

     After completing the M.M.Ed. at North Texas State
University, Jackson obtained a first prize at the Royal
Conservatory in Brussels in 1974 as a student of Elie
Apper.  He has given recitals in Washington, D.C. at the
National Gallery of Art (22 February 1976) and at the

Kennedy Center for the Performing Arts (11 June 1982). He
has also been featured on TV and radio broadcasts in the
U.S. and Europe. He was appointed to Howard University
(Washington, D.C.) in 1975 and also teaches at the University of Maryland. He is the leader of The Washington Sax-
opnone Quartet; other members are James Steele, Richard
Parrell, and Herman Tessman.

Recordings:

> Music for Saxophone and Piano (Musical Heritage MHS
> 3623, 1977, music by Duijck, Gotkovsky, Lantier,
> Lunde, Poot, Vivaldi); Reginald Jackson (cassette,
> Roncorp EMC 002, 1983, music by Albinoni, Absil,
> Koechlin, Milhaud, Stein); The Washington Saxophone
> Quartet (cassette, Roncorp EMS 027, with James
> Steele, Richard Parrell, and Herman Tessman, music
> by Absil, Bach, Dubois, Françaix, Niehaus).

Composition dedicated to R. Jackson:

> Norman Heim (b. 1929): Suite, opus 83 (1984, 13').
> Norcat.


JACOBSON, MICHAEL N.
b. Burley, Idaho
   6 September 1955

Studying with Robert Miller and Joseph Wytko, Jacobson obtained the B.M. in Theory, Composition, and Jazz
Performance at Arizona State University in 1978. Subsequently he completed the M.M. at Indiana University as a
student of Eugene Rousseau. He was saxophone teacher at
Mansfield State College (Pennsylvania) and the National
Membership Director for NASA; in 1984, he was appointed
to the faculty of Baylor University.

Composition dedicated to M. Jacobson:

> William Calhoun: Sonata for Soprano Saxophone. Dorn.
> Prem. May, 1982.

Recording:

> Michael Jacobson (cassette, Roncorp EMS 031, music by
> Arma, Benson, Dahl, Husa).


JOHNSTON, MERLE
b. Watertown, New York      d. United States
   c. 1897                     c. 1978

Born into a musical family, Johnston first played
the piano, drums, and brass instruments. In 1917, he

enrolled in the Clarkson Institute of Technology and while
there, learned to play the tenor sax.  He formed a dance
band, the Clarkson Melody Boys, which became the training
ground for his saxophone style, sound, and embouchure,
leading him to his early successes.  After graduating in
1921 with a B.S. in Electrical Engineering, Johnston went
to New York and became a free-lance studio musician as well
as a well-known sax teacher.  He filled in with such groups
as Paul Whiteman's Orchestra, Sam Lanning's Band, and Benny
Rolfe's Lucky Strike Orchestra.  By the early 1930s, he had
worked for every phonograph company in the city and performed on most of the major radio broadcasts from New York.
He played with Elfie Evans and Arnold Brilhart in what was,
acording to Larry Teal, "the top section in New York."[7]
Johnston specialized in the tenor saxophone and formed a
quartet, setting a high standard of excellence; this group
was featured in the well-known 1928 recording of "Always
in All Ways," from the picture Monte Carlo.  In the 1930s
most areas of the country lacked outstanding teachers, so
Larry Teal went to New York to study with Johnston; this
made a significant impact on Teal's teaching philosophy
and performance.  Teal recalled:

> Johnston was the man who revolutionized saxophone pedagogy in
> this country through his method of teaching embouchure, vibrato,
> and throat position.  Merle was also the first American saxo-
> phonist to teach the regulated jaw vibrato and was the founder
> of the New York school of saxophone playing."[8]

With the outbreak of World War II, Johnston moved to
Los Angeles, where he used his technological training in
the manufacturing of weaponry.  He remained active as a
teacher long after the end of the war.

Compositions:

> Valse Elégante, Morning Glory, Blue Streak, Tip Toes
> (sax-a. or C melody, Robbins, 1928); 36 Time and
> Rhythm Exercises for Daily Practice; 36 Technical
> Exercises; 36 Staccato Exercises (published privately,
> 1930, OP); Crystal Suite (AATB, with B. Bonnel, 1936,
> transferred to PAS, 1945, OP); Deep River (AATB, with
> B. Bonnel, 1937, transferred to PAS, 1945, OP); Pro-
> cession of the Sardar (AATB, with B. Bonnel, trans-
> ferred to PAS, 1945, OP); Liebestraum, My Old Ken-
> tucky Home (AATB, PAS, 1945, OP).

JORDHEIM, STEVEN H.
b. Fargo, North Dakota
   28 September 1957

After completing the B.M. at the University of North
Dakota, Jordheim studied with Frederick Hemke, earned the
M.M. from Northwestern University in 1980, and went to

Bordeaux, France, for additional studies with J. M. Londeix.
He has made solo appearances in Grand Forks (with the University of North Dakota Wind Ensemble, 1980) and on Wisconsin Public Radio (Madison, 21 November 1982). He received
the first nomination for the Silver Medal at the 1983 Concours at Geneva. He has performed Martin's Ballade with
the Suisse Romande Orchestra and the Société de l'Orchestre
de Bienne (Switzerland). Other solo appearances include
Ibert's Concertino da Camera with the Orchestre Symphonique
du Rhin (Basel, Switzerland) and on 16 September 1983 in
Mulhouse, France. He is Assistant Professor at the Conservatory of Music at Lawrence University (Appleton, Wisconsin). In 1984, he was a winner of the Concert Artists
Guild Award.

## Compositions dedicated to S. Jordheim:

> Leslie Bassett (b. 1923): Duo Concertante (1984, 15').
> Prem. 21 May 1985, NYC.
> Michael Halstenson (b. 1956): Ballade (sax, ch. orch.,
> 13'). Prem. 13 May 1984, Appleton, Wisconsin.
> _____: Essay for Saxophone and Piano. Prem. fall,
> 1982.
> _____: Trio (1984, fl., sax, pf., 8'). Prem. 20 .
> Jan. 1985, Fargo N.D.


KLOCK, LYNN
b. Toledo, Ohio
   12 August 1950

A pupil of Larry Teal, Klock completed the M.M. at
the University of Michigan and was the baritone saxophonist with the Detroit Saxophone Quartet. After his debut
recital in New York at Carnegie Hall, 29 January 1978, he
was the first saxophonist to appear on the Warsaw (Poland)
Philharmonic Recital Series on 20 October 1981. He also
appeared on radio and TV in Warsaw. Other tours have
taken him to the American and British Virgin Islands
(1980, 1981, and 1982). He has been a guest soloist with
orchestras in Ohio, New Hampshire, and Massachusetts and
with various university bands in Arkansas, Tennessee,
Ohio, and Florida. He has taught at the University of
Massachusetts (Amherst) since 1980.

## Compositions dedicated to L. Klock:

> Charles Argeersinger: Doxology Variations (sax, w.
> ens.). Prem. 15 Feb. 1983, Amherst.
> Charles Bestor (b. 1924): Suite for Saxophone and
> Percussion. Prem. 15 Feb. 1983, Amherst.
> Marc-Antonio Consoli: Saxoldie. Prem. 20 Oct. 1980,
> Warsaw, Poland.
> Andrzej Dutkiewicz (b. 1942): Capriccio (sax, hn.,
> 1984, 9'). Prem. 11 Sep. 1984, Amherst.

    \_\_\_\_\_: <u>Dance Triste</u> (13'). A.A. Prem. 28 July 1978, NYC. (Part two only).

    Steve Fernadino: <u>Klockwork Rag</u>. Prem. 4 May 1980, Iowa City.

    Walter S. Hartley (b. 1927): <u>Sonata for Baritone Saxophone and Piano</u> (10'30). Dorn, 1977. Prem. 8 March 1977.

    Salvatore Macchia: <u>Concerto</u> (sax, w. ens., 1984).

    \_\_\_\_\_: <u>In a Dark Time</u>. Prem. 6 March 1980, Amherst.

    Claire Polin (b. 1926): <u>A Klockwork Diurnal</u> (sax, hn., bn.). Prem. 25 Jan. 1977, NYC.

## Recording:

Detroit Saxophone Quartet (Mark Records, 1975).


KNUESEL, RITA E.
b. St. Cloud, Minnesota
   2 February 1953

    In 1972, Knuesel was the Grand Award winner of the Young Artists Competition, and she appeared as soloist with the Minnesota Orchestra. A pupil of Jerry Luedders, she earned the B.M. at the College of St. Benedict (St. Joseph, Minnesota), and in 1975 was accepted at the CNSM in the class of Daniel Deffayet. After two years, Knuesel was the first woman in the school's history to win a first prize in saxophone. In 1978, the Concert Artists Guild awarded her a first prize, and she made her debut at Carnegie Recital Hall, 10 April 1979. Knuesel has appeared at the WSC meetings in Evanston and Nuremberg and, since 1977, she has been a member of the music faculty at the College of St. Benedict where she teaches sax and flute and is Chairperson of the Music Department.

## Compositions dedicated to R. Knuesel:

    Jerome Coller (b. 1929): <u>Sonatine</u> (1966). Prem. 30 June 1979, Evanston.

    \_\_\_\_\_: <u>Trio</u> (1985, 2 saxes, pf.). Prem. 19 Oct. 1985, St. Cloud, Minnesota.

    Gregory Walker (b. 1951): <u>Four Sketches</u> (sax solo). Prem. 9 July 1982, Nuremberg.

    \_\_\_\_\_: <u>Sonatine</u> (sax, tpt., 1981).

## Recording:

Rita Knuesel (cassette, Roncorp EMS 022, music by Boutry, Coller, Gotkovsky, Tomasi).


KOVAL, NESTOR N.
b. Pittsburgh, Pennsylvania
   12 December 1928

Koval has been on the music faculty of Duquesne University since 1964, where he holds the rank of Associate Professor and teaches clarinet and saxophone. A graduate of the CNSM in 1952, he was the first American to win a first prize in clarinet, as a pupil from the class of Ulysse Delécluse. He is the founder and soprano saxophonist of the Pittsburgh Saxophone Quartet.

Composition dedicated to N. Koval:

DiSalvo:  Rhapsody for Soprano Saxophone (1973).


KRAMER, MARTIN
b. Philadelphia, Pennsylvania
   3 March 1907

After studying violin, conducting and harmony with William F. Haptich, Kramer, at 17, began to play the saxophone and traveled to New York to take lessons from Merle Johnston. In 1930, he performed in theatres in Philadelphia and had a studio near the Academy of Music. Stokowski invited him to play saxophone parts, when needed, with the Philadelphia Orchestra. Kramer wrote several works for the saxophone, and his earlier compositions were mainly in the romantic style. His Concerto for Saxophone, written in 1933, was probably one of the first large American concerti written for the instrument. Premiered by the composer with saxophone and piano, it was later performed by Lou Ingber with the Pennsylvania Symphony Orchestra. Kramer's Symphony (1939) called for four saxophones and was written in a conservative style to show how these instruments would blend in the symphony orchestra; the work was premiered by the Symphony Club Orchestra. Stokowski was interested in programming one movement for a Latin American tour; however, the composer would not permit a cut version of his symphony. This work and his later compositions were written in a more contemporary harmonic and rhythmic idiom.

Compositions:

Concerto (c. 1933, 26'); Symphony No. 1 (1939, contains 4 saxes, Fleischer); Lawd (fantastic spiritual, 6 saxes, Pro Art, 1938, OP); Waltz Allegro (ded. to C. Leeson, Pro Art, 1938, OP); Swing Fugue (3 saxes, Pro Art, 1938, OP); American Quintet (clar., str. quar., ded. to Artie Shaw).


KYNASTON, TRENT P.
b. Tucson, Arizona
   7 December 1946

At the University of Arizona, Kynaston was awarded the B.M. with Distinction (1968) and the M.M. in Composi-

tion (1969). After teaching in secondary schools in Arizona and California from 1968 to 1973, he was appointed to
the music faculty of Western Michigan University (Kalama-
zoo). Continuing saxophone study with Larry Teal until
1975, he has concertized much in the Midwest and appeared
at WSC meetings in the U.S. and England. He taught at the
Interlochen Arts Academy in 1975-76 and is currently an
Associate Professor and Head of the Wind and Percussion
Division at Western Michigan University. During his sab-
batical leave, 1979-80, he studied with J. M. Londeix at
the CNRM, Bordeaux, where he earned the Médaille d'Honneur
for Saxophone and Chamber Music.

Compositions:

>Concerto for Saxophone and Wind Orchestra (Dorn, 1981);
>Phil Woods Solos (tran.-ed., CPP, 1980); Jazz Impro-
>visation (with R. Ricci, Prentice-Hall, 1978); Espejos
>(Master Solos, HL, 1976); Dance Suite, opus 15 (WIM,
>1966); Dawn and Jubilation; Symphony No. 1 (orch.);
>Social Comment (wind ens.); Daily Studies (CPP, 1981);
>Sonata Duet (sax, cl., WIM); Corybant-Bleu (1980, SpSS
>AAATTBBBs).

Compositions dedicated to T. Kynaston:

>Curtis Curtis-Smith (b. 1941): Unisonics. Presser.
>Robert Muczynski (b. 1929): Concerto, opus 41 (sax,
>    sm. orch., 17'30). Presser, 1983. Prem. 1 Nov.
>    1981, Kalamazoo.
>_____: Sonata, opus 29. Schirmer, 1973. Prem. 13
>    Dec. 1970.

Recordings:

>The Chamber Music of Robert Muczynski (Coronet
>S 3004); Trent Kynaston, Saxophone (Coronet S 3035,
>with S. Hesla, pf.); Sonatas for Saxophone (Coronet
>S 3044, T. Turner-Jones, pf.); Sonorous Explorations
>(Composers Recordings CRI SD 388, with C. Curtis-Smith,
>pf.); Concerto for Saxophone and Wind Orchestra (Mark
>Records MC 1418, with Western Michigan U.); Hazel's
>Gone; Here Comes Sheba! (Western Michigan U. School of
>Music, SMR 1981-1, music by Brown, Kern, Maschewitz,
>Pettiford, Ricci, Sherwin); Fanfares and Celebration
>(Western Michigan U. School of Music SMR 1983-1, music
>by Bassett, Creston, Denisov, Muczynski).

LADARIO, TEXIERO DE
b. South America              d. Unknown
   Unknown

Little is known about the amazing South American performer, de Ladario, and what became of him. He was a stur-

dily built man, below average height, blind, and very mod-
est about his abilities.  Horwood quotes an observer in
the Selmer Company office at 4, Place Dancourt about two
years after World War I:

> His tongue articulation was amazing, and he gave proof of this
> when he played for me a transcription of the Scherzo tarantelle
> for violin and piano by Wieniawski that served to demonstrate
> his finger technique that was wonderful in its complete command
> over the most formidable demands that could be contemplated.[9]

He commanded a compass of four octaves, making use
of a highly developed embouchure and some additional keys.

Publication:

    Tablature pour saxophone (Henri Selmer, 1930, OP).


LANG, ROSEMARY R.
b. Weisburg, Indiana       d. Indianapolis, Indiana
   29 April 1920          5 February 1985

    After early saxophone study with James Spear and
Robert Prietz, Lang attended the Jordan College of Music,
where she completed the B.M.Ed. and the M.M. in 1952.  She
played professionally on clarinet, oboe, bass clarinet,
and saxophones in Indianapolis; she also performed on the
saxophone with the Indianapolis Symphony when needed.
From 1944 until her death, she was an associate professor
at Butler University.

Publications for Saxophone:

    Beginning Studies in the Altissimo (1971, rev. 1978,
Lang); Principles of the Saxophone (Lang, 1974).


LANSING, JEAN A.
b. New Buena Vista, Iowa
   15 May 1949

    Lansing completed the M.M. in 1975 at Indiana Univer-
sity as a pupil of Eugene Rousseau and is a candidate for
the D.Mus. at the same institution.  In addition to solo
appearances there, she has given recitals at the University of Michigan and Bucknell University and plays tenor
sax in the Rousseau Saxophone Quartet.  Since 1979, she
has been Instructor of Saxophone at Wichita State University.

Compositions dedicated to J. Lansing:

    David Baker (b. 1931): Fantasy.  Prem. April, 1977,
      Bloomington, Indiana.

Christina Kusmych:  Shapes and Sounds IV.  Prem.
May, 1983.

Recording:

Yamaha Suite (Golden Crest 4224, with Rousseau Quartet,
music by Carisi, Heiden, Linn, and Paich).


LAVALLE, PAUL (JOSEPH USIFER)
b. Beacon, New York
   Unknown

At ten years of age, Lavalle gained a working knowledge of musical instruments by playing in his brother's
band.  After graduation from high school, he went to study
Law at Columbia University, but a musical scholarship mo-
tivated him to transfer to Juilliard, where he became a
student of Joseph Schillinger.  Although he specialized
in clarinet and saxophone performance, he geared his ambitions mainly toward conducting and composing.  In the 1930s,
he was hired by NBC and was chosen for clarinet and saxophone solos with the NBC Symphony Orchestra by Arturo Tos-
canini.  His composition Symphonic Rhumba was premiered
by the NBC Symphony, conducted by Stokowski.  The saxophone
section at NBC in the middle thirties included Lavalle as
well as Artie Shaw, Jimmy Dorsey, Benny Goodman, Arnold
Brilhart, Alfie Evans, and Henry Wade.

Lavalle's association with NBC led to his creating
and organizing a number of imaginative radio programs, such
as "Chamber Music Society of Lower Basin Street," "Highways
of Melody," and "The All-Stradivare Orchestra."  In 1948,
Lavalle launched "The Band of America," which by 1960 had
a weekly program; by 1964, a tour covering 45 cities; and
a few years later, a 15-week transcontinental itinerary.
It was appointed the official band of the New York World's
Fair in 1964.  Lavalle continued as its guest conductor
for a number of important events in the East, and this
led to his appointment on 1 January 1968 as Director of
Music and Conductor for the Radio City Music Hall.  Currently, he is known nationally for his work in creating
and directing the All-American High School Band (sponsored by McDonald's).

As a composer and arranger, Lavalle is strongly represented on popular LP albums released by MGM and RCA-
Victor.  (The most distinguished example is "Lavalle with
his Band of America," which set the incredible sale of
over five millions LPs.)


LEESON, CECIL BURTON
b. Candon, North Dakota
   16 December 1902

At the age of 17, while studying mechanical engineering at the University of Arizona, Leeson became interested in the saxophone and purchased his first instrument. In those days the only means of saxophone study was with clarinetists, self-teaching tutors, and recordings of early soloists, especially Rudy Wiedoeft's Valse Erica (1917). The only school to offer saxophone instruction leading to a degree was Dana's Musical Institute in Warren, Ohio; and Leeson enrolled there in 1921. He graduated in 1925 with a B.M., and assisted in the teaching of saxophone in his senior year. In 1925, he gave his first official public recitals in Arizona. Commercial playing, an important aspect of the era, began for Leeson in 1920, when he returned to the East to play in several organized big bands in Buffalo, Detroit, and Cleveland. In Cleveland, he began teaching saxophone as director of his own school, which he was persuaded to take over from Carmen Lombardo.

In 1923, he moved to California and became the saxophone instructor of the Hollywood Conservatory of Music. After many solo appearances, he gave a highly acclaimed recital there on 11 June 1931. Featured on the program was the Concert Waltz, opus 109, dedicated to him by Francesco Magliocco, which was lost when Leeson moved from New York to Chicago late in 1940.

Cecil Leeson's debut at Town Hall on 5 February 1937 was the first saxophone recital given in this hall. The program included works by Debussy, Glazunov, Creston, and Mana-Zucca, and arrangements by the soloist. The Glazunov Concerto, with Paul Creston playing the piano, was the first performance of this work in America, and eleven reviews were written of this historic occasion. In later years Creston said, "Cecil Leeson has been the greatest stimulus for the enrichment of the saxophone repertory, and I am most grateful for having been chosen a contributor to the repertory."[10] Leeson's solo appearance with the Rochester Philharmonic Orchestra under José Iturbi on 13 January 1938 featured the American premiere of the orchestral version of the Concerto in Eb by Alexander Glazunov. Some of his other important orchestral appearances were with the New York Philharmonic (under Rudolf Ganz) and the Montreal Symphony Orchestra (under Douglas Clarke).

World War II broke out before Leeson could make a European tour, and he enlisted in the Navy, serving for three years in the Chicago area. Additional studies earned him the M.M. and the D.F.A. at Chicago Musical College. He began teaching at Northwestern University in 1955, continued concertizing in the Midwest, and, in 1961, Ball State University brought him to Muncie, Indiana, where he later became Chairman of the Woodwind Division (1971-77). At his retirement in 1977, the Leeson Archival Saxophone Collection was established at the Bracken Library. This exhibit features antique saxophones (including original

saxophones built by Adolphe Sax and Son), manuscripts of
first editions, correspondence, recordings, historical
materials from the Conn and Buescher Archives, and other
memorabilia.

Compositions:

> Three Children's Pieces (1946); Concertino for Alto
> Saxophone and Winds (or ch. orch., 1948, SMC, 1st
> mov't. Prem. 10 Jan. 1952, entire work prem. 5 April
> 1956, Evanston, Ill.); Concerto No. 1 (1947, prem. 27
> Jan. 1965); Concerto No. 3 (1952, prem. 10 Jan. 1952,
> Urbana, Ill.); Sonata No. 1 (1953, rev. 1979, SMC,
> 1984); Sonata No. 2 (1966); Concerto No. 2 (1st mov't,
> 1948); Concerto for Tenor Saxophone (c. 1960, 1st
> mov't. Prem. by Dale Baker, 18 Feb. 1969).

Leeson transcribed compositions for saxophone and
piano from the works of Kreisler, Bach, and Glazunov;
they were released by Charles Foley and Hill-Coleman and
are now out of print. The following were released by the
Southern Music Company in 1984: Rimsky-Korsakov: Flight
of the Bumble Bee, Schubert: L'Abeille (The Bee), and
Glazunov: Sérénade Espagnole.

Solo Compositions dedicated to C. Leeson:

> Garland Anderson (b. 1933): Sonata for Tenor Saxo-
> phone and Piano. SMC, 1968. Prem. by N. Bright-
> man, May 1971.
> Anton Bilotti (1906-1963): Sonata (1939). Presser.
> Prem. c. 1939-40.
> Bernard Brindel (b. 1912): Suite (1938). Presser.
> Paul Creston (1906-1985): Concerto, opus 26 (1941,
> band/orch., 17'). Schirmer, 1963. Prem. by V.
> Abato with N.Y. Philh., 1944.
> _____: Sonata, opus 19 (1939, 13'). Sha. Prem. 9
> Jan. 1940, Heidelberg Col., Tiffin, Ohio, and
> 15 Feb. 1940, NYC.
> _____: Suite, opus 5 (1935, 10'). Sha. Prem. 4
> March 1936, 1st mov't only.
> Morris Knight (b. 1933): Sonata (1964). SMC. Prem.
> 16 April 1967.
> Charles Kuhn: Sonata (1969-70). Prem. 15 Feb. 1970,
> Muncie, Ind.
> Claude Lapham (b. 1890): Concerto in Ab (1937).
> Leeds. Prem. 6 March 1940, NYC.
> Lawson Lunde (b. 1935): Scherzo, opus 38a (1970,
> sax-b., from Sonata, opus 38). Composer.
> _____: Sonata opus 30 (1968, sax-t., pf., 15').
> Composer.
> _____: Sonata No. 2, opus 38 (1970, 12'). Composer.
> Edvard Moritz (b. 1891): Concerto, opus 97 (1939-40,
> 35'). Fleischer. Prem. 26 May 1940, Pennsylvania
> WPA Orch.

_____ : Sonata No. 1, opus 96 (1938). SMC. Prem.
7 Nov. 1939, Akron, Ohio.
_____ : Sonata No. 2, opus 103 (1940). SMC.
_____ : Sonata No. 1 for Tenor Saxophone and Piano,
opus 154 (1963). Prem. by N. Brightman, April,
1967, Muncie, Indiana.
William Presser (b. 1916): Concerto for Tenor Saxo-
phone and Piano (1965). Prem. by N. Brightman,
5 Nov. 1969.
Sam Raphling (b. 1910): Sonata (1945). SMC, 1980.
Prem. 2 Nov. 1945, Chicago.
_____ : Sonata for Tenor Saxophone and Piano (1969).
Prem. by Randall Gage, 8 Dec. 1976.
Robert Sherman (b. 1921): Sonata (sax-t., pf.). SMC,
1984.
Leon Stein (b. 1910): Sonata for Tenor Saxophone and
Piano (1967, 14'). SMC, 1970.
Burnet Tuthill (1888-1982): Concerto for Tenor Saxo-
phone, opus 50 (orch./band, 1965). SMC. Prem. by
N. Brightman, April, 1967, Muncie, Indiana.
_____ : Sonata, opus 20 (1939). SMC, 1966. Prem. 18
April 1962.
_____ : Sonata for Tenor Saxophone and Piano, opus 56
(1968). SMC.
Jaromir Weinberger (1896-1967): Concerto (1940).
SMC. Prem. 11 Dec. 1946, Chicago.

Chamber Music and Miscellaneous Works Written for C. Leeson
(saxophone quartet AATB unless otherwise specified):

Carl Dawson: Quartet (1968).
Serge DeGastyne (b. 1930): Suite Rhetaise (1961, sax,
strs.).
Morris Knight (b. 1933): Quartet No. 2 (1968). SMC,
1973. Prem. 18 Feb. 1969.
Lawson Lunde (b. 1935): Sonata, opus 25 (Duet AT,
10'). SMC, 1981.
_____ : Suite, opus 11 (1959, SATB or AATB, 9').
Composer.
Mana-Zucca (1887-1981): Walla-Kye (c. 1936).
Sprague-Coleman (OP).
Edvard Moritz (b. 1891): Quartet, opus 181 (1961).
SMC.
_____ : Trio Sonata (1963, sax, vn., pf.).
William Presser (b. 1916): Quartet (1969).
Robert Sherman (b. 1921): Trio Sonata (1963, sax,
vn., pf.). Prem. 27 Jan. 1965, Muncie, Indiana.
_____ : Variations (1962, sax, hn., pf.). Prem. 18
April 1962.
Elie Siegmeister (b. 1909): Around New York (1939).
Prem. 15 June 1939, NYC.
Leon Stein (b. 1910): Quintet (1956, sax, strs.,
13'38). Cor. Prem. 10 April 1958.
_____ : Sextet (1958, sax, ww. quin., 12'30). Cor.
Prem. 23 Feb. 1959.

_____: Suite for Saxophone Quartet (1962). SMC.
_____: Trio Concertante (1961, sax, vn., pf., 16').
    Dorn, 1978. Prem. 9 April 1962.
Burnet Tuthill (1888-1982): Quartet, opus 52 (1966).
    SMC.
David Van Vactor (b. 1906): Andante and Allegro
    (1972, sax-a., str. quar.). Prem. 16 Dec. 1973.
Richard Weinhorst: Trio Sonata (1963, sax, vn., pf.).

Recordings:

    Cecil Leeson and the Lyric Arts String Quartet (En-
    chanté ENS 2001, quintets by E. Moritz and L. Stein);
    The Art of Cecil Leeson, Vol. I (Enchanté ENS 2002,
    sonatas by Anderson, Moritz, and Tuthill); The Art
    of Cecil Leeson, Vol. II (Enchanté ENS 2003, sonatas
    by M. Knight and L. Lunde); The Art of Cecil Leeson,
    Vol. III (Enchanté ENS 2004, Stein: Trio and Raphl-
    ing: Sonata); The Art of Cecil Leeson, Vol. IV (En-
    chanté ENS 2005, Creston: Concerto and Sherman: Trio);
    The Art of Cecil Leeson, Vol. V (Enchanté ENS 2006,
    sonatas by Creston and Moritz); The Art of Cecil
    Leeson, Vol. VI (Enchanté ENS 2007, 1952 and 1977 per-
    formances of Weinberger: Concerto); The Art of Cecil
    Leeson, Vol. VII (Enchanté ENS 2008, music by Bilotti
    and Maurice.


LEFEBRE, EDOUARD A.
b. Holland                  d. Brooklyn, New York
   c. 1834                     22 February 1911

    E. A. Lefèbre, the soloist with Gilmore's band for
19 years (until the leader's death in 1892), was unquestionably the outstanding saxophone soloist in America from
the 1870s to the 1890s. "The Saxophone King" (as he was
called) joined the Sousa Band in 1893. Popular with audiences for both the novelty of the instrument and his impressive technique, he remained in the U.S., becoming an
American citizen in 1884. By 1905, he formed a saxophone
quartet which played transcriptions and toured both the
U.S. and Europe; by 1907, the quartet had traveled to such
frontiers as Alaska and the Philippines.

    (See chapter 3 for additional information.)

Publications:

    Jean-Baptiste Singelée (1812-1875): Allegro de Con-
        cert (1st mov't from Grand Quatuor Concertant,
        1862, SATB or AATB). CF, 1912.
    _____: Fantaisie Pastorale, opus 89. CF, 1900 (OP).
    _____: Fantaisie sur "La Somnambule," opus 49. CF,
        1900 (OP).

    (A publication dated 1900 lists no fewer than 25 solos,

including the above arranged and edited by Lefèbre.)


LILEY, THOMAS L.
b. Topeka, Kansas
    29 September 1948

   A pupil of George Etheridge and Eugene Rousseau, Liley
was awarded the B.M.Ed. at the University of Kansas (1971)
and the M.M. at Catholic University (1974).  In 1983, he
completed the course work for the D.M.A. at Indiana University.  He was a soloist at regional and national meetings of NASA and at the 8th WSC.  From 1981 to 1985, he
taught at the University of Florida (Gainesville) and, in
1985, he was appointed to the faculty at the University of
Kansas.  He is editor of The Saxophone Symposium, the
quarterly journal of the North American Saxophone Alliance.

Compositions dedicated to T. Liley:

   William Davis (b. 1949):  Recitative and Scherzo.
      Prem. Jan., 1984.
   Frederick Fox (b. 1931):  Annexus (10'). Prem. March,
      1981.  Composer.

Recording:

   Thomas Liley Plays Saxophone (cassette, Roncorp EMS
   017, 1983, music by Beethoven, Fox, Heiden, Mucsynski,
   Platti.


LINDEMANN, HENRY
b. and d. unknown

   A well-known radio saxophonist, Lindemann had teaching
studios in New York and Philadelphia, and designed a saxophone mouthpiece.

Compositions:

   18 Modern Hot Saxophone Solos (with Blanchard; Mills,
   1936, OP); Henry Lindemann Method  (Mills, 1936); Pi-
   miento (with Blanchard; Mills, 1937, OP); Wisteria
   (Mills, OP); Quicksilver (OP); In Schoen Nacht (OP);
   Nocturno (OP).


LUEDDERS, JERRY D.
b. Sturgis, Michigan
    27 June 1943

   Luedders studied with Larry Teal at the University of
Michigan until 1965 and completed the M.M. at Indiana University with Eugene Rousseau in 1967.  Additional studies fol-

lowed with Daniel Deffayet at the Conservatoire at Nice
and in Paris. After serving as Chairman of the Music Department at the College of St. Benedict, St. Joseph, Minnesota, Luedders became the Director of the School of Music
at Lewis-Clark College, Portland, Oregon in 1977.

Composition dedicated to J. Luedders:

> Stanislaw Skrowaczewski (b. 1920): Ricercari Notturni
> (S, A, B saxes, 1 perf., orch.). European Ameri-
> can, 1977. Prem. 15 Jan. 1978, Minneapolis; re-
> peated at Kennedy Center, 17 Sep. 1978, and San
> Antonio, 25 Jan. 1982).

LULLOFF, JOSEPH P.
b. Milwaukee, Wisconsin
   23 May 1960

An active performer in both classical and jazz idioms,
Lulloff holds the B.M. (1980) and M.M. (1984) from Michigan State University, where he studied with Elaine Zajac
and James Forger. His other teachers have included J. M.
Londeix, Stanley De Rusha, and Eugene Rousseau. Lulloff
has won numerous solo competitions in Michigan and was
named the outstanding soloist in the Ohio State and the
Notre Dame University Collegiate Jazz Competitions. A
performer at the sixth and seventh WSCs, he was a winner
of the 1984 Concert Artists Guild Award and made his Carnegie Hall debut on 15 January 1985. Lulloff made two ensemble recordings at Michigan State University (1981 and
1983), and in 1984, was appointed to the faculty of the
University of Illinois.

Composition dedicated to J. Lulloff:

> Ronald Newman: Music for Alto Saxophone and Piano.
> Prem. Feb., 1979.

MASEK, DOUGLAS H.
b. Cleveland, Ohio
   30 December 1947

A student of Vincent Abato, Masek earned the M.M. at
Ohio State University in 1971 and the D.M.A. in 1978 at the
University of Southern California, where he has been on the
faculty ever since. In addition to solo appearances in the
U.S. and at the 1982 WSC in Nuremberg, he has performed
with the Los Angeles Philharmonic, Ojai Festival, and with
American chamber orchestras.

Compositions dedicated to D. Masek:

> Michael Anderson: Sonata. Prem. Dec. 1977.
> Tony Fox: Symmetry. Prem. March, 1979.

Jerry Grant:  Dance Frames.  Prem. 31 March 1981.
Randy Love:  Passerine Aria.  Prem. 31 March 1981.
Deon Price:  Mesurée.  Dorn.  Prem. March, 1980.
_____ : Vectoral Rhapsody.  Prem. Feb., 1981.
William Schmidt (b. 1926):  Concerto (w. ens., 20').
    WIM.  Prem 27 April 1983.
Jenö Takács (b. 1902):  Two Fantastics.  Prem. 29
    April 1969.
David Van Vactor (b. 1906):  Lento and Allegro (sax,
    strs.).  Prem. 14 May 1972.

## Recording:

Deon Nielsen Price:  A Composer's View (Town Hall
    S 34, 1983).


## MASINO, RENE
b. Montréal, Québec, Canada
   8 November 1939

In 1965, Masino won the First Prize at the Conservatoire de Musique in Montréal and in May of the same year
made his debut in a recital in Québec.  His teachers were
Arthur Romano, Gilles Moisan, and Pierre Bourque.  Since
1979, he has served as Professeur Agrégé at the University
of Montréal; he is also on the faculty at the Centre D'Arts
d'Orford in Québec.  A member of the Quatuor de Saxophones
de Montréal with David Clark, Simon Stone, and composer-
saxophonist Walter Boudreau, Masino also performs with
l'Ensemble de la Société de Musique Contemporaine du Québec.

## Compositions dedicated to R. Masino:

Walter Boudreau (b. 1943):  Cocktail Music.  Prem.
    Jan., 1985.
Paul Théberge:  A void not filled with words.  Prem.
    April, 1985.
Alain Thibault:  E.L.V.I.S.  Prem. March, 1984.

## Recording:

Montréal Saxophone Quartet (NSE, 1985, music by Lei-
bowitz, Pousseur, Vivier, Wood).


## MAUK, STEVEN G.
b. Greenville, Tennessee
   29 November 1949

After graduation from the University of Tennessee,
where he was a pupil of Anthony D'Andrea, Mauk earned the
M.M. (1973) and the D.M.A. (1976) as a student of Larry
Teal and Donald Sinta at the University of Michigan.  In
1975, he was appointed to the faculty of Ithaca College.

In addition to solo performances for NASA, he was a soloist
with the U.S. Navy Band (12 January 1979) and played Villa-
Lobos' Fantasia at Alice Tully Hall on 14 January 1978.
As a 1980 winner of the East and West Artists' Interna-
tional Competition, he gave a solo recital at Carnegie
Recital Hall in December, 1980.

## Compositions dedicated to S. Mauk:

> Jane Brockman (b. 1949): Divergencies (fl., sax-s.,
> pf.). Prem. 1975.
> David Deason (b. 1945): Gossamer Rings (sax-s.,
> Band). Prem. 28 Jan. 1983, Washington, D.C.
> _____: Quartet (SATB, 1982). Prem. 18 Sep. 1982
> (1st mov't only), Ithaca, New York.
> John Hilliard: Fantasy (sax-s., pf.). Prem. 29 July
> 1976.
> Malcolm Lewis: Poem for Soprano Saxophone. Dorn,
> 1978. Prem. 29 July 1976.
> Samuel Pellman (b. 1953): Before the Dawn (sax-s.,
> symph. w. ens.). Prem. 28 June 1979.
> _____: Horizon (sax-s., w. ens., mixed chor., nar.).
> Prem. 14 Oct. 1979.
> Greg Woodward: Concerto (symph. w. ens.).
> _____: Parapter for Alto Saxophone. Prem. 26 May
> 1979.

## Recordings:

> Horizon, by Samuel Pellman (Cornell University Wind
> Ens., Record No. 26, 1979); Concertino for Alto Saxo-
> phone and Band, by Jerry Bilik (Cornell Univ. Wind
> Ens., Record No. 35, 1983); Poem for Soprano Saxophone
> by Malcolm Lewis (Open-Loop Records, Dorn, 1978);
> Divertimento for Marimba and Alto Saxophone, by Akira
> Yuyama (MAI Records, Paul Smadbeck, 1982).

MENARD, REMI
b. Jonquière, Québec, Canada
   25 September 1944

Before studying with Pierre Bourque at the Conserva-
toire in Québec (1959-65), Ménard was a pupil of Maurice
DeCelles. Accepted at the CNSM in Paris, he worked with
Mule and Deffayet from 1966 to 1969 and won a first prize.
A former member of the Pierre Bourque Quartet, after his
appointment to the faculty at the Ecole de Musique of the
University of Laval in 1969, he formed his own saxophone
quartet.

## Compositions dedicated to R. Ménard:

> J. Clément Isabelle (b. 1948): Duo Concertant (1982).
> _____: Quatuor (1973, 15').

_____ : Sonate (1974, sax-s., pf.).
Alain Gagnon: Fantaisie Lyrique, opus 28 (1982).

Recording:

Quatuor de Saxophone Pierre Bourque (RCA LSC 3141, 1969).


MILLER, FRANK A.
b. Trenton, New Jersey
   27 November 1935

A student of Vincent Abato, Miller completed the B.A. at Trenton State College (1977) and the M.A. at Brooklyn Conservatory (1979). In addition to performing in New York and teaching woodwinds, he is a musical consultant and studio conductor/arranger of background music on ABC.

Compositions dedicated to F. Miller:

Jeffrey Lesser: Last Saxophone on Earth (sax, br.
   quin., 1979).
_____ : Saxophone Quartet (1979).
_____ : Suite for Clyde (1979). Dorn, 1980.
David Uber: Saxophone Quartet (1977). Presser.


MINOR, BRIAN M.
b. Muncie, Indiana           d. Chicago, Illinois
   14 December 1938             1 September 1981

After saxophone instruction with Charles Hubbard, Minor became a pupil of Cecil Leeson and earned the B.A. and M.M. at Northwestern University. As a Fulbright Scholar, he studied with Marcel Mule while at the same time perfecting his French at the University of Besançon, the University of Montpellier, and the Alliance Française in Paris. A Carnegie Fellow at Ball State University (1972-74), he completed the D.M.A. in 1975. Between 1968 and 1977, he taught French at Muskegon Community College, and saxophone at Western Michigan University and Hope College. At the retirement of Cecil Leeson in 1977, Minor was named Associate Professor of Music at Ball State University. On 18 November 1974 Minor made his New York debut at Alice Tully Hall.

Under the management of Thea Dispeker, Minor's European tours included numerous broadcasts and recitals from the Netherlands, the Bavarian, and the Saarbrucken Radios. Performances were given in Paris, Bordeaux, Amsterdam, Rotterdam, Munich, the Soviet Union, and Mainland China as well as the U.S. and Canada.

Compositions dedicated to B. Minor:

Lawson Lunde (b. 1935):  Alsacian Serenade, opus 31
    (1969, sax, vcl., 4'). Composer.
_____: Celtic Paean, opus 36 (1969, 4'). Composer.
_____: Hommage to Shostakovitch, opus 35 (1969, sax,
    vcl., 4'). Composer.
_____: Music, opus 21a (1964, sax solo, 10', from
    Sonata, opus 21). Composer.
_____: Sonata No. 1, opus 12 (1958-63, 4'). SMC,
    1967. Prem. 4 May 1963, Muncie, Indiana (mov'ts.
    2 and 3; see J. Bestman).
_____: Sonata, opus 21 (1964, sax solo, 16'). Com-
    poser.
_____: A Trip to Pawtucket (after Oliver Shaw, 1964,
    1'). Composer.
Vincent Persichetti (b. 1915):  Parable XI (1972-73,
    6'42). Elkan-Vogel.
Leon Stein (b. 1910):  Phantasy for Solo Saxophone.
    Dorn, 1971.
_____: Trio (cl., sax, pf., 1969, 20'30). Dorn, 1974.

Recordings:

Brian Minor Plays Saxophone (Crystal S 151, with the
Chicago Str. Quar., music by Lunde, Persichetti,
Stein). Brian Minor, Saxophone (Crystal S 154, 1978,
with the Westwood Ww. Quin., music by Creston, Heiden,
Stein).


MOEREMANS, JEAN H.B.
b. Belgium                     d. Belgium
    Unknown                        c. 1922

    (See chapter 3).

    Moeremans returned to Belgium about 1921, where he
died a short time later.

Composition:

Swell of the Day (air and variations, 1906, Victor
Records 4035, 7-inch, OP).

Compositions dedicated to J. Moeremans:

John Philip Sousa (1858-1932):  Belle Mahone (1885).

Recordings. Listed in Victor Catalog, Jan., 1906, the
    following 10-inch recordings were made in 1904:

Old Folks at Home; The Carnival of Venice; The
Merry Postillion (No. 1971); The Gypsy's Serenade
(No. 4034).

MOORE, JOHN S.
b. Hardinsburg, Kentucky
   15 November 1952

   A student of Sigurd Rascher, Pamela Farmer, and Pa-
trick Meighan, Moore completed the M.M. at Florida State
University in 1978.  Specializing in the tenor saxophone,
he is a member of The Trio and The Saxophone Sinfonia.
He has been heard as a solo performer at the 1979 WSC,
NASA regional meetings, and the University of Louisville
Saxophone Institute.  The following remarks by Sigurd Ras-
cher praise his solo performance:

   Mr. Moore plays with a delightfully mellow tone that is thor-
   oughly controlled and expressive.  This enables him to render
   a melodic line with complete conviction.  Combined with remarkable technique control of the instrument, this places Mr. Moore
   in the ranks of first-rate musicians.[11]

Moore has taught at the University of Kentucky (1978-80)
and now teaches in the central Kentucky area.

Compositions for tenor saxophone dedicated to J. Moore:

   Walter S. Hartley (b. 1927):  Sonorities VII (sax-t.,
      pf.).  Composer.
   Marc Satterwhite:  aprilmourningmusic (1985, 10').
   Marc Alan Taggart (b. 1956):  Concerto for Tenor
      Saxophone (1981).  "Réverie" (2nd mov't).  Prem.
      April, 1982, Ithaca, New York.
   John Worley (b. 1919):  Sonata No. 2 (1985, sax-t.,
      pf.).  Composer.

Recordings:

   (See D. Bilger and L. Patrick.)


MOORE, MORRIS C. III
b. Baltimore, Maryland
   8 November 1948

   After earning the B.M. in clarinet at the University
of Texas (Arlington), Moore attended North Texas State
University and received the M.M. in 1979.  His saxophone
teachers were James Riggs, Elie Apper, and Norbert Nozy.
Moore continued his study with Apper at the Royal Conservatory in Brussels, where he was awarded the Superior Diploma in Saxophone and a first prize in Chamber Music in
1980.  In France, he studied with André Beun at the CNRM
at Lille and won the certificate of Superior Examination.
Since his international debut at the WSC, London, he has
appeared as a soloist with the Fort Worth Symphony Orchestra and given recitals in Texas.  He has taught saxophone at Texas Christian University.

Compositions dedicated to M. Moore:

> Merrill Ellis (b. 1916): <u>Dream Fantasy</u> (cl., sax,
> per., tape, 1976). CF.
> William Latham (b. 1917): <u>Ex Tempore</u> (sax solo).
> Dorn, 1978. Prem. 29 June 1979, Denton, Texas.

MOROSCO, VICTOR
b. United States
   1936

A student of Vincent Abato, Daniel Bonade, and Joseph
Allard, Morosco received the B.S. and the M.S. from Juilliard. In 1962, he gave his first Carnegie Hall Recital
and was also featured in the premiere of Harold Farberman's
<u>Concerto for Saxophone</u> with the Orchestra of America. Ad-
ditionally, he has performed with the New York Philharmonic,
the NYC Ballet, the American Symphony (under Stokowski),
and the Symphony of the Air. Morosco has been active in
commercial recordings, TV, and films, and has played in
jazz groups in New York and Los Angeles. He is a studio
musician in Los Angeles, a member of the Los Angeles Quartet, and a teacher.

Compositions:

> Blue Caprice (sax solo); Six Contemporary Etudes
> (duet form, Artisan, 1974).

Composition dedicated to V. Morosco:

> Phil Woods (b. 1931): <u>Sonata</u>. Kendor, 1980.

Recordings:

> Contemporary Chamber Ensemble (Nonesuch Records
> 71221, music by Schwantner); Bach: <u>The Art of the
> Fugue</u> (Protone Records PR 146, Los Angeles Sax Quar-
> tet); Double Exposure (Protone Records PR 153, with
> Phil Woods and Joseph Roccisano).

NASCIMBEN, MICHAEL D.
b. Buffalo, New York
   17 August 1942

After studying with William Willett, Sigurd Rascher,
and Joseph Allard, Nascimben studied at the University of
Michigan with Larry Teal and earned a D.M.A. in 1971. He
has performed with the Austin Symphony, the Meadowbrook
Symphony, and the Buffalo Philharmonic. He has taught at
the University of Texas and at SUNY, Buffalo, and is currently teaching instrumental music in western New York.
He is Music Director of and alto saxophone in the Amherst
Saxophone Quartet, which was established in 1978 and made

its debut in Carnegie Hall in May, 1982.

Compositions dedicated to the Amherst Quartet:

> Eubie Blake/Manny Albam:  Eubie Medley (1982, SATB, Orch.).
> Rocco DiPietro:  Phantom Melos (1981).
> Duke Ellington/Manny Albam:  Sophisticated Lady (1982, SATB, orch.).
> George Gershwin/Manny Albam:  Strike Up the Band (1982, SATB, orch.).
> Jerome Kern/Manny Albam:  All the Things You Are (1982, SATB, orch.).
> Leila Lustig:  The Language of Bees (1983).
> Robert W. Mols:  Enchainment (1981).
> Stephen Parisi:  Introduction and Capriccio (1980).
> William Schimmel:  Quartet for Saxophones (1982).
> Richard Shulman:  Peace in Jerusalem (1984).
> Phil Sims:  Ellington-Medley (1982).
> Leo Smit:  Tzadik (1983).
> Andrew Stiller:  Chamber Symphony (1982).

Recordings:

> An American Classic:  Eubie Blake (Musical Heritage Society MHS 4368, 1981); Saxophone Quartets by Creston, Mols, Parisi, and Wilder (Mark Records, 1984).

PARENTI, ANTHONY (TONY)
b. New Orleans, Louisiana          d. New York, New York
   6 August 1900                      7 April 1972

Parenti first studied the violin, then switched to clarinet.  He attended Saint Philip's School in New Orleans, and later studied with Joseph Tavermo, playing in his Italian band for 18 months.  From 1916, he played in small bands for dances and movie houses until he led his own band in New Orleans.  He made his recording debut in January, 1925.  In the late 1920s, Parenti began to perform in New York and was a staff musician at CBS.  He led his saxophone quartet on radio and in a short Warner Brothers film.  The other members of the Saxophone quartet were Ted Greenberg (2nd alto), "Doc" Opsahl (tenor), and S. C. Thompson (baritone).  The quartet was called the "Singing Saxophones," and S. C. Thompson did the arrangements, many of which were published by Alfred in the early 1930s.  After spending four years in the Radio City Symphony Orchestra, Parenti left in 1939 to join Ted Lewis and remained with him until 1945.  He led his own band and also worked in Chicago until January 1949.  During the 1950s, he worked in Florida for four years, moved back to New York in 1954, and continued active performing until 1971.

PARME, FREDERIC
b. France                    d. United States
   Unknown                      Unknown

    Because Leopold Stokowski was a great innovator with
orchestral sound, he engaged Frederic Parme, a French bass
clarinetist and saxophonist, to double the string bass
part with the contra-bass clarinet in the Philadelphia Orchestra from 1925 to 1927.  On 22 April 1927, Parme was
saxophone soloist in Debussy's Rapsodie.  Although the
program notes do not claim this was the first performance
of the work in the United States, it was certainly one of
its earliest performances in North America.  Parme is also
remembered for his work in the development of saxophone
mouthpieces.

Composition:

    Serenade (c. 1922, CF, OP).


PATRICK, LEE
b. Oneonta, New York
   17 November 1938

    A student of Sigurd Rascher, Patrick completed degrees
at Ithaca College (B.M.), Ball State University (M.M.), and
the University of Kentucky (D.M.A.).  He is a member of the
faculty at the University of Louisville and founded the
University of Louisville Saxophone Institute in 1975.  In
1978, he organized The Trio in order to explore the artistic potential of the saxophone trio.  Most of the literature performed is for ATB.  Its current members are Rick
Morgen, alto saxophonist with the Lexington Philharmonic
and the Louisville Orchestra; John Moore, tenor sax, professor at the University of Kentucky (Campbellsville);
and Patrick, baritone sax.  Patrick has performed with the
18-member Saxophone Sinfonia and is the current Director
of Scholarly Publications for The Saxophone Symposium.
He has made six arrangements for saxophone and sax quartet,
which have been published by Belwin, Bourne, Presser, and
Ethos.

Compositions:

    Sea Songs (1980, ATB); Folk Song Miniatures (1981,
    ATB); Tribute to JB (1980, ATB).

Compositions dedicated to L. Patrick and The Trio:

    Werner Wolf Glaser (b. 1910):  Trio for Saxophones.
        STIM, 1980.
    Walter S. Hartley (b. 1927):  Trio for Saxophones.
        Presser.  Prem. 20 June 1984.
        _____:  Sinfonia No. 6 (1984-85, SSAAATTBBBs).  Ethos.

Prem. 23 June 1985, Louisville.
Frederick Mueller (b. 1937):  Five Etudes for Saxo-
phone Trio (1984).
Marc Satterwhite:  9 Aphorisms for 3 Saxes (1983).
Marc Taggart (b. 1956):  A Round O'trios (1978-1981).

Recordings:

The Trio (Dinant Records 404035); The Saxophone Sinfonia (see D. Bilger).


PELCHAT, ANDRE
b. Montréal, Québec, Canada
   28 July 1945

After study at the Conservatoire de Québec at Val
d'Or, Pelchat won first prizes in saxophone and chamber
music at the Conservatoire de Montréal (1973) and the
"Maîtrise" at the University of Montréal (1975).  In 1979,
he studied with J. M. Londeix at the CNRM at Bordeaux.  He
plays soprano sax with the Quatuor de Saxophones de l'Info-
nie, which has been in existence since 1974.  A member of
the Société de Musique Contemporaine du Québec, he has
been heard on Radio-Canada and has recorded compositions
and arrangements by Walter Boudreau.

Compositions:

Exploration (1980, sax-t. solo, CMC).   Impro Binantine
(sax-sp. solo, CMC).

Composition dedicated to A. Pelchat:

Walter Boudreau (b. 1947):  Le Cercle Gnostique IV
(SATB).  Prem. 1 July 1979, WSC, Evanston.


PITTEL, HARVEY
b. Montana
   22 June 1932

Beginning as a clarinetist, Pittel became interested
in the saxophone while attending Northwestern University,
where he studied with Frederick Hemke.  During his service
in the U.S. Military Academy Band, he studied with Joseph
Allard.  A winner of the Concert Artists Guild Award,
Pittel made his debut at Carnegie Recital Hall on 8 November 1973.  He has appeared with numerous symphony orchestras, including the Boston Symphony, New York Philharmonic,
Baltimore Symphony, Los Angeles Philharmonic, Louisville
Symphony, Suisse-Romande, and the London Sinfonietta.  Pittel was awarded the Silver Medal at the Concours International d'Exécution Musicale in Geneva.  While teaching at
the University of Southern California, he organized the

Harvey Pittel Saxophone Quartet with James Rotter, Roger Greenberg, and Mark Watters. Pittel is also well known as a teacher, having taught at the Mannes College in New York and schools in Boston, Tanglewood, and Aspen. Since 1980, he has been an associate professor at the University of Texas.

Pittel performed Ingolf Dahl's Concerto many times and assisted in the editing of the work, pubished by European-American Music.

Compositions dedicated to and premiered by H. Pittel:

> Paul Chihara (b. 1938): Concerto. Prem. 29 Jan. 1981, Boston.
> Ernst Kanitz (1894-1978): Little Concerto (sax solo). Artisan, 1971. Prem. 15 Dec. 1970, WSC, Chicago.
> Howard Quilling (b. 1935): Suite (1970, sax, w. orch. or pf.). Artisan.
> John Rodby (b. 1944): Concerto for Saxophone and Orchestra (1971).
> Robert Rodriguez (b. 1946): Sonata in One Movement (1973).
> Anthony Vazzana: Studi for Saxophone Alone (1978). Prem. 30 June 1979, WSC, Evanston.
> Emmett Yoshioka (b. 1944): Duo Concertino. Composer.
> _____: Sonata (1973). Composer.

Recordings:

> Bach: The Art of the Fugue (Protone PR 146/2, with the Los Angeles Saxophone Quartet); Harvey Pittel Saxophone (Crystal S 105, music by Maurice, Rodriguez, Stevens); Harvey Pittel Trio (Crystal S 157, music by Bach, Creston, Ellington, Villa-Lobos); Sextuor à vent (Crystal S 352, with the Westwood Ww. Quin., music by Dubois, Heiden, Milhaud); John Rodby: Saxophone Concerto (Crystal S 500, with the London Sinfonietta); Harvey Pittel Saxophone Quartet (Crystal S 155, 1980, music by Bach, Bozza, Desenclos, Joplin, Niehaus, Rivier); Paul Chihara: Concerto for Saxophone (LS 781).

PITUCH, DAVID ALAN
b. Corry, Pennsylvania
   17 July 1947

An American saxophonist of Polish Heritage, Pituch earned the B.M. from the Baldwin-Wallace College-Conversatory (1969) and the M.M. from the University of Colorado (1976). From 1976 to 1978, he attended the Musicology Institute of Warsaw on a Fulbright research grant. In 1980, he formed the Duo Esztényi-Pituch with the Hungarian pianist Szabolcs Esztényi, which has given numerous recitals throughout Poland, Austria, East Germany, and the United

States.  In 1980, Pituch established the first class in
saxophone at the Chopin Academy in Warsaw.

Publication:

The Saxophone and Saxophone Playing (New York, Scrib-
ner, 1984).

Compositions dedicated to or premiered by D. Pituch:

Krzysztof Baculewski (b. 1950): Partita (1980, sax,
harpsichord, 12-15'). AA. Prem. 1983.
Augustyn Bloch (b. 1929): Notes for Saxophone
(7-8'). AA. Prem. 1981, Salzburg.
Jan Fotek (b. 1928): Musiquette (1983, 3 saxes, 3').
Sonoton.
____: Variations (1985, 10').
Roman Palester (b. 1907): Concertino (1938, rev.
1978, sax, ch. orch., 16'). Prem. 28 May 1981,
Cracow.
Zbigniew Penherski (b. 1935): Jeux Partie (sax,
per., 7'). Prem. International Festival "Warsaw
Autumn," 1984.
Boguslaw Schaeffer (b. 1929): Proietto (sax, tape,
12'). Prem. 1983, Warsaw.
Ryszard Szeremeta (b. 1952): Amphora Snake Dance
(1984, sax-t., tape). Prem. 1985, West Berlin.
Zbigniew Wiszniewski (b. 1922): Duo für Altsaxophon
und Marimba (1982, 12'). Sonoton. Prem. 21 Feb.
1983, Warsaw.
____: Duo für Altsaxophon und Violoncello (1983,
14'). Sonoton. Prem. International Festival "Warsaw Autumn," 1984.

Recordings:

David A. Pituch Plays New Compositions for the Saxo-
phone (Pro Viva ISPV 122, music by Bloch, Dutkiewicz,
Fotek); Dutkiewicz: Danse Triste (Polskie Nagrania
SX 2091); P. Moss: Quatre Poésies (Pro Viva); Warsaw
Autumn 1984 Chronicle (PN SX 2409, music by Penherski).

RADNOFSKY, KENNETH
b. Bryn Mawr, Pennsylvania
31 July 1953

Radnofsky received the B.M. cum laude from the University of Houston in 1974 and the M.M. with honors from
the New England Conservatory in 1976.  With the Pittsburgh
Orchestra and the Oregon Symphony Orchestra, he performed
the Concerto by Gunther Schuller.  He has taught at the
New England Conservatory, Yale University (1981-84), and
since 1983, at Boston University.  In 1984, he was appointed for additional teaching at the Hartt College-Con-

servatory. He was a recipient of a grant from the National
Endowment for the Arts (with John Sampen and James Forger)
for 1986-88, and will play commissioned works for saxophone
by Milton Babbitt, Donald Martino, and Morton Subotnick.

Compositions dedicated to and premiered by K. Radnofsky:

> David Amram (b. 1930): Concerto for Saxophone and
>     Orchestra. Prem. 17 March 1981, Portland, Maine.
> Roger Bourland: Minstrels (1982, sax-s., bn., strs.).
> _____: Quintet (sax, str. quar.). Prem. Feb., 1985,
>     Portland.
> Alan Hovhaness (b. 1911): Concerto (1981, sax-s.,
>     strs.).
> Shirish Korde (b. 1945): Constellations (1974, SATB).
>     Dorn, 1980.
> Thomas Oboe Lee (b. 1945): Sourmash (winner of the
>     Koussevitzky Prize). Dorn, 1980.
> Gunther Schuller (b. 1925): Saxophone Concerto.
>     AMP. Prem. 17 Jan. 1984, Pittsburgh.
> Ezra Sims (b. 1928): Sextet (1982). Composer.
> _____: Solo (1982). Composer.

Recordings:

> Berg: Violin Concerto (Deutsche Grammophon DG 2531
> 110, with BSO, Perlman); Korde: Constellations
> (Spectrum 128); New Music (Gunmar, 1985, music by
> Bourland and others); Northeastern Records (music
> by Sims and others); Happy Feet (Crest, 1976, music
> by P. Whiteman).


RAMSAY, W. NEAL
b. Nashville, Tennessee
  28 June 1952

A student of Vincent Abato, James Riggs, and Don Cas-
sel, Ramsay completed degrees at George Peabody College
(1974) and Texas State University (1976). His national
debut recital was at the Lisner Auditorium, JFK Center,
Washington, D.C. on 17 October 1978. Since 1980, he has
served on the faculty of the Blair School of Music, Van-
derbilt University. He has arranged music for saxophone
and piano, published by Shawnee and Dorn (1978-82).

Compositions dedicated to or premiered by N. Ramsay:

> Victoria Bond (b. 1949): Notes From Underground.
>     Prem. 11 Nov. 1985, Carnegie Recital Hall.
> _____: Scat (1984).
> Fred Geissler: Timelife I.
> Marvin Lamb: A Ballad of Roland. Dorn.
> _____: Final Roland.
> Oscar Smith (b. 1951): Symbols. Prem. 28 Feb. 1983, NYC.

Gary Weaver:   A Tribute to Paul Desmond.
Jeffrey Wood:   Moortown Elegies.

# Recordings:

Saxophone Alone (Cumberland NSW 101, 1979, music by
Bach, Bonneau, Bozza, Hartley, Lamb, Noda); Neal Ram-
say in Recital (Cumberland CRP 1757, 1982, music by
Creston, Handel, Milhaud, Robert, Wiedoeft); Neal
Ramsay (cassette, Roncorp EMS 009, 1983, music by
Creston, Handel, Milhaud, Robert, Wiedoeft); Four
Moods (Cumberland CRP 8451, music by Handel, Maurice,
Smith, Woods).


RASCHER, SIGURD MANFRED
b. Elberfeld (now Wuppertal)
   West Germany
   15 May 1907

Rascher is of Scandinavian extraction.  After matricu-
lating at the Stuttgart Musikhochschule in 1930, where he
studied clarinet with Philipp Dreisbach, Rascher decided to
become a saxophonist.  He began teaching in elementary
schools and, with hard work, was soon in constant demand
as a saxophonist.  By 1932, Rascher was already playing a
three-and-a-half-octave range, much to the chagrin of German music professors of the time, who believed the instrument's range was limited to only two-and-a-half octaves.
On 3 October 1932, he was invited to Hannover to play the
premiere of the Saxophone Concerto by Edmund von Borck;
this was followed by performances in Berlin (November, 1932
and 6 January 1933).  During a contemporary music festival
at Strasbourg, directed by Hermann Scherchen in the summer
of 1933, Rascher became acquainted with the famous singer
Marya Freund.  After she heard him perform von Borck's
Concerto, she offered to introduce him to some composers
in Paris, including Jacques Ibert who was inspired to
write the famous Concertino da Camera for Rascher.

The political and social upheaval in Germany, which
started in the 1920s, became so extreme that, in 1933, the
Ministry of Propaganda and Enlightenment was obliged to
take measures to boycott the saxophone; this resulted from
the ban on so-called "Negro music."  Rascher left Germany
in 1933 to teach saxophone at the Royal Danish Conservatory,
Copenhagen, and a year later in Malmo, Sweden; he held both
posts until 1938.  Since his debut in the U.S. in 1939,
Rascher has appeared as soloist with most of the principal
symphony orchestras in the U.S., Europe, Australia, Central
America, and Cuba.  His final appearance was on 14 May 1977.
In addition to his distinguished musicianship, brilliant
agility, and sweetness of tone, Rascher has had a phenomenal success as a teacher.  He taught at the Manhattan
school (1940-42) and at Eastman School of Music, and has

appeared at many conferences and workshops throughout the U.S.

In 1969 he formed the Rascher Saxophone Quartet (with his daughter Carina, Bruce Weinberger, and Linda Bangs), for which many noted composers have created new works. Upon Rascher's retirement in 1981, John Edward Kelly was invited to join the quartet as an alto saxophonist. The Rascher Saxophone Ensemble was formed as an outgrowth of several summer saxophone institutes held by Rascher with his loyal and enthusiastic students.

The spring 1982 issue of The Saxophone Symposium presented a special feature honoring Sigurd Rascher on his 75th birthday. Patrick states:

> Through the years Mr. Rascher continued to grow as an artist
> and his performance became more and more insightful. . . .
> Perhaps a proof of this would be his final solo appearance
> (May 14, 1977); there are knowledgeable critics who believe
> that this was the most beautiful and deeply moving performance
> of his career.[12]

In addition to 84 transcriptions published by Belwin-Mills, Bourne, Chappell, and McGinnis and Marx, from works of Bach, Eccles, Fasch, Gershwin, Martini, Mozart, Schumann, Vivaldi, and others, Rascher has composed and edited the following works:

> 24 Intermezzi (1958, Bourne); Top Tones  (1941-61, CF);
> Complete Scales Chart (CF); 158 Studies (1935-68, Han-
> sen); Scales (1965, MM); The Carnival of Venice (pf.
> by Glaser, Chappell, 1937); Quartettino (by Wm. Schu-
> man, 1939, AATB, Peer, 1959); Sextuor (c. 1844, by G.
> Kastner, SSATBBs, Ethos, 1982); Gleanings from Six
> Centuries (AATB with L. Patrick, MM, 1981).

## Compositions dedicated to S. M. Rascher:

> Samuel Adler (b. 1928):  Line Drawing After Mark Tobey
>     (SATB, 1978).
> Henk Badings (b. 1907):  La Malinconia (8'). Don.,
>     1948.
> Warren Benson (b. 1924):  Cantilena (2'30). B.H.,
>     1954.
> _____: Concertino (1955, 13'). MCA.
> _____: Invocation et Dance (1960, 4'30). MCA.
> Jørgen Bentzon (1897-1951):  Introduction, Variations
>     et Rondo (1938, 17'). Ska.
> _____: Racconto, opus 25 (1935, fl., sax, bn., db.,
>     13'). Ska.
> Edmund von Borck (1906-1944):  Capriccio in A, opus 11
>     (vn., sax, pf., 1935).
> _____: Concerto, opus 6 (1932, 17'). Prem. 3 Oct.
>     1932, Hannover.

René Borel: Fugato in F (SATB). Bourne, 1976.
Henry Brant (b. 1913): Concerto (20'). CF, 1941.
     Prem. 12 May 1945, NYC.
Hans Brehme (1904-1957): Saxophone Sonata (c. 1932).
Eric Coates (1886-1957): Saxo-rhapsody (1936, 11').
     B.H. and Chappell. Prem. Folkestone Festival, 1937.
Henry Cowell (1897-1965): Air and Scherzo (1961).
     Sch., 1963.
Ingolf Dahl (1912-1970): Concerto (sax, w. orch., 1949,
     rev. 1953, c. 18-19'). EAM, 1979.
Erwin Dressel (1909-1972): Bagatelles. Ries.
_____: Concerto (1932, 24'). Ries, 1932. Prem. 4
     March 1934, Göteborg, Sweden.
_____: Partita. Ries, 1965.
Will Eisenmann (b. 1906): Concerto, opus 38 (15').
     Uni., 1948.
_____: Duo Concertante, opus 33 (11'). CF, 1966.
_____: Mouvements für Atlsaxophon, opus 68 (1962, 5').
_____: Nevermore (Ballade), opus 28, Kendor, 1969.
Frank Erickson (b. 1923): Concerto (with band, 13').
     Bourne, 1966.
Everett Gates (b. 1929): Incantation and Ritual
     (1963, sax solo, 4').
Fritz Gerhard (b. 1911): Fantaisie Ben Venga Amore
     (1970, SATB).
Roberto Gerhard (1896-1970): Quartet.
Werner Wolf Glaser (b. 1910): Allegro, Cadenza, and
     Adagio (1950, orch./pf.). STIM.
_____: Canto (sax, strs., 1970). STIM. Prem. 2 June
     1971.
_____: Concertino (1935). STIM.
_____: Drei Sonaten im alten Stil (1934, sax solo).
     STIM. Prem. 18 Feb. 1966, Buffalo.
_____: Little Pieces for Four Saxophones, opus 8a,
     (SAAT, 6'). Presser, 1977.
_____: Little Quartet (sax, vn., vla., pf., 1970).
     STIM.
_____: Quartet (sax, vn., vla., vcl., 1950). STIM.
_____: Quintet for Five Saxophones (SAATB, 1964-77,
     15'). STIM. Prem. 2 Nov. 1978, NYC.
_____: Suite (1935, 12'). STIM.
_____: Three Pieces for Eleven Saxophones (1981,
     SSAAAATTBBBs, 12'). STIM.
Alexander Glazunov (1865-1936): Concerto in E$^b$, opus
     109 (1934, 14'). Leduc. Prem. 26 Nov. 1934,
     Nyköping, Sweden.
Renata Grisoni: Albumblat, opus 60. Peters.
_____: Sonatina, opus 64. Curci.
_____: Suite Italien, opus 26. Peters.
Walter S. Hartley (b. 1927): Aubade (SAATBBs). Ethos.
     Prem. 15 May 1985.
_____: Chamber Music (1960, sax, ww. quin., for S.
     Rascher and R. Resnik, 8'30). FEMA, 1972.
_____: Octet (1975, SAAATTBBs, 8'30). Dorn, 1980.
_____: The Saxophone Album (1974, 4 pieces for divers

saxes). Dorn, 1982.
_____: Suite for Saxophone Quartet (11'). Phil.,
1972.
Paul Hindemith (1895-1963): Konzertstück (1933, AA).
MM, 1978.
Emil Hlobil (b. 1901): Quartet for Saxophones, opus
93 (1974). Schirmer.
Karel Husa (b. 1921): Concerto (1967, sax, w. ens.,
17'). AMP. Prem. 17 March 1968.
_____: Elégie et Rondeau (1960). Leduc. Prem. 29
July 1960, with pf.; 6 May 1962, with orch.
Jacques Ibert (1890-1962): Concertino da Camera
(1934-35, 11'). Leduc. Prem. 2 May 1935, Paris,
mov't I; 11 Dec. 1935, Winterthur, entire work.
Wolfgang Jacobi (1894-1972): Barcarole (1964, 2 saxes).
_____: Serenade and Allegro (1961, sax, orch., 11').
_____: Sonata (1964, 10'30). Bourne
Ernst Lothar von Knorr (1896-1973): Chamber Concerto
(sax, pf., chor., ch. orch.).
Erland von Koch (b. 1910): Bagatella Virtuosa (1978,
SATB, 2'). STIM.
_____: Cantilena (1978, sax-s. solo, 3'). CG.
_____: Cantilena e vivo for Saxophone Quartet (1978,
3'). CG.
_____: Concerto for Saxophone and String Orchestra
(1958, 19'). Peer. Prem. 22 Sep. 1959.
_____: Concerto Piccolo (1962, S, A, strs., rev. for
winds, 1976, 13'). Br. H.
_____: Dance No. 2 (1938, rev. 1967, S or A, orch.,
2'). STIM.
_____: Dialogue for Soprano and Alto Saxophones
(1975, 5'). STIM.
_____: Miniatures for Saxophone Quartet (1970, 12').
Br. H.
_____: Moderato e Allegro for Saxophone Chamber Or-
chestra (1981, SSAAAATTBBBs, 9'). STIM. Prem. 6
Oct. 1982, Hattiesburg, Miss.
_____: Monolog Nr. 4 (1975, sax solo). CG.
_____: Saxophonia (1976, SATB, w. orch., 18'). STIM,
Fleisher. Prem. 4 Feb. 1977, Stockholm.
Peter Korn (b. 1922): Konzert (1956, 20'). Bourne.
Prem. 6 Jan. 1957, Elkhart.
John David Lamb (b. 1935): Alto Saxophone Concerto
("Cloud Cuckoo Land," c. 1971).
_____: Barefoot Dances (1962, AA). MM, 1971.
_____: Night Music (1956, sax, band). Composer.
_____: Three Antique Dances (1961, sax solo). Composer.
_____: Three Flourishes (1961, AA).
_____: Three Pieces (1963, sax-b., pf.). Romp (Bel.,
1964); Finney's Folly; Frolic.
Lars-Erik Larsson (b. 1908): Konzert, opus 14 (1934,
20'). CG. Prem. 27 Nov. 1934, Norrköping, Sweden.
William Latham (b. 1917): Concerto Grosso (1960, S,
A, band/orch., 18'). Prem. 16 Dec. 1960 with band,
Chicago; 30 Oct. 1962 with orch., Hilversum, Holland.

Clair Leonard (b. 1901):  Recitativo and Abracadabra.
    Bourne, 1962.
Zdenek Lukás (b. 1928):  Rondo per 4 Saxofoni (1970).
Otmar Macha (b. 1922):  Plâc Saxofonu (1969, 6'30).
    CMIC.
_____ : The weeping of the Saxophone (1968).  CMIC.
Frank Martin (1890-1974):  Ballade (15').  Uni., 1938.
Albert Moeschinger (b. 1897):  Concerto Lyrique, opus
    83 (1958, 15').  B.H.
Roman Palester (b. 1907):  Concertino (1938, rev.
    1978, 14').  Polish.
Armand Russell (b. 1932):  Particles (1965).  Bourne,
    1967.
Takefusa Sasamori:  Variations, "Taki Kojo no Tski."
    Peer, 1963.
Albert Schmutz (1887-1975):  Sonata (1961).  Peer,
    1968.
Robert Starer (b. 1924):  Light and Shadow (1977,
    AATB).  MCA, 1978.
Marshall Turkin:  Sonata.  Presser, 1958.
Waldemar Welander (b. 1899):  Arietta (1947, 3'55).
    CF, 1965.
_____ : Concertino (1964).  STIM.
Maurice Whitney (b. 1909):  Introduction and Samba
    (sax, band/pf., 8'16).  Bourne
_____ : Rhumba.  Bourne, 1949.
Carl Anton Wirth (b. 1912):  Beyond These Hills
    (c. 1965).  CPP.
_____ : Dark Flows the River.  CPP.
_____ : David (triptych, sax, winds, per.).  Prem. 31
    Oct. 1978, San Jose.
_____ : Idlewood Concerto (1954, 20').  Presser.
    Prem. 22 Oct. 1956, Chattanooga.
_____ : Jephta (1958, S, A, strs., pf., per.).
John Worley (b. 1919):  Claremont Concerto (1962, 23').
    Prem. April, 1963, Lynn, Mass.  Composer.
_____ : Sonata (1974).  CF, 1979.

Recordings:

Debussy Rhapsodies (Col. M 56659, N.Y. Philharmonic);
Sigurd Rascher Plays a Classical Recital on the Saxo-
phone (CHS 1156); Sigurd Rascher Plays the Saxophone
(Grand Award Series, 2 vols., AAS 703, 708); von Koch:
Saxophone Concerto (EMI, Sweden, HMV 061 34016); Amer-
ican Concertos (VC 81047, reissue, Cincinnati Symph.
Orch., Brant: Concerto); The Rascher Saxophone Quar-
tet (Coronet, Vol. 1, LPS 3021, music by Bach, Gates,
Gerhard, Hartley, Koch, Lukas; Vol. 2, LPS 3030 music
by Borel, Glaser, Hindemith, Hlobil, Lamb, Patachich;
Vol.3, LPS 3032, music by Bach, Farmer, Frescobaldi,
Handel, Haydn, Jacobi, Mendelssohn, Obrecht, Praeto-
rius, Purcell, Worley); The Rascher Saxophone Ensemble
(Coronet, Vol. 1, LPS 3022, music by Bach, Bellman,
Bull, Grieg, Odstricil, Vivaldi, Wirth, Worley; Vol. 2,

LPS 3031, music by Bach, Grieg, Handel, Hartley, Kastner); von Koch: Saxophonia (Mark Records MC 20161,
1980, with the Clarence High School Band, N.Y.).

Film:

The Saxophone (c. 1957, Buescher Band Instrument Co.
and Oklahoma City U.).


RASCHER-PETERS, CARINA
b. Shushan, New York
   7 August 1945

     Daughter of the famous virtuoso Sigurd Rascher,
Rascher-Peters specializes in the soprano saxophone (pre-
fering the older, curved model).  She showed phenomenal
talent at an early age and has been heard both as a soloist in her own right and in joint concerts with her father.
In a tour of Europe in 1962, they won the highest praises
from music critics in Stockholm, Munich, Groningen, Arnhem,
and Amsterdam.  Now teaching in Tübingen, Germany, Rascher-
Peters continues to lead the quartet, which, since 1971,
has given hundreds of concerts in such halls as Stockholm's
Konserthus, Zurich's Tonhalle, New York's Carnegie Hall,
and Prague's Smetana House, as well as many radio and TV
appearances.

Compositions dedicated to C. Rascher-Peters:

     Siegfried Borris (b. 1906): Konzert für Soprano Sax-
        ophone (1966). SZ.
     Everett Gates (b. 1921): Incantation and Ritual
        (1963, sax solo, 4').
     Harald Genzmer (b. 1909): Sonata (sax-s., pf.). RE.
     Fritz Gerhard (b. 1911): Rhapsodie (1980, sax-s.,
        pf.).
     Werner Wolf Glaser (b. 1910): Konzert für Soprano
        Saxophone (1980, 17'). STIM.  Prem. 7 July 1982,
        WSC, Nuremberg.
     Erland von Koch (b. 1910): Concerto Piccolo (1962,
        S, A, strs., rev. for winds, 1976, 13').  Br. H.
        _____: Dance No. 2 (1938, rev. 1967, S/A, orch., 2').
        STIM.
        _____: Dialogue for Soprano and Alto Saxophone (1975,
        5').  STIM.
     John David Lamb (b. 1935): Sonata (c. 1962, sax-s.,
        pf.).
        _____: Three Flourishes (1961, AA).
     William Latham (b. 1917): Concerto Grosso (1960, SA,
        band/orch., 18').  Hilversum, Holland.

Compositions dedicated to the Rascher Saxophone Quartet
        after 1981:

     John Boda (b. 1922): Opus for Saxophone Quartet (1984).

Michael Denhoff (b. 1955):  Gegen-Sätze (1984).
Violeta Dinescu (b. 1953):  Drei Miniaturen für Saxo-
    phonquartett (1982).
Harald Genzmer (b. 1909):  Quartett for Saxophonen
    (1982).
Werner Wolf Glaser (b. 1910):  Four Phantasies for
    Four Saxophones (c. 1982, 12'). STIM.
Walter S. Hartley (b. 1927):  Antiphonal Prelude
    (1984, SATB, org.). Composer.
_____ :  Solemn Postlude (1985, SATB, org.).  Composer.
_____ :  Toccata Concertante (1984-85, SATB, org.).
    Composer.
Maurice Karkoff (b. 1927):  Ernst & Spass, opus 156
    (1984, SATB).
Miklós Maros (b. 1943):  Quartett for Saxophones
    (1984).


Recordings:

(See Sigurd Rascher Saxophone Quartet and Saxophone
Ensemble.)


REGNI, ALBERT B.
b. Johnson City, New York
   11 August 1936


A pupil of William Osseck, Regni received the B.M. at
Eastman in 1958 and studied additionally with Gino Alistri
at the Manhattan School, where he completed the M.M.  He
performs freelance engagements in New York and has recorded
with the New York Philharmonic, Contemporary Chamber Ensemble, and numerous other groups on such labels as Nonesuch,
Columbia, RCA, and CTI.  In 1980-81, he was Associate Professor of Music at the University of Texas.

Compositions dedicated to A. Regni:

Bernard Hoffer:  Concerto for Alto Saxophone (1983,
    sax, w. ens.).
Karl Korte (b. 1928):  Symmetrics (1973, sax, per.).
Barton McLean (b. 1938):  Dimensions III and IV
    (1979, sax, tape).


Recordings:

Extended Saxophone (Composers Recordings CRI SD 431);
Five Songs of Experience (John Harbison:  Bermuda Triangle, CRI S 313); Darius Milhaud:  La Création du
Monde (Nonesuch 71122); William Walton:  Façade (Columbia M 33980).

REX, HARLEY E.
b. Lehighton, Pennsylvania
   29 March 1930

Rex completed the B.S. and the M.M. degrees at Mansfield State University and the D.M.A. in 1971 at the University of Michigan. His teachers were Sigurd Rascher and
Larry Teal. A saxophonist and arranger with the U.S. Army
Band (1954-62), he has made many solo appearances with the
MENC in Fort Worth, Ann Arbor, and Washington, D.C. (1962,
1964, 1968, 1973, and 1976). He was the saxophonist with
the Houston Symphony Orchestra (1965-73), has conducted
the Houston Municipal Band since 1966, and teaches at Sam
Houston State University. Over 26 of his arrangements for
sax ensemble are available from Dorn Music Publishers.

Compositions:

> Preludio and Movendo (sax, pf./band, Mills, 1962);
> Saxophone Rhapsody; Shenandoah (SATB); Scherzo (cl.
> quar.); Washington Sonata (sax, pf./band, 1974, Dorn);
> Four Pastels (AATB, Dorn); Andando and Brillante
> (sax, band, Dorn, 1982).


RICHTMEYER-TRUAX, DEBRA
b. Lansing, Michigan
   19 January 1957

Richtmeyer-Truax studied with Frederick Hemke and
earned the B.M.Ed. (1979) and the M.M. (1980) at Northwestern University. She was a semifinalist at the World
Saxophone Competition in Gap, France in 1978, and a winner
at Northwestern University Concert Competition (1979) and
the Chicago Women's Farwell Competition (1980). She has
been soloist at WSC meetings in Evanston, Illinois (1979),
Nuremberg (1982), the University of Maryland (1985), and
various regional meetings for NASA. Since 1981, she has
been teaching at North Texas State University and performing, when needed, with the Dallas Symphony Orchestra.

Compositions dedicated to D. Richtmeyer-Truax:

> Amy Quate: Light of Sothis (1982). Leduc. Prem. 8
>    July 1982, WSC, Nuremberg.
> Bert Truax: Romance and Burlesque (sax-s., tpt., pf.).
>    Prem. 28 June 1985, WSC, U. of Maryland.

Recordings:

> NTSU Wind Ensemble (ERS 830217, 1983, Finney: Concer-
> to); Dallas Symphony Orchestra (RCA, ARC1-4573, 1983,
> Mussorgsky-Ravel: Pictures at an Exhibition).

RIED, MICHAEL J.
b. Portville, New York
   11 April 1939

A student of Sigurd Rascher and William Willett, Ried completed the M.S. degree at SUNY, Fredonia in 1969. He began teaching at the Clarence Central Schools, Clarence, New York, in 1970, and has performed in recitals and concerts since 1961.

Compositions dedicated to or premiered by M. Ried:

Persis Vehar (b. 1937): Four Pieces (1975). Tenuto, 1980.
_____ : Quintus Concertino (sax, w. ens.). Prem. 6 Nov. 1981.


ROTTER, JAMES
b. San Diego, California
   21 October 1948

A student of Harvey Pittel, Rotter received the M.M. from the University of California, Los Angeles. He is a member of the Los Angeles and the Harvey Pittel Saxophone Quartets and has participated in WSC meetings in Bordeaux and Evanston. He is an instructor of saxophone at the University of Southern California, University of Redlands, and San Diego State University.

Compositions dedicated to J. Rotter:

Barney Childs (b. 1926): The Word From Department R. Prem. 1 July 1979, Evanston.
Howard Quilling (b. 1935): Suite for Saxophone and Wind Orchestra.
David Ward-Steinman (b. 1936): Golden Apples. Prem. 4 Dec. 1981, San Diego.
Ronald Yates (b. 1947): Concerto (1970, sax, str. orch., per., 14').

Recordings:

(See Harvey Pittel Saxophone Quartet.)


ROUSSEAU, EUGENE E.
b. Blue Island, Illinois
   23 August 1932

Rousseau began his study of the saxophone at the age of nine under the tutelage of Elda Jansen Bengston. He later studied with Horace Frederick, Sam Meron, and Albert Freedman at the Chicago Musical College, where he completed the B.M.Ed. He holds the M.M. from Northwestern University

(oboe, 1954) and the Ph.D. from the University of Iowa
(clarinet pedagogy, 1962). During the course of his work
at Iowa, he was awarded a Fulbright Grant to study with
Marcel Mule in Paris (1960-61). Rousseau has been a member of the faculty of the School of Music at Indiana University since 1964 and has served as Chairman of the Woodwind Faculty for six years.

Rousseau made a highly successful solo debut at Carnegie Hall in January, 1965. In 1969, he appeared at Wigmore Hall (London), Concertgebouw (Amsterdam), and the
Conservatorium (Berlin). In 1968, he performed at the
Musikverein (Vienna) and the Salle Gaveau (Paris). As
Visiting Professor at the Hochschule für Musik in Vienna,
in October, 1981, he was the first saxophone teacher at
that institution. A President of NASA from 1978 to 1980,
he played at some of the WSC meetings. Rousseau has given
many clinics, lecture-recitals, and solo appearances on
all educational levels throughout the U.S., Canada, Europe,
and Asia. He was a consultant for the G. Leblanc Company
and now holds a similar position with the Yamaha Company.

Book:

> Marcel Mule: His Life and the Saxophone (Etoile
> Music, Inc., 1982).

Publications:

> Saxophone Method (2 vols., Kjos); Debussy: Rapsodie,
> 1903 (rev. sax, pf., Etoile, 1975); Solo Albums for
> Alto and Tenor Saxophones (Etoile); Saxophone High
> Tones (Etoile, 1978); Helpful Hints for Saxophone
> (vols. for A, T, B, Belwin); 27 educational solos
> (9 each for A, T, B, Belwin); arrangements for sax
> solos and quartets (Etoile, 1982).

Compositions dedicated to E. Rousseau:

> Jindrich Feld (b. 1925): Concerto (1980, SAT, 1 perf.,
>     orch.). BH. Prem. 9 July 1982, WSC, Nuremberg.
>     (w. orch., 1985, Kjos; pf., Ars Nova). Prem. with
>     w. orch., 27 June 1985, Washington, D.C.
> Frederick Fox (b. 1931): Visitations (1982, AA, 10').
>     Composer.
> Bernhard Heiden (b. 1910): Solo. AMP. Prem. 16 Dec.
>     1969, WSC, Chicago.
> J. Orrego-Salas (b. 1919): Quattro Liriche, opus 61
>     (1967). Peer. Prem. 1968, London.

Recordings:

> Saxophone Concertos (Deutsche Grammophon DGG 2530
> 209, 1971, music by Dubois, Glazunov, Ibert, Villa-
> Lobos); Eugene Rousseau Plays Saxophone (Coronet 1292,

music by Desenclos, Granados, Handel, Ibert, Maurice,
Van Delden); The Virtuoso Saxophone (Coronet 1601,
music by Bonneau, Chopin, Dubois, Hindemith, Platti,
Ruggiero); Saxophone Duos (Coronet 1703, with J.
Rezits, pf.); Saxophone in Chamber Music (Coronet
1709, with Indiana U. Faculty Ww. Quin., Berkshire
Str. Quar., music by Bentzon, Heiden, Ibert); Music
for Two Saxophones (Crystal S 156, with D. Bamber,
music by Cunningham, Glenn, Lamb, Loeillet); Yamaha
Suite (Crest 4224, 1982, Eugene Rousseau Saxophone
Quartet, with S. Goacher, J. Lansing, D. Bamber, music
by Carisi, Heiden, Linn, Paich).

RUNYON, ALFRED (SANTY)
b. Chanute, Kansas
   18 April 1907

At the age of eight, Runyon started his musical career playing the drums in his father's movie house in Oklahoma; and, at eleven, he began to play the saxophone.  For
two years, he studied at Oklahoma State University, the University of Missouri, and the University of Tulsa, while performing and leading bands in the Southwest.  Additionally,
he studied the flute with Kincaid in Philadelphia and with
Ernest Liegle in Chicago.  Moving to Chicago (after the
Chicago World's Fair), he played with Michel Ayres, WGM
Radio, and Henry Weber's Orchestra.  Runyon worked at the
Chicago Theater for ten years, had a successful private
studio, and also taught at Northwestern University and
Wheaton College.  Several important saxophonists studied
with him, including Sonny Stitt, Lee Konitz, John Boswell,
Paul Desmond, Wolf Tane, and the members of the saxophone
section of the original Lawrence Welk Band.  In 1941, he
began making jazz saxophone mouthpieces; his factory is
now located in Opelousas, Louisiana.

Compositions:

Santy Runyon's Modern Saxophone Studies (1944, Gorns-
ton, now Bay); Dynamic Etudes (1949, Gornston, now
avail. from the comp.); Exotic (1953, from Dynamic
Etudes, pf. acc. by H. Huffnagel, Gornston, 1957);
Dreams of Yesterday (song, with Duplantis, 1966);
Spring Come Again (song, with E. Lyttle, 1969).

Composition dedicated to S. Runyon:

Arsene Siegel: Pasquinade (sax/cl., pf, 7'). Seesaw,
1946.

SAMPEN, JOHN W.
b. Bloomington, Illinois
   10 April 1949

One of America's outstanding soloists, Sampen studied

with Frederick Hemke, Larry Teal, and Donald Sinta, completing the M.M. in 1972 at Northwestern University.  He
was soloist at several meetings of the WSC and a winner in
the Geneva Concours of 1970 as well as in another international competition in Belgium in 1979.  Sampen has taught
at Wichita State University and since 1977 has been Professor of Saxophone at Bowling Green State University.  In
1984, he completed a doctorate at Northwestern University
and, in 1985, was the recipient of a grant from the National Endowment for the Arts for 1986-1988; he will play commissioned works by Babbitt, Martino, and Subotnick.

### Compositions dedicated to J. Sampen:

Burton Beerman (b. 1943):  Concerto (sax, tape).
   ACA.  Prem. 1980.
_____ :  Moment (1978).  ACA.  Prem. Aug., 1979.
Derek Bell (b. 1923):  Honest Pleasures (1981, sax,
   ch. ens.).
William Bolcom (b. 1938):  A Short Lecture on the
   Saxophone (sax solo).  Prem. 29 June 1979, WSC,
   Evanston.
Sydney Hodkinson (b. 1934):  Three Dance Preludes.
   Prem. July, 1982.  Composer.
D. Mariacy:  Private Eye (1982, sax-s., tape).
Walter Mays (b. 1941):  Concerto.  Bel.  Prem. 5 July
   1974, WSC, Bordeaux.
Elliott Schwartz:  Chamber Concerto IV.  Prem. April,
   1981.
Marilyn Shrude (b. 1946):  Evolution V (sax, SATB).
   ACA.  Prem. July, 1976.
_____ :  Masks (SATB, pf.).  ACA.  Prem. 8 July 1982,
   WSC, Nuremberg.
_____ :  Music (sax-s., pf.).  ACA.  Prem. 5 July 1974,
   WSC, Bordeaux.
_____ :  Quartet for Saxophones.  SMC, 1972.
Alan Stout (b. 1932):  Suite for Saxophone and Organ.
   ACA.  Prem. May, 1972.
Charmian Tashjian:  Antiphonies I (sax, ch. ens.).
   Prem. April, 1977.
Vladimir Ussachevsky (b. 1911):  Mimicry (sax-s.,
   tape).  Prem. 8 July 1982, WSC, Nuremberg.

### Recording:

Walter Mays:  Concerto (CRI 361, 1976).


SAMYN, NOEL G. L.
b. Menin, Belgium
   24 December 1945

A student at the Conservatoire Royal in Brussels,
where he won a first prize (1962-66), Samyn was a pupil of
François Daneels.  His first recital was for the Jeunesses

Musicales in Brussels on 5 March 1968.  Moving to Canada,
he first taught at the Conservatory in Val d'Or, Québec.
In 1978, he was appointed Professor of Saxophone at the
Conservatoire de Musique du Québec at Hull.

Compositions:

> 5 Trios (2 cl., sax, Bil., 1976); 9 Etudes Transcen-
> dantes (Bil., 1977); Romance (Bil., 1977).


SANNELLA, ANDY
b. New York, New York          d. New York, New York
   11 March 1900                  1961

Sannella, a violinist, steel guitarist (Hawaiian-
style), pianist, and conductor, began his career in the
early 1920s in Panama City and picked up the saxophone,
playing with Ray Miller from 1920 to 1922.  From the late
1920s through the 1930s, he was a leading studio artist
known for his sweet alto saxophone sound.  A member of the
first saxophone octet organized by Clyde Doerr, he taught
saxophone seriously in New York, conducted orchestras for
such radio shows as Manhattan Merry-Go-Round (1934-37),
Community Sing (with Milton Berle, 1936-37), and the Gil-
lette Show (which ended in 1937).  In Hollywood in the
late 1930s, he was a pianist/organist.  He remained active
on TV until the late 1940s, and was still making recordings
in the 1950s.

Compositions (the following publications were copyrighted
          and published in 1928 by Spier & Coslow, Inc., and
          are all out of print):

> Aileen; Jack & Jill (with J. Shilkret); Millicent
> (with J. Shilkret); Saxannella (with H. Klickman);
> S.O.S. (song, with Ross and B. McClean, Marman Music,
> 1953); Intervals (studies, 1932).

Recordings:

> Jack and Jill, Aileen (Columbia 1414-D); Love's Golden
> Dream, Valse Jewel (Harmony 1026-11); Hula Blues
> (Rounder, 1012).  (For additional recordings, see
> Roger Kinkle, The Complete Encyclopedia of Popular
> Music and Jazz, vol. 3, pp. 1705-6.)


SCHNEIDER, ARTURO ERIC
b. 22 August 1929
   Casilda, Santa Fé, Argentina

A student of John Grisigrione and Ruggiero Lavecchia,
Schneider studied at the Grande Castelli Hermanos in Buenos
Aires until 1947.  He performed with the National Symphony

of Argentina (1966), was one of the founders of the Astor
Piazzola Orchestra, and plays flute and tenor sax with his
own quartet.  For the last 20 years, he has been heard in
the house orchestra for Channel 13 TV in Buenos Aires and
has had a large saxophone class of private students.  On
24 May 1976, he was a feature sax-soloist with Astor Piazzola and his New Group, at Carnegie Hall's 85th Anniver-
sary Concert in an evening of Argentinian music, performing compositions by Astor Piazzola.

Composition:

        Coctel De Ritmos (1954).

Recordings:

        Maria de Los Buenos Aires (TROVA TLS 5020/2, music by
        Piazzola); Pulsacion (TROVA TLS 5038, 1969, music by
        Piazzola); Music by Osvaldo Berligier (1984).


SIBBING, ROBERT V.
b. Quincy, Illinois
   9 February 1929

        After receiving the B.M. at the University of Iowa,
Sibbing completed the Ed.D. at the University of Illinois
in 1969.  He has been Professor of Saxophone at Western
Illinois University (Macomb) since 1969.  He was the soprano saxophonist and founder of the Illinois Saxophone
Quintet, which has performed frequently at the WSC and
NASA meetings.  In 1985, Sibbing resigned his leadership
and the ensemble became a quartet with Keith Zimmerman
playing soprano saxophone.  Other current members of the
Illinois Saxophone Quartet are John Tavenier, Robert Kies-
ler, and Janet Schisler-Lulloff.  Sibbing made many arrangements for the saxophone quintet which are available from
Etoile.

Compositions:

        Moments (sax, bn., db., 1976, Etoile); Sonata (sax-s.,
        pf., 1981, Etoile); Vocalise (1980, Etoile); Pastiche
        (sax, hn., Presser).


SIGMON, C. MILLER
b. Hickory, North Carolina
   26 September 1947

        After receiving the B.M. and while completing the
M.M. at the University of Michigan, where he studied with
Larry Teal and Donald Sinta, Sigmon taught saxophone at
the University of Toledo from 1969 to 1971.  He was a
member of the U.S. Marine Band in Washington from 1971 to

1975 and taught at George Mason University from 1972 to
1975. Following his military service, he went to Bordeaux
for additional study at the CNRM with J. M. Londeix. Returning to the U.S., he served as Artist-in-Residence at
Rockingham Community College (Wentworth, N.C.), and in 1979,
he became the Performing Arts Coordinator for the North
Carolina Arts Council in Raleigh. He was soloist for WSC
meetings in Toronto, Bordeaux, and Evanston.

## Compositions dedicated to or premiered by C. M. Sigmon:

Walter S. Hartley (b. 1927): Quartet for Reeds (ob.,
    cl., sax, bn., 9'30). Dorn, 1977.
Annette Le Siege: Suite. Seesaw, 1979.
Andreas Makris (b. 1930): Fantasy and Dance (12').
    Mediterranean. Prem. 4 July 1974, Bordeaux.
Jerzy Sapieyevski (b. 1945): Air for Alto Saxophone
    and String Quartet. Presser, 1976.
D. Werts: Sigmonody (1972, sax solo). Dorn.


SINTA, DONALD J.
b. Detroit, Michigan
    16 June 1937

One of America's most gifted soloists, Sinta was a
pupil of Larry Teal. He received the B.S. (1959, Mus. Ed.)
at Wayne State University and the M.M. (1962) from the University of Michigan. He has concertized widely in the
U.S., has made concert appearances in Europe and Canada,
and is a clinician for the H. and A. Selmer Company. Before his appointment to the University of Michigan (following Larry Teal's retirement in 1974), he taught at
Ithaca College and Hartt School of Music. In 1984, he was
awarded a fellowship grant as a soloist from the National
Endowment for the Arts, and in 1985 and 1986, will perform
commissioned works by William Albright, William Bolcom,
and David Diamond.

## Compositions dedicated to D. Sinta:

Samuel Adler (b. 1928): Canto IV (1971). Dorn.
William Albright (b. 1944): Doo-Dah (1975, sax trio).
    Dorn.
_____: Sonata (1984).
Georges Andrix (b. 1932): 4 Pieces.
Wayne Barlow (b. 1912): Concerto (1969, sax, band).
    Prem. May, 1970, East Strousburg, Pa.
Leslie Bassett (b. 1923): Music for Saxophone and
    Piano (1968, 10'). Peters. Prem. Aug., 1968,
    by E. Zinn-Ervin, in Tempe, Arizona.
Frank Bennet: Song (1975).
Warren Benson (b. 1924): Farewell (2'). MCA, 1964.
    Prem. Feb., 1964.
_____: Star Edge (1966). CF, 1978. Prem. May, 1966.

William Bolcom (b. 1938): Lilith (1984). Marks.
Stephen Chatman (b. 1950): Quiet Exchange (sax, 2
     suspended cym., 5'10). Dorn.
Laura Clayton (b. 1943): Simichai-ya (sax, tape,
     1976).
Paul Cooper (b. 1926): Concerto (1982). Prem. 14
     Oct. 1982, Stockholm, Sweden.
Ellwood Derr (b. 1932): I Never Saw Another Butter-
     fly, opus 11 (sop., sax, pf., 12'). Dorn, 1966.
_____ : One in Five in One, opus 10 (1965-72). Dorn,
     1972.
David Diamond (b. 1915): Sonata (1984).
Edward Diemente (b. 1923): Diary, Part II (sax,
     tape). Dorn, 1972.
_____ : Mirrors VI. Dorn, 1974.
Arnold Franchetti (b. 1906): Sonata. Dorn. Prem.
     March, 1970, Chicago.
Steven Galante: SAX Sound II. Diminishing Returns,
     1979.
Jerome Grant (b. 1936): Duo I (sax, tape). Dorn.
Walter S. Hartley (b. 1927): Concerto (sax, band).
     Tenuto, 1966. Prem. Feb., 1967.
_____ : Duo ((5'30). Tenuto, 1964.
_____ : Sonorities IV (3'). Dorn, 1976.
Jack Hale: Sintage (1964).
John Huggler (b. 1928): Elaboration (1967).
Edward Jay Miller (b. 1930): Fantasy Concerto (1971,
     sax, band, 10'). ACA.
Robert Myers (b. 1941): Concerto (1967).
Jeffrey Steinberg: Diary of Changes (1980).
_____ : Tones (1978).
Alec Wilder (1907-1980): Concerto (c. 1966, sax,
     band). Margun.
_____ : Sonata (1969, 11'30). Margun.

Recordings:

     American Music for Saxophone (Mark Educ. Records MRS
     2268, music by Benson, Creston, Hartley, Heiden);
     Ingolf Dahl: Concerto (U. of Michigan SM 0009); The
     Revelli Years (vol. 2, Crest CRS 4211, Creston: Con-
     certo); Music for Saxophone and Piano (New World 109,
     1968, music by Babbitt, Bassett, Smith, Wuorinen).

SMIALEK, THOMAS W., JR.
b. Newport, Rhode Island
     16 July 1955

     A pupil of Philip DeLibero (Westfield State College,
1977), Smialek studied with Frederick Hemke at Northwestern University and obtained the M.M. in 1979. He won the
Saxophone Service Performance Award in 1978 and 1980 (presented by Dorn Publications) and is currently Visiting
Artist at Halifax Community College (Weldon, N.C.). Since

1981, he has been active in performances with the North
Carolina Artists Program.

Composition dedicated to T. Smialek:

> Robert Lombardo (b. 1932):  Cantabile (sax, vib.).
> Composer. Prem. 31 May 1981.


SMITH, HOWIE
b. Pottsville, Pennsylvania
   25 February 1943

Smith studied with Donald Sinta, J. Carl Borelli, and
Willis Coggins and earned music education degrees at Ithaca
College (1965) and at the University of Illinois (1968).
He established the first jazz studies program on a terri-
tory level in Australia at the New South Wales State Conservatorium in Sydney (1973-75), and in 1975, he was one
of the featured artists at the Sydney Opera House.  Since
1976, he has been a clinician for the Yamaha Corporation
and was a freelance musician in San Diego (1976-79).  In
1979, he was appointed to the faculty of Cleveland State
University and performs jazz in addition to classic styles.
Smith has been a soloist with the Cleveland Orchestra (15
January 1984) and the Cleveland Chamber Symphony (15 November 1982 and 15 April 1984).  He has presented numerous
concerts and workshops at Cleveland State University and
schools in the U.S. and Canada.  Many of these programs
included original compositions by the soloist.

Selected Compositions:

> Helix III (1984, sax, ch. orch.); Illoda (1965, sax,
> w. ens.); Let the Games Begin (1983, SATB); Life on
> Earth:  Coming Soon (1982, sax, amplified vla., elec-
> tronics); Metaforest (1978, sax, tape, electronics);
> New York Still Life (1975, S and A); Passages (1981,
> sax-a., strs.); Prelude, Post-Prelude and Finales
> (1975, SATB); Schizerzo (1983, sax, tuba).  Smith has
> composed numerous works for the jazz saxophonist with
> large jazz band or combo; all his works are available
> from Otama.

Compositions dedicated to H. Smith:

> Edwin London (b. 1929):  Balls.  Composer.  Prem. 11
>     April 1985, Cleveland, Ohio.
> _____ :  Pressure Points (sax, orch.).  Composer.
>     Prem. 14 July 1972, Cleveland, Ohio.
> Elliott Schwartz (b. 1936):  Cleveland Doubles (sax
>     and cl. soloists, w. ens.).  Composer.  Prem. 16
>     Oct. 1981, Cleveland, Ohio.
> Martin Westley-Smith (b. 1945):  Doublets II (sax,
>     tape, 8').  Uni.  Prem. 3 Dec. 1974, Australia.

Recordings:

> Smith has participated in over 15 jazz recordings,
> most of which are distributed by Phillips.


STEPHENS, HAROLD B. (STEVE)
b. Circleville, Ohio          d. United States
   22 July 1897                  March, 1983

Stephens began studying the $E^b$ clarinet at the age of
ten.  He joined the old John H. Sparks Circus Band in 1915
and spent three years circus "trouping."  At the age of
20, he enlisted in the 1st U.S. Cavalry Band and served
from 1917 to 1919.  In Los Angeles (1920-23), he played
for dances, concert bands, and theatres.  On 15 November
1923, he was engaged as the saxophone soloist with the
Long Beach Municipal Band; and from 1925 to 1926, he was a
member of the Sousa Band.  He then returned to Long Beach,
where he remained until 1962.

(For additional information, see chapter 3.)


STOLTIE, JAMES M.
b. Galesburg, Illinois
   10 July 1937

After graduating from Knox College (Galesburg, 1959),
Stoltie completed the M.A. (1960) and the Ph.D. at the
University of Iowa (Woodwind Literature and Pedagogy, 1962).
He has been active in NASA and performed in several re-
gional meetings and at the sixth WSC at Northwestern Uni-
versity.  Since 1968, he has been Professor of Music at
Crane School of Music, SUNY, Potsdam.

Compositions dedicated to J. Stoltie:

> David Deason (b. 1945):  Blues Walk (sat-t., pf.).
>    Prem. 22 Sep. 1984, Potsdam.
> Elliot Del Borgo (b. 1938):  Canto for Saxophone
>    Alone.  Dorn.  Prem. 1 Oct. 1973.
> _____ :  Concertino for Alto Saxophone and Strings.
>    Prem. 21 July 1972.
> _____ :  Sonata No. 1.  Prem. 26 May 1973.  Dorn.
> _____ :  Sonata No. 2.  Prem. 23 Oct. 1983.
> Arthur Frackenpohl (b. 1924):  Air for Alto (1979).
>    Kendor, 1980.
> _____ :  Dorian Elegy (on a melody by Stoltie, 1981).
>    Kendor, 1982.
> _____ :  Intrada (sax ens.).  Prem. 22 Sep. 1984,
>    Potsdam.
> _____ :  Rhapsody for Solo Saxophone (3'30). Kendor, 1984.
> _____ :  Variations for Alto Saxophone and Piano.
>    Sha., 1974.

Paul Steinberg:  Troika (sax, tape, 1983).
Persis Vehar (b. 1937):  Sounds of the Outdoors (sax
    solo, 7'40).  Kendor, 1985.  Prem. 22 Sep. 1984,
    Potsdam.

Recordings:

James Stoltie Plays Music for Saxophone Alone (coro-
net LPS 3036, 1975, music by Bach, Debussy, Del Borgo,
Gates, Hartley, Noda, Persichetti); Lyrical Music for
Saxophone and Piano (Redwood ES 18, 1981, music by
Diemente, Frackenpohl, Gretchaninoff, Hartley, Kosteck,
Schmidt, Skolnik, Still, Welander, Wirth).


STREET, WILLIAM H.
b. Detroit, Michigan
   26 July 1949

   Street completed the B.M. and the M.M. at Catholic
University as a student of George Etheridge.  He studied
at the CNRM in Bordeaux with Jean-Marie Londeix and won a
Premier Prix de Saxophone in 1975 and the Médaille d'Honneur in 1977.  A teaching assistant at Northwestern University, he completed the D.Mus. in 1983 and was a student of
Frederick Hemke.  His dissertation, Elise Boyer Hall, Ame-
ca's First Female Concert Saxophonist, is available on University Microfilms International.  In addition to giving
numerous recitals in Illinois, Iowa, and Michigan, he has
performed with symphony orchestras in Chicago, Grant Park,
Milwaukee, and Southwest Iowa.  In 1983, he was appointed
to the faculty of Cornell College, Mount Vernon, Iowa.

Compositions dedicated to Wm. Street:

Jean-Michel Defaye (b. 1932):  Concerto (1984).
Alf Houkom (b. 1935):  Shadows (1984).
Patrick Kavanaugh (b. 1957):  Debussy Variations No. 5
    (1977, sax solo).  CF.
_____:  Hommage to C. S. Lewis (1978, sax, ww. quin.).
_____:  Quintus Rotus (1980, sax, tape).
Albert Potts (b. 1958):  Five Lyric Etudes (1984).
Jeremy Young (b. 1948):  Concerto (1983).
_____:  Hassle for Saxophone (1970, rev. 1979, sax
    solo).


TAGGART, MARK ALAN
b. Cleveland, Ohio
   16 September 1956

   A pupil of Sigurd Rascher and Lee Patrick, Taggart
graduated with honors from the University of Louisville in
1978 and completed the M.F.A. and D.M.A. in Composition at
Cornell University in 1983.  All his compositions include

the saxophone, and part of his dissertation was the <u>Ballade</u>
for orchestra, which calls for SAATBBs. From 1983 to 1985,
Taggart was a teacher at Wabash College (Crawfordsville,
Indiana) and, in the fall of 1985, he was appointed com-
poser-in-residence at East Carolina University (Greenville,
North Carolina).

Compositions:

> Two Sad Songs (1976, SSAAATTBBBs, Ethos, 8'); Red and
> White (1978, poem by C. Sandburg, ten., sax, vib.,
> prem. 25 March 1975, 10'); Death (1978, poem by Wm.
> Carlos Williams, mezzo sop., sax, vcl., pf., prem.
> 25 March 1975, 19'); A Round O'Trios (1978-83, ATB,
> prem. Dec., 1981, Ithaca); Concerto for Tenor Saxo-
> phone (1981, 18'); Serenade (1981, AATB, 3'); Con-
> certo for Chamber Ensemble (1983, cl., sax, bn., tpt.,
> db., pf., prem. 24 April 1983, Ithaca, 20'); Lament
> and Credo (1984, SSAAAATTBBBs, prem. 24 June 1984,
> Louisville).

Compositions dedicated to M. Taggart:

> David Conte:  <u>Sonata for Soprano Saxophone and Piano</u>
>     (1979).
> Garth Drozin: <u>Parabolics</u> (1981, sax, per.).
> John Hilliard (b. 1930): <u>Dolphy</u> (1981, sax-s., tape).
>     ACA.
> Brian Israel: <u>Concertino</u> (1982, SAATTBBs). Ethos,
>     1984. Prem. June, 1982.
> _____ : <u>Sonata</u> (1981).
> C. L. Mais: <u>Gossamer Piece</u> (1981, sax-s., pf.).
> _____ : <u>Licksody</u> (1980).
> Stephen May: <u>Sonatinissima</u> (1979).
> Mark Simon: <u>Concerto</u> (1981, sax, orch.).
> Steven Stucky: <u>Notturno</u> (1981). ACA.


TEAL, LAURENCE LYON (LARRY)
b. Midland, Michigan          d. Ann Arbor, Michigan
   26 March 1905                 11 July 1984


Teal's first experience in music was with an old Meyer
System flute; then his father, who had a small orchestra,
encouraged him to take up the saxophone. In 1917, he received his first saxophone--a tenor with two manual octave
keys, made by Evette and Schaefer. At 12, he was learning
to read the cello parts in the orchestra and, shortly
afterward, started earning money playing for dances and
in the local theatre. Reaching college age, he entered
the University of Michigan as a pre-dentistry major. Teal
soon became involved with a fine jazz band, and in 1925,
the group left for a European tour (three months each in
Paris and Madrid).

After the tour, Teal played in several bands in the
Detroit area and was an original member of the Casa Loma
Orchestra, performing on the tenor saxophone with Glen
Gray Knoblaugh playing lead.  In 1928, the orchestra moved
to New York, where it eventually became the Glen Gray Orchestra.  For the next three years, Teal played clarinet
and saxophone in orchestras at the Capitol and Fischer
Theatres in Detroit.  One summer, in the mid-1930s, Teal
studied with Andrew Jacobson, a former tenor saxophonist
with the Sousa Band who had settled in Boston, where he had
a society orchestra in which Teal played.  He also studied
briefly in New York with Merle Johnston.  In those days
there were very few saxophone teachers, and Teal said
"Jacobson and Johnston were the most outstanding."13  From
1931 to 1943, Teal was a member of the studio orchestra of
radio station WJR, Detroit, where he appeared several times
as a soloist on local and network programs.  He doubled on
various instruments (flute, clarinet, saxophone, and bass
clarinet), and was invited to play bass clarinet with the
Detroit Symphony Orchestra by the conductor, Karl Krueger.
Among other activities, he was featured with the WPA Orchestra in the first performance of Glazunov's Concerto on
7 April 1938.  It was during this time that he met Bernhard
Heiden, who had just arrived from Germany with his wife,
Cola, a fine pianist.  Heiden, impressed with Teal's tone
quality and musicianship, promised to compose a work for
him; the result was the famous Sonata, premiered on 8 April
1937.  Teal played Ibert's Concertino da Camera with a
chamber group on 8 March 1937 and with the Detroit Symphony
on 27 February 1947.  In the early 1940s, Teal completed
musical studies at Wayne State University and at the Detroit Institute of Musical Arts, where he earned his Ph.D.
in 1943.  With a busy schedule of radio shows, other performances, and teaching at his private studio, Teal resigned from the Detroit Symphony.  Later he was invited to
rejoin the orchestra (this time in the flute section) under
the conductor Paul Paray.

By 1953, Teal was a well-known orchestral performer
and teacher and was appointed to the faculty of the Uni-
of Michigan.  The earliest professor of saxophone at a Big
Ten University, he began the first doctoral program in
saxophone in the United States.  Teal attributed his success as a saxophonist and teacher to these factors:  his
study of various instruments (clarinet with Albert Luconi
and flute with John Wummer and Georges Barrère); a wide
range of practical experience; and a lot of sound musical
advice from fine musicians.  In 1974, Teal retired from the
University of Michigan and remained active as a teacher,
guest professor, and writer.  Fourteen of Teal's arrangements and transcriptions for solos and ensembles have been
published by G. Schirmer, Hal Leonard, Presser, and Etoile.

Books:

The Art of Saxophone Playing (Summy-Birchard, 1963,

translated into Japanese); The Saxophonist's Manual
(University Music Press, 1978).

## Methods:

Saxophonist's Workbook (trans. into Japanese); Stu-
dies in Time Division (University Music Press, 1954);
Daily Studies for the Development of the Saxophone
Technique (Etoile, 1972); Introducing the Alto Saxo-
phone (GIA Publ., with J. Froseth, 1976); Introducing
the Tenor Saxophone (GIA Publ., with J. Froseth, 1977);
Introducing the Alto Clarinet, Introducing the Bass
Clarinet (GIA Publ., with J. Froseth, 1977).

## Compositions dedicated to L. Teal:

Jerry Bilik (b. 1933): Concertino (sax, band). Com-
    poser. Prem. 26 July 1973, Ann Arbor, by D. Sinta.
Ross Lee Finney (b. 1906): Concerto for Saxophone
    and orchestra of Winds (1974, 13'15). Peters
    (ossia passage in mov't. II, by P. Cohen).
Frederick Fox (b. 1931): S.A.X. (1979, sax, SATB).
    Composer.
Bernhard Heiden (b. 1910): Sonata (1937). Schott.
Jean-Marie Londeix (b. 1932): Gammes et Modes
    (2 vols.). Leduc, 1970.


THOMPSON, KATHRYNE E.
b. United States              d. United States
   Unknown                       Unknown

A student of E. A. Lefèbre during the 1920s, Thompson
taught saxophone in Los Angeles, where she and her staff
maintained a constant enrollment of 100 students.  She was
also the director of the Southern California Saxophone Band
and organized a quartet of three saxophones and piano
called The Melody Four.  As a soloist, her biggest success
came from performances of Felix Arndt's Nola (Fox, 1926),
and such songs as Herbert's A Kiss in the Dark, Openshaw's
Love Sends a Little Gift of Roses, and The World Is Wait-
ing for the Sunrise, by Seitz.  A few of Thompson's talented students were provided with catchy stage names which
often bordered on the ludicrous; according to Hemke, Mary
Gillespie was known as "America's little Pavlova" and Mary
Campbell as "Miss America."[14]

Compositions (the following were published by the Southern
    California Music Co., Los Angeles, 1920):

Thompson Progressive Method; Thompson Practical Studies (advertised as studies in bass clef and a neces-
sity for all players desiring to do any branch of orchestra work); The Ragtime Saxophone (suggestions and
models for ragging on the saxophone); Barcarolle (for

alto and C melody with piano acc., solo or duet);
Bubble and Squeak (for alto and C melody, solo or
duet); Carolyn--Melodie (solo for alto or C melody
with piano); Valse Caprice (solo for alto or C melody
with piano).


TIMMONS, TIMOTHY M.
b. Tulsa, Oklahoma
   12 March 1948

   After receiving the B.M. from the University of Tulsa,
where he studied with Dwight M. Daily, Timmons earned the
M.M. at Northwestern University as a student of Frederick
Hemke (1971). After three years as a member of the Tulsa
Philharmonic, he went to Ithaca College, where he was an
instructor of saxophone and theory. He made many appearances with high school and college bands and has been the
Assistant Dean and Professor of Saxophone at the University
of Missouri-Kansas City Conservatory since 1977.

Recording:

   T. Timmons, Saxophone Soloist/Ithaca College Band
   (Crest CRS 4124, 1974, Concerti by Dahl and Husa).


TRAXLER, A.
b. United States          d. United States
   Unknown                   Unknown

   Traxler received the highest honors at the Dana Musical Institute (Youngstown, Ohio), completed the four-
year  course in Clarinet and Saxophone in three years, and
later studied with E. A. Lefèbre. As a composer, Traxler
won first prize for his Tarantelle in the All Southern
Contest of 1925. He performed with Pryor's Band (two
years), Bellstedt Band (two years), Duss Band (two years),
and Innes Band (five years).

Compositions:

   Grand Virtuoso Saxophone Studies (tran. from the
   Clarinet Method by Lazarus, Bel., 1928. Grand
   Artistic Duets (Bel.). Romance (Bel., 1935).


UNDERWOOD, DALE W.
b. Cortland, New York
   23 November 1948

   While attending Onondaga Community College and Ithaca
College, Underwood studied with Donald Sinta from 1964 to
1967. Accepted in the U.S. Navy Band in July, 1968, he
became the principal saxophone soloist in July, 1969 and

has been featured in concerts in Washington, D.C., and on
the many tours throughout the U.S.  Participating in international festivals, he gave recitals for the WSC in
London (1976), the Symposium in Brussels (1977), the WSC
in Evanston (1979), and the seventh WSC in Nuremberg (1982).
In addition to many recitals at universities, he appeared
as soloist with the Boston Pops Orchestra in 1976, and has
organized the Navy Band's  Annual International Saxophone
Symposium since 1978.  He has taught privately in the
Washington, D.C. area and at Catholic University since
1979.

## Compositions dedicated to D. Underwood:

> Urban Carvalho:  <u>Song and Dance</u> (1971, sax, band/pf.).
> Presser.  Prem. Dec., 1971, Chicago.
> Jay Chattaway:  <u>Double Star</u> (1984, A, T, tape).
> _____ :  <u>Nocturne and Ritual Dance</u>.  Prem. July, 1976,
> WSC, London.
> Elliot Del Borgo (b. 1938): <u>Soliloquy and Dance</u> (1979,
> sax, band).  Dorn.  Prem. March, 1979.
> Clare Grundman (b. 1913):  <u>Concertante</u> (1972, sax,
> band/pf.).  B.H.  Prem. Jan., 1973, Washington, D.C.
> Harley Rex (b. 1930):  <u>Andando and Brillante</u>.  Dorn.
> Prem. Fall, 1982.
> Joe Roccisano:  <u>Contrasts for Alto and Tenor Saxophone</u>
> (band).  Prem. 25 Jan. 1985, Washington, D.C.
> Claude T. Smith (b. 1932):  <u>Fantasia</u> (1983, sax, band).
> Winsert.  Prem. 28 Jan. 1983, U. of Maryland.
> Mary Jeanne Van Appledorn:  <u>Liquid Gold</u>.  Dorn, 1982.
> Prem. 10 July 1982, WSC, Nuremberg.
> David Ward (b. 1917):  <u>Concert Piece for Alto Saxophone
> and Band</u> (1978).  Dorn.
> _____ :  <u>Encore for Saxophone</u> (1974,  sax, band).
> Prem. June, 1974, Washington, D.C.

## Recordings:

> Dale Underwood with Metropolitan Wind Ensemble (Crest
> CRS 4136, 1975, music by Creston, Grundman, Hartley,
> Whitney); Dale Underwood--Saxophone (Crest RE 7067,
> 1976, music by Bassett, Handel/Rascher, Hartley,
> Heiden, Lane); Dale Underwood--Saxophone (Crest RE
> 7091, 1979, music by Bozza, Creston, Del Borgo, Ec-
> cles/Rascher, Ibert); Dale Underwood--Saxophone
> (Crest RE 7101 digital, music by Bozza, Del Borgo,
> Makris, Tull, Van Appledorn, Ward).

VEREECKEN, BENJAMIN (BEN)
b. United States          d. United States
   Unknown                   Unknown

   Vereecken joined the Sousa band in time for the World
Tour of 1910.  An advertisement dated 23 October 1915

listed him in the Pan-American Pacific Exposition in San
Francisco. (For further information, see chapter 3.)
Barnhouse released five original compositions in 1908; at
that time, Vereecken was soloist with the Arthur Pryor
Band. He wrote over 25 arrangements and fantasy variations, which were published by Fischer in 1922. Many of
these solos were for Eb, Bb, or C melody saxophone.

Compositions:

> Bouquet de fleurs, Cheerfulness, Admirations, A Shep-
> herd's Dream, Waternymphs (all Barnhouse, 1908);
> Foundation to Saxophone Playing (CF, 1917); The Saxo-
> phone Virtuoso (CF, 1919); Complete Chart for All Sax-
> ophones (CF); Autumn Life, Blue Bells of Scotland,
> Last Rose of Summer, Mocking Bird, Then You'll Remem-
> ber Me (All for Eb or Bb sax, CF, 1922); Junior Saxo-
> phone Method (Rubank); 16 Artistic Duets (Rubank,
> 1926).

VILLAFRUELA-ARTIGAS, MIGUEL ANGEL
b. Holguin, Cuba
26 January 1955

In 1965, Villafruela began early musical studies at
the José Maria Ochoa Conservatory in Holguin. In 1970,
he continued at the National School of the Arts in Havana,
with Carlos Averoff as his teacher, where he obtained the
baccalaureate in sciences and letters in 1974. In 1979,
Villafruela went to Europe and became a Laureat winner in
the Young Interpreters Contest in Bratislava. Admitted to
the CNSM in 1980 in the class of Daniel Deffayet, he won a
first prize in 1982, gave recitals in Paris and at the
seventh WSC in Nuremberg, and that same year, was appointed
Professor of Saxophone at the Instituto Superior de Arte
in Havana.

Compositions dedicated to M. Villafruela:

> Andrés Alén: Tema con Variaciones (1978).
> Hector Angulo and Juan Blanco: Bucolica (sax, tape,
>     13'). Prem. May, 1985, Havana, Cuba.
> Jorge López Ma: La Palabra (c. 1983, sax solo).

WATTERS, MARK E.
b. Irving, Texas
25 May 1955

A student of Earl Haberkamp and of Harvey Pittel,
Watters is a graduate of the University of Southern California (1977). Since 1979, he has appeared as baritone
saxophonist in approximately 79 concerts on tour with the
Harvey Pittel Saxophone Quartet. He has also performed in

concerts with the Los Angeles Philharmonic and the Calvin
Simmons and Ojai Festivals under Michael Tilson Thomas.
He is also a composer, arranger, and conductor.

Composition:

Rhapsody (1983, sax-b., orch., or w. orch.).  Prem.
16 April 1983.

Compositions dedicated to M. Watters:

Robert Linn (b. 1925):  Saxifrage Blue (sax-b., pf.).
Prem. Oct., 1977.
Mario Pelusi (b. 1951):  Concert Piece for Baritone
Saxophone (brass quar., per., 12'30).  Prem.
April, 1978.

Recordings:

Mark Watters--Baritone Saxophone (Crystal S 152,
1979). (See Harvey Pittel for quartet recordings.)

WAXMAN, CARL
b. Philadelphia, Pennsylvania
4 September 1910

Waxman has had a long and varied career, from road
houses, burlesque, vaudeville, and radio to the Philadelphia Orchestra.  He still performs with the Lester Lavin
Orchestra, a society ensemble which was invited to play
for the wedding of Prince Charles and Lady Diana.  His
saxophone teachers were Abe Belov and Milton Schatz, and
he studied clarinet with Edward Vozzela, Joseph Musemci,
Michael Guerra and Robert McGinnis.  In spite of his lack
of formal musical education, Waxman constantly improved
his abilities and performed with some of the greatest musicians who, as he says, "were gracious and kind if you
had the desire to learn."[15]  He premiered many saxophone
compositions, but unfortunately, the records of these performances were not kept.  Some of these compositions still
exist at the Settlement School of Music in Philadelphia.
Beginning in 1948, he played all the saxophone solos, when
needed, with the Philadelphia Orchestra, and, from 1950
to 1965, he participated in the recordings of the following works released by Columbia:

Honegger:  Joan of Arc; Ravel:  Bolero (both sop.
and ten. solos); Prokofiev:  Lt. Kije and Romeo and
Juliet; Rameau:  "The Hen" from Holiday for Orchestra;
Walton:  Facade; Rachmaninoff:  Symphonic Dances; Mus-
sorgsky-Ravel:  Pictures at an Exhibition; Kodaly:
Hary Janos Suite.

WIEDOEFT, RUDY C.
b. Detroit, Michigan              d. Queens, New York
   3 January 1893                    18 February 1940

There have been many tributes to Rudy Wiedoeft, prais-
ing his brilliance of performance, the characteristic style
of his saxophone compositions, and his great impact on his
pupils as well as on the hundreds who were inspired to
learn the saxophone after listening to his many solos and
recordings.  For more detailed information the reader is
referred to the ASCAP Biographical Dictionary and to the
two articles for Hobbies Magazine by Jim Walsh; the latter
were reprinted in the Winter 1981 issue (Vol. VI, No. 1)
of The Saxophone Symposium.  A member of a musical family,
young Rudy began playing clarinet in his father's family
orchestra at the age of eleven.  Ten years later, he was
the first chair clarinetist with Porter's Catalina Island
Band, San Francisco.  He took up the saxophone in 1914 as
an experiment, soon fell in love with the instrument, and
dropped the clarinet altogether.  After playing the saxophone for less than four years, Wiedoeft made his first
recording for Edison in 1917.  In early 1918, he enlisted
in the Marines and was stationed at Mare Island in San
Francisco Bay.  Late in 1918, he was discharged and was
back in New York recording for Emerson by 1919.  He appeared in two outstanding musical groups, the Palace Trio
and the Wiedoeft-Wadsworth Quartet.  (The latter included
Wiedoeft and his great rival for saxophone honors at the
time, Frank Wheeler Wadsworth, and two pianists--Robinson
and Harry Akst.)  Both groups were active in 1920.  Besides
his many recordings and compositions for the saxophone,
Wiedoeft wrote songs with Al Bernard (one of the most brilliant comedians of the time) and other pianists and lyri-
cists (see list of compositions).

In 1921, Wiedoeft formed his own orchestra, Rudy
Wiedoeft's Californians, which was active until 1922.  It
is believed that he turned it over to his brother, and the
group became the Herb Wiedoeft's Cinderella Roof Orchestra.
Rudy joined the Eight Famous Victor Artists (not an orchestra, but a group of singing, touring, and recording artists)
and remained with them until 1926, when he felt he could
earn more by giving recitals "on his own."  The International Musician's Tribute (of April, 1940) mentions that
he appeared in Paris in 1925; it was probably during this
tour that he recorded double-faced, 10-inch Columbia records in London.  When Henri Selmer heard him in Paris, he
said, "I have never heard a saxophonist to equal Wiedoeft,
and I doubt if there will be any to excel him, his staccato
is so rapid, his execution so brilliant."[16]

On 17 April 1926, Wiedoeft was back in the U.S. and
gave a concert at Aeolian Hall, assisted by two singers,
three pianists, and three other saxophonists--Arnold Brilhart, Alford Evans, and Harold Sturr.  With the hall filled

to capacity and the concert carried on radio in New York
and other cities, at a conservative estimate, five hundred
thousand to a million people listened to this concert.
Among the many top-ranking players inspired and taught by
Wiedoeft was Hubert Pior Vallee, who changed his name to
Rudy and became a saxophonist and, later, a prominent orchestra leader.  In summing up Wiedoeft's brilliant, but
short career, Walsh says:

> After that came teaching and increasingly poor health which led
> to an early death in 1940 [cirrhosis of the liver].  But one
> thing is certain:  Rudy Wiedoeft was regarded in his day as a
> genius; he is still remembered as one, and as long as records
> of his playing are collected, his memory will live as that of
> the wizard who during his lifetime was The King of the Saxo-
> phone.[17]

Compositions (most of the following were published for
         both C melody and alto saxophone and are out of print):

Valse Erica (ded. to Mrs. Erica Noll, 1917, Robbins,
1921); Valse Vanity (1917, Robbins); Waltz Llewellyn
(1917, Robbins); Saxophobia (1918, Robbins); Bupkis,
Cloudy Days, Grand and Noble (1919); Just For Today
(with Al Bernard, Robbins, 1919); Love O' Mine, Northern Lights, Oriental Blues, Very Soon, Karavan (with
Abe Olman, Forster, 1919); Lone Star (with Al Bernard,
Mayfair, 1919); Fancies (with Louis Weslyn, Robbins,
1920); Jonteel (with Jan Ricky, Wiedard, 1920); Ta-Hoe
(with Carl Fenton & Geo. O'Neil, 1920); Saxema (Robbins, 1920); Saxophone Blues (with Al Bernard, Handy
Bros., 1920); Na-Jo (with W. Holliday & Geo. O'Neil,
Sam Fox, 1920); Wee Bit of Love (with D. Ringle, Mayfair, 1922); Valse Yvonne, Saxarella, Vision d'Amour
(Robbins, 1923); Sax-O-Phun, Rudy Wiedoeft's Collec-
tion of Famous Classic Transcriptions, Rudy Wiedoeft's
Simplified Photographic Saxophone Chart, Melodie
(tran. from Tschaikovsky), Souvenir (Robbins, 1924);
Sax-Serene, Valse Mazanetta (Robbins, 1925); Rudy
Wiedoeft's Collection of Transcriptions of World Fa-
mous Love Songs (with D. Savino), Dans l'Orient (with
D. Savino), Sax-O-Doodle (with Hugo Frey), Sax-O-Trix
(with D. Savino), Carry Me Back to Old Virginny (tran.
from J. Bland, Robbins, 1926); The Sweetest Story Ever
Told (tran. from R. Stults, 1926); Forgotten (tran.
from E. Cowles, 1926); A Dream (Robbins, 1926); Sweet-
est Kiss of All (with Leo Robin, Harms, 1926); Valse
Marilyn, Rudy Wiedoeft's Complete Modern Method for
the Saxophone (Robbins, 1927); Andantino (tran. from
E. Limare), Londonderry Air (traditional), Rudy Wied-
oeft's Folio of Easy Saxophone Solos (with Hugo Frey),
Rudy Wiedoeft's Advanced Etudes and Studies for the
Saxophone, vols. 1 & 2 (Robbins, 1928); Bitter Sweets,
Valse Pamela, Rubenola (with Hugo Frey, Robbins, 1929);
Rudy Wiedoeft's Folio of Saxophone solos and Duets

(with Leon Rosebrook, Robbins, 1931); Lightnin',
Valse Sonia (with Hugo Frey), A Southern Sketch,
Frolic (with J. R. Robinson, Robbins, 1932); Strange
Butterfly (Cesare Ciociano, 1933); Claraphobia (Rob-
bins, 1935); Blue Lotus, Cleo, Sax-O-Minute Waltz,
Vera (with J. Ring & F. Hager, Robbins, 1937); Rudy
Wiedoeft's Secret of Staccato for the Saxophone (Rob-
bins, 1938); Saxophone (based on Rubenola, with Hugo
Frey, Robbins, 1955).

## Compositions dedicated to R. Wiedoeft:

Mayhew L. Lake: Wiedoeft's Rubato (sax-a., pf.).
   Robbins, 1925.
Gunther Schuller (b. 1925): Tribute to Rudy Wiedoeft
   (sax, band). BTM. Prem. 11 Dec. 1978, Milwaukee.

## Recordings:

Wiedoeft made over 100 cylinder and disc recordings
from 1917 to 1927, with Edison, Emerson, Brunswick,
Columbia, Victor, and other companies. Among his
last ones was La Golondrina (with Arnold Brilhart, 2
Dec. 1927), released by Columbia.


WOLFE, GEORGE W.
b. Corry, Pennsylvania
   21 March 1948

A student of Eugene Rousseau, Richard Kemper, David
Baker, and Daniel Deffayet, Wolfe holds a B.S. from Mansfield State College and the M.M. from Indiana University.
A soloist at international meetings of WSC (1979 and 1985),
he has performed in recitals in the eastern and midwestern
states. An original member of the American Saxophone Quartet, he is currently Assistant Professor at Ball State University and a performing artist/clinician for the Yamaha
Company.

## Compositions:

Rewards of Ambition (1981, operetta, ch. winds);
Randomization No. 1 (sax-s., mar., Percussion Plus,
1982); Five Scriabin Etudes (Kjos, 1985); Prepara-
tory Method for Saxophone (Roncorp, 1985); Persian
Dance (pic., bn., xyl., drone instr., tabla, Percussion Plus, 1982).

## Compositions premiered by G. Wolfe:

Paul Arma (b. 1905): Phases Contre Phases (sax-s.,
   pf.). Lemoine. Prem. 12 Dec. 1978.
_____ : Six Mobiles (sax solo). Prem. Nov. 1978.
Thomas Beveridge: Alborada. Prem. 12 Feb. 1981,
   Harrisonburg, Va.

Recordings:

> Recital Music for Saxophone (Coronet LPS 3046, 1977,
> music by Charpentier, Hartley, Orrego-Salas, Tomasi);
> American Saxophone Quartet (Coronet 2755, 1972, music
> by Arma, Schmitt, Schumann); George Wolfe (cassette
> Roncorp EMS 007, 1983, music by Blavet, Bozza, Handel,
> Hartley, Koechlin, Still, Wolfe); American Saxophone
> Quartet (cassette, Roncorp EMS 008, music by Arma,
> Pierné, Scarlatti, Schmitt, Schumann/Teal).

WYMAN, F. S. LAURENCE
b. Elgin, Illinois
   26 November 1935

After saxophone study with Sigurd Rascher and Orville
Kiltz, Wyman completed the Ph.D. in Music Theory at the
Eastman School in 1972.  Since 1965, he has been Professor
of Saxophone at SUNY, Fredonia.

Compositions:

> Deltangi (1964, sax, 4 vcl.); Djiwa (1971, sax solo);
> Rainfall (1972, sax-t., pf.).  (These are available
> from the composer.)

Compositions dedicated to L. Wyman:

> Lucas Mason: Lay-Alla-Allah (sop., fl., sax, pf.).
>     Prem. 25 Jan. 1972.  Composer.
> _____: Romance (sax, guit.).    Prem. 21 March 1978.
>     Composer.
> _____: Song & Dance (sax solo).  Prem. 24 Jan. 1983.
>     Composer.
> Louis Richardson (b. 1924): Adagio (1984).  Composer.
> Freda Swain (b. 1902): Fantasy-March (1983).

WYTKO, JOSEPH
b. Morgantown, West Virginia
   19 May 1949

After earning the B.M.E. from West Virginia University
(1971), Wytko completed the M.M. (1974) and the D.M.A. at
Northwestern University as a student of Frederick Hemke.
His first major appearance was with the Pittsburgh Symphony
Orchestra on 31 October 1974; he has also performed with
the Chicago and Grant Park Orchestras.  He is a co-founder
and saxophonist of the Tosart Ensemble and also plays with
the Phoenix Symphony Orchestra.  He is active as a clini-
cian and soloist for the Selmer Company and Director of
Region 2 of NASA.  Wytko is Chairman of the Performance
Division and Associate Professor of Music at Arizona State
University.  In 1984, he was awarded a fellowship grant as

a solo recitalist from the National Endowment for the Arts
for 1985-1986 and he will perform commissioned works by
W. Albright, W. Bolcom, and D. Diamond.

## Compositions dedicated to J. Wytko:

William Albright (b. 1944): Sonata (1984).
Tommy Joe Anderson (b. 1947): Concerto, opus 23
   (1976).
_____ : Liebeslied, opus 20 (1975). Dorn.
_____ : Sonata, opus 10 (1970, 4'28). SMC, 1971.
_____ : Sonata No. 2, opus 17 (1973). Dorn, 1976.
William Bolcom (b. 1938): Lilith (1984). Marks.
Thomas Canning (b. 1938): Concert Piece (1974).
James DeMars: Seventh Healing Song of John Joseph
   Blue (1982, sax, 4-channel tape).
David Diamond (b. 1915): Sonata (1984).
Grant Fletcher (b. 1913): Sax-Son I (1977).
Glenn Hackbarth: Metropolis (1978).
Russell Howland (b. 1911): Quartet No. 3 (1976).
   Hill.
William Karlins (b. 1932): Catena II (1982). ACA,
   1983.
Gregory LaTraille: Lyric Concerto (1972, rev. 1978,
   sax-s., ch. ens.).
Bruce Maiman: Quartet No. 1 (1979).
Robert Rabinowitz: Echoes For Forever (1983, sax,
   4-channel tape).
Stephen Syverud (b. 1938): Field of Ambrosia (1975).

## Recording:

Recital Music for Saxophone (Brewster Records BR-
1295, 1978, music by Anderson, Bassett, Husa, Noda,
Reutter).


ZAJAC, ELAINE U.
b. Detroit, Michigan
   12 June 1940

   A student of Larry Teal, Zajac completed the B.M.
(1969) and M.M. (1970) at the University of Michigan. She
served as a graduate assistant at the University of Michigan, taught at the National Music Camp in the summers of
1972 and 1973, and was a member of the faculty at Michigan
State University from 1971 to 1978. She has 53 published
arrangements and has collaborated with Larry Teal in his
publications. Her arrangement of the band accompaniment
of Ibert's Concertino da Camera is available on rental
from Leduc.

## Compositions:

Five Miniatures (SATB, Etoile, 1974; recorded by the

Indiana Saxophone Quartet, see K. Fischer); Elabora-
tions (HL, 1976, Master Solos, Interm.).

Recording:

Master Solos (HL, 1976, cassette with solo collection).

# 7.

# Annotated Bibliography of Saxophone Soloists in Europe

ACKERMANN, HANS
b. Basel, Switzerland     d. Basel, Switzerland
    7 October 1902          12 August 1979

     A violinist, studying at the Basel Conservatory and the Ecole Normale in Paris, and later a saxophonist, Ackermann became a member of the Basel Symphony Orchestra. After World War I, he had numerous engagements as a saxophone soloist in Paris, Italy, Algeria, and Morocco. His repertoire, in addition to Debussy, Glazunov, Ibert, and d'Indy, included such composers as Paul Bonneau (b. 1918), Hans Brunner (1898-1958), Albert Jenny (b. 1912), Roger Vuataz (b. 1898), and Will Eisenmann (b. 1906).

Composition dedicated to H. Ackermann:

     Will Eisenmann (b. 1906): <u>Concerto da camera</u> (1948, sax, orch. or pf., 15'). Uni.


APPER, ELIE
b. Ukkel, Belgium
    22 July 1933

     A pupil of M. Hanssens, M. Van Guchte, and François Daneels, Apper attended the Royal Conservatory in Brussels from 1952 to 1956, where he received the First Prize. Since 1970, he has been a professor of saxophone at the Royal Conservatory in Brussels (Flemish section); has concertized in England, France, Germany, and the Unites States; and served as a visiting professor at North Texas State University. He also leads his own saxophone quartet and the Saxofonio Ensemble, whose members include N. Nozy, R. Van Der Meirsch, F. Couche, J. Lauwers, and F. Commeene. He was also the tenor saxophonist with the Quatuor Belge de Saxophones.

Compositions dedicated to E. Apper and the Saxofonio
    Ensemble:

    Peter Cabus:  Facetten (1974, sax, strs.).  Maurer.
    _____: Praeludium and Rondo (1979, SAATTB).  Maurer.
    _____: Rapsodie (1974, A and T, per., pf.).  Maurer.
    Marcel De Jonghe:  3 Bagatelles (1982, SATB).
    Paul Harvey (b. 1935):  Common Market Suite (A, T,
        per., pf.).  Maurer.
    Frederich Koch (b. 1923):  Soundings (1974, sax, band).
        Maurer.
    Vic Legley (b. 1915):  Parades II, opus 93, No. 2
        (SAATTB).  Schott, 1980.  Prem. 1 Oct. 1978.
    Willem Pelemans (b. 1901):  Concerto (1976).  Maurer,
        1977.  Prem. 10 Feb. 1977.
    Fernand Ruelle (b. 1921):  Le Gille (1976, sax, per.,
        pf.).  Maurer.
    Anna Van Haute:  Lucioles (SATB).  Maurer, 1982.
        Prem. 7 March 1980.

Recordings:

    Saxofonio Ensemble (EUROP ER 3028, 1976); Saxo-Rama
    (ZEPHYR Z 08, Schott, 1981, music by Arma, Gilson,
    Leduc, Legley) - (Also see François Daneels.)


BARAGLIOLI, JEAN-PIERRE
b. Paris, France
    3 August 1957


    After receiving a Médaille d'Or à l'Unanimité in sax
in 1975, Baraglioli was awarded a Prix National at the Concours de Saxophone in Aix-les-Bains in 1977.  After two
years of study at the CNSM in the class of Daniel Deffayet,
he won a Premier Prix in 1979.  In addition to his appointment to the Garde Républicaine (beginning in 1979), he has
performed with the Concerts Colonne and the Ensemble de
Chambre Français.  He is also a professor in various regional conservatories in Paris.  Since 1980, he has led the
Quatuor de Saxophone Gabriel Pierné, playing the soprano
sax; this ensemble is made up of first prize winners of the
CNSM and was a Laureate of the Yehudi Menuhin Foundation in
1982.  Other quartet members are Philippe Portejoie, alto;
Sylvain Frydman, tenor; and Jean-Pierre Solvés, baritone.

    Baraglioli has premiered the following compositions
of Aubert Lemeland (b. 1932):

    Capriccioso, opus 68 (sax solo, 6').  Prem. 1978.
    Cinq Portraits, opus 49 (cl., sax, 8').  Bil.  Prem.
        July, 1976.
    Divertissement No. 1, opus 45 (fl., cl., sax, 9').
        Bil.  Prem. July, 1978.

Epitaph to John Coltrane, opus 86 (sax-s., pf., 5').
Bil. Prem. Dec., 1979.
Figures qui bougent un peu, opus 79 (sax, vla., vib.,
guit., 10'). Prem. June, 1978.
Quintet, opus 37 (sax, str. quar., 14'). Bil. Prem.
Jan., 1979.
Terzetto, opus 69 (ob., cl., sax, 8'). Bil.
Trio, opus 106 (ob., sax, vcl., 10').

Compositions dedicated to J. P. Baraglioli and A. Beghin
(Saxophone and Percussion Duo):

Marc Bleuze (b. 1937): Proper (sax, per.).
Jacques Casterède (b. 1926): Pièces (sax, per.).
Jean-Claude Fohrenbach (b. 1925): Week Chronicle
(sax, per.).
Aubert Lemeland (b. 1932): Walkings, opus 105 (sax-s.,
vib., 8'30). Bil. Prem. April, 1980.
Yves Queyroux (b. 1946): Sonate (sax-s., per.).

Compositions dedicated to the Quatuor de Saxophones
Gabriel Pierné:

Gustavo Beytelmann: Momentos.
Jacques Casterède (b. 1926): 3 Nocturnes.
Jean-Claude Fohrenbach (b. 1925): Pièces.
François Jeanneau (b. 1935): Suite pour Quatuor de
Saxophones.
Jean-Pierre Solvés: A Night Maw.

Recording:

Quatuor Gabriel Pierné avec Jean-Claude Fohrenbach
(Productions Patrice Caratini, CARA 008, music by
P. Pierné, J. Casterède, P. Woods, J. C. Fohrenbach).


BEAUFRETON, BERNARD
b. Luynes, France
3 June 1939

After his studies at the CNRM in Tours (1952-1957),
Beaufreton went to the CNRM at Versailles (class of Marcel
Josse), and, after two years of study, won a first prize
in 1961 at the CNSM in Paris (class of Marcel Mule). Beaufreton has been a tenor saxophonist with the Garde Républicaine since 1966. In chamber music, he has been active
as a member of the Quatuor Jacques Desloges, the Quatuor
Garde Républicaine, and the Quintette de Saxophones de
Paris. The last group has performed in Japan, the U.S.,
the Soviet Union, and other European countries.

Music dedicated to B. Beaufreton:

Paul Méranger (b. 1936): Diptuka, opus 15 (sax-t.,

pf.)  SEMI, 1979.  Prem. 30 July 1976, WSC, London.
Lucie Robert (b. 1935):  <u>Rythmes Lyriques</u> (S, T,
  11'20).  Bil., 1984.

Recordings:

>   (See Jacques Desloges and André Beun for sax quartets
>   and André Beun for sax quintet listings.)


BENSMANN, DETLEF
b. Berlin, Germany
  1958

   Coming from a musical family, Bensmann entered the
Orchesterschule der Hoche Schule Konservatorium in Berlin
in 1975, where he studied saxophone and contrabass.  In
1977, he was a student at the Hochschule der Kunste.  From
1979 to 1981, he was a contrabassist with the Deutsche
Oper in Berlin; and in 1979, he played sax with the Berlin
Orchestra.  He is a soloist in many radio broadcasts from
Berlin and also teaches music there.

Recording:

>   Virtuoso Saxophone Concertos (Schwann Musica Mundi
>   VNS 2065, LC 1083, 1980, music by Glazunov, Martin,
>   Rivier, and Villa-Lobos).


BERNARD, JACQUES
b. Dole, Jura, France
  8 August 1931

   A pupil of Marcel Mule, Bernard won a first prize in
sax at the CNSM in 1951.  He also studied composition with
Jean Rivier and Darius Milhaud.  Since 1967, he has been
a professor of saxophone and clarinet in five conservatories near his home in Sucy-en-Brie.

Compositions:

>   Andante et Scherzo (1965, SATB, 10'40); L'Opéra de
>   l'espace (1970, ww. quar., speaker on poems by Chas.
>   Dobzijnski); Dialogue d'anches (1969, ob., cl., sax,
>   bn., E.F.M., 13'); Climats (1975, sax, mallet per.,
>   Intersong); Six miniatures (1978, sax solo, 8'30,
>   Andel).


BEUN, ANDRE
b. Saint-Pol-sur-mer, Nord, France
  19 February 1937

   Studies with Maurice DeFere and Marcel Josse at the

CNRM of Lille and Versailles (1957 and 1958) led Beun to
the saxophone class of Marcel Mule at the CNSM, from 1959
to 1961, where he graduated with a first prize.  A member
of the Garde Républicaine, he became the saxophone soloist
as well as leader of the Garde Républicaine Saxophone Quartet at the retirement of Michel Nouaux in 1979.  From 1978
to 1982, he served as a professor at the CNRM at Lille.
Beun is often called to play saxophone solos for the Orchestre de Paris, Orchestre de l'Ile de France, Concert
Pasdeloup, and Concerts Colonne.  He has participated in
numerous recitals in Paris and has toured both as a soloist
and with saxophone quartets.  In addition, he has performed
under the direction of Pierre Boulez with the Ensemble In-
tercontemporain.

Since 1980, Beun has been the director of the Quin-
tette de saxophones de Paris, which has toured in Japan,
England, Switzerland, Belgium, Russia, and the United
States.

Compositions dedicated to A. Beun:

Jacques Bernard (b. 1931):  Climats (1976, sax, mallet
    per.).  Intersong.
_____: Six Miniatures (1978, sax solo, 8'30).  Andel.
Dino Castro (b. 1920):  Concerto (1978, SAB, 1 perf.,
    ch. orch.).
Eric Fischer (b. 1961):  Concerto (1982, sax-s.,
    orch.).
Raymond Lamote:  Chant Lyrique (4'50).  Bil., 1981.
    Prem. 19 Jan. 1980.
Jean-Claude Naude (b. 1933):  Sun-Sand-Sea (SAATB).
Jean-Louis Petit (b. 1937):  Samu 92 (SAATB).  E.F.M.
Lucie Robert (b. 1935):  Flammes et Fumées, opus 53
    (SAATB).  Prem. 7 July 1982.
_____: Perpetuum mobile (1985, sax solo).  Prem. 29
    June 1985, WSC, U. of Maryland.
_____: Rythmes Lyriques (1984, S, T).  Bil.
Claude Terranova:  Métamorphoses (SAATB).

Recordings:

Quatuor Garde Républicaine (AFA 20772, 1970, music by
Bagot, Bozza, Desenclos, Sciortino); Quatuor de Sax-
ophones de la Garde Républicaine (AFA 20893, 1973,
music by Bagot, Bernard, Lemeland, Sciortino); Au
Delà du Hasard (Jean Baraque Ensemble, Musique Inter-
nationale de Champigny, 1978); Tomasi: Ballade pour
Saxophone (Corélia 79116); Quintette de Saxophones de
Paris (Corélia, 1983, music by Robert, Defaye, Naude,
Terranova); Solos with composer-pianists (Corélia
CC 682.372, music by Boutry, Delerue, Gotkovsky);
André Beun (Corélia CC 78080, music by Bernard, Cheva-
lier, Gotkovsky).

BICHON, SERGE
b. Jaunay-Clan, Vienne, France
   29 November 1935

    Bichon studied with Louis Fourré, André Delage, Mar-
cel Josse, Fred Lockwood, Marcel Mule, and Daniel Deffayet.
He won first prizes at the CNSM in Saxophone (1960) and
Chamber Music (1961).  Since 1956, he has been Professor
of Saxophone at the CNRM at Lyon.

    Bichon is one of the most respected teachers of saxo-
phone in France.  In addition to serving on the juries for
the CNSM and the Concours Centralisés de nomination de Pro-
fesseurs, he was the founder and organizer of the Concours
d'Aix-les-Bains, the Concours International de Gap, and
the Stages pour Saxophonistes amateurs.  Many of his students have been admitted to the CNSM and have qualified for
teaching certificates; more than 30 former students are
professors in schools of music in France and foreign
countries.

Publications edited by S. Bichon:

    Jouez du saxophone (2 vols., Chou., 1977); Collection
    S. Bichon (sax ens., Chou.); Gammes pour tous (Chou.).

Compositions dedicated to S. Bichon:

    Jean-Claude Amiot (b. 1939): Quatuor No. 1.
    Raoul Barthalay: Mini-Variations sur une vieille
        ronde française (1978, AAA, 2'15).  Bil., 1983.
    Alain Bonnard (b. 1939): Sonate No. 1 (sax-s., pf.).
        E.F.M., 1974.
    _____ : Treble (1979, ob., sax, pf.).
    Jean Bouvard (b. 1905): (Numerous small ens. for sax,
        publ. by Bil., Chou., and Martin).
    Pierre-Max Dubois (b. 1930): Trois miniatures (1981,
        AATB).  Ly.
    René Leibowitz (1913-1971): Variations pour quatuor
        de saxophones.  Prem. May, 1969.
    Lucie Robert (b. 1935): Supplications (1981, ob.,
        sax, vcl., 10').  Dorn.
    Antoine Tisné (b. 1932): Espaces irradiés.  Chou.,
        1980.
    Alain Weber (b. 1930): Assonances (1980, ob., sax,
        vcl.).

Recordings:

    Quatuor de saxophone Rhônes-Alpes (REM 10.826, music
    by Desenclos, Gotkovsky, Schmitt); Serge Bichon et
    le saxophone (music by Arma, Bouvard, Debussy, Hummel,
    Leibowitz, Scarlatti); Oeuvres pour saxophones
    d'Alain Bonnard; Trio Evolution (ob., vcl., sax,
    REM 10.875, music by Robert).  (Participation with

l'Orchestre Symphonique de Lyon and l'Harmonie Municipale de Lyon.)


BOGAARD, ED
b. Weesp, Holland
   1943

Studying at the conservatories in Amsterdam and
Utrecht, Bogaard won, with distinction, the first soloist
diploma ever awarded in Holland to a saxophonist. He appears regularly in concert, on radio and TV in Holland and
has also performed in the Scandinavian countries, Germany,
England, France, Italy, Poland, Rumania, and Israel. In
1983, he served on the Jury for the Concours International
de Genève. He is Professor of Saxophone at the Sweelinck
Conservatory in Amsterdam, give master classes in Holland
and Belgium, and is a professor at the Académie d'été in
Nice. In 1969, he founded the Netherlands Saxophone Quartet, which performs on recordings and tours.

Compositions dedicated to Ed. Bogaard:

Walter Hekster (b. 1937): Between Two Worlds (1977,
    sax, orch., 12'). Don.
Tristan Keuris (b. 1946): Concerto (11'). Don.
    Prem. 9 Oct. 1971, Radio Philharmonic.
Hans Kox (b. 1930): Concertino (sax, 10 winds).
    Don. Prem. 29 Nov. 1982.
Erich Eder de Lastra: Drei Tempi (sax-t., pf.).
David Porcelijn (b. 1947): Pulverization II (1973,
    sax, orch., 15'). Don.
Hendrik de Regt (b. 1950): Musica, opus 9 (1971, 10').
Ted Ponjee (b. 1953): The Square World (1984, 15'). Don.
Leo Samama (b. 1951): Capriccio (1976). Don.
Joep Straesser (b. 1939): Intersections V-1 (1977,
    ob., cl., sax, bn., 11'). Don.
Diderik Wagenaar (b. 1946): Kaleidofonen (1971).
(See L. van Oostrom for Netherlands Saxophone
    Quartets.)

Recordings:

Tristan Keuris: Saxophone Concerto (CV 7703, with the
Rotterdam Phil. Orch.); Ed Bogaard (Telefunken 642841
AZ); Ed Bogaard (Donemus 7374/4 CV 8002 and CV 8001);
Ed Bogaard (Attacca 8203-3, Polydor 2441 035). (See
L. van Oostrom for saxophone quartet recordings.)


BOK, HENRI JOSEPH
b. Rotterdam, Holland
   9 March 1950

A pupil of Leo van Oostrom, Bok attended the Conservatory of Rotterdam from 1973 to 1980 and, since 1981, has

served as Professor of Bass Clarinet at that Institution.
In the Rijnmond Saxophone Quartet (founded in 1973), with
Tom de Vette, J. van der Lee, and J. de Ligt, he plays
tenor sax. He has numerous compositions in manuscript form
dedicated to him.

Compositions dedicated to H. Bok and the Rijnmond Saxophone
    Quartet:

    Bernard van Beurden (b. 1933): Psychophony. Don.
        Prem. 19 Feb. 1979, Rotterdam.
        ____: Triptyque.
    Yvonne Desportes (b. 1907): Dedicace. Prem. 29 June
        1979, WSC, Evanston, Ill.

Compositions dedicated to H. Bok and Evert le Mair, percus-
    sionist:

    David Babcock: Fenêtres Prismatiques, opus 8 (1982,
        sax/bcl., mar./vib.).
    Zbigniew Bargielski: Ikar (1981, sax/bcl., mar./
        vib.).
    László Borsody: Duo (1983, sax, vib.).
    Giuseppe Colardo: Divertimento (1983, sax/bcl.,
        mar./vib.).
    William Duckworth (b. 1942): Midnight Blue (1976,
        sax, self-prepared tape). Composer.
    Andrew Ford: Boatsong (1982, sax/bcl., per.).
    Geza Frid (b. 1904): Vice Versa (1982, sax, mar.).
        Don.
    Milos Haase: Echoes (1982, sax, vib.).
    Mike Irik: Interaction III (1983, sax/bcl., mar./
        vib.).
    Daniel Kessner: Arabesque (1983, sax, vib.).
    Michal Kosut: Honeymoon (1981, sax, mar./vib.).
    Zdenek Lukás: 2 + 2 (1982, sax/bcl., mar./vib.).
    Paul-Baudoin Michel: Masscom (1983, sax, vib.).
    Fabio Nieder: Lega (1983, sax, mar.).
    Per Nørgård: Proteus (1983, sax per.).
    Tiberiu Olah: Concerto Notturno (1983, sax/bcl.,
        mar./vib.).
    Vladan Radovanovic: Duet (1983, sax/bcl., mar./vib.).
    Endre Székely: HeBem-Music (1982, sax/bcl., mar./
        vib.).
    Jim Theobald: Lewis Carrolls (1983, sax/bcl., mar./
        vib.).
    Mark Verhaegen: Etchings (1982, sax/bcl., mar./vib.).
    Anatol Vieru: Doubles Duos (1983, sax/bcl., mar./vib.).
    Ferdinand Weiss: Méditation et danse (1982, sax, vib.).
    Zbigniew Wiszniewski: Duo (1982, sax, mar.).

Recordings:

    Het Rijnmond Saxofoon Kwartet (ORESTE 6814.743, June
    1982 and RCS 468, Aug., 1981).

BOUHEY, ALAIN
b. Dijon, France
   16 February 1949

A pupil of Michel Nouaux and Jean-Marie Londeix,
Bouhey attended the CNRM, Dijon, from 1960 to 1964, where
he won a first prize and also earned the Maîtrise de
Lettres Modernes in literature.   In 1974, he won the Médaille d'Argent at the first Concours National d'Aix-les-
Bains.   He was Professor of Saxophone at the National Institute of Arts in Dakar, Senegal, from 1972 to 1978.   In
Cambrai he taught at the National Conservatory from 1978 to
1980.   He is on the faculty of the Ecole Normale de Musique
in Paris, and since 1980, he is also a professor at the
CNRM at Rennes and the Conservatoire Municipal du XVI Arrondissement in Paris.   Bouhey performs alto sax with the
Ensemble de Saxophone Français.

Compositions dedicated to A. Bouhey:

André Ameller (b. 1912): Entrée et dance (sax solo,
   4'). Combre. Prem. August, 1981.
Paul Arma (b. 1905): Deux Convergences (sax, tape, pf.,
   7'20). Prem. July, 1976.
Gilles Boizard (b. 1933): Concert (sax-s., vcl., hp.,
   14'). Prem. March, 1981.
Ida Gotkovsky (b. 1933): Eolienne (sax, hp., 14').
   Bil.  Prem. July, 1979.
Victor Martin (b. 1921): Orbitales III (sax, org.,
   8'). Prem. 10 July 1982).
Franz Tournier (b. 1923): Prophéties (sax, org., 10').
   Prem. 10 July 1982.
Alain Voirpy (b. 1955): Méditation sur un Sanctus
   (sax, org.). Lem., 1982. Prem. 10 July 1982.


BRIARD, RAYMOND
b. France                    d. France
   Unknown                      Unknown


A member of the Garde Républicaine Band, Briard followed M. A. Lambert (who worked for the saxophone manufac-
turer Couesnon) as soloists at the opera in the 1920s.
Both men played the saxophone as it had been played for
decades--like a clarinet and without vibrato.   Briard had
been a clarinetist before playing the tenor saxophone in
the Garde.   After his retirement from the Garde, Marcel
Mule succeeded him and also began playing, at the opera,
the sax solos in Massenet's Werther.   Briard made many
transcriptions of saxophone solos, which were published
by Salabert, Durand and Leduc.   His 239-page Nouvelle
Méthode contained solos from Werther by Massenet, L'Arlésienne by Bizet, and many early saxophone solo compositions.

Compositions:

Pastorale et Tarentelle (Marg., OP); Nouvelle Méthode
pour l'étude de tous les saxophones (Bil., c. 1920).

Compositions dedicated to Briard:

François Combelle (1880-1953):  Sur l'Essonne (Barca-
rolle, 1920).  H.S., OP.
René Brancour (1862-1948):  Suite (sax-t., pf., 1923).
OP.


BRYMER, JACK
b. South Shields, England
27 January 1915

Principal clarinetist of the Royal Philharmonic (1957-
1963), the BBC Orchestra (1963-1971), and the London Symphony (1971-to date), Brymer is also a skilled saxophonist.
He took over the leadership of the Michael Krein Saxophone
Quartet when its founder died in 1966 and still plays soprano sax in that group.  Brymer is the director of the
London Wind Soloists and a member of many well-known chamber music ensembles.  He has made many solo appearances and
recordings as a clarinetist and played the first performances in England of saxophone concerti by Gilbert Vinter,
Phyllis Tate, and Ronald Binge.

Recordings:

The Best of Eric Coates (EMI Studio Two Series TWO
223, Saxo-Rhapsody with the Royal Liverpool Phil.
Orch.); William Walton:  Facade 2 (Argo ZRG 649).


BUMCKE, GUSTAV
b. Berlin, Germany          d. Germany
18 July 1876                   1963

Merit for being the first German musician to pay
attention to the saxophone must go to Gustav Bumcke.  As
a young man, he played the trumpet and studied with Julius
Kosleck.  He also studied composition with Max Bruch and
Englebert Humperdinck for two years.  From 1900 to 1903,
he was a director in several theaters and tried to arouse
interest in the saxophone among wind players.  As early as
1902, he wrote a symphony which included a part for the
instrument; his later compositions were quite successful.
Richard Strauss gave him the responsability of premiering
his Suite for thirteen winds.  In 1902, when he went to
Paris to study with the son of Adolphe Sax and with Victor
Thiels, he brought back eight saxophones to Berlin and
began a saxophone class the next year.  In 1926, he wrote
the first German method for saxophone; his sax studies and

exercises were published between 1927 and 1932. His writing included material learned from Sax, Victor Thiels, and his own experience.

In 1931, Bumcke organized and conducted the first German saxophone orchestra (1 sopranino, 2 sopranos, 7 altos, 3 tenors, 1 baritone, and 1 bass), and in 1932, his Berlin Saxophone Quartet included Engrid Larssen, Emil Mantz, Carl Petzell, and himself playing the baritone. Because of Nazi regulations and World War II, his long association with the Stern Conservatory came to an end and he resigned himself to teach privately and at the Scharwenka Conservatory. Financial difficulties during these years obliged him to sell, one by one, his collection of 32 saxophones.

Compositions by G. Bumcke (the following were published by Anton Benjamin Co.; those with an asterisk are available from Simrock [AMP]):

*Saxophon Schule (1926); Grifftabelle für saxophon; Morceaux instructifs choisis (sax, pf.); Sextet, opus 19 (1908, cl., eng. hn., bcl., sax, hn.); Sextet, opus 20 in Ab (AA, eng. hn., bcl., bn.); 2 Quartets, opus 23 (1908, SATB); *36 Leicht Original Etüden, opus 43 (2 vols.); *36 Einfache Etüden, opus 43; *Tägliche, Technische Ubunger, opus 43; *Konzert-Valse, opus 48; *Tonkeiter Etüden, opus 70 (Scale Exercises); La Promenade (8 winds); Amour et Douleur (6 winds); *Jazz Studies, opus 43.

CAENS, JEAN-PIERRE
b. Rabat, Morocco
   15 October 1948

Caens began his saxophone studies with Jean-Marie Londeix (1958-1968). He won a First Prize at the CNRM at Dijon, and later studied with Daniel Deffayet, won the First Prize at the CNSM in 1973, and was a Laureat at the Concours International de Genève in 1970. Since 1974, he has been Professor of Saxophone at the CNRM at Besançon and Professor of Musicology at the Faculté de Lettres.

Compositions dedicated to or premiered by J. P. Caens:

André Ameller (b. 1912): Capriccio (sax solo). Combre. Prem. 4 July 1974, Bordeaux.
J. Paul Baumgartner (b. 1932): Cycle IV (1982, sax, cl., ob., bn.).
Dieter Einfeldt (b. 1935): Imaginationen II. Prem. 10 July 1982, WSC, Nuremberg.
N. Zourabichvili de Pelken (b. 1936): Pointillés (1979, sax, tape).
_____: Winterleid (1984, ob., cl., bn., sax, 18'). Prem. 28 June 1985, WSC, U. of Maryland.

CHARLES, JACQUES
b. Poitiers, France
   25 January 1952

   After receiving the Licence es Lettres from the University of Poitiers, Charles studied at the CNSM with
Daniel Deffayet and won first prizes in Saxophone (1975)
and Chamber Music (1977).  He has performed on the soprano
saxophone with the Quatuor de Saxophones Contemporain since
its creation in 1975.  Other members of the quartet are
Pierric Leman, alto; Ghislain Mathiot, tenor; and Max Jézouin, baritone.  Charles has appeared as soloist and with
his quartet in France, Switzerland, Holland, Italy, Germany,
and the United States.  He has been Professor at the Conservatoire National de la Rochelle since 1976, and is a member
of the Jury at the CNSM in Paris.  He is currently Editor
of the As.Sa.Fra. Bulletin.

Compositions dedicated to or premiered by J. Charles and
       The Quatuor de Saxophones Contemporain:

   Bruno Bontempelli (b. 1948):  Jeu d'anches (SATB).
      Prem. 29 July 1979, WSC, Evanston.
   Thérèse Brenet (b. 1935):  Calligramme (SA, 1 perf.).
      Prem. 8 July 1982, WSC, Nuremberg.
   Thierry Carré-Chesneau (b. 1950):  2 Pièces (1978, SA).
   Bernard Cavanna:  Quatuor (1982).
   Philippe Dulat:  Quatuor à l'enfant malade (1980,
      SATB).
   Jacqueline Fontyn (b. 1930):  Fougères (SA, pf.).
      Sal., 1982.
      _____ :  Mime 3 (SA, pf.).  Chou., 1982.
   Claude Foray (b. 1933):  Quatuor.
   Jean-Marc Laureau (b. 1946):  Etat Limité (1982,
      SATB).  Prem. 11 July 1982, WSC, Nuremberg.
   Edith Lejet (b. 1941):  Aube Marine (SATB).  Sal.
      Prem. July, 1982, WSC, Nuremberg.
   Jean Lemaire (b. 1927):  Entre chien et loup (1980,
      6 saxes, pf.).
   Aubert Lemeland (b. 1932):  Concertino (1980, SATB).
      _____ :  Noctuor, opus 93 (SATB).  Bil. 1983.
      _____ :  Trio, opus 106 (1982, ob., sax, vcl.).
   Vivienne Olive (b. 1950):  Music (2 saxes, orch.).
      Prem. 11 July 1982, WSC, Nuremberg.
   Etienne Rolin (b. 1952):  Maschera (1981, SAB,
      1 perf., orch.).
      _____ :  Tightrope (SATB).  Prem. 1980, Garches.

Recordings:

   Quatuor de Saxophones (Phillips 0181, 1981); Inté-
   grale des Quatuors de Saxophones d'Aubert Lemeland
   (Cybélia CY 654); Quatuor de Saxophones Contemporain (Auvidis, music by Singelée, Weill, Scarlatti,
   Lejet).

CHAUTEMPS, JEAN-LOUIS (JAY)
b. Paris, France
   6 August 1931

     In 1949, Chautemps took up the saxophone. He studied
harmony with Olivier Gixo and clarinet with M. Dauwe. In
1951, he became a professional jazz musician as a student
of Claude Bolling. In the 1960s, he performed in jazz
clubs and with groups in Paris, studied classical saxophone
with D. Deffayet, taught jazz improvisation, wrote Jazz Ex
with B. Parmegiani, and composed music for films. In the
1970s, he worked on the flute with R. Hériché and was heard,
like Michel Portal and other well-trained commercial musicians, in Musique Vivante concerts, where he played in festivals and tours in France and the United States. He participated in Luciano Berio's "Circle" in 1974 and in other
avant-garde concerts, and he founded the group RHIZOME. He
is a professor of saxophone at the Conservatory of Bagneux,
leads a saxophone workshop at the Châteauvallon Festival,
and performs in a saxophone quartet he founded (other members are F. Jeanneau, P. Maté, and J. Di Donato).

Composition premiered by J. L. Chautemps:

     Paul Méfano (b. 1937):  Périples (1978, sax-t. solo,
        14').  Sal.

Recordings:

     Stravinsky:  Ebony Concerto (dir. P. Boulez); Jay
     Cameron's International; Jacques Denjean; Philly Joe
     Jones; Chet Baker in Paris (MAS/ALVIM).


CHAUVET, GEORGES
b. France, 1906

     An original member of the Garde Républicaine Saxo-
phone Quartet, Chauvet played the baritone saxophone. The
premiere of the quartet was on 2 December 1928 in La Rochelle. According to Rousseau,

     Chauvet contributed greatly to the success of the Quartet.
     Believing firmly in the medium, he spent countless hours
     copying parts for the various transcriptions that made up the
     bulk of the early quartet repertory. In addition, he used
     his energy and organizational ability to book numerous con-
     certs for the Quartet.[1]

In 1936, Chauvet, Mule, and Romby left the Garde, and the
name of the quartet was changed to Le Quatuor de Saxophones
de Paris. The fourth member, Fernand Lhomme, remained in
the band and was replaced by Georges Charron on tenor saxophone. In 1948, after a brilliant career, Chauvet retired
from the quartet.

Publications by G. Chauvet:

> Etudes de Perfectionnement (Combre); Le Saxophone classique (2 vols., Combre); Quatuor Concertant (Besson, OP); 15 Grandes Etudes (Barret, AB or ST, Combre).

Compositions dedicated to G. Chauvet:

> Robert Clérisse (b. 1899): Sérénade Mélancolique (SATB). Leduc.
> François Combelle (1880-1953): Sérénade Italienne. H.S. (OP).


COHANIER, EDMOND
b. Geneva, Switzerland
   Unknown

    After studying solfège, flute, and clarinet, Cohanier received his first lesson on the saxophone on 11 November 1918. In 1925, he left for Paris with the intention of studying clarinet at the CNSM, but he decided to concentrate on the saxophone. Unfortunately, at that time the only teachers in Paris were members of the Garde Républicaine Band, who did not play with a vibrato. He began performing in small orchestras for silent films in some of the Paris theaters and soon began playing with various American jazz orchestras in the French capital. In 1930, after a tour to South America, he started performing in a large jazz orchestra at the Paramount Theater in Paris. During World War II, he returned to Switzerland, where he was heard in various Swiss cities and soon received an invitation to lead his eighteen-piece orchestra for the Beromunster Radio broadcasts and variety shows. Shortly after, the conductor Hermann Scherchen formed a symphonic orchestra in Zurich; he offered Cohanier a contract to play solo saxophone and bass clarinet, and, consequently, Cohanier performed solo works and incidental orchestral passages.

    In 1960, he began the Edmond Cohanier Saxophone Quartet with André Vivian, alto; Maurice Hourier, tenor; and Anton Schöb, baritone. The quartet played on Swiss Radio and toured in Germany, Belgium, Spain, and Italy.

Composition:

> Silhouette (valse caprice, Bil., 1976, 3'20).

Compositions dedicated to or premiered by E. Cohanier:

> Paul Guilmain: Espoir et Impatience (SATB).
> Rolf Liebermann (b. 1910): Petit Rondo in F (1952, a sight-reading piece for the Concours International de Musique de Genève, 6').
> Boris Mersson (b. 1921): Concerto (1966, sax, band).

_____ : Suite pour saxophones, opus 17.  Br.H., 1960.
Jules Semler-Collery (b. 1902):  Petite Marche Burlesque (SATB).

Recordings:

Quatuor de Saxophones Edmond Cohanier (Vols. 1, 2, 3, Gallant).

COMBELLE, FRANÇOIS
b. Marcigny, Saone & Loire,   d. Paris, France
   France, 26 July 1880          3 March 1953

Originally an oboist, Combelle entered the Garde Républicaine in 1902 and eventually became the saxophone soloist.  In 1923, he urged Marcel Mule to undertake the competitive audition, and the latter entered the band in August at the age of 21.  According to Mule in a conversation with E. Rousseau:

Combelle was without question a brilliant soloist and gifted virtuoso who played solos often with the band, although the music consisted of fantaisies, variations, etc.[2]

When the Selmer Company purchased the remains of Adolphe Sax's plant from his estate in 1920, Combelle became the tester and advisor.

Compositions:

1er Solo de Concert (ded. to M. Pilot, Bil., OP);
1er Solo de Concert (B or T, 1911, Alfred, 1927);
Esquisse (H.S., OP); Grande Méthode Moderne (1910, ded.
to G. Pares, H.S., 1911, OP); Le Barbier de Séville
No. 1 (1920, H.S., OP); Sur L'Esson, Barcarole (1920,
to Briard and Raffy, H.S., OP); Fantaisie Mauresque
(c. 1920, to E. Hall, Rubank, 1959, ed.  H. Voxman);
Sérénade Italienne (ded. to Chauvet and Légé, H.S.,
1920, OP); Triolette Mazurka (H.S., 1920, OP); Rapsodie
Cypriote (1932, ded. to H. Selmer, H.S., OP); Malbrough
(Bil., 1938); Ballade et Divertissement (sax solo,
H.S., OP); Five Duets (Rubank, 1958, ed. H. Voxman).

Composition dedicated to F. Combelle:

Maurice Decruck (1896-1954) and Fernande Breilh:
Chant Lyrique, opus 69.  H.S., 1932 (OP).

DANEELS, FRANCOIS
b. Tubize, Belgium
   4 November 1921

Through his many solo appearances in the United States,

Canada, Germany, Switzerland, Hungary, and Czechoslovakia,
Daneels has earned a great reputation for his artistic
finesse and sensitive musical interpretations. He first
studied with Bageart in Belgium and, in June, 1939, won
the First Prize with Great Distinction at the Royal Conservatory in Brussels; this was followed by his first important appearance on Radio Belge in September. In 1954, he
was appointed Professor of Saxophone at the Conservatory,
succeeding Maurice Van Guchte (1897-1953). In 1953,
Daneels founded the Quatuor Belge de Saxophones with A.
Jacquet, E. Apper, and J. Cunche, and the group made fre-
quent international tours; later he founded the Septuor
Belge de Saxophones. Daneels is also known internationally
through his pupils, who are professors in Belgium, the
United States, and Canada.

Compositions:

> Suite (sax solo, Schott, 1973, ded. to the Royal
> Cons.); Quatre miniatures (Schott, 1982); Le Saxophon-
> iste en herbe (beg. method, Schott, 1969); 14 Etudes
> pour saxophone (Schott, 1983); Sax-retro, (1984).

Solos and concerti dedicated to F. Daneels:

> Jean Absil (1893-1976):  Fantaisie Caprice, opus 152.
> Lemoine, 1971.
> René Barbier (b. 1890):  Pièce Concertante, opus 95
> (1959, 10'). CBDM.
> Edward Boguslawski (b. 1940):  Musica Concertante
> (sax, orch.).
> Roger Calmel (b. 1921): Concerto. Chou., 1972.
> _____ : Suite (1961, 8').
> Raymond Chevreuille (b. 1901): Double Concerto, opus
> 34 (1963, sax, pf./orch.). CBDM.
> Jeanne Colin (b. 1924): Fantaisie pour saxophone,
> opus 27 (sax solo, 9'). Bil., 1978.
> Franz Constant (b. 1910): Concerto (1963, 13').
> Metropolis.
> _____ : Fantasia. Bil.
> Pierre-Max Dubois (b. 1930): Circus Parade (sax, per.,
> 15'). Leduc, 1965.
> _____ : Grave et Scherzo Mécanique. R.R., 1973.
> _____ : Sonatine (8'). Leduc, 1966.
> Guy Duyck: Introduction et danse. Maurer.
> Jacqueline Fontyn (b. 1930): Dialogues (1969).
> Ida Gotkovsky (b. 1933): Brillance (13'). E.F.M.,
> 1974.
> Wolfgang Hildemann (b. 1925): Concerto Coreografico.
> William Latham (b. 1917): Sisyphus. Bil., 1971.
> Jacques Leduc (b. 1932): Rhapsodie. Schott.
> Victor Legley (b. 1915): Concert d'Automne, opus 85.
> (11'15). Bil., 1975.
> Marcel Poot (b. 1901): Ballade (8'). Schott, 1948.
> _____ : Concerto (14'10).

Jules Semler-Collery (b. 1901):  <u>Barcarolle et Danse</u>
(6'30).  Esc., 1968.

<u>Chamber Music dedicated to F. Daneels (N.B.: saxophone
quartet unless otherwise indicated.)</u>:

Jean Absil (1893-1976):  <u>Divertissement</u>, opus 86
(SATB, Ch. orch.).  CBDM.
_____ :  <u>Suite d'après le folklore Roumain</u>, opus 90
(1956, 17').  CBDM.
Karel Albert (b. 1901):  <u>Quatuor Voor Saxofones</u> (1960).
René Barbier (b. 1890):  <u>Quatuor</u> (1961, 14').  CBDM.
Pierre Bartholomée:  <u>Ricercare</u>  (1974, SATB).
Charles Becker (b. 1944):  <u>Triade</u> (1974).
Jeanne Colin (b. 1924):  <u>Quatuor</u>.
Franz Constant (b. 1910):  <u>Quatre Séquences</u>  (1966,
12').  CBDM.
_____ :  <u>Triade</u> (1967, voice, sax, pf., per., 8').  CBDM.
Edgar Cosma (b. 1925):  <u>7 Séquences</u> (1963, 12'30).
Jean Cunche (b. 1930):  <u>Introduction et Tarentelle</u>
(1958, 6').
René Défossez (b. 1905):  <u>Mouvement Perpétuel</u>.
Michel Deom:  <u>Le pêcheur d'ombres</u>, opus 7 (1980, 16'30).
Bil., 1980.
Jean-Marie Depelsenaire (b. 1914):  <u>Concertino</u>.
Philippo, 1972.
Victor Douliez:  <u>Prélude et Scherzo</u>.
Pierre-Max Dubois (b. 1930):  <u>Variations</u> (1968, 16').
Leduc.
Fernand Marcel Fontaine:  <u>Concertino de Dinant</u>.  Sha.
Prem. 20 Nov. 1975.
Paul Harvey (b. 1935):  <u>Three Movements</u> (1975, 15').
Nestor Higuet:  <u>Thème, variations et fugue</u>.
Edgard Leclercq:  <u>Impressions Romantiques</u> (5').
_____ :  <u>Introduction et Scherzo capriccioso</u> (5').
Maurer.
_____ :  <u>Prélude et mouvement perpétuel</u> (4').  Maurer.
Jacques Leduc (b. 1932):  <u>Sortilèges Africains</u> (1967,
voice, sax, pf., per., 10').
_____ :  <u>Suite en quatuor</u>, opus 15 (1966, 12').  Schott.
Victor Legley (b. 1915):  <u>Cinq miniatures</u>, opus 54
(1958, 8').  CBDM.
Arthur Meulemans (1884-1966):  <u>Concertino</u> (1962, SATB,
orch.).  CBDM.
_____ :  <u>Concerto Grosso</u> (1958, SATB, orch., 13'30).
CBDM.
_____ :  <u>Quatuor</u> (1953, 14').  CBDM.
Lucien Poliet (b. 1921):  <u>Versailles</u> (1960, suite, 11').
Marcel Poot (b. 1901):  <u>Concertino</u> (1963).  CBDM.
_____ :  <u>Scherzo</u> (1941, 4').  CBDM.
_____ :  <u>Thema con variazioni</u> (sax octet).
Henri Pousseur (b. 1929):  <u>Vue sur les jardins inter-</u>
<u>dits</u>.  BH.
Marcel Quinet (b. 1915):  <u>Concerto Grosso</u> (SATB, orch.).
_____ :  <u>Pochades</u> (1967, 8').  Bil.

Roland Renerts: Cinq danses (sax septet).
Max Vandermaesbrugge (b. 1933): Saxofolies, opus 40
   (1974, sax septet).
Maurice Vaute: Divertissement.  CBDM.
_____ : Impromptu.  CBDM.

Recordings:

Recital de Saxophone (Buffet Crampon BCB 101, music by
Rivier); François Daneels (Buffet Crampon BCB 102,
music by Semler-Collery); Recital de Saxophone (Buffet
Crampon BCB 105, music by Absil, Latham, Dubois); Quatuor de Saxophones (ALPHA DR 43, music by Absil, Meulemans, Poot); Quatuor de Saxophones (ALPHA DR 90,
music by Bertouille, Moulaert); François Daneels (BMF
214, music by Constant, Fontyn, Quinet, Langlois);
Facétie (Decca 153006); Jean Absil: Phantasmes (Decca
143235); Saxophone and Orchestra (His Master's Voice,
music by Brenta, Legley); Prestige du Saxophone (Cla-
sijaz Cl. 201, music by Binge, Poot, Dubois, Schuhoff);
Quatuor de Saxophones (Musica Magna, music by Barbier,
Françaix, Leduc, Simonis); SAXO RETRO (Schott Frères
Z 07); Saxophone in concert (Schott Frères Z 23, music
by Harvey, Legley, Martin, Villa-Lobos).


DECOUAIS, RENE
b. Tours, France
   1938

     As a student at the CNSM in Paris in the class of
Marcel Mule (1951-1955), Decouais won a first prize.  He
is Professor of Saxophone at the Conservatoire National in
Limoges, concertizes, and leads the Quatuor de Saxophones
de Limoges.  He has arranged Jean Rivier's Concerto for
saxophone and trumpet for band accompaniment, which is
published by Billaudot.

Compositions:

35 Etudes Techniques (Bil., 1973); Trois Pièces en
concert (Bil., 1983, 8').

Compositions dedicated to R. Decouais:

Julien Porret (b. 1896): 19e Solo de Concours (sax-s.,
   pf.).  Mol.
Jean-Pierre Leguay (b. 1939): Sève (13').  Lem.
   Prem. 4 July 1974, WSC, Bordeaux.

DECRUCK, MAURICE
b. France                    d. France
   1896                         1954

     Decruck, saxophone soloist on call for the New York

Philharmonic, published numerous works in collaboration
with his wife, the French composer, Fernande Breilh. The
French musicologist, Robert Bernard, said, "[It is] pleas-
ant and easy [to listen to]."[3]

Compositions:

>       Chant Lyrique, opus 69 (1932, H.S., OP); Ecole moderne
>       du saxophone (1932, Leduc); Selméra-Sax (1934, H.S.,
>       OP); The Golden Sax (1934, ded. to R. Wiedoeft, Ed.
>       Paris, OP); Rex Sax (ded. to C. Sauvage, Ed. Paris,
>       OP); Duos (2 saxes, Ed. Paris, OP); 3e Chant Lyrique
>       (Leduc); 5e Chant Lyrique (Leduc); 8 Pièces Françaises
>       (c. 1943, Bil., 17', OP); Sonate en Do# (1944, Bil.,
>       16'); Variations Symphoniques (SATB, Ed. Paris, OP);
>       Sicilienne (SATB, Ed. Paris, OP); Pavanne (SATB, Ed.
>       Paris, OP); Printemps (SATB, Ed. Paris, OP); Saxo-
>       phonie (SATB, Ed. Paris, OP).


DEFFAYET, DANIEL
b. Paris, France
   23 May 1922

Deffayet began the study of solfege at seven, the
violin at eight, and the saxophone at twelve. He was admitted to the CNSM in the violin class of A. Tourret. Entranced by the warmth and beauty of the saxophone's tone
quality heard through the recordings of Marcel Mule in the
1930s, Deffayet began the study of this instrument with
Mule in April, 1938; when the class for saxophone was established in 1941, Deffayet was a member. In the spring
of 1943, he won the Premier Prix, Premier Nommé; he later
earned other prizes in Chamber Music (1944) and a second
prize in Violin (1945). In October, 1940, he began replacing Mule for various engagements at the Opéra and the
Opéra Comique. As an orchestral musician, Deffayet has
performed under the direction of such famous conductors as
Dorati, Kubelik, Boulez, Bernstein, Maazel, Markevitch,
Martinon, Monteux, Munch, Leinsdorf, Paray, and Ozawa.
Since 1966, Herbert von Karajan has called on him to play
important solos and make recordings with the Berlin Philharmonic Orchestra.

Beginning his teaching career in 1948, Deffayet was
professor at municipal conservatories in Paris, the Ecole
Municipale de Beauvais, and the Conservatoire du Mans
(1951-1957). When Mule decided to retire in 1968, after
25 years of exceptional teaching, Deffayet was the unanimous choice to continue the spirit of the French School
of saxophone playing. In addition to his teaching and
many solo appearances, he is the tester and advisor for
Buffet-Crampon and Vandoren.

In 1953, the year of his debut as a soloist, playing

Ibert's <u>Concertino da Camera</u>, he formed the Quatuor de
Saxophones Daniel Deffayet, with Jacques Mafféi, Jacques
Terry, and Jean Ledieu; their first concert took place on
12 April 1956 at Alençon.   In the same year, Mafféi was
appointed Director of the Ecole Municipale d'Alençon, and
Henri-René Pollin replaced him as the alto saxophonist;
since then, there has been no change in personnel.  Besides
numerous concerts in France, important tours have taken
the quartet to England, Sweden, Denmark, Germany, Switzerland, Canada, the United States, Japan, and Korea.

## Compositions dedicated to D. Deffayet:

Traditionally, composers commissioned to write "solos
de concours" for the CNSM, dedicate their works to the
current professor.  The following test pieces for saxophone
have been dedicated to Deffayet since 1970:

| Year | Composer | Title | Publisher |
|------|----------|-------|-----------|
| 1970 | Jean-Paul Rieunier b. 1933 | Linéal | Leduc |
| 1971 | Désiré Dondeyne b. 1921 | Concerto | Chou. |
| 1972 | Roger Calmel b. 1921 | Concertino (Andante and Final) | Chou. |
| 1973 | Pierre Sancan b. 1916 | Lamento et Rondo | Dur. |
| 1974 | Alain Margoni b. 1934 | Cadence et Danses | E.F.M. |
| 1975 | Jean-Pierre Beugniot b. 1935 | Sonate | Bil. |
| 1976 | Jean-Michel Defaye b. 1932 | Ampélopsis | Leduc |
| 1977 | Georges Delerue b. 1925 | Prisme | ET |
| 1978 | Marcel Bitsch b. 1921 | Aubade | Leduc |
| 1979 | Roger Boutry b. 1932 | Cadence et Mouvement | Unpublished |
| 1980 | Ida Gotkovsky b. 1933 | Variations Pathétiques | Bil. |
| 1981 | Serge Lancen b. 1922 | Prélude et Scherzo | Bil. |
| 1982 | Pierre-Max Dubois b. 1930 | Respirations | Bil. |
| 1983 | Pierre Ancelin b. 1934 | Saxophonies | Bil. |
| 1984 | Alain Bernaud b. 1932 | Rhapsodie | Chou. |

## Etudes and unaccompanied solos dedicated to D. Deffayet:

René Decouais (b. 1938):   <u>35 Etudes Techniques</u>.
Bil., 1933.

Pierre-Max Dubois (b. 1930): Sonate d'étude (15').
   Leduc, 1970.
Guy Lacour (b. 1932): 28 Etudes (sur les modes à
   transpositions limitées d'Olivier Messiaen). Bil.,
   1972.
Jeanine Rueff (b. 1922): Sonate (1967, 12'20). Leduc,
   1969.
Gilles Senon: 16 Etudes Rythmo-Techniques. Bil.,
   1979.
Henri Tomasi (1901-1971): Evocations (1968). Leduc.

Solo compositions dedicated to D. Deffayet:

Pierre Bauzin (b. 1933): Concerto, opus 32 (22').
   : 2nd Concerto, opus 55 (18').
Alain Bernaud (b. 1932): Sonate (SB). Prem. 6 July
   1974, WSC, Bordeaux.
Marc Carles (b. 1933): 3 Chants Incantatoires. E.M.Tr.
Jerome Coller (b. 1929): Trio (1984, 2 saxes, pf.).
   Prem. 19 Oct. 1985, St. Cloud, Minnesota.
Yvonne Desportes (b. 1907): Blablabla (1971, 2 saxes).
Pierre-Max Dubois (b. 1930): Sonate (20'). Leduc,
   1956.
Guy Lacour (b. 1932): Divertissement (sax, per.,
   12'30). Bil.
Nicole Philiba (b. 1937): Concerto (1962, 14').
   Bil., 1968. Prem. 1964, Nice.
   : Sonate (1964, 17'). Bil., 1968.
Alain Weber (b. 1930): Linéaire I (17'). E.F.M.
   Prem. 6 July 1974, WSC, Bordeaux.

Saxophone Quartets dedicated to D. Deffayet:

Maurice Bagot (b. 1896): Quatuor (1965).
Henri Barraud (b. 1900): Quatuor (1977).
Jacques Bernard (b. 1931): Andante et Scherzo (1965).
Georges Boeuf (b. 1937): Parallèles (1967, 12').
   CANF.
Thérèse Brenet (b. 1935): Tétrapyle (1979, SATB,
   pf.). Prem. July, 1979, WSC, Evanston.
Roger Calmel (b. 1921): Quatuor méditerranéen (1982).
Marc Carles (b. 1933): Cycliques. Prem. July, 1976,
   WSC, London.
Edgar Cosma (b. 1925): Sept Séquences (1963, 12'30).
Jean-Michel Damase (b. 1928): Quatuor (1975). Lem.,
   1978.
Marcel Dautremer (b. 1906): Tetra venti (1975).
Raymond Depraz (b. 1915): Symphonie II (SATB, orch.,
   1973, 32'30). E.F.M. Prem. 19 April 1973, Stras-
   bourg.
   : Quatuor No. 2 (1974, 17'). E.F.M.
Marcel Despard (b. 1920): Quatuor.
Pierre-Max Dubois (b. 1930): Les Métamorphoses (24').
   Bil., 1983. Prem. 11 July 1982, WSC, Nuremberg.
Jindrich Feld (b. 1925): Quatuor (1982, 26'). Leduc.

U. S. prem. 25 June 1985, WSC, U. of Maryland.
Graciane Finzi (b. 1945): Cinq Séquences pour Quatuor
   de Saxophones (1982, 10').
Edmond Gaujac (1895-1962): Rêves d'enfant.
Jean-Paul Holstein (b. 1939): Cinq énigmes (1981).
Edith Lejet (b. 1941): Quatuor en cinq mouvements
   (12'). E.F.M.
Jean Lemaire (b. 1927): Quatuor (1982, SATB, orch.).
Jean Martinon (1910-1976): Concerto Lyrique (1976,
   SATB, orch., 21'). E.F.M.
Nicole Philiba (b. 1937): Quatuor (1959, 16'30).
Jean-Pierre Rivière (b. 1929): Parallèles (1982).
Antoine Tisné (b. 1932): Alliages (1971, 15'). Bil.,
   1974. Prem. 11 Oct. 1972.
Arkadi Trebinski (b. 1897): Double Quatuor (1977,
   SATB, str. quar.).

Recordings:

Ibert:  Concertino da Camera (Epic LC 3478, OP); Woodwind Music (Musical Heritage MHS 732, music by Gallois-
Montbrun, Glazunov); Double Concerto (RTF-Barclay 995
006, OP); Debussy: Rapsodie (ERATO STU 70719);
Daniel Deffayet, Alto Saxophone (Crest RE 7051, music
by Boutry, Gallois-Montbrun, Rueff); George Bizet:
L'Arlésienne Suites 1 & 2 (Deutsche Grammophon 2530
128); Oeuvres de P. M. Dubois, Challan, Planel (EMI C
069 16369); Le Quatuor de Saxophones Deffayet (CBS/
Sony SOLN 2, music by Rueff, Tisné, Pascal); Quatuors
de Saxophones (EMI 2 C 069 14187, music by Desenclos,
Pierné, Rivier, Schmitt); L'Art suprême du quatuor de
saxophones (CBS/Sony 25 AG 487, music by Bach, Scar-
latti, Boccherini, Mozart, Schumann, Tchaikovsky,
Albéniz, Debussy); Pièces Classiques Célèbres (London
SLA 6 348, music by Bach, Corelli, Couperin, Handel,
Leclair, Lully, Rameau, arr. by M. Mule); Le Quatuor
de Saxophones Deffayet (Crest, 1985, music by Glazunov,
Feld, Schmitt).


DELABRE, MAURICE
b. Uzes, Gard, France
   10 April 1936

     After studies at conservatories in Nîmes and Le Mans,
Delabre obtained a unanimous First Prize at the CNSM in
the class of Marcel Mule in 1959. A year later, he won
the First Prize in Chamber Music in the class of René
Leroy. Admitted into the Garde Républicaine Band in 1962
as a baritone saxophonist, he is a member of the Quatuor
de Saxophones de la Musique de la Garde.

Recordings:

(For quartet recordings, see Michel Nouaux.)

DELAMARRE, PIERRE
b. La Baule, France
   6 May 1947

A first prize laureate of the Conservatoire de la Ville de Paris in 1971, Delamarre studied with Jacques Terry and Daniel Deffayet.  A composer, he has been Professor of Saxophone and Theory at the Ecole municipale at Saint-Nazaire, where he has also served as Director of the Municipal Band since 1978.

Compositions:

> Quatuor pour rire (Bil., 1978, 2'45); Rhapsodie pour saxophone et orchestre d'Harmonie (1979, 5'); Composer. (He has written 8 other works which are unpublished.)

DELANGLE, CLAUDE
b. Lyon, France
   4 June 1957

Delangle studied from 1966 to 1975 at the CNRM in Lyon in the class of Serge Bichon. He became a member of the class of Daniel Deffayet at the CNSM, Paris, in 1975, and won a first prize in Saxophone in 1977.  In 1978, he obtained the Licence de concert à l'unanimité from the Ecole Normale de Musique in Paris and won the Premier Second Prix and the Prix spécial pour l'interprétation de l'oeuvre imposée at the Concours International de Saxophone at Gap. He was also awarded the Premier Prix de Musique de Chambre à l'unanimité at the CNSM in 1979.  One of France's most brilliant young saxophone soloists, he has concertized extensively and was heard as soloist with Radio France, Monte Carlo, and the Paul Kuentz Orchestra.  Since 1982, he has been Professor of Saxophone at the CNRM for Boulogne-Billancourt.  He also edits sax music for Lemoine in Paris.

Compositions dedicated to or premiered by C. Delangle:

> Claude Ballif (b. 1924): Solfeggietto, opus 36, No. 8 (sax solo).  Prem. May, 1982.  E.M.Tr., 1982.
> Thomas Bracht: Concertino (sax, str.).  Prem. 11 July 1982, WSC, Nuremberg.
> Patrick Busseuil (b. 1956): Arène.  Prem. Dec., 1981, Lyon.
> Marius Constant (b. 1925): Concertante.  Prem. 18 May 1979, Antibes.
> Yvonne Desportes (b. 1907): Per Sa Pia (sax, per.). Prem. 30 Nov. 1978, Paris.
> Denis Dufour: Cueillir à l'arbre un petit garçon (sax, synth.).  Prem. 2 Feb. 1979, Lyon.
> Alain Louvier (b. 1945): Cinq éphémères (sax-s., pf.).  Prem. Jan., 1982, Paris.
> Miroslav Miletić (b. 1925): Sonate.  Prem. Feb.,

1982, Zagreb, Yugoslavia.
Lucie Robert (b. 1935): Rhapsodie (sax solo, 5').
    Dorn, 1981. Prem. 11 Jan. 1978, Paris.
Patrice Sciortino (b. 1922): Sapiaxono. E.M.Tr.
    Prem. 26 Jan. 1979, Sceaux.
Antoine Tisné (b. 1932): Espaces Irradiés. Prem. 17
    Oct. 1980, Aubervilliers.

## Recordings:

Debussy: Rapsodie (ERATO STU 71400, Orchestre National
de l'Opéra de Monte Carlo); Claude and Odile Delangle
(REM 10864, music by Charpentier, Tisné, Messiaen,
Dufour, Constant).


DEMEY, WILLY J.
b. Ingelmunster, Belgium
   25 November 1951

A pupil of François Daneels at the Royal Conservatory
in Brussels in 1969, Demey was a laureate of the national
competition (pro Civitate, 1968, in Mechelen) and of the
Tenuto competition in 1973. He has also appeared as a
soloist with orchestras in Belgium, Germany, and Sweden.
A former professor at the Royal Conservatory in Antwerp,
he is now professor at the Royal Conservatory at Ghent and
director of the Royal City Band in Izegem. A past member
of the Quatuor Belge and the Septuor de Saxophones, he currently plays alto sax with the Brussels Saxophone Quartet.

## Compositions dedicated to W. Demey:

François Daneels (b. 1921): Quatre Miniatures (sax
    solo). Schott, 1982.
Jean Decadt (b. 1914): Concerto No. 1 (1973). CBDM,
    1981.
Herman Verschraegen (b. 1936): Concerto (1981).
    Peryns, 1982.
André Waignein: Feeling (1970). Scherzando, 1971.

## Recordings:

Jean Decadt: Concerto (J. J. Production 78.013 MARL,
Germany); The Brussels Saxophone Quartet (LP 5114).


DESLOGES, JACQUES J.
b. Paris, France
   2 September 1934

In the class of Marcel Mule at the CNSM from 1952 to
1954, Desloges won the Premier Prix, the Prix d'Honneur,
and other prizes in Chamber Music (1954), History of Music
(1958), Harmony (1959), and Counterpoint (1962). He also

received a Diploma in Orchestral Conducting from the Schola
Cantorum (1969). Appointed as Professor of Saxophone at
the CNRM in Versailles in 1975, he has been assistant conductor of the Musique de la Police Nationale since 1982,
and was the first editor of the Bulletin for As.Sa.Fra.,
serving until 1981. Desloges has been active as a soloist
with various orchestras and has appeared as a recitalist
and with his saxophone quartet on tours and for WSC meetings. The other members of the Quatuor de Saxophones
Jacques Desloges are Michel Trousselet, alto; Bernard Beaufreton, tenor; and Michel Lepève, baritone.

Compositions:

> Rondo (SATB, CANF, Toulouse, 1972); Prélude et Danse
> (ob., bn., cl., sax, Paris, 1983); 6 Pièces faciles
> (1978); Prélude et Rondo français (edit. from P. Vel-
> lones, SATB, Lem., 1975); Jardin de Bêtes Sauvages
> (edit. from P. Vellones, SATB, Dur.); 2nd Sonatine,
> opus 194 (1943, sax-s., edit. from Ch. Koechlin,
> Eschig, 1983); Le repas de Tityre (sax-s. solo, edit.
> from Ch. Koechlin, Eschig, 1983); Fabliau (A or T,
> pf., Martin, 1985).

Solo Compositions dedicated to J. Desloges:

> Paul Arma (b. 1905): Comme une improvisation (sax
> solo). Dorn, 1981. Prem. 28 June 1979.
> _____: 3 Contrastes (sax solo). Chou., 1972. Prem.
> 18 Jan. 1974.
> André Arnold (b. 1910): Mélopée (5'). Prem. 17 Dec.
> 1972.
> _____: Thème varié (sax, org.). Prem. 23 March 1979.
> _____: Védéa (10'). Arpèges, 1983. Prem. 4 March
> 1971.
> Michelle Foison (b. 1942): Variations. Prem. 15
> Oct. 1970, Paris.
> Serge Lancen (b. 1923): Dédicace (sax, band/orch.).
> Mol., 1983. Prem. 6 July 1974, Bordeaux.
> Pierrette Mari (b. 1929): Corollaire d'un songe.
> Arpèges, 1983. Prem. 3 March 1976, Paris.
> _____: Jaserie (sax-s., pf.). Combre, 1960. Prem.
> 13 Dec. 1975, Paris.
> _____: Trio (SAT). Prem. 19 Nov. 1956, Paris.
> Gérard Massias (b. 1933): Dialogues (sax, bcl.).
> Bil. 1968. Prem. 17 Nov. 1966.

Saxophone Quartets dedicated to J. Desloges:

> Paul Arma (b. 1905): Petite Suite. Lem., 1976.
> Prem. 27 May 1972.
> André Arnold (b. 1910): Quatuor, opus 50. Prem. 2
> March 1974.
> Jacques Barat: Descente sur la neige. Prem. 7 April
> 1974.

_____ : Karanguez (1'30). Prem. 16 June 1972.
Jean-Pierre Beugniot (b. 1935): Pièces en quatuor.
    E.F.M., 1974. Prem. 31 March 1971.
André Bondon: Movimenti. Esc., 1982. Prem. 17 Nov.
    1981, Paris.
Yvonne Desportes (b. 1907): 4 Fuguettes. Prem. 2
    Dec. 1977.
Gérard Gastinel (b. 1949): Gamma 415. Prem. 30 July
    1976, WSC, London.
Roland Gérin: Suite en quatuor. Prem. 12 Feb. 1978,
    Paris.
Jean-Claude Henry: 2 Pièces. Prem. 20 Nov. 1956,
    Paris.
Suzanne Joly (b. 1914): Séquences. (12'). E.F.M.,
    1974. Prem. 2 March 1973.
André Jorrand: Quatuor dans le style ancien. Prem.
    22 Nov. 1981, Paris.
Pierrette Mari (b. 1929): De Trois à Quatre. Prem.
    4 July 1974, WSC, Bordeaux.
Paul Méranger (b. 1936): Quatuor d'Automne. Prem.
    25 Nov. 1978.
_____ : Suite Pittoresque. Prem. 3 March 1974.
Michel Merlet (b. 1939): Variations. Leduc, 1983.
    Prem. 6 July 1982, WSC, Nuremberg.
Jeanine Richer: Quatuor. Prem. 27 Jan. 1962.
Edmond Romano: Séquences alternées. Prem. 29 Jan.
    1981, Paris.

Recordings:

Quatuor de Saxophones Jacques Desloges (K.O. JD 001,
1974, music by Absil, Boeuf, Desloges, Beugniot);
Saxophone Alto et Piano et Quatuor (EFM-ORTH 012,
1975, music by Beugniot, Calmel, Koechlin, Pichaureau,
with A. M. Desloges, pf., awarded Prix du Disque de
l'Académie du Disque Français); Un Bon Petit Diable
(Libellule 1 3005, 1980, sax, band); Comme une Improvisation (Gasparo GS 214, 1981, music by Arma).


DRUET, ROBERT
b. France, 1920

    A first prize recipient as a member of the class of
Marcel Mule at the CNSM from 1946 to 1949, Druet has taught
in Rouen for a year and is presently the Director of the
National Conservatory at Perpignan.

Compositions:

L'Ecole Française du saxophone (3 vols., 1963, Bil.);
Air et Danse (Bil., 1976); Mélodie (Bil.).

Composition dedicated to R. Druet:

Julien Porret (b. 1896): Concertino No. 9. Martin.

ENGLISH SAXOPHONE QUARTET
Formed 1976

Playing for festivals, colleges, schools, music soci-
eties, radio, and TV, the English Saxophone Quartet, in
both its recordings and its appearances, has featured
diverse programs. The ensemble has appeared in most parts
of the United Kingdom and played at WSC meetings in Evanston, Illinois, and in Nuremberg. Members, performing and
teaching around the Manchester area, are Mark Jordan, soprano; Alan Andrews, alto; Neville Duckworth, tenor; and
Raymond Scott, baritone.

Compositions dedicated to the English Saxophone Quartet:

Colin Cowles (b. 1940): Four Features (1979, 12').
    Prem. 10 March 1981.
Terence Greaves (b. 1933): Three Folk Songs (1978).
    Stanza Music. Prem. April, 1980.
Laurie Holloway: Running Buffet. Lorimar Music.
    Prem. July, 1981.
Joseph Horovitz (b. 1926): Variations on a Theme of
    Paganini (c. 1977, 8').
Daryl Runswick (b. 1921): Family Group (15'). Prem.
    Feb., 1979.
John Tilstone-Ellis (b. 1929): Ollersett Suite.
    BMIC. Prem. July, 1978.
Peter Wishart (b. 1921): Aquarelles, opus 84 (1982).
    _____: Barquarolles. Prem. May, 1982.

Recordings:

A Study in Contrasts (ESQ AS 31, July, 1979, music
by Absil, Françaix, Joplin, Gershwin, Ellis); Saxophone Sundae (White Tower Records, March, 1981, music
by C. Cowles).


FOUCHECOURT, JEAN-PAUL
b. Blanzy, Saône & Loire, France
    30 August 1958

Fouchécourt began the study of the saxophone at the
age of twelve. He completed his studies at the National
Conservatory in Dijon in 1976, winning the Médaille d'or
à l'unanimité in the class of Jean Arnoult. Two years
later, he won the Premier Prix de Saxophone at the CNSM in
the class of Daniel Deffayet. In July, 1978, he was third
prize winner at the Concours International de saxophone at
Gap, and, in September of the same year, the First Prize
at the Concours International d'instruments à vents in
Ancona, Italy. He received a unanimous first prize in
Chamber Music at the CNSM (class of J. Lancelot). Fouchécourt has been the Professor of Saxophone at the national
Conservatory of Chalon-sur-Saône and founder and director

of the Orchestre Departemental of Saône-et-Loire. He has
made many solo appearances for Radio France and was a soloist at the sixth and seventh WSCs, Evanston and Nuremberg,
in 1979 and 1982.

Compositions dedicated to J. P. Fouchécourt:

> Raffi Ourgandjian:  Chant Elégiaque (1979).  Prem. 29
>     July 1979, WSC, Evanston.
> Claude Prior (b. 1918):  Concerto pour Saxophone alto
>     et Harmonie (1981).  Prem. 10 July 1982, WSC,
>     Nuremberg.

Recording:

> Le Saxophone Classique et son Repertoire (Pathé-
> Marconi JPF 0181, music by Boutry, Creston, Dubois,
> Maurice).

FOURMEAU, JEAN-YVES
b. Roubaix, France
   8 July 1958

Fourmeau studied at the Conservatoire de Roubaix
(class of René Desmons), and was awarded the Première médaille à l'unanimité in saxophone, solfège, sightreading,
and chamber music.  From 1975 to 1977, he continued his
education at the CNSM in Paris and won the Premier Prix,
Premier nommé in the class of Daniel Deffayet.  He was one
of the winners in the Concours International de Gap in 1978.
He has been active in concerts and recitals for French
radio and TV and has toured Germany, England, Belgium,
Switzerland, and the United States.  He has performed in
orchestral concerts under the direction of Bernstein,
Maazel, Ozawa, Dorati, Boulez, Marriner, Tilson-Thomas,
and Jean-Claude Casadesus.

Compositions dedicated to J. Y. Fourmeau:

> Pierre-Max Dubois (b. 1930):  Conclusion (sax solo).
>     Leduc.  Prem. 28 June 1979, WSC, Evanston.
> Odette Gartenlaub (b. 1922):  Dialogue.  Prem. 9 July,
>     1982, WSC, Nuremberg.
> Raymond Guiot (b. 1930):  Opium (sax solo).  Bil.
>     Prem. 28 June 1979, WSC, Evanston.
> Jean-Paul Holstein (b. 1939):  Suite Irréverentieuse.
>     Bil.  Prem. 9 July 1982, WSC, Nuremberg.
> Roger Tessier (b. 1937):  AVAZ.  Prem. Jan., 1979,
>     Lille.
> Antoine Tisné (b. 1932):  Music for Stonehenge.  Chou.
>     Prem. 30 July 1976, WSC, London.

GARDNER, FREDDY
b. England                    d. London, England
   c. 1911                       26 July 1950

     During the early 1930s, Ray Noble was leading one of
the greatest sweet bands of all time in England.  Musicians
were chosen from Lew Stone's and other leading London orchestras, and one of the most outstanding was Freddy Gardner
who played lead saxophone and was soloist on many of Noble's
HMV labels from England (issued later on U.S. Victor).
Gardner's lilting tone and vibrato was important to the
band's beautiful ensemble sound.  When Noble came to the
United States in 1934 to form a new band, this beautiful
sound was never duplicated.  Gardner continued to be active
in England as a freelance musician and leader.  In the late
1940s, he attracted some attention in the United States
when several of his saxophone solo recordings were issued.
At the time of his death, he was working with the Peter
Yorke Orchestra as a soloist.

Recordings:

     In addition to 21 recordings with Ray Noble's band
     and 11 solo recordings, he made the following LPS:
     Freddy Gardner (Col. 10" CL 6187); Freddy Gardner
     (Mon-Ever MES 7044); Ray Noble (Mon-Ever MES 6816,
     7021, 7027, 7039, 7040).


GARBAREK, JAN
b. Norway, 1947

     Garbarek, the best-known saxophonist in Norway, has
performed in a number of European countries as well as in
the United States, and has become internationally known
through his more than 30 recordings.  He is a composer
of jazz and other styles of music, and has arranged much
of the music which he performs; he has also written for
stage, film, and TV.


GOURDET, GEORGES
b. Pruniers, Loire & Cher, France
   26 February 1919

     At 16 years of age, Gourdet became serious about
music and studied with musicians in his region.  At the
outbreak of World War II, he served with the 131st Infantry
Regiment and on 3 September 1940 was captured.  The time
in captivity was not lost, as it permitted Gourdet to study
several languages, philosophy, and various musical subjects
which proved to be of considerable use later.  He was released from the service on 5 May 1945 and, the next October,
he was accepted at the CNSM in the class of Marcel Mule.
He won First Prizes in Saxophone (1947), History of Music
(1948), and Chamber Music (1949).

When Georges Charron of the Mule Quartet died in 1951, Gourdet was invited to replace him on tenor saxophone; in 1960, he moved to the alto position when André Bauchy retired. Gourdet's knowledge of musical literature and his ability to speak to audiences at all levels was a great asset to the quartet's popularity.

In 1957, Gourdet made his first concert tour and gave 30 recitals and lectures in Canada. Continuing as a concert artist, he participated in some 600 concerts in various European countries, Africa, and Asia Minor. Serving as Director of the Conservatoire municipal de Suresnes in 1970, he was invited the following year to be the Professor of Saxophone and Music at the Ecole Nationale de Caen. He has written numerous articles; written and made several translations for the record firms of Decca, Philips, Deutsche Grammophon; and contributed to encyclopedias. He is an editor of a saxophone series for the Gérard Billaudot Editions.

## Books by G. Gourdet:

"Saxophone" [in vol. III, Encyclopédie de la musique, ed. F. Michel (Fasquelle: Paris, 1961)]; Les Instruments à vent (Puf collection "Que sais-je?" 1967); Debussy (Hachette, 1970).

## Collections edited by G. Gourdet, Editions G. Billaudot:

Musique de chambre pour saxophone et divers instruments; L'enseignement moderne du saxophone; L'école Française du saxophone (with R. Druet, 1963).

## Compositions dedicated to G. Gourdet:

Jean Absil (1893-1976): Sonate, opus 115 (11'). Lem. 1963.
Amédée Borsari (b. 1905): Concerto (1947, 18'20). Bil., 1982. Prem. 22 May 1961.
Yvon Bourrel (b. 1932): Sonate, opus 18 (14'). Bil., 1964.
Roger Calmel (b. 1921): Concertino (10'). Heu., 1952.
Jacques Charpentier (b. 1933): Gavambodi 2 (10', 1966). Leduc, 1969.
Marcel Dautremer (b. 1906): Concerto, opus 61. Lem., 1962.
Pierre-Max Dubois (b. 1930): Mazurka, Hommage à Chopin (4'). Leduc, 1961.
_____ : 2 Mini Romances. Bil., 1981.
_____ : Prélude et Rengaine (A or T, pf.). Bil., 1979.
_____ : Suite Française (16'). Leduc, 1962.
Isabelle Duha (b. 1951): Scherzo. Bil., 1981.
Marc Eychenne (b. 1933): Sonate (16'). Bil., 1963.
Guy Lacour (b. 1932): 25 Etudes Atonales Faciles. Bil., 1975.

Gérard Massias (b. 1933):  Suite Monodique (11').
  Bil., 1954.
Albert Moeschinger (b. 1897):  Images (1958, sax, fl.,
  vcl., vn., 18').  Bil.  Prem. June, 1966.
Lucie Robert (b. 1936):  Double Concerto (sax, pf.,
  orch., 30').  E.F.M., 1968.
_____ :  Quintette (sax, str. quar., 19').  Bil.,
  c. 1960.

Recordings:

Music for Saxophone Quartet (Musical Heritage MHS 817,
music by Absil, Desenclos, Pierné, Rivier). (Also
see M. Mule Quartet.)


GRØN, CHRISTIAN ANCHER
b. Copenhagen, Denmark
  10 April 1943

An avant-garde jazz flutist and conductor from 1962
to 1965, Grøn received the highest diploma from the Royal
Danish Academy in 1973 after earning his teaching diploma
in 1972.  From 1973 to 1975, he was in Paris studying
privately with Daniel Deffayet.  He has given radio and
concert performances in Copenhagen with the Royal Academy
Orchestra, the Radio Symphony, and the Royal Opera.  Other
concert appearances have taken him to Norway, Sweden, and
WSC meetings in London and Bordeaux.  In addition to teaching, he has been a columnist for a publication for the
Danish Music Teachers Asssociation and the As.Sa.Fra. Bulletin in France.

Compositions dedicated to or premiered by C. A. Grøn:

Niels Viggo Bentzon (b. 1919):  Sonata, opus 320
  (1973).
Hermann David Koppel (b. 1908):  Ternio No. 2, opus
  92 (1973).
Bo Nilsson (b. 1937):  Portrait de femme No. 2 (sax,
  strs.).  Prem. 19 March 1976.
Jens Ole Malmgren:  Trio (1972, fl., ob., sax).
Paul Rovsing Olsen (b. 1922):  Aria (1976, sax, alto
  voice, pf.).


HARLE, JOHN
b. Newcastle, Tyne & Wear, England
  20 September 1956

Since leaving the Royal College of Music in London,
Harle has been the winner of numerous performance awards.
At 17, he was Solo Saxophonist with the Coldstream Guards;
later he became the first saxophonist to attain the ARCM
degree in saxophone at the Royal College, as a pupil of

Stephen Trier.  In 1978, he was awarded the Dannreuther
Prize for his performance of Ibert's Concertino da Camera;
he has also performed the British premiere of Frank Martin's Ballade.  After a year of study with Daniel Deffayet
in Paris, Harle established himself as an orchestral and
chamber music performer, working regularly with the London
Philharmonia and the BBC Orchestra under the batons of Muti,
Boulez, Maazel, Tilson-Thomas, Haitink, and Rattle.  A
winner of the 1983 Concert Artists Guild competition, he
made his New York debut on 14 February 1984.

Compositions and Edited Publications:

> Saxophone Studies (Universal, 1981-1983); Ballade
> (F. Martin's orchestral piece, arr. for sax and pf.,
> with J. Lenehan, Uni.); Three-Penny Opera (1928,
> by Kurt Weill, arr. for SATB, Uni.).

Compositions dedicated to J. Harle:

> Luciano Berio (b. 1925):  Sequenza IX b (from Sequenza
> IX for clarinet).  Uni.  Prem. Feb., 1981.
> Jonty Harrison (b. 1952).  EQ (1980, 13'30).
> David Heath:  Out of the Cool.  Prem. Feb., 1982.
> _____ :  Rumania.
> Jonathan Lloyd (b. 1948):  John's Journal (AS, pf.,
>     15').  B.H.  Prem. Nov., 1981; U.S. prem. 14 Feb.
>     1984.
> Ned Rorem (b. 1923):  Picnic on the Marne (Seven
>     Waltzes for Saxophone and Piano).  B.H.  Prem. 14
>     Feb. 1984, NYC.

Recordings:

> James Dawson, Soprano Saxophone (Crystal, S 158,
> Harle, bcl.); Two Saxophone Concertos (Huperion, with
> London Sinfonietta, music by Ibert, Villa-Lobos);
> Mainly for Pleasure (BBC); Walton: Facade (Decca,
> with London Sinfonietta); The Draughtsman's Contract
> (Piano Records, music by M. Nyman); Betrayal (sound-
> track by Pinter and Spiegl, 1982).


HARVEY, PAUL M.
b. Sheffield, Yorkshire, England
    14 June 1935

    A clarinet student of Frederick Thurston, Ralph Clarke,
and William Tomlinson, Harvey also studied composition and
received the LRAM and ARCM degrees.  After performing in
the Bournemouth Symphony Orchestra, he was appointed Professor of Clarinet at the Royal Military College, Kneller
Hall.  Active as a free-lance musician and performing on
various clarinets and saxophones, he became the leader of
the London Saxophone Quartet, founded in 1978 by Christopher

Gradwell, who plays tenor saxophone and teaches at Trinity
College of Music. The L.S.Q. made its debut in April, 1971
at Queen Elizabeth Hall, London. Other members of the
quartet are Hale Hambleton (of the English National Opera,
alto sax) and David Lawrence (member of the Band of the
Royal Horse Guards, baritone sax). An earlier alto saxophonist with the L.S.Q. was Peter Ripper (b. 1939), who is
in demand for both commercial and classical performances in
London.

Compositions and Publications:

    Harvey has composed 15 clarinet compositions; the
following are his works for the saxophone:

    The Agincourt Song (1976, SATB, Novello); Alto Saxo-
    phone Solos (2 vols., Chester, 1977); Bubble and
    Squeak (Sp., Bs., Composer); Christmas Fantasy (SATB,
    Composer); Concerts Duets (AT, Roncorp, 1981); Con-
    certinos (1974-75, for sax, sax-b., sax-t., each for
    orch./band, Maurer, prem. 1976, WSC, London); Concer-
    tino Grosso (1975-76, SATB, orch./band, 13', Maurer,
    prem. 1976, WSC, London); The Hartfleur Song (SATB,
    2', Novello, 1978); Pieces of Nine (1979, SATB, 2
    tpts., hn., trb., tuba, 5'); Robert Burns Suite (SATB,
    9', Novello, 1979); The Saxophonist's Bedside Book
    (Fentone, 1981); Saxophone Quartets (3 vols., SATB,
    Chester, 1980-82); Seven Saxophonian Folk Dances
    (SATB, parts only, 10', Kjos, 1976); Three Movements
    (1975, SATB, 15', Composer); Tenor Saxophone Solos
    (2 vols., Chester, 1979); Trio for Flute, Clarinet,
    and Alto Saxophone (Composer, prem. 26 April 1981).

Compositions dedicated to P. Harvey and the London Saxo-
    phone Quartet:

    Colin Cowles (b. 1940): Concertante for Saxophone
        Quartet and String Quartet (1973).
        _____: From Barrack Hill No. 2 (4 S, 4 A, 4 T, 4 B,
        1979, 8').
        _____: Six Easy Quartets in Recognizable Forms
        (1975, 15').
    Gordon Jacob (1895-1984): Duo for Soprano and Alto
        Saxophones (1980, 9'). Emerson.
        _____: Miscellanies (sax, band, 13'). Emerson.
        Prem. 28 July 1976, WSC, London.
        _____: Quartet No. 1 (1972, 12'). Emerson. Prem.
        WSC, 1974, Bordeaux.
        _____: Quartet No. 2 (14'). Emerson.
    John Mitchell: Pod (1975, SATB, 5-6'). BMIC.
    James Patten (b. 1936): Trochee (1972, SATB, 5').
        _____: Two Short Pieces for Saxophone Quartet
        (1972, 2'). BMIC.
    Paul Patterson (b. 1947): Diversions (1976, SATB,
        12').

John Reade (b. 1943):  Quintet for Saxophone and Wind
    Instruments.  BMIC.  Prem. WSC, 1976, London,
    rev. 1977.
    _____: Saxophone Quartet (1979, 7').
Neil Richardson:  Jazz Suite for Saxophone Quartet
    (1978, 21'25).
John Rushby-Smith:  Saxophone Quartet (1972, 12').
    Sim, 1976.

Recordings:

    London Saxophone Quartet (Transatlantic TRA 308);
    London Saxophone Quartet (Argo ZRG 4851); From Med-
    ieval to Jazz (Decca Argo ZK 79, music by Blyton,
    Harvey, Richardson); Betjeman's Banana Blush (Charis-
    ma CAS 1086, Sir John Betjeman, Poet Laureate, music
    arr. J. Parker); Late Flowering Love (Charisma CAS
    1096); The Little Big Band (Cannon CNN 5966); Winds
    of Change (EMI EMA 791, arr. for SATB and ww. doubles);
    The London Saxophone Quartet (cassette, Roncorp EMS
    020, 1983, music by Absil, Cordell, Dubois, Harvey,
    Jacob).


HECHT, CHRISTIANE
b. Roubaix, Nord, France
    9 October 1949

    Hecht studied at the conservatories at Roubaix (with
René Desmons, from 1965 to 1969) and Paris in the 10th
arrondissement (with J. Terry, from 1970 to 1971).  She
was a member of the class of Daniel Deffayet at the CNSM
from 1971 to 1975.  She was the first French woman to win
a first prize in saxophone at the Paris Conservatory and
to obtain the Certificat d'Aptitude à l'enseignement.  She
taught at the National School of Music in Lorient (1974-
1977) and at the National Conservatory, Region of Douai
(1977-1981).  Since 1978, she has been Professor at the
Conservatoire National de Tourcoing.  In 1981, she was appointed to teach additionally at the CNRM in Lille.
Hecht plays saxophone with the Opéra du Nord, the Orchestre National de Lille, and the North Saxophone Quartet.
Other members of the N.S.Q. are Jacques Defer, soprano;
Yves Tanguy, tenor; and René Vanoverberghe, baritone.


HURUM, HELGE
b. Norway, 1936

    Hurum is not only an important jazz composer but has
also made a name for himself in other genres.  He plays
the clarinet, flute, and saxophone and has studied with
Richard Kjelstrup, among others.  Hurum has led a number
of his own jazz groups, as well as larger jazz orchestras.
As a composer, he has used jazz as his primary point of

departure.  His compositions include works for jazz orchestras, symphony orchestras, and combinations of the two.
An example of the last-mentioned is "Concentus ad libitum"
(1977), for jazz quintet and symphony orchestra; and "On-
gura" (1971), for song and jazz orchestra.  His symphonic
works include "Norva Impulsa" (1972) and "Jazz på tunet"
(1977).  Hurum has also composed chamber music and music
for the stage.[4]


ITALO, MARCONI
b. Arezzo, Italy
   30 June 1939

     A pupil of Eraclio Sallustio of Della R.A.I-TV in
Rome, Italo studied the clarinet at the conservatory G. B.
Martini in Bologna in 1972.  He is the founder of and alto
saxophonist with the Quartetto Italiano di Sax and has performed with the symphonic orchestra "del Maggio Musicale"
in Florence.  Italo has been heard as soloist in Pontedera
(Glazunov: Concerto and Villa-Lobos: Fantasia, 20 June
1981), and in Naples (Ibert: Concertino da Camera, 17
November 1983).  He is Professor of Clarinet at the G. Rossini Conservatorio in Pesaro.

Compositions dedicated to M. Italo:

     C. Luyo: Geometriche Etudie (sax, org.).  Prem 23
       Nov. 1981.
     Eraclio Sallustio: Lunaris (sax, strs.).  Prem. 10
       May 1980).
     Ottavio Terreni: Xeres (sax, org.).  Prem. 23 Nov.
       1981.
     A. Zimmerman: Rip-Torn.  Prem. 5 Feb. 1980.


JEZOUIN, MAX
b. Nîmes, France
   4 April 1950

     A student at the Conservatory at Nîmes from 1956 to
1969, Jézouin was admitted to the CNSM in 1972, class of
Deffayet, and won a first prize in saxophone in 1976 as
well as a first prize in chamber music in 1977.  Earlier
saxophone teachers were J. Pierson and J. Terry.  Professor of Saxophone at the Conservatory in Asnières since
1974, he was appointed professor at Angoulême in 1982.

Compositions dedicated to M. Jézouin:

     Thérèse Brenet (b. 1935): Phoenix (sax solo).  Lem.
     François Bourdin: Fugue (ob., sax).  Prem. 19 May
       1984.
     _____: Quatuor.  Prem. March, 1985.
     _____: Rêverie (fl., sax, pf.).  Prem. 19 May 1984,
       Angoulême.

François Leclère (b. 1950): <u>Périphéria</u> (1977, SATB).
Edith Lejet (b. 1941): <u>Emeraude et Rubis</u> (2 saxes,
   3'). E.M.Tr. Prem. 19 May 1984.
____: <u>Jade</u> (sax, per., 3'30). Sal. Prem. June,
   1981.
____: <u>Saphir</u> (sax-b., pf., 4'30). Sal. Prem. 22
   April 1982, Sèvres.
Charles Leval (b. 1908): <u>Saxophonia</u> (1983, SATB).
Etienne Rolin (b. 1952): <u>Miniatures</u> (SATB, 4').
   Prem. 19 May 1984, Angoulême.
____: <u>Sablier</u> (SATB, 3'30). Lem. Prem. 19 May
   1984, Angoulême.
____: <u>10 Aphorismes</u> (sax solo, 12'). Prem. 12 Dec.
   1984.

## Recordings:

(See Jacques Charles for saxophone quartets.)


JOHNSSON, CHRISTER
b. Smöland, Sweden
   4 April 1956

A student of Jules de Vries at Ingesund and Sölve
Kingstedt at the State Academy in Stockholm, Johnsson also
studied with Jean-Marie Londeix at the CNRM in Bordeaux.
He was a member of the Ensemble International de Saxophones
in 1978. Johnsson performs throughout Scandinavia and
teaches saxophone at the Swedish State Colleges in Stockholm, Arvika, and Göteberg.

## Recording:

Lars-Eric Larsson: <u>Concerto for Saxophone</u> (Caprice
Records CAP 1242, 1983).


JOSSE, MARCEL
b. Ermont, Val d'Oise, France
   27 June 1905

Principal cellist with the Ballets Sakharoff at 16
years of age, Josse was appointed a year later as a re-
placement in the orchestra at the Opéra Comique. After
developing a weakness in his wrist, he had to abandon the
cello and hopes of a diploma at the CNSM. In 1925, Josse
became interested in the saxophone, and, although there
were no study books for this instrument, he adapted certain techniques from the cello. He studied harmony with
Marcel Cariven and counterpoint with Julien Fack, and began teaching the saxophone in 1933. Josse also perfected
his saxophone playing with Marcel Mule, who, in 1935, invited him to join his quartet, replacing Paul Romby. In
1948, when Georges Chauvet retired, Josse moved to the

baritone sax and performed in this position until the quartet was disbanded in 1966, on the retirement of Mule.

Josse has also had an active career as an administrator. Beginning in 1948, he served for 28 years as a professor of saxophone at the CNRM at Versailles, 10 years at la Schola Cantorum, and 15 years at l'Ecole de Musique de Melun, where in 1960, he became the Director. Since World War II, 52 of his students have entered the CNSM in Paris, where they received first prizes. Wishing to do something permanent for the saxophone, in 1972 he established a fund to underwrite a composition contest called the Concours de composition Josse. A jury of experts selects three winners for each competition, a prize is awarded, and the works are published.

## Compositions dedicated to M. Josse:

Guy Lacour (b. 1932): 50 Etudes faciles et progressives (2 vols.). Bil., 1972.

## Recordings:

Music for Saxophone Quartet (MHS 817; see M. Mule).

KIENTZY, DANIEL
b. Périgueux, France
13 June 1951

After studies at the National Conservatory in Limoges with René Decouais, Kientzy obtained a first prize in Saxophone at the CNSM in the class of Daniel Deffayet (1976) and a first prize in Chamber Music. He was awarded the Prix de la SACEM in 1983, has made a study of avant-garde music, and has written an essay on multi-sounds published by Salabert, where he is director of the collection "Saxophone." He plays all members of the sax family and has performed at various times with orchestras and on radio in the Paris area. His ensemble, Saxtuor, features all saxophone combinations from one to five performers.

## Publication:

Les sons multiples aux saxophones (Sal., 1982).

## Compositions dedicated to or created by D. Kientzy:

Eric Brabant (b. 1941): Saxodrome (1982, Sp.SATB, 1 perf., tape).
Anna Buczkowna: Hipostaza (1984-85, SAT, fl., vcl., vib., sop.).
Bernard Cavanna: La Vilette (1984-85, Sp.STBs., db., tape).
_____: Sax déminé (SA: 1 perf., TB: 1 perf., tape, sop., ten.).

Michel Celarianu: <u>Janvier</u> (1984-85, sax-s., fl.,
2 db., per.).  Sal., 1983.
_____ : <u>Ouverture</u> (sax, bcl., per.).
Gérard Condé (b. 1947): <u>Monarch of Gods and Demons</u>
(1983, all saxes, 1 perf., musical theater).
Michel Decoust: <u>Olos</u> (1984-85, sax-t., tape).
Yvonne Desportes (b. 1907): <u>Une fleur sur l'étang</u>
(1977, sax, hp.).  Dorn.
Bertrand Dubedout: <u>Cycle de Transparence</u> (1984-85,
sax, tape).
Alain Fourchotte: <u>Disgression III</u> (1983, sax solo).
Sal.
_____ : <u>Disgression V</u> (1984-85, sax-b. solo).
Gérard Garcin (b. 1947): <u>Enfin/après/elle arriva</u>
(Sp.AB, tape).  Sal., 1981.
Claudy Malherbe: <u>Non-Sun</u> (1984-85, sax-t., ob., bn.,
cl.).
Costin Miereanu (b. 1943): <u>Boléro des Balkans</u> (1983,
Cb.Bs.TSSp., 1 perf.).  Sal.
_____ : <u>Do-Mi-Si-La-Do-Ré</u> (1980, SATBBs., 1 perf.,
tape, film).  Sal.
_____ : <u>Jardins retrouvés</u> (sax, tape).  Sal.
_____ : <u>Kammer Concert No. 1</u> (1984-85, Sp.SATBs., ens.).
_____ : <u>Tercafeira</u> (1984-85, Sp. SATB, tape).
_____ : <u>Variant-Invariant</u> (sax, tape).  Sal., 1983.
Stefan Niculescu: <u>Cantos</u> (1984-85, Sp.ATB, orch.).
Horatiu Radulescu: <u>Astray</u> (1984-85, Sp.SATBBs.,
prepared pf.).
_____ : <u>Capricorn's Nostalgic Crickets</u> (sax, tape).
_____ : <u>Sky</u> (1984-85, sax, cl., fl., 2 bn., 2 db.,
per.).
_____ : <u>"X"</u> (1984-85, sax, cl., 2 bn., 2 db., per.).
Etienne Rolin (b. 1952): <u>Tourbillons</u> (1982, SA,
1 perf., per.).
Louis Roquin: <u>Machination VII</u> (sax ens.).
_____ : <u>Machination VIII</u> (1983, SATBCb., 1 perf.,
tape).
_____ : <u>Soli Solo et Solissimo</u> (1984-85, SATCb., tape).
François Rossé (b. 1945): <u>Level</u> (1983, sax, recorder,
fl., synth.).
_____ : <u>Quartz</u> (1982, 3 saxes).
_____ : <u>Sonate en arcs</u> (2 saxes, 1 perf.).  Sal., 1983.
Rudolf Ruzicka: <u>Tibia I</u> (1984-85, sax-s., tape).
Marc Tallet (b. 1951): <u>Mnémosyne et l'oubli</u> (1982,
sax, tape, 5').  Sal.
_____ : <u>Permutations pentatoniques</u> (1977, sax, fl.,
pf.).
Daniel Tosi: <u>Multitude No. 2</u> (1984-85, sax, Sp.SAT,
fl., vib., tape, 2 per., 3 soloists).
_____ : <u>Surimpressions II</u> (SATB, 1 perf., tape).
Sal., 1982.

<u>Recordings</u> (from Salabert):

Daniel Kientzy: <u>Saxophones et électroacoustiques,</u>

2 vols. (SC 003, music by Méfano, Levinas, Miereanu,
Borenstein); (SC 004, music by Miereanu, Tallet,
Tosi); Daniel Kientzy: Les Sons Multiples, 2 vols
(SC 001, SC 002, cassettes); Daniel Kientzy (Poly
Art Record PAR 5304).


KLOSE, HYACINTHE ELEONORE
b. Corfu, Greece            d. Paris, France
   11 October 1808            29 August 1880

     Arriving in France at an early age, Klosé joined a
military band and perfected his clarinet playing under the
instruction of Frederic Berr. After Berr's death in 1838,
Klosé became the Professor of Clarinet at the Paris Conservatory, a post he held until 1868. During this long tenure,
he was enormously successful in Paris as a soloist and
earned the highest praise; he rarely travelled and probably
never crossed the frontiers of France. Devoting all his
time to his many pupils, Klosé developed, with Buffet, a
system of clarinet fingering based on Boehm's principles
and similar to that of the saxophone.

     A skilled performer and composer of many pieces for
the clarinet, Klosé also took an interest in the saxophone,
took some lessons from Adolphe Sax, and wrote two saxophone
solos and several books for the study of the instrument.
It was Klosé who first taught the saxophone to his clarinet
student, L. A. Mayeur, in the 1850s. After his graduation
from the Conservatoire in 1860, Mayeur studied with Adolphe
Sax and earned much praise from Paris music critics for
his beautiful playing.

Compositions for the saxophone:

     Solo (1858, ded. to A. Sax, ed. G. Corroyez, 1926,
     Leduc, OP, PBN); Solo (1859, ded. to Monsieur Escudie,
     for Eb alto or Bb sop. sax, Sax, OP, PBN); Fantaisies
     on mélodies by Depas and Schubert (1869-1880, rev.
     Corroyez, Leduc, OP, PBN); Méthode Complète de saxo-
     phone (1877, rev. by E. Gay, Leduc, 1950); Méthode
     (2 vols., ed. Juijer, Mol.); Méthode Elémentaire pour
     saxophone alto (1877, Leduc, 1886, OP, PBN); Méthode
     Elémentaire pour saxophone ténor (1877, Leduc, 1886,
     OP, PBN); Méthode Elémentaire complète de saxophone
     baryton Mi bémol (1879, Leduc, 1886, OP, PBN); Mé-
     thode Elémentaire complète de saxophone soprano Si
     bémol (1881, Leduc, rev. 1886, OP, PBN).

     Klosé also adapted some of his clarinet studies for
the saxophone; these collections of studies have gone
through several revisions and the following are still
available:

     25 Etudes de mécanisme (first publ. 1881, ed. Mule,

1955, Leduc); 25 Exercices journaliers (1882, ed.
Mule, 1951, CF); 15 Etudes chantantes (1883, ed. Mule,
1948, Leduc); 20 Studies (Fox).


KREIN, MICHAEL
b. England, 1908                    d. England, 1966

The son of Jascha Krein, a famous Russian violinist,
Michael served his apprenticeship as a clarinetist.  He
was employed full time by the BBC for over 20 years.  He
also doubled as a sax soloist, arranger, and orchestral
conductor.  He formed his sax quartet about the same time
he joined the BBC (c. 1941).  Michael Krein and Walter Lear
have the distinction of being the first serious saxophonists of this century in England.  They worked hard to gain
respectability for the saxophone at a time when the general
public was rather narrow-minded about the instrument.
Krein had a great reputation as a wit and raconteur, and
could relate stories for hours on end to his fellow musicians without repeating himself.  The Krein Saxophone Quartet played quality performances of music in a lighter vein.
When Krein died in 1966, Jack Brymer took over the leadership of the quartet.

Compositions:

Serenade (NWM, 1960); Valse Caprice (SATB, c. 1930,
NWM, 1960, 5'); Krein's quartet library includes 17
original and 24 arranged works (for more information,
see J. Dawson:  Music for Saxophone by British Composers.  Dorn, 1981).



LACOUR, GUY
b. Soissons, Aisne, France
   8 June 1932

A student of Marcel Josse at the CNRM at Versailles,
Lacour received a first prize in 1950; at the CNSM in 1952,
he won the First Prize in the class of Marcel Mule, and
in 1956, the First Prize for Chamber Music.  He also
studied harmony and composition during his military service
and was invited by Mule, in 1961, to play tenor sax in the
famous quartet until it disbanded in 1966.  Lacour is now
a member of the Ensemble de Saxophones Français and a consultant for the Selmer Company.  A tenor sax soloist for
WSC meetings, he has performed in Paris with several orchestras and with Radio France.  He has recorded Ravel's
Boléro with von Karajan and the Berlin Philharmonic Orchestra.  Lacour has been a professor at the conservatories
of Genevilliers, Clichy, and the Fifth Arrondissement of
Paris.  In 1975, he was appointed Director of the Ecole
Municipale de Musique at Mantes-la-Ville.

Compositions:

>    Huit études brillantes (Leduc, 1963); Divertissement
>    pour saxophone alto et percussion (Bil., 1968); Pré-
>    cis pour l'étude des gammes (Bil., 1968); Quatuor
>    (Bil., 1969); Suite en duo (2 saxes, Bil., 1971,
>    10'10); 50 Etudes faciles (2 vols., Bil., 1972); 28
>    Etudes sur les modes à transpositions limitées d'Oli-
>    vier Messiaen (Bil., 1972); Hommage à Jacques Ibert
>    (sax, orch./pf., Bil., 1972); 24 Etudes atonales fa-
>    ciles (Bil., 1975); Pièce concertante (A or T, 13
>    instr./pf., Bil., 1976, prem. 28 July 1976, WSC, Lon-
>    don); 100 Déchiffrages manuscripts (2 vols., Bil.);
>    Tendre mélodie (A or T, pf., Bil., 1977); Noctilènes
>    (A or T, pf., Bil., 1985).

Compositions dedicated to or premiered by G. Lacour:

>    Pierre Hasquenoph (1922-1982): Concertino (sax-t.,
>        orch./pf.). Esc., 1976.
>    Serge Lecussant: Yesterday, Today and Forever (sax-t.,
>        pf.). Prem. 30 June 1979, WSC, Evanston.
>    Marcel Mihalovici (b. 1898): Chant Premier, opus 103
>        (sax in Bb, pf.). Heugel. Prem. 3 July 1974, WSC,
>        Bordeaux.

Recordings:

>    Music for Saxophone Quartet (NHS 817, see M. Mule);
>    L'Ensemble de Saxophones Français (Sonopress 70504,
>    music arr. from J. S. Bach for 3-8 saxes).


LEAR, WALTER
b. England                    d. Hereford, England
1894                          25 December 1981

    Lear came from a musical family (his father was an out-
standing clarinetist). For over 70 years, he performed on
the clarinet, basset horn, bass clarinet, and saxophones
in the Royal Opera House and the BBC (1930 to 1953), the
London Symphony and Royal Philharmonic (1954 to 1974), in
many other orchestras and chamber ensembles, and as a soloist. He was Professor of Saxophone at Trinity College
of Music for 50 years and influenced generations of pupils.
Disliking the term "doubling," he preferred to call himself
a "multiple player," and gave many distinguished performances of saxophone concertos. He played an original
Boosey and Hawkes Imperial bass clarinet with independent
speaker keys, preferring this instrument because it gives
the freedom to use the "wrong" speaker or the occasion
for harmonics. On retiring in the 1970s, Lear took up
water color painting and showed just as great a skill at
that.

Compositions dedicated to or premiered by W. Lear:

> Peter Racine Fricker (b. 1920): Aubade (4'). Schott,
> 1952.
> Joseph Holbrooke (1878-1958): Concertino in Bb, opus
> 88 (15'). B.H., 1928.
> Gordon Phillips: Recitative and Slow Dance (bcl.,
> pf.). Schott, 1950.


LEDIEU, JEAN
b. Breteuil, Oise, France
   2 May 1929

Ledieu began to study the violin at the age of six,
but switched to the saxophone and became a pupil of Marcel
Josse in 1945. Two years later he was admitted to the
class of Marcel Mule at the CNSM. In 1949, he received a
first prize. The following year, while in the chamber
music class of Ferdinand Oubradous, Ledieu became interested in the baritone sax. In 1953, the Deffayet Saxophone Quartet was formed, with Ledieu as the baritone
player. He has taught at several conservatories in the
Paris area, was the Professor at the Conservatoire National
at Beauvais in 1960, and is now Professor at the CNRM in
Nancy. He has performed at WSC meetings, both as a soloist
and as a member of the Deffayet Quartet.

Compositions dedicated to J. Ledieu:

> Alain Bernaud (b. 1932): Humoresque (sax-b., pf.).
> Prem. 11 July 1982, WSC, Nuremberg.
> _____ : Sonate (S,B). Prem. 6 July 1974, WSC, Bordeaux.
> Thérèse Brenet (b. 1935): Incandescences (1984, sax-
> b., pf.). Prem. 27 June 1985, WSC, U. of Maryland.
> Alain Margoni (b. 1934): Sonate (sax-b., pf.). Prem.
> 28 July 1976, WSC, London.
> Jean-Paul Rieunier (b. 1933): Volume 7 (sax-b.,
> winds). Prem. 6 July 1974, WSC, Bordeaux).
> Jeanine Rueff (b. 1922): Deux pour Trois (sax-b.,
> pf.). Prem. 11 July 1982, WSC, Nuremberg.

Recordings:

> (See Daniel Deffayet.)


LEMAN, PIERRIC
b. Roubaix, France
   28 April 1953

A student of René Desmons at the Conservatoire National at Roubaix, Leman was admitted to the CNSM in 1971
(class of Deffayet) and won the Premier Prix à l'unanimité
in 1975. In 1977, he won a first prize in Chamber Music.

He has played alto sax with the Quatuor de Saxophones Contemporain since its creation in 1975, has been a soloist
for Radio France, and has performed with the Concerts Colonne Orchestra.  In addition to solo appearances in several
countries, he premiered Vivienne Olive's Music (for two
saxophones and orchestra with Jacques Charles on 11 July
1982, in Nuremberg).  Since 1981, he has been professor at
the National Conservatory at Cambrai.

Compositions dedicated to the Quatuor de Saxophones
        Contemporain:

        (See Jacques Charles.)

Recordings:

        (See Jacques Charles.)


LETELLIER, ROBERT
b. St. Omer, Pas-de-Calais, France
   c. 1918

        A student of Marcel Mule in the first class established
at the CNSM in 1942, Letellier won a first prize in 1943.
Admitted to the Musique de l'Air, he became the solo saxophonist, and with three other saxophonists from the band
(Corbières, Lavoix, Violeau), he formed a saxophone quartet.

Compositions and Publications:

        Ballade (Mar.); 14 Nouveaux duos et trios (Mar., Mol.);
        40 Etudes de style (Mar., Mol.); Melancoly Song (Mar.);
        Pièce récréative d'après Gluck (3 saxes, Mar.); Re-
        cueil de Duos et Trios (Mar., Mol.); Tablature pour
        tous les saxophones (Mar.); 38 Etudes faciles pour le
        style et l'interprétation (Mar.); Méthode nouvelle
        (Mar., Mol.).


LIGER, DANIEL
b. Tours, France
   20 May 1950

        Liger was graduated from the Conservatoire National
in Tours in 1966 as a pupil of Alfred Lockwood.  He began
studies at the CNSM with Deffayet in 1967 and received the
Premier Prix, Premier nommé in 1970.  From 1970 to 1977,
he gave recitals in Paris and Switzerland both as a soloists and as a member of the Quatuor de Saxophones de
Paris, playing soprano sax (other members of the ensemble
are F. Caumont, alto; A. Jousset, tenor; and A. Legros,
baritone).  In 1977, he was appointed professor of Saxophone at Tours.

Compositions dedicated to the Quatuor de Saxophones de
    Paris:

    Patrick Choquet (b. 1947):  Quatuor de Saxophones.
        Prem. 24 Jan. 1975, Paris.
    Gérard Gastinel (b. 1949):  Cinq poèmes anciens (SATB,
        Mezzo-sop., pf.). Prem. 3 July 1974, WSC, Bordeaux.
    Roselyne Masset-Lecocq (b. 1950):  2 Pièces Brèves.
        Prem. 19 April 1977, Paris.
    Jacques Petit (b. 1946):  Saxorch.  Prem. 30 April
        1976, Paris.


LONDEIX, JEAN-MARIE
b. Libourne, Gironde, France
    20 September 1932

    As a student of Pierre Ferry at the CNRM in Bordeaux
from 1942 to 1946, Londeix was already developing into a
fine soloist.  In the class of Marcel Mule at the CNSM in
Paris (1951-1952), he won the Premier Prix and the Prix
d'Honneur.  He has become one of the world's most presti-
gious saxophone soloists, with more than 600 recitals and
orchestral appearances in Europe, Japan, and North America.
A charter member of the World Saxophone Congress, which
was established in 1969, he founded the As.Sa.Fra. in 1972
and was the principal organizer for the Fourth WSC, at
Bordeaux University in 1974.

    Londeix was Professor of Saxophone and Solfège at the
Conservatory of Dijon; he was Guest Professor at the University of Michigan in 1968; and since 1970, he has been Professor at the CNRM, Bordeaux.  He has had over 70 foreign
students at the CNRM; and in 1977, he founded the Ensemble
International de Saxophones de Bordeaux.  Several important
compositions have been dedicated to this ensemble, which
has performed in France, Germany (in 1982), and the United
States (in 1985).  Londeix has made over 350 arrangements
and transcriptions for saxophone, of which about 50 have
been published by Leduc, Jobert, Salabert, Schott, and
others.

Books, Compositions, and Study Materials:

    Exercices mécaniques (1961-1964, 3 vols., Lem.);
    Le Saxophone en Jouant (1963-1971, 4 vols., Lem.);
    Gammes conjointes et en intervalles (1963, Lem.);
    Le Détaché (1968, Lem.); Gammes et Modes d'après
    Debussy, Ravel, Bartok (1969, Leduc); 125 Ans de
    Musique pour Saxophone (1960-1970, Leduc); Planche
    des doigtés comparés des harmoniques (1971-1976,
    Leduc); Quatre Tableaux Aquitains (sax, pf., Leduc,
    1974); Méthode de Rythme à l'usage des instrumental-
    istes (3 vols., Leduc); Le Beau Dion (sax-t., pf.,
    Combre, 1976); Saxophon spielend leicht (2 vols.,

Schulz); De la Justesse d'Intonation (Leduc, 1981);
Music for Saxophone (Vol. II, 1969-1984, Roncorp,
1985).

## Compositions dedicated to J. M. Londeix:

André Ameller (b. 1912): <u>Azulerous de Valencia</u> (1965,
    sax, ww. quin.).
    _____: <u>Concertino</u>, opus 125 (1959, sax, strs., fl.,
    12'30). Phil. Prem. 29 Nov. 1959, Reims.
    _____: <u>Jeux de Table</u> (8'30). Lem., 1954. Prem. 4
    Feb. 1954, Barcelona.
    _____: <u>Suite d'après Rameau</u> (1960, sax, strs., ww.
    quin., pf., 9'). E.M.Tr. Prem. 17 Oct. 1960,
    Mainz, Germany.
Pierre-Philippe Bauzin (b. 1933): <u>Cinq Pièces Brèves</u>.
    Prem. 8 June 1961, Lyon. Composer.
    _____: <u>Concerto</u>, opus 18 (1959, sax, strs., per., 16').
    Composer.
    _____: <u>Poème</u>, opus 20 (sax, orch., 14'). Prem. 23
    Feb. 1962, La Rochelle. Composer.
    _____: <u>6 Esquisses</u>, opus 57 (1967-1968, sax solo).
    Composer.
    _____: <u>Sonata</u>, opus 15 (1959, 15'). Prem. 16 May
    1963, Dijon. Composer.
Conrad Beck (b. 1901): <u>Nocturne</u> (1959). Lem. Prem.
    1 April 1962, Bâle.
Jean-Pierre Beugniot (b. 1935): <u>Anamorphose</u> (ob.,
    sax, hn.). Prem. 6 March 1977, Bordeaux.
Edvard Hagerup Bull (b. 1922): <u>Sextuor</u> (1965, sax,
    ww. quin.).
Jacques Charpentier (b. 1933): <u>Concert No. 5</u> (sax,
    strs.). Leduc. Prem. 6 July 1974, WSC, Bordeaux.
Paul Creston (1906-1985): <u>Rapsodie</u>, opus 108 (sax,
    org.). Prem. 29 July 1976, WSC, London.
Edison Denisov (b. 1929): <u>Concerto Piccolo</u> (4 saxes,
    1 perf., per. ens., 22'). Leduc, 1982. Prem. 28
    April 1979, Bordeaux.
    _____: <u>Sonate</u> (13'30). Leduc. Prem. 14 Dec. 1970,
    Chicago.
Pierre-Max Dubois (b. 1930): <u>Concerto</u> (sax, strs./
    pf., 17'). Leduc,. Prem. 9 Oct. 1959, Bordeaux.
    _____: <u>Le Lièvre et la Tortue</u> (1957, sax, orch./pf.,
    4'30). Leduc. Prem. 4 Nov. 1958, Lyon.
    _____: <u>Pièces Caractéristiques</u> (16'30). Leduc.
    Prem. 16 Feb. 1962, Paris.
    _____: <u>Sinfonia da Camera</u> (sax, ww. quin., 17').
    Leduc. Prem. 14 May 1964, Dijon.
Marc Eychenne (b. 1933): <u>Sextuor</u> (sax, ww. quin.,
    12'15). Prem. 14 May 1964.
Aleksander Glinkowski (b. 1941): <u>Sequentia</u> (1971, 11').
Suzanne Haik-Vantoura (b. 1912): <u>Les Visages d'Adam</u>
    (sax, orch., 20'). Prem. 27 April 1966, Dijon.
Guy Lacour (b. 1932): <u>Hommage à Jacques Ibert</u> (1972,
    sax, orch./pf.). Bil. Prem. 27 March 1973, Bordeaux.

Leslaw Lic (b. 1930): <u>Concerto</u>. Dorn, 1983.
Ivan Markovitch (b. 1929): <u>Complainte et Danse</u>.
    Leduc. Prem. 13 Oct. 1964, Charleroi, Belgium.
Jean-Michel Meyer (b. 1910): <u>Novelette</u>. Schott,
    1962.
Jacques Murgier (b. 1912): <u>Concerto</u> (sax, strs.).
    E.M.Tr. Prem. 29 Nov. 1959, Reims.
Ryo Noda (b. 1948): <u>Improvisation I</u> (sax solo).
    Leduc. Prem. 27 March 1973, Bordeaux.
Julien Porret (b. 1896): <u>18e Solo de Concours</u>. Mol.
Hermann Reutter (b. 1902): <u>Pièce Concertante</u> (1968,
    11'30). Schott. Prem. Dec. 1969, Geneva.
Lucie Robert (b. 1936): <u>Strophes</u>. Dorn. Prem.
    April, 1978, Ithaca.
François Rossé (b. 1945): <u>Le Chêne Egaré</u> (sax solo,
    10'). Bil. Prem. 30 June 1979, WSC, Evanston.
Henri Sauguet (b. 1901): <u>Concert à Trois pour Fronsac</u>
    (fl., sax, hp., 12'). Prem. 24 June 1979, Fronsac.
    _____: <u>Oraisons</u> (4 saxes, 1 perf., org.). Bil.
    Prem. 29 July 1976, WSC, London.
    _____: <u>Sonatine Bucolique</u> (10'30). Leduc. Prem. 13
    Oct. 1964, Charleroi, Belgium.
Hans-Ludwig Schilling (b. 1927): <u>Sonatine</u> (sax solo,
    10'30). Bil., 1978.
    _____: <u>Trisax</u> (1978, ATB). Composer.
Maurice Thiriet (1906-1972): <u>Adagio</u> (5'). Leduc,
    1965.
Henri Tomasi (1901-1971): <u>Printemps</u> (sax, ww. quin.,
    10'). Leduc, 1963. Prem. 14 May 1964, Dijon.

<u>Compositions dedicated to the Ensemble International de
    Saxophones de Bordeaux</u>:

Pierre-Philippe Bauzin (b. 1933): <u>Folk-Rapsodie</u> (sax,
    chorus, sax ens., winds). Prem. 2 June 1978. Com-
    poser.
    _____: <u>5 Mouvements en Forme de Musique</u> (10 saxes).
    Composer.
Walter Boudreau (b. 1943): <u>Demain les Etoiles</u> (1980,
    12 saxes, 18'). Prem. 21 March 1981, Fronsac.
Jean Courtioux (b. 1931): <u>Les Quatre Eléments</u> (Ballet
    for 12 saxes, electric pf., per.). Dorn.
    Prem. 8 May 1981, Bordeaux.
Pierre-Max Dubois (b. 1930): <u>Hommage à Hoffnung</u>
    (Ballet for 11 saxes, per., 25'). Prem. 8 May
    1981, Bordeaux.
Viktor Ekimovski (b. 1947): <u>Cantus Figuralis</u>, opus
    32 (1980, 12 saxes, 14'). Prem. 5 Feb. 1981,
    Talence.
Arnaud Fusté-Lambezat (b. 1959): <u>Blanc et Noir</u>
    (1981, 12 saxes, 12'). Prem. 4 March 1982,
    Mérignac.
Michel Fusté-Lambezat (b. 1934): <u>Mouvements</u>
    (1978, 13 saxes, 13'). Prem. 8 April 1979,
    Bordeaux.

Nicolas Korndorff (b. 1943): <u>Musique Primitive</u>
(1981, 12 saxes, 26').
Trent Kynaston (b. 1946): <u>Corybant Bleu</u> (1979, 12
saxes).
Christian Lauba (b. 1952): <u>Devil's Rag</u> (1984, 12
saxes, 8').
_____ : <u>La Forêt Perdue</u> (12 saxes, 12'). Prem. 5 May
1982, Villenave d'Ornon.
_____ : <u>Mutation-Couleurs IV</u> (1985). Prem. 29 June
1985, WSC, U. of Maryland.
Jacques Murgier (b. 1912): <u>Suite Française</u> (1983-84,
12 saxes, 12'). Prem. 16 May 1984, Bordeaux.
Sergei Pavlenko (b. 1952): <u>Concerto Brève</u> (1980,
12 saxes, 15'). Prem. 5 Feb. 1981, Talence.
François Rossé (b. 1945): <u>Spath</u> (1981, 12 saxes,
16'). Prem. 6 July 1982, WSC, Nuremberg.
Henri Sauguet (b. 1901): <u>L'Arbre</u> (Ballet for 11
saxes). Prem. 25 May 1981, Bordeaux.
Ludwig Schilling (b. 1927): <u>Grande Saxophonie</u> (1979,
12 saxes, 13'). Prem. 8 July 1982, WSC, Nuremberg.
Composer.
Alain Voirpy (b. 1955): <u>Sylphe</u> (1983, 12 saxes, 10').
Prem. 16 May 1984, Bordeaux.

## Recordings:

Musique de chambre avec saxophone (Voix de son Maître
C 063-10734, 1970, and EMI-Japan AA 8703, 1971, music
by Beck, Charpentier, Hindemith, Jolivet, Koechlin,
Tomasi, Villa-Lobos); Debussy: <u>Rapsodie</u> (Vox-Candide
CE 31 069, 1972, with Luxemburg Orch.); Jean-Marie
Londeix (Voix de son Maître CE 12805, 1973, music by
Absil, Creston, Denisov, Noda); Debussy: <u>Rapsodie</u>
(Voix de son Maître CE 165-12791/6, 1974, with Or-
chestre National de France, "Grand prix du Disque");
Ensemble de Saxophones Français (Selmer LPL 4011,
1974, works of J. S. Bach, arr. for 3-8 saxes by Lon-
deix and Lacour, OP); Duets for Saxophone (Crest RE
7062, 1975, music by Telemann and Leclair, arr. by
Londeix); Jean-Marie Londeix and Anne-Marie Schielin
(Crest RE 7066, 1976, music by Delvincourt, Desenclos,
Milhaud, Robert); Jean-Marie Londeix and Lucie Robert
(Crest RE 7098, 1979, music by Finzi, Koechlin, Lou-
vier, Robert); Jean-Marie Londeix and Carmen Picard
(Société Nouvelle d'Enregistrement, Montréal, 1984,
music by Denisov, Gotkovsky, Hindemith, Pilon); The
Revelli Years (vol. 2, Crest CRS 4211, music by
Gershwin, Rimsky-Korsakov).


MAYEUR, LOUIS-ADOLPHE
b. Menin, Belgium               d. Cannes, France
   21 March 1837                   1894

(See Chapter 1.)

Compositions for Saxophone:

Mayeur wrote nine solos for saxophone and piano, but they are out of print. The following study material is still available:

> Grande Méthode (1896, rev. and expanded by M. Perrin, Leduc, 1963); Scales, Arpeggio Exercises and Studies in Interpretation (CF); 21 Studies (Fox); 10 Duos (2 saxes, rev. P. de Ville, CF, 1907); 20 Studies (rev. P. de Ville, CF, 1911); Grande Collection of Scales, Arpeggios, Exercises and Studies in Interpretation (CF, 1925).

MAZZONI, MASSIMO
b. Civitanova Marche, Italy
   28 November 1959

A student of Romano Mauriello, Mazzoni attended the Conservatory of Pesaro from 1978 to 1979 and studied with Jean-Marie Londeix at the CNRM in Bordeaux from 1980 to 1981. He has performed in recitals in Venice (Biennale Musica, 1979) and Turin (Teatro Regio, 1980). He has been a professor at the Conservatory of Fermo since 1982.

Compositions dedicated to M. Mazzoni:

> Ruggero Lolini (b. 1932): Solitudini Declinate (2 saxes). Prem. 27 June 1985, WSC, U. of Maryland.
> R. Paniccia: Study on sound variations. Prem. 22 Jan. 1984.
> Sergio Rendine (b. 1954): Ianua (2 saxes). Prem. 27 June 1985, WSC, U. of Maryland.

Recording:

> Spiegel (Fenit Cetra LMA 3002, Sep. 1979, music by F. Cetra).

MELZER, JACQUES
b. Lens, France
   1934

A student of Marcel Mule at the CNSM from 1951 to 1954, Melzer received the Premier Prix and the Prix d'Honneur. He is the Professor of Saxophone at the National Conservatory at Nice and founded the Ensemble de Saxophones Français. The ensemble played many concerts in France and other countries; its original members were J. Melzer, soprano; J. M. Londeix, alto; G. Lacour, tenor; and R. Audefroy, baritone.

Compositions dedicated to J. Melzer and R. Audefroy:

> Guy Lacour (b. 1932):  Suite en duo (2 saxes, 10'10).
>   Bil., 1971.
> Rudolphe Palombo (b. 1931):  Quatuor.

Recording:

> L'Ensemble de Saxophones Français (Sonopress 70504,
> music arr. from J. S. Bach for 3-8 saxes).

## MICHAILOV, LEV
b. Russia, 1928

When J. M. Londeix gave recitals in Moscow and Leningrad in 1970, he attracted the attention of the cultural
officials in Russia.  As a result, Lev Michailov, a clarinetist and saxophonist, was appointed the first Professor
of Saxophone at the Moscow Conservatory in October, 1972.
However, this institution still requires students to learn
to play the clarinet as their first instrument.  Michailov
performed at the Fourth WSC, at Bordeaux in 1974.

Compositions dedicated to L. Michailov:

> Viacheslav Artiomov:  Recitative I (sax solo).
>   Soviet Composers' Pub., 1978.
> Edison Denisov (b. 1929):  Deux Pièces (1974, 5'10).
>   Leduc, 1978.  Prem. 4 July 1974, WSC, Bordeaux.
> Alexander Feifman:  Romance.  Soviet Composers' Pub.
> German Lukijnov:  Quartet in Bb.
> Igor Katayev:  Sonata (1976).
> Boris Tobis:  Aria.  Soviet Composers' Pub., 1978.
> Alexander Vustin:  Autumn Sonatina.  Soviet Composers'
>   Pub., 1978.

Recording:

> Glazunov:  Concerto and Quartet (Odys./Mel. Y 35205,
> with Oseichuk, Vorontsov, and Eremin).

## MIJAN, MANUEL
b. Toledo, Spain
   6 January 1953

Studying at the Royal Conservatory of Madrid from
1970 to 1980, Mijan won several honors; his saxophone
teacher was Antonio Minaya.  From 1981 to 1982, with the
help of a scholarship from the French government, he
studied in the class of J. M. Londeix and won a first
prize at the CNRM in Bordeaux.  He has given numerous recitals in Madrid, appeared on radio and TV, and toured in
the provinces.  He was also heard at the Symposium Festival

in Belgium (1981) and the WSC in Nuremberg (1982). He is
saxophone soloist with the Bande Municipal de Madrid and
has taught at the Royal Conservatory of Madrid since 1982.
In 1984, the Alpuerto S.A. published his translation of
J. M. Londeix: Le Saxophone en Jouant (El Saxofón Ameno).

Composition:

Técnica de Base (Real Musical, 1983).

Compositions dedicated to M. Mijan:

Romain Alis (b. 1935): Ambitos, opus 135 (1982).
  EMEC, 1984.
M. Angulo: Bisonante (1983).
M. Balboa: Sombra Interrumpida (1980). EMEC, 1982.
N. Clément: Sonate (1983).
M. Davia: Quatuor (1981).
R. Diaz: Quatuor (1980).
F. Otero: Double Suggestion (1980).
D. Stéfani: Quintette (SATB, pf.). Alpuerto S.A.,
  1983.
Jésus Villa Rojo: Eclipse (1982). EMEC, 1983.
_____: Quatuor (1984).


MONDELCI, FEDERICO
b. Ostra Vetere, Ancona, Italy
  1958

Mondelci won the First Concours International Prix
Ancona 1978 and the Concours International de Stresa Prix
Franco Verganti 1979. He studied with J. M. Londeix at
the Académie Internationale d'Eté de Nice and at the Conservatory of Bordeaux in 1981, where he received the Médaille d'or à l'unanimité. In addition to appearances in
Italy and Bordeaux, he was a soloist with the Nuremberg
Symphony Orchestra at the Seventh WSC in 1982. He is a
professor at the Conservatory in Pesaro.

Compositions premiered by F. Mondelci:

Ruggero Lolini (b. 1932): Solitudini Declinate (2
  saxes). Prem. 27 June 1985, WSC, U. of Maryland.
Sergio Rendine (b. 1954): Ianua (2 saxes). Prem.
  27 June 1985, WSC, U. of Maryland.
Aurelio Sahori (b. 1946): Cadenze (1982). Prem.
  9 July 1982, WSC, Nuremberg.


MULE, MARCEL RENE ARTHUR
b. Aube, Normandy, France
  24 June 1901

Mule began to study saxophone at the age of eight with
his father, an excellent amateur musician and director of

a band at Beaumont-le-Roger (Eure).  He started to study
the violin at nine and the piano at ten.  As early as 1912,
he won prizes at Alençon and Rouen and showed much aptitude for musical performance.  His musical studies were
interrupted when his father sent him to the Ecole Normale
d'Instituteurs at Evreux in 1917; three years later, he was
appointed a teacher at Beaumont-le-Roger.  His military
service in Paris allowed him to renew contact with music
and he became saxophone-soloist in the 5th Infantry Regiment band for two years.  During that time, he was able to
study violin with Gabriel Willaume and harmony, counterpoint, and fugue with Georges Caussade; these studies made
an enormous influence on his future artistic career.

    In 1922, he met François Combelle, soloist with the
Garde Républicaine, who suggested that he audition for a
vacancy in that organization.  In 1923, at the age of 21,
he was accepted into the famous band; two months later,
he succeeded Combelle in the solo position, where he remained for 13 years.  At that time, saxophonists in Paris
were not using vibrato, which was heard in popular dance
orchestras on tour from America.  Although this vibrato
was experimental and often too pronounced, Mule was won
over and decided to develop his own style.  Rousseau says:

> Although Marcel Mule was not greatly taken with nonclassical
> music, he derived enormous benefit from his experience of
> playing jazz.  He became increasingly aware of the saxophone's
> potential power and versatility, and he experimented with vi-
> brato.  At that time, he used vibrato only during his after-
> hours jobs, never with the Guard.[5]

    By 1928, Mule and three of his colleagues from the
Garde Républicaine established the saxophone quartet instrumentation and began regular rehearsals.  They gave
their premiere on 2 December 1928 at La Rochelle.  The
original members of the Quatuor de la musique de la Garde
Républicaine, in addition to Mule as leader and soprano
sax, were René Chaligné, alto; Hippolyte Poimboeuf, tenor;
and Georges Chauvet, baritone.  By 1932, they added the
vibrato to their excellent musicianship, became widely
known, and were in demand for both radio and live concert
performances.  The personnel of the quartet changed very
little during its 40 years of existence; replacements over
the years included Paul Romby, Fernand Lhomme, Georges
Charron, Marcel Josse, Georges Gourdet, André Bauchy, and
Guy Lacour.  In 1936, the name was changed to Quatuor de
saxophones de Paris, when Mule, Chauvet, and Romby left
the Garde.  Shortly after 1951, it was changed again to
Quatuor de Saxophones Marcel Mule, to distinguish it from
other emerging quartets in Paris.  The early repertoire
consisted mostly of transcriptions, and the first original
quartets were by Pierre Vellones and Robert Clérisse.
When Alexander Glazunov composed his Quartet, opus 109 in
1932, he dedicated it "Aux artistes de saxophones de la

Garde Républicaine"; in 1936, Gabriel Pierné dedicated his
Introduction et variations sur une ronde populaire to Mule.
The quartet's 1937 recording of Pierné's composition earned
Le grand prix du disque.

    Starting in 1925, Mule gave numerous solo concerts in
France, England, Switzerland, Germany, Holland, Belgium,
and Luxemburg, creating and inspiring many new works.  His
orchestral engagements included appearances at the Opéra
Comique, where he played the saxophone part in Massenet's
Werther.  According to Mule, his first complete presenta-
tion of a concerto was with the Pasdeloup Orchestra on 16
November 1935, of the Concerto  by Pierre Vellones.  In
1958, he received one of the greatest honors of his career
when Charles Munch invited him to perform Concertino da
Camera by Ibert and Ballade by Tomasi in twelve concerts
with the Boston Orchestra.  During this tour Mule gave a
special recital in Elkhart, Indiana, which was an inspiration to American saxophonists.  Although he received many
offers for more tours in America and  Europe, Mule decided
to curtail his solo career in 1960, at the height of his
abilities, but continued with his sax quartet and his
teaching.

    At the age of 41, with a reputation as a virtuoso
well established, Mule was appointed Professor at the CNSM
by the new Director, Claude Delvincourt.  This was indeed
a historic moment for the saxophone, since many years had
elapsed after the termination of Adolphe Sax's class in
1870.  Hemke says, "In 1942 [Mule] culminated a system of
teaching the concert saxophone when he became Professor
at the Paris Conservatory."[6]  When he retired from the
CNSM on 1 January 1968, after 26 years, no fewer than 87
of Mule's pupils had received first prizes and were car-
rying on the high standards of the French school in Europe, Canada, and the United States.  In 1958, Mule was
made Chevalier de la Légion d'honneur, the highest distinction awarded for outstanding contributions in France.
As an early teacher of the saxophone, he was confronted
by a lack of suitable materials, and he arranged and
transcribed more than 100 classic studies from the early
repertoire of other instruments.  Many of these masters,
such as Berbiguier, Terschak, Rode, and Ferling, are still
available from Leduc and used throughout the world.  Mule
has also made excellent transcriptions of solos and sonatas from the Baroque, Classic, and Romantic periods for
saxophone and piano.  In these transcriptions, he preferred to keep the original solo part for the sax, and
transposed the piano accompaniment to agree with the Bb
or Eb instruments.  In addition to many solo and quartet
compositions dedicated to Marcel Mule, the following
solos de concours (commissioned for the termination of
studies at the Conservatoire) have been dedicated to
him:

| Year | Composer | Title | Publisher |
|------|----------|-------|-----------|
| 1943 | Henri Busser (1872–1973) | Au pays de Léon et de Salamanque, opus 116 | Leduc |
| 1944 | Paul Pierné (1874–1952) | Prélude et scherzo | Bil. |
| 1945 | Edmond Marc (1899–1982) | Pierrot et Colombine | Bil. |
| 1946 | Marcel Dautremer (1906–1978) | Tango et tarentelle | Leduc |
| 1948 | Claude Pascal (b. 1921) | Sonatine | Dur. |
| 1949 | Henri Tomasi (1901–1971) | Concerto (I) | Leduc |
| 1950 | Jean-Michel Damase (b. 1928) | Concertstück, opus 16 | Leduc |
| 1951 | Jeanine Rueff (b. 1922) | Concerto (II, III) | Leduc |
| 1952 | Henri Martelli (1899–1980) | Cadence, interlude et rondo, opus 78 | Esc. |
| 1953 | Robert Bariller (b. 1918) | Rapsodie Bretonne | Leduc |
| 1954 | Marius Constant (b. 1925) | Musique de concert | Leduc |
| 1956 | Alfred Desenclos (1912–1971) | Prélude, cadence et finale | Leduc |
| 1959 | Pierre-Petit (b. 1922) | Andante et fileuse | Leduc |
| 1961 | Eugène Bigot (1888–1965) | Prélude et danses | Leduc |
| 1963 | Pierre Lantier (b. 1910) | Allegro, arioso et finale | Lem. |
| 1964 | Roger Boutry (b. 1932) | Divertimento | Leduc |
| 1965 | Jules Semler-Collery (b. 1902) | Fantaisie caprice | Esc. |
| 1966 | Ida Gotkovsky (b. 1933) | Concerto (II, III) | E.M.Tr. |
| 1967 | Georges Dandelot (1895–1975) | Sonatine | Esc. |

## Additional solos and study material dedicated to M. Mule:

Albert Beaucamp (1921–1967): Tarentelle. Leduc, 1946.
Louis Beydts (1895–1953): Romanesque (3'). Leduc, 1935.
Serge Bichon (b. 1935): Jouons du Saxophone. Chou., 1969.
Jean-Robert Blanc (b. 1907): Aubade et Impromptu, opus 29. Bil., 1956.
Paul Bonneau (b. 1918): Caprice en forme de valse (sax solo, 4'). Leduc, 1950.
_____ : Concerto (15'30). Leduc, 1944.
_____ : Pièce concertante dans l'esprit jazz (10'). Leduc, 1944.

_____: Suite (7'). Leduc, 1944.
Eugène Bozza (b. 1905): Aria. Leduc, 1936.
_____: Concertino (15'). Leduc, 1938.
_____: Etudes caprices. Leduc, 1944.
_____: Improvisation et caprice (sax solo). Leduc, 1944.
_____: Pièce Brève (sax solo). Leduc, 1955.
_____: Pulcinella, opus 53a. Leduc, 1944.
_____: Scaramouche, opus 53b. Leduc, 1944.
Charles Brown (b. 1898): Arlequinade (7'30). Leduc, 1969.
Henri Busser (1872-1973): Asturias. Leduc.
René Challan (b. 1910): Concerto (20'). Leduc, 1946.
René Corniot (b. 1901): Eglogue et Danse Pastorale (14'). Leduc, 1946.
Maurice Decruck (1896-1954) and Fernande Breilh: 8 Pièces Françaises (17'). Bil.
_____: Sonate en Do# (1944, 16'). Bil.
Jules-Albert Douane (b. 1891): Capriccio. Lem., 1960.
Robert Druet (b. 1920): L'Ecole Française du Saxophone (3 vols., 1963). Braun/Bil.
Pierre-Max Dubois (b. 1930): Divertissement (10'). Leduc, 1953.
Vladimir Dyck (1882-1943): 1re Légende Hébraique. Bil., 1936.
_____: 2e Légende Hébraique (sax-s., pf.). Bil., 1936.
Jean Françaix (b. 1912): 5 Danses Exotiques (6'). Schott, 1962.
Marius-François Gaillard (1900-1973): Nuite Sobre o Tejo (3'). Bil., 1934.
Armand Heck (1878-1947): Concertino in G, opus 41, (4'). Combre, 1946.
Leo Laurent: King-Saxo (2'30). Bil., 1939.
Daniel Lazarus (1898-1964): Sonate (sax solo, 8'). Dur., 1948.
Paule Maurice (1910-1967): Tableaux de Provence (1954-59, 12'). Lem.
Jules Mazelier (1879-1959): Quick. Lem., 1953.
_____: Spleen. Lem., 1953.
René Monfeuillard (1886-1958): 2 Pièces. Leduc, 1938 (only the second piece, entitled Dialogue joyeux, is still in print).
Claude Pascal (b. 1921): Impromptu. Dur., 1953.
_____: Sonatine (8'). Dur., 1948.
Paul Pierné (1874-1952): 3 Pièces. Bil.
Julien Porret (b. 1896): Papillons, Caprice, opus 407. Martin.
Jules Semler-Collery (b. 1902): 10 Etudes Concertantes. Esc., 1964.
Henri Tomasi (1901-1971): Ballade (14'). Leduc, 1939.
_____: Concerto (18'30). Leduc, 1949.
Romuald Vandelle (1895-1969): Prélude et Gigue (5'). Leduc, 1958.

Marc Vaubourgoin (1907-1983):  6 Petites Pièces (1951,
11'). E.F.M.
Pierre Vellones (1889-1939):  Concerto in F, opus 65.
Lem. Prem. 16 Nov. 1935, Paris.
Heitor Villa-Lobos (1887-1959):  Fantasia, opus 630
(sax-s., 3 hns., strs., 9'45). SMPC, 1948.

## Saxophone Quartets dedicated to M. Mule:

Jean Absil (1893-1976):  1er Quatuor, opus 31 (1937,
10'). Lem.
_____ :  3 Pièces en Quatuor, opus 35 (1954). Lem.
Eugène Bozza (b. 1905):  Andante et Scherzo. Leduc,
1938.
_____ :  Nuages. Leduc, 1946.
Charles Brown (b. 1898):  Quatuor (20').
Roger Calmel (b. 1921):  Concerto Grosso (SATB, strs.,
per., 17'). Heu., 1956.
_____ :  Quatuor de Saxophone (1957).
Robert Clérisse (1899-1973):  Cache-Cache. Leduc.
Alfred Desenclos (1912-1971):  Quatuor (15'30).
Leduc, 1964.
Jean Dupérier (b. 1886):  3 Airs pour un soir de Mai.
Lem., 1936.
Julian Falk (b. 1902):  Prélude et Fugue (1949).
Jean Françaix (b. 1912):  Paris à nous deux (1954,
opéra buffa).
Alexander Glazunov (1865-1936):  Quatuor, opus 109.
Bela., 1932.
Georges Migot (1891-1976):  Quatuor (1955).
Claude Pascal (b. 1921):  Quatuor (17'). Dur., 1961.
Gabriel Pierné (1853-1937): Introduction et variations
sur un thème populaire (1936, 7'46). Leduc, 1938.
Robert Planel (b. 1908):  Burlesque (1942).
Jean Rivier (b. 1896):  Grave et Presto (1938, 8').
Bil., 1966.
Jeanine Rueff (b. 1922):  Concert en Quatuor. Leduc,
1955.
Florent Schmitt (1870-1958):  Quatuor, opus 102
(14'16). Dur., 1941. Prem. 3 Feb. 1943, Paris.
Jules Semler-Collery (b. 1902):  Arlequinade (1950,
13'). Marg.

## Recordings:

Since 1930, Mule has made about 30 solo and quartet
recordings in 78 rpm. and four LPs, which brought a profound awareness of fine tone quality and musicianship to
saxophonists in Europe and America. The following two
albums have been reissued and are still available:

Marcel Mule (Selmer, Paris, music by Bonneau, Bozza,
Creston, Dubois, Granados, Maurice, Tomasi); Music
for Saxophone Quartet (Musical Heritage Society MHS
817, music by Absil, Desenclos, Pierné, Rivier).

NET, JACQUES
b. Le Bouscat, Gironde, France
   18 February 1944

Net received a first prize from the CNRM at Bordeaux
as a pupil of Pierre Ferry.  He was admitted to the CNSM
in 1964 in the class of Marcel Mule and won the First Prize
in 1967.  He was appointed Professor of Saxophone at the
CNRM at Grenoble in 1972 and began the directorship of the
Orchestre d'Harmonie de Grenoble in 1978.  He has arranged
music by Bach, Bartok, and Gershwin for large saxophone
ensembles; the music is in manuscript form.

Compositions dedicated to J. Net:

> Gérard Gastinel (b. 1949): Concerto (sax, strs., 1984).
> _____: Improvisation II (12'30).  Chou.  Prem. 20 July
>     1978.
> _____: Suite pour saxophone seul.  Prem. 8 July 1982.


NOUAUX, MICHEL
b. Achicourt, Pas-de-Calais, France
   12 October 1924

After winning a first prize from the CNRM at Lille,
Nouaux entered the class of Marcel Mule; he won a first
prize at the CNSM in 1944.  In 1952, he was awarded the
Premier Prix à l'unanimité at the Concours International
de Genève, the only person ever to win this honor in Geneva.
He has been soloist at the Radio Française, the Orchestre
de Paris, and the Garde Républicaine Band.  While in the
Garde, he played the soprano saxophone with the Quatuor
de Saxophones de la Musique de la Garde Républicaine.  Other
members of the quartet were André Beun, alto; Bernard
Beaufreton, tenor; and Maurice Delabre, baritone.  In 1980,
he retired from the Garde and became the soprano saxophonist with the Ensemble de Saxophones Français, which includes Alain Bouhey, alto; Guy Lacour, tenor; and Roland
Audefroy, baritone.  Nouaux is Professor of Saxophone at
conservatories in Montreuil and Bobigny, was the advisor
for the saxophone manufacturers Couesnon and Yamaha, and
is now with Selmer.

Compositions dedicated to M. Nouaux, the Quatuor de Saxo-
     phones de la Musique de la Garde Républicaine, and
     the Ensemble de Saxophones Français:

> Maurice Bagot (b. 1896): Saxophonie à quatre (SATB,
>     9').  Ed. Cont.
> Aubert Lemeland (b. 1932): Arioso, opus 24 (1972,
>     SATB, 6').  Composer.
> _____: Epilogue Nocturne, opus 22 (1971, SATB, 8'15).
>     Bil., 1976.  Prem. June, 1972.
> René Nicolas (b. 1926): Passim (SATB, 8'35).  Ed. Cont.

Lucie Robert (b. 1936):  <u>Cadenza</u> (10'). E.F.M., 1974.
_____: <u>Tétraphonie</u> (SATB). Prem. 11 July 1982,
    Nuremberg.
Patrice Sciortino (b. 1922): <u>Agogik</u> (1974, SATB, 11').
    Chou.
_____: <u>Danse païenne</u> (1960, SATB, 4'20). Chou.

Recordings:

Quatuor de Saxophones de la Musique de la Garde Républicaine, 2 vols. (AFA 20.772, music by Bozza, Desenclos, Sciortino, Bagot; AFA 20.893, music by Bernard,
Bagot, Lemeland, Sciortini).


NOZY, NORBERT H. J.
b. Halen, Belgium
    9 September 1952


A student of François Daneels and Elie Apper, Nozy
received first prizes in Percussion and Chamber Music in
1973 at the Conservatory in Brussels, and the Diplome Supérieur de Saxophone from the same institution in 1975.
He also studied harmony and counterpoint at the Lemmens
Institute at Leuven and was a Laureate of the International
Gaudeamus Competition for avant-garde music in Rotterdam
in 1973. A member of the Quatuor Belge de Saxophones from
1972 to 1975, he has been active at WSC meetings and was
appointed Visiting Lecturer at North Texas State University
(1973 to 1974). He is presently a saxophone teacher at the
Maastricht Conservatory in Holland and at the Lemmens Institute of Musical Arts in Leuven. Since 1975, he has been
saxophonist with the Royal Guides Orchestra in Brussels
and, since 1983, Assistant Conductor; he is also a member
of the Saxofonia Ensemble.

Compositions dedicated to N. Nozy:

Peter Cabus: <u>Trio</u> (AT, pf., per.).
Claude Coppens (b. 1936): <u>Wheels within wheels</u> (1973,
    sax solo). CBDM.
François Daneels (b. 1921): <u>Quatre miniatures</u> (sax
    solo). Schott, 1982.
F. Geusen: <u>Saxo Trio</u> (AT, pf., per.).
F. Gyselinck: <u>Sorrow</u> (sax, vib.).
A. Van Belle: <u>Koan V</u> (sax solo).


Recordings:

Pro Civitate (Alpha SP 6011, 1970); Gaudeamus (Gaudeamus 73002, 1973). (For Quartets and Ensembles,
see E. Apper and F. Daneels.)

OLSSON, BIRGIT
b. Enköping, Sweden
   1956

    After leaving the Enköping School of Music, Olsson
continued her saxophone study at the College of Music in
Stockholm with Sölve Kingstedt (1974 to 1978). From 1978
to 1979, she was a student at the CNRM in Bordeaux in the
class of Jean-Marie Londeix. Olsson is presently teaching
saxophone at the Stockholm Institute of Musical Education
and the Enköping School of Music.

Composition dedicated to B. Olsson:

       Torbjörn Iwan Lundgvist (b. 1920): Concitato (1980,
          sax solo). Prem. July, 1982, WSC, Nuremberg.


OOSTROM, LEONARDUS VAN
b. The Hague, Holland
   17 July 1942

    A student of clarinet of Jolle Huckriede and of saxo-
phone of Adriaan Bosch at the Royal Conservatory in The
Hague, van Oostrom graduated in 1966 and was awarded the
Fock medal. Since 1969, he has been the soprano saxophonist with the Netherlands Saxophone Quartet; the group received the Johan Wagenaarprize in 1980. A teacher of saxophone at the Conservatories of Rotterdam and The Hague,
and of Improvised Music at the Amsterdam Conservatory, he
has led international courses and been soloist for the WSC
in London (1976). He has also performed with the Rotterdam
Philharmonic and the Concertgebouw Orchestra. Other members of the Netherlands Saxophone Quartet are Ed Bogaard,
alto; Adri Van Velsen, tenor; and Jacques Landa, baritone.
In addition to his quartet concerts, van Oostrom has made
a study of lighter saxophone compositions written between
1915 and 1940; he performs these novelties on the C melody
saxophone.

Compositions dedicated to L. van Oostrom or premiered by
    the Netherlands Saxophone Quartet:

       Hank Alkema (b. 1944): Sonatine (1980, 8'). Don.
       Dick Borstlap (b. 1943): From Here to Eternity (1966,
          6'). Don.
       Rokus de Groot (b. 1947): Kontur (1982, 25'). Don.
          Prem. 24 Sep. 1983.
       Otto Ketting (b. 1935): Symphony for Saxophones and
          Orchestra (1978, SATB, 6 hns., 5 tpts., 4 trbs.,
          tuba, pf., per., strs., 31'). Don. Prem. 18 March
          1979, Concertgebouw, Amsterdam.
       Tristan Keuris (b. 1946): Quartet (1970, 8'10). Don.
       Klaas de Vries (1944): 2 Koralen (1974, 5'55). Don.
          Prem. 5 July 1974, WSC, Bordeaux.

Recordings:

> Ragtime Sax (RR 0105, 1976, music by Wiedoeft, Dorsey,
> Alter); Netherlands Saxophone Quartet (CBS 71087 and
> 71094, 1979-80, music by Françaix, Glazunov, Dubois,
> Pierné, Rivier); Waterland Ensemble (WM 001 and 002,
> music by Loch Dekker); Jean Françaix: Paris à nous
> deux (Nonesuch H 71402, 1982, also quartets by Pierné,
> Rivier); Otto Ketting: Symphony for Saxophones and
> Orchestra (Donemus CV 8001); Netherlands  Saxophone
> Quartet (Donemus CV 8002, music by Keuris, Petersma,
> de Vries, Wagemans).


PAREILLE, PAUL
b. Tannay, Nièvre, France
   4 May 1926

Early studies in 1947 with Marcel Josse led Pareille
to the CNSM in the class of Marcel Mule, where he received
the First Prize in 1952.  In the same year, he won a Première Médaille in Chamber Music and was appointed Professor
at the Conservatory of Amiens.  In 1953, he was admitted
to the Musique de l'Air de Paris.  After he had performed
with various jazz groups (Henri Rossoti, Benny Bennet,
Jacques Helian, and others), a class of jazz studies was
created under his direction at the Conservatory of Amiens.
In 1968, he founded the Quatuor d'Anches Français (oboe,
clarinet, sax, and bassoon), and subsequently performed in
198 concerts, broadcasts, and tours with the ensemble.  In
1969, the Quatuor won the First Prize with Honor at the
Concours International de Musique de Chambre at Colmar.
25 compositions were written for Pareille and dedicated to
the quartet; 12 were published by Leduc, Editions Françaises de Musique, and Billaudot.  He founded and became
the Director of the Municipal Conservatory at Chatou in
the Paris area.  The Ensemble Instrumental Paul Pareille
(of 12 strings), which he organized in 1976, has presented
over 212 concerts to date.

Compositions dedicated to P. Pareille and the Quatuor
d'Anches Français (woodwind quartet unless otherwise
specified):

> Jacques Bernard (b. 1931): Dialogue d'anches (13').
>     E.F.M., 1969.
>     _____: L'Opéra de l'Espace (1970, ww. quar., speaker).
> Monic Cecconi-Botella (b. 1936): Ariette.  Combre,
>     1962.
>     _____: Silences (10').  E.F.M.  Prem. 5 Feb. 1972.
> Pierre Max-Dubois (b. 1930): Les trois Mousquetaires
>     (10').  Leduc, 1966.
> Marcel Goldmann (b. 1936): Hével II (1970, 10').
>     E.F.M.  Prem. 29 May 1972, Paris.
> Charles Jay (b. 1911): Andante (sax, pf., 8'40).

Lem., 1977. Prem. June, 1971, Epernay.
_____: Fantaisie burlesque (1962, 7'). Combre.
_____: Lied (1942, 6'). Combre.
Aubert Lemeland (b. 1932): Nocturne, opus 10 (8').
  E.F.M.
Alain Louvier (b. 1945): Cinq portraits et une image.
  Leduc, 1975.
Gérard Massias (b. 1933): Variations (1956, 8'). Bil.
Daniel Meier (b. 1934): Kuklos (12'). E.F.M.
Denise Roger (b. 1924): 3 Mouvements (11'). E.F.M.
Patrice Sciortino (b. 1922): Flammes (1979).
_____: Rapsodique.
Jules Semler-Collery (b. 1902): Quatuor d'anches
  (1964, 9').

Recordings:

Le Quatuor d'anches Français (Centre National d'art
Français M 10 009, 1974, Calmel: Cantata Liberté);
Le Quatuor d'anches Français (E.F.M. "O.R.T.F." 001,
1974, music by Cecconi, Goldmann, Lemeland, Meier).


PERRIN, MARCEL JEAN
b. Algiers, Algeria
  1 June 1912

Guided by his father, an eminent trumpeter, Perrin
studied at the Conservatory of Algiers and won first prizes
in violin, saxophone, harmony, and counterpoint. In Paris,
he studied with Marcel Mule and received the title of Professor d'éducation musicale. He returned to Algiers as a
teacher and concert artist. He formed the Quatuor de saxophones d'Alger in 1935, and gave concerts on tours and
broadcasts until 1962. In addition, he has toured with his
wife, the pianist Suzanne Perrin Valls, and has made orchestral appearances in Belgium, France, Germany, Holland,
Italy, Portugal, Sweden, and Switzerland from 1933 to 1980.
This long and impressive career has led to contacts with
many composers who have dedicated works to him. Perrin's
many compositions and his book, Le Saxophone, earned him,
in 1954, the award Officier dans l'ordre des Palmes Acadé-
miques. He was one of the earliest French saxophone soloists to bring the saxophone to audiences in many
countries.

Book:

Le Saxophone (1955, Edition d'Aujourd'hui, Paris).

Compositions:

Rêves (1936, Leduc, 1938, 2'45); Mirage (1938, sax,
pf./orch., Leduc, 1950, 2'30); Poème (1942, Leduc);
Berceuse (1941, Leduc, 1950, 2'); Elégie (1941, S/A,

pf., Delrieu, 1950, 2'); Mélodie (1941, S/A, pf.,
Delrieu, 1950, 2'); Arlequins (1943, Leduc, 1950,
1'50); Nocturne (1945, sax, pf./org./orch., Delrieu,
1959, 7'30); Fantaisie Tzigane (sax, orch./band, 1941,
Delrieu, 1959, 5'); Caprice (atonal étude, 1951,
4'50); Agilité (chromatic étude, 1951, 4'); Tourbillon
(technical étude, 1951, Delrieu, 1957, 4'); 22 Exercices Transcendants (Leduc, 1950); Technique du Saxophone (Delrieu, 1957); Bagatelle (1951, S/A, pf.,
3'10); Complainte (1951, S/A, pf., Combre, 1960, 3'15);
Esquisse (Dorn, 1983, 2'45); Mélopée (2'30); Reflects
(S/A, pf., Dorn, 1983, 2'10); Nouvelle Méthode (edit.
from L. A. Mayeur, Leduc, 1963); Cinq Pièces (SATB,
1941, Dorn, 1984); Evocations (1958, sax solo, Dorn,
1983).

**Compositions dedicated to or premiered by M. Perrin:**

Michel Buono (1899-1951): Concertino (sax, orch., 11').
    Prem. 18 June 1942.
Roger Calmel (b. 1921): Les Caractères (sax, fl.,
    pf., 15').
Henry Defosse (1883-1956): Bucolique Nocturne (7').
    Prem. 24 Jan. 1932.
    _____: Elégie (sax, ch. orch., 6'). Prem. 11 Sep.
    1952.
    _____: Gavotte (sax, ch. orch., 1'30). Prem. 21 Feb.
    1942.
    _____: Sicilienne (sax, ch. orch., 1'50). Prem. 14
    June 1941.
Marc Eychenne (b. 1933): Cantilène et Danse (sax,
    vn., pf., 13'). Bil. Prem. 25 Nov. 1961.
Raphael Génin (1896-1975): Sonate, opus 36. Prem.
    1 April 1969.
Guido Guerrini (1890-1965): Chant et Danse dans un
    style rustique (SATB). Prem. 17 Dec. 1946.
Manfred Kelkel (b. 1929): Concertino (16'). Prem.
    8 May 1961.
    _____: Lanterna Magica (sax, pf., per.).
    _____: Musique Funèbre (sax, orch., 9'). Prem. May,
    1960.
    _____: Rhapsodie, opus 12 (18'). Ricordi, 1961.
    Prem. 19 Aug. 1961.
Bernhard Krol (b. 1920): Antifona, opus 53a, (sax,
    org., 7'). BB.
    _____: Aria e Tarantella, opus 37 (12'). Hof. 1953.
    Prem. 22 Sep. 1962.
    _____: Elegia Passionata, opus 69a (1979, 8'). BB.
    Prem. 27 Sep. 1979.
    _____: Intermezzo amabile, opus 79 (4'30). BB, 1981.
    Prem. 7 July 1981.
    _____: Litania Pastorale, opus 62 (sax-s., org., 12').
    Sim., 1962. Prem. 2 May 1976.
Félix Loup (b. 1906): Pavane à un héro disparu (1939,
    SATB, 8'10). Prem. May, 1945.

Dominique Marchal (b. 1952):  Bonus est Dominus (sop.,
    sax, org., 5'). Prem. 15 March 1981.
_____: Sonatine (sax solo, 8'40). Prem. June, 1981.
Edward Michael (b. 1921): Pièce Brève (9'). Prem.
    16 June 1967.
Roland Saint-Aulaire (1886-1964): Visages d'enfants
    (SATB, 10'30). Prem. 12 April 1938.
Gilbert Vinter (1909-1969): Concerto Burlando (1962,
    14'). BMIC. Prem. 12 Oct. 1964.

Recordings:

Marcel Perrin (Colosseum COLOS Stm. 525, music by
Debussy, Martin, with Nuremberg Sym.; Ursina Mocette
M 2008, sax, org., at Wiesbaden with K. Weber; Link-
shaendle Records LR 0381, sax, pf.).


POLLIN, HENRI-RENE
b. Troarn, Calvados, France
   8 July 1921


    Polin began his studies at the Conservatoire de Mu-
sique at Caen on both clarinet and saxophone with Fernand
Blachet and received the First Prize on both instruments
in 1941.   In the same year, he was admitted to the CNSM as
a clarinetist in the class of Auguste Périer, but, in 1943,
he changed his emphasis to saxophone and was accepted in
the class of Marcel Mule.   Pollin became a member of the
Garde Républicaine Band in 1947.   In 1949, he won both the
Premier Prix and the Prix d'Honneur at the CNSM.   Since
1950, he has served as Professor of Saxophone at the CNRM
at Rouen.   He is also Director of the municipal band of
that city.   Since 1956, he has been playing alto saxophone in the Deffayet Saxophone Quartet, which has performed for many radio and TV broadcasts, concerts, and
tours in Europe, the United States and Asia.

Composition dedicated to H. R. Pollin:

Albert Beaucamp (1921-1967):  Chant Elégiaque.
Leduc, 1951.

Recordings:

Villa-Lobos:  Sextuor mystique (MUSIDISC 19 026).
(Also see D. Deffayet for quartet recordings.)


PORTE, GEORGES
b. Marseille, France
   1946


    Upon graduation from the conservatory of his native
city in 1963, Porte entered the class of Jean Guichard

at the Conservatory in Toulon, and a year later, received
the Premier Prix. In 1965, after studying with Daniel
Deffayet, he was admitted to the CNSM in the class of Marcel Mule; he received a unanimous first prize for saxophone
in 1967. Admitted to the Garde Républicaine, Porte also
performed with l'Orchestre d'anches de Paris and played
with the Paris Philharmonic and Lyric Orchestras of Radio-
France. After winning the First Prize at the Concours
d'Aix-les-Bains in 1974, he was soloist at that city's
festival the following year, accompanied by the string
ensemble of Radio-France. A member of the Quatuor de Saxophones d'Ile-de-France with Jean-Louis Bousquet, Daniel
Martin, and Maurice Delabre, he also performs with the
Quatuor de Saxophones de la Garde Républicaine and the
Quintette de Saxophones de Paris.

## Composition dedicated to G. Porte:

Paul Méranger: Solo 24 (1981, 7'15). Bil.

## Recordings:

Music by Paul Bonneau (Chappell Editions, sax, hp.).
(See A. Beun for saxophone quintet recordings.)


PRATI, HUBERT
b. Villerupt, M. & M., France
   25 June 1939

A student of Jacques Genvrin at the Conservatoire de
Metz, Prati studied with Marcel Mule and Daniel Deffayet
at the CNSM from 1961 to 1964. He was soloist in the
Concerto by Paul Bonneau in Metz in 1964 and was appointed
Professor of Saxophone at the Conservatory in 1968.

## Compositions:

L'alphabet du saxophoniste (beg. method, Bil., 1980);
17 études faciles et progressives (Bil., 1981); 29
études progressives très faciles (Bil., 1981).

## Compositions dedicated to H. Prati:

Félix Lemaire (b. 1927): Suite Brève. Bil., 1980.
_____ : Trois Pièces. Bil., 1980.


PRIESNER, GUNTHER
b. Burglzunstadt, Bavaria, West Germany
   13 November 1951

A 1979 graduate of the University of Würzburg, major-
ing in saxophone, Priesner studied with Richard Kätzel and
Jean-Marie Londeix. He has been a professor of saxophone

at the Fachakademie Konservatorium, Nuremberg, since September, 1982. He was the Host Chairman for the Seventh WSC, Nuremberg, in July, 1982, and was elected President of the Arbeitsgruppe Saxophon e.V. Priesner has participated in saxophone meetings in Brussels, Luxemburg, and Ghent in 1977, 1978, and 1980.

## Compositions dedicated to G. Priesner:

Helmut Bieler: Reprisen (sax, pf., per.). Prem. 17 March 1983.
_____: Sounding Colours (SATB). Prem. 28 June 1985, WSC, U. of Maryland.
Heinrich Hartl (b. 1953): Quartet, opus 16 (1984, 8'). Tonger. Prem. 27 May 1984.
Winfried Jentzsch (b. 1941): Maqam (1983, sax solo, 6'). Prem. 7 Nov. 1983.
Gottfried Müller (b. 1914): Sonate (sax solo). Sik. Prem. 14 Feb. 1979.
_____: Recitativo, Canzonetta e Fuga (SATB, 7'). Prem. 28 June 1985, WSC, U. of Maryland.


ROMBY, PAUL
b. Nouvion, Aisne, France
   26 November 1900

A student of François Combelle, Romby became a member of the Garde Républicaine Band and, in 1932, replaced René Chaligné as alto saxophonist in the Garde saxophone quartet. In 1936, he left the Garde, along with Mule and Chauvet, and the ensemble's name was changed to Le Quatuor de Saxophone de Paris. Romby retired from the quartet in 1945 and was replaced by Marcel Josse. Romby was a teacher, composer, and arranger of early twentieth-century sax literature. He wrote some twenty compositions (published by Paul Buescher) and a method (published by Margueritat); they are all out of print.

## Composition dedicated to P. Romby:

Julien Porret (b. 1896): Dialogue, opus 237. Martin.


ROTH, IWAN
b. Basel, Switzerland
   8 June 1942

Roth was a student of Marcel Josse at the CNRM in Versailles from 1957 to 1959. He attended the CNSM in the class of Marcel Mule from 1959 to 1961 and won the First Prize. He also studied flute with Robert Hériché and Gaston Crunelle before his appointment in 1970 as Professor of Saxophone at the Conservatory in Basel. He is a highly respected teacher, and his saxophone class

grew from 12 to more than 50 students, from Switzerland,
Denmark, France, the United States, Germany, Italy, and
Hungary.  From 1970 to 1980, Roth played over 800 services
with principal symphony orchestras in Switzerland, Germany,
and Austria.  On 9 March 1982, he was a featured soloist at
La Scala, Milan, for the creation of the opera La Vera
Storia by Luciano Berio; the performance included an eight-
minute ballet, accompanied by the saxophone, based on the
composer's Sequenza IX.  Roth also plays the soprano sax
and leads the Quatuor de saxophones suisse, which has given
concerts in eleven countries.  The other members of the
quartet are Michel Surget, Urs Schoch, and Jean Georges
Koerper.

Compositions dedicated to I. Roth:

> Luciano Berio (b. 1925):  Sequenza IX b (1980, sax
>     solo).  Uni.  Prem. 28 April 1981.
> Paul Creston (b. 1906-1985):  Suite (1978, SATB).
>     Sha.  Prem. 30 June 1979, WSC, Evanston.
> Rudolf Kelterborn (b. 1931):  Saxophonquartett (1978).
> Boris Mersson (b. 1921):  Fantasia, opus 37.  Kunzel-
>     mann.  Prem. 29 June 1979, WSC, Evanston.
> Jean-Charles Perrin (b. 1920):  Duo Concertant.  Bil.
>     Prem. 3 July 1974, WSC, Bordeaux.
> Lucie Robert (b. 1936):  Variations (8'20).  Bil.
>     Prem. 17 Oct. 1978.
> Armin Schibler (b. 1920):  Konzertante Fantasie.  Eul.
>     Prem. 26 Jan. 1979.
> _____ : Quatuor sonores.  Prem. 30 June 1979, WSC,
>     Evanston.
> Robert Suter (b. 1919):  Conversazioni concertanti.
>     Prem. 2 March 1979.
> _____ : Jeux à quatre (1977).
> Jacques Wildberger (b. 1922):  Konzertante Szenen.
> _____ : Portrait (7').  Uni.  Prem. 31 Sep. 1983.
> _____ : Prismes (1976).  Gehrig.

Recordings:

> Virtuoses Saxophon (Basilisk ST-7801, music by Bon-
> neau, Demerssemann, Milhaud, Robert, Wildberger);
> Saxophone Recital (Colosseum SM 640, music by Bozza,
> Denisov, Françaix, Hindemith, Milhaud); The Magic
> Saxophone (Colosseum 596, music by Bozza, Chopin, De-
> merssemann, Milhaud, Monti, Rimsky-Korsakoff, with
> Nuremberg Sym. Orch.); Musique de compositeurs suisses
> (Jecklin disc 568, music by Beck, Mersson, Perrin,
> Schibler, with orch.); Iwan Roth et l'orchestre radio-
> symphonique de Bâle (CTS. Pl., Moeschinger: Concerto);
> Quatuor de saxophones suisse (Basilisk ST-7702, music
> by Albeniz, Bach, Gibbons, Rivier, Suter, Tchaikovsky);
> Quatuor de saxophones suisse (Duraphon HD 388, Pfiff-
> ner:  Tentatio); Quatuor de saxophones suisse (Musica
> Helvetica MH 44 MS, Sutter: Jeux à quatre).

SAVIJOKI, PEKKA
b. Helsinki, Finland
   1952

   Savijoki began his saxophone studies at the Sibelius
Academy in Helsinki and continued at the CNSM in Paris
with Daniel Deffayet from 1973 to 1975. In 1977, he received his diploma with distinction at the Sibelius Academy. He is presently a free-lance artist and teaches at
his alma mater. In addition to appearances in Scandinavia, Savijoki has made solo performances in France, England, and the Netherlands.

Compositions dedicated to or premiered by P. Savijoki:

      Erik Bergman (b. 1911): Mipejupa, opus 96 (fl., sax,
         gui., per., 17'). Prem. 20 Nov. 1981, Helsinki.
         _____: Solfatara, opus 81 (1977, sax, per., 15').
         Pan. Prem. 16 Jan. 1978.
      Daniel Börtz (b. 1943): Monologhi 7 (1979, sax solo,
         8'). CG. Prem. 23 Oct. 1979, Stockholm.
      Eero Hämeeniemi (b. 1951): Chamber Music Book (1980,
         fl., gui., sax, per.). Prem. 6 April 1981, Helsinki.
      Paavo Heininen (b. 1938): Discantus III opus 33 (1976,
         sax solo, 13'). Prem. 11 May 1977, Helsinki.
         _____: Saxophone Concerto, opus 50 (30'). Prem. 29
         Aug. 1983, Helsinki Festival.
      Usko Meriläinen (b. 1930): Simultus for four (fl.,
         sax, gui., per., 16'). Pan. Prem. 1979, Hämeenlinna.
         _____: Sonata (1982, 13').
      Esa-Pekka Salonen (b. 1950): Concerto (22'). Hansen.
         Prem. 22 Sep. 1981, Finnish Radio Sym. Orch.
      Leif Segerstam (b. 1944): Episode No. 7 (sax, per.,
         10'). Prem. 14 Oct. 1979, Hämeenlinna.
         _____: Epitaph No. 2c (1977, 9'). Prem. 7 April 1978,
         Helsinki.
      Jarmo Sermilä (b. 1939): Contemplation II (1978, sax,
         tape, 11'). Prem. 3 July 1979, Hämeenlinna.

Recordings:

      The Virtuoso Saxophone (BIS LP 159, music by Creston,
      Hindemith, Jolivet, Koch, Maurice); The French Saxo-
      phone (BIS LP 209, 1982, music by Boutry, Françaix,
      Ibert, Milhaud); Saxophone concerti (BIS LP 218, music
      by Glazunov, Larsson, Panula).


SCHOLLAERT, LUC
b. Enghien, Belgium
   30 July 1949

   A student at the Conservatoire Royal de Musique from
1965 to 1974 in the class of François Daneels, Schollaert
won first prizes in Saxophone (1969) and Chamber Music

(1970). He has been soloist on the alto and soprano saxophones with various Belgian orchestras and is now involved
in music productions for Belgian TV. Since 1970, he has
been a professor of woodwinds, chamber music, and percussion at academies in Alsemberg and Brussels. A former
participant with the Quatuor Belge and the Belgian Saxophone Septet (directed by François Daneels) he is presently the soprano saxophonist in the Brussels Saxophone
Quartet, which first performed on 24 March 1969. The group
has appeared at international meetings in Colmar, France
(1970), Bordeaux (1974), London (1976), and Evanston (1979).
Other tours have taken the quartet to the United States
and Australia in 1977 and 1978, the latter tours including
concerts in Indonesia, Malaysia, Singapore, Thailand, and
India. Other members of the Brussels Saxophone Quartet
are Willy Demey, Christian Vangeyte, and Freddy Vanatten-
hoven.

## Compositions dedicated to the Brussels Saxophone Quartet:

The following Belgian composers have written works
which have been premiered since 1969 and are still in
manuscript form:

W. Carron, I. Ceulemans, F. Constant (b. 1910),
B. Couroyer, J. Decadt, R. Decancq, F. Engelen-Costy,
F. Nuyts, M. Poot (b. 1901), F. Quinet (1898-1971),
A. Souffriau.

## Recordings:

The Belgian Saxophone Quartet (LP Foon cw 1308;
LP Selection 5114).


TANGVOLD, ERIK
b. Norway
   3 June 1944

Tangvold studied saxophone with Frederick Hemke. He
now teaches in Norway and is a member of the Harald
Bergersen Saxophone Quartet. He performed at the WSC at
Northwestern University in 1979.

## Compositions dedicated to E. Tangvold:

Terge B. Lerstad (b. 1955): Saxophone Concerto No. 2,
    opus 171 (1984, sax, cl. choir).
Yngve Slettholm (b. 1955): Four Profiles for Saxo-
    phone Solo, opus 3 (1978, 14'). Lyche. Prem. 29
    June 1979, WSC, Evanston.
    _____ : Introduksjon og Toccata (sax, per.). NMI,
    1981.

Pierre-Max Dubois (b. 1930): <u>Dessins Animés</u> (1978, S,A, cl., bcl., 16'). Frost.

Composition dedicated to the Bergersen Saxophone Quartet:

Kristian Evensen (b. 1953): <u>Quartet for Saxophones</u> (1983, 10'). NMI. Prem. April, 1984.


TERRY, JACQUES HENRI
b. Ermont, France
   25 October 1922

   At age 15, Terry studied the clarinet and saxophone with Fernand Blachet at the Conservatory in Caen. Later, he was a student of the famous clarinetist Gaston Hamelin. In 1942, Terry was accepted at the National Conservatory in Paris in the clarinet class and in Marcel Mule's first saxophone class. After two years of study, he was called in the military service and sent to Germany. Returning to the CNSM in 1945, he won the First Prize in Saxophone at the end of the school year (1946) and became a member of the Garde Républicaine, playing tenor sax. He is an original member of the Daniel Deffayet Saxophone Quartet (since 1953) and has performed with the Paris Opera and other orchestras in France. With Deffayet, he has been invited to play with the Berlin Philharmonic Orchestra conducted by von Karajan. A respected teacher, he has been Professor of Saxophone at the Conservatoire in Argenteuil since 1968 (a class begun by Deffayet) and also teaches at the Municipal Conservatory of the 10th Arrondissement in Paris.

Recordings:

   (See D. Deffayet saxophone quartet recordings.)


TRIER, STEPHEN
b. Newbury, England
   13 March 1930

   Trier graduated from the Royal College of Music in London as a clarinet pupil of Frederick Thurston (1945-1950); he also studied the bass clarinet with Walter Lear (1947-1950). Trier was engaged as bass clarinetist with the Royal Philharmonic Orchestra under Sir Thomas Beecham; and from 1956 to 1968, he was a member of the London Philharmonic Orchestra. In about 1955, Michael Krein encouraged him to learn the saxophone in order to play some of the necessary saxophone solos, and since 1956, Trier has recorded most of the major orchestral saxophone parts. He is Professor of Bass Clarinet and Saxophone at the Royal College and also teaches at the Guildhall School of

Music and Drama. He translated Jean-Marie Londeix' Le
Saxophone en jouant (3 vols.) for Lemoine in 1974.

Composition dedicated to S. Trier:

>    Gordon Jacob (1895-1984): Variations on a Dorian
>        Theme. Emerson, 1973.


VAN GUCHTE, MAURICE
b. Monceau, Belgium              d. Brussels, Belgium
   1897                            1953

As early as 1924, Van Guchte was a soloist with the
First Regiment of the Belgian Guides. He was Professor of
Clarinet and Saxophone at the Conservatoire Royal de Musique at Ghent from 1924 to 1949 and served in the same
capacity at the Conservatoire Royal de Musique in Brussels
from 1950 to 1953. He was also a soloist in the orchestra
of the Chapelle Musicale Reine Elisabeth.

Composition dedicated to M. Van Guchte:

>    Robert Bréard:  Premiere Suite. Leduc, 1929.


VAPIROV, ANATOLY
b. Russia
   1946

While studying clarinet with P. N. Sukhánov at the
Leningrad Conservatory, Vapirov enjoyed playing the saxophone with jazz and variety groups. In 1975, he became
the first Russian to receive a first prize on the saxophone;
a year later, he was appointed to teach a five-year specialized diploma course in saxophone at the conservatory.
The resident specialist for the Leningrad State Symphony
Orchestra and the Kirov Opera and Ballet Theater, he is
also committed to contemporary jazz, and was voted the
USSR's number one tenor saxophonist. During an interview
with McCarraher, Vapirov said:

>    I am not concerned with the difference between contemporary
>    jazz and contemporary classical music, to me it is all fas-
>    cinating. . . . In my time I have studied classical music,
>    Dixieland, Swing, Mainstream, and Bebop Jazz. However, there
>    came a time when I had to finish with the old ways and begin
>    to experiment, but the basis of my experimental music is clas-
>    sical music and past jazz styles. [7]

In the same article, McCarraher reports some historic
background of the saxophone in Russia:

>    In 1904 Count Sheremetev (of Moscow Airport fame) employed
>    five saxophonists in his personal orchestra, who formed a

quartet.  There is then a gap till the 1920s when the saxophone,
as in the West, came into its own in dance bands, Music Hall,
the State Circus, and Variety.  The earliest Soviet recording
of the Glazunov Concerto was in the 1960s by Gebopgen. . . .
The Moscow Conservatory, according to Vapirov, has not followed
that lead [of specialized sax instruction] and insists on
students taking clarinet as their first instrument.[8]

## VENTAS, ADOLFO RODRIGUEZ
b. Amposta, Terragona, Spain
   31 January 1919

From 1932 to 1936, Ventas studied the saxophone with
Marcelino Bayer at the Municipal Conservatory in Barcelona.
Ventas returned in 1959 for additional study of the clarinet and saxophone, as well as other musical subjects.  He
received the First Prize with Honor for saxophone and clarinet in 1969.  Since 1959, he has been a soloist, mostly
playing the soprano sax, with the municipal band in Barcelona.  Although most of the conservatories in Spain have
clarinetists teaching the saxophone, Ventas specializes on
the instrument, and since 1970, he has been a professor at
his alma mater.  With three other teachers, he formed the
Barcelona Saxophone Quartet (the other members are Francisco Alias, alto; Salvador Lopez, tenor; and Juan Bonet,
baritone).  Ventas has been a pioneer in creating interest
for the saxophone in Spain, and composers have written
works for him and the Barcelona Quartet.  The following
have submitted unpublished works in manuscript form to
Ventas:

Salvador Brotons, Jordi Cervello, F. Fleta Polo,
Rogelio Groba, and Riba Rosa.

Ventas has made a number of transcriptions for saxophone
and has written three original compositions for sax quartet, which are unpublished.

Study material by A. Ventas:

Gimnasia Técnica y Mecánica del Saxofon  (2 vols.,
Quiroga); Huit Etudes (Quiroga); Arpèges (Boileau);
Chromatismes (Boileau); 28 Etudes-Caprice.

## VERMEEREN, JEAN-PIERRE
b. Roubaix, Nord, France
   21 September 1948

Vermeeren studied with René Desmons from 1960 to 1967
at the National Conservatory in Roubaix.  He was accepted
at the CNSM in the class of Daniel Deffayet the following
year.  In 1970, he received the First Prize in Saxophone
and became tenor sax soloist with the Musique de l'Air in
Paris.  At the WSC in Bordeaux, he premiered P. M. Dubois'

Triangle (for soprano, alto, tenor, and piano) on 4 July
1974; the composition was published by Rideau Rouge in
1975.  He has won the Bronze medal (First named) in 1970
at the Concours International de Genève, and the First
Prize at the Concours National d'Aix-les-Bains in 1977.
He performs with the Ensemble de Saxophones de Paris and
teaches at various municipal conservatories in the Paris
area.


VIARD, JULES
b. France                    d. France
   1890                         1935

    Formerly an oboist, Viard took up the saxophone and
specialized in lighter music, capitalizing on the novelty
and popular appeal of the instrument in the 1920s and '30s.
He was a vaudeville musician and performed at the Folies
Bergères and the Casino de Paris.  In addition to arranging music for publication, shows, and films, he was also
successful in producing and selling a few recordings of
arranged solos.  In an interview with Rousseau, Mule says:

> Perhaps the most amusing thing I recall of Viard is that he
> wished to play the saxophone with a vibrato but was not able
> to do so in the normal manner.  So he produced a kind of undu-
> lation by sitting down and moving his knees rapidly while he
> played, causing a somewhat regular movement of the saxophone
> that he called a vibrato.[9]

Many of Viard's arrangements are still available from
Leduc, Durand, and Salabert.  The following were arranged
for alto or tenor sax and piano:

> Ravel: Pièce en forme de Habanera (Leduc, 1930);
> Debussy: La Fille aux cheveux de lin;  La Plus que
> Lente (Dur., 1931); Leoncavallo:  Aubade; Friml:
> Indian Love Call (Sal., 1939).


Compositions published by Salabert:

> 3 Oeuvres originales (Scherzetto, Menuet, Ecossaise,
> A/T sax, 1935); Grande Méthode de Saxophone (1935);
> Variations sur "Le Carnaval de Venise;" Jota; Sicil-
> ienne; Tarentelle; Douce Berceuse; Rondo; Capriccio;
> Slap and Laugh; La Dernière Rose d'été (c. 1935).


Compositions dedicated to J. Viard:

> Manuel Rosenthal (b. 1904):  Saxophon' Marmelade (sax,
>     orch./pf.).  Esc., 1929.
> Joseph Strimer (1881-1962):  Orientale.  Leduc, 1933.
> _____ :  Sérénade (sax-t., pf.).  Leduc, 1933.

VRIES, JULES HENDRIK DE
b. Amsterdam, Holland          d. Karlstad, Sweden
   17 December 1905              5 December 1981

When de Vries was two, his family moved to Germany,
where his father, a flutist, was engaged to play in the
Berlin Opera. At the age of six, de Vries started his
musical education with the piano; from age 10 to 17 he
studied the cello with the Russian cellist Alexander Schus-
ter. De Vries grew up in a musical family (his mother was
a fine violinist) and sang in several choirs. He always
felt that he belonged in music, and, in 1922, he attended
the Musicalische Hochschule. Because of inflation and political unrest, the family moved to Norway in 1924. Shortly
after this, Jules's father left for the United States to
play at the Metropolitan Opera. It was about this time
that Jules studied the clarinet with B. Valdar in Oslo; he
also worked as a jazz musician and often sang in theaters.
He was one of the first European musicians to play the famous glissando solo for clarinet in Gershwin's Rhapsody in
Blue.

His desire to perform on an instrument resembling the
human voice led de Vries to a career as a saxophonist.
Without formal instruction, he taught himself the saxophone.
He had his own quartet from 1932 to 1939; and in 1936, he
began his radio debut as a saxophone soloist. When Norway
was invaded by the German army in 1942, de Vries fled to
Sweden.

After studying with Marcel Mule in Paris from 1946 to
1948, de Vries began a busy and successful career as a saxophonist, as both a recitalist and an orchestral soloist.
He toured continuously for six years, performing a size-
able repertoire. He recorded eighteen concerts for radio
broadcasts in all of the Central European countries, but
not in England (which would not grant him a work permit).
In 1954, he became afflicted with a severe cramp in his
jaw, which brought an end to his intensive six-year career
as a saxophone soloist.

De Vries then returned to Sweden and played cello as
a principal in orchestras and toured the Scandinavian
countries performing chamber music. He continued to teach
cello and saxophone, and his active life and love of people gave him great insight as a teacher. He also had considerable success leading a youth orchestra in his home
city of Karlstad.

Compositions dedicated to J. de Vries:

    Henk Badings (b. 1907): Cavatina (sax-s., pf., 5').
       Don., 1952.
    Göte Carlid (1920-1953): Triad (1950, 5'). STIM.
    Lex van Delden (b. 1919): Sonatina, opus 36 (1952). Don.

Esteban Eithler (1913-1960): Concerto. Prem. season
of 1953-54.
Hans Gál (b. 1890): Suite, opus 102b. Sim., 1973.
Wolfgang Jacobi (1894-1972): Aria (sax, orch.).
Sven-Eric Johanson (b. 1919): Fem expressioner
(1950, 5'). STIM. Prem. 16 Dec. 1950.
Maurice Karkoff (b. 1927): Nio Solominatyrer, opus 8b
(sax solo, 6'30). STIM.
_____: Rapsodisk Fantasi, opus 8a (1953, 4'). STIM.
Friedrich Leinert (b. 1908): Sonate (1952, 12'30).
Br.H.,1956.
Walter Lessing: Concertino (sax, pf., orch.). Prem.
season of 1953-54.
Günter Raphael (1903-1960): Concertino, opus 71
(1951, 16'). Br.H.
_____: Divertissement, opus 74 (1953, sax, vcl.,
13'30). Br.H.
_____: Recitatif (1958, 4'). Leduc.
Lars-Eric Sanner (b. 1926): Sonatin (1954). STIM.
Erwin Schulhoff (1894-1942): Hot Sonate (1930).
Schott.
Eduard Tubin (b. 1905): Sonate (1951, 14'). STIM.
Hans Zender (b. 1936): Concertino, opus 5 (1952).
Br.H. Prem. season of 1953-54.

Recording:

Debussy: Rapsodie (Lyrichord Lyr LP 738 E, with
Frankenland State Symphony).


VRHOVNIK, OTO
b. Dravograd, Yugoslavia
10 September 1950

After studies at the Conservatory of Marburg, Yugoslavia, Vrhovnik attended the Hochschule für Musik in Graz, Austria, where he received a diploma. In 1978, he studied in Paris at the Ecole Normale with Roland Audefroy, and a year later, he received the Licence de Concert. Additional studies followed at the summer Académie Internationale in Nice in 1981, with Jean-Marie Londeix, and in 1982, with Daniel Deffayet. Vrhovnik was appointed Professor of Saxophone at the Steiermark Regional Conservatory in Graz in 1979, and in October, 1985, he was guest professor at the Musikhochschule in Vienna. He has been heard in concerts and radio broadcasts in Austria, Italy, Yugoslavia, and Bulgaria, and participated in the WSC meetings in Evanston and Nuremberg.

Compositions dedicated to O. Vrhovnik:

Lilcho Borisov (b. 1925): Concertino (sax, orch).
Prem. 11 Feb. 1984, Sofia Bulgaria.

Eugen Brixel (b. 1939): Saxophonissimo (sax solo).
Prem. Nov., 1983, Sofia, Bulgaria.
_____: 3 Bagatellen. Prem. Nov., 1983, Sofia, Bul-
garia.
Franz Cibulka (b. 1946): Capriccio. Prem. 4 Oct.
1980, Graz, Austria.
_____: Kaleidoskop (sax, orch.). Prem. 1982, Austria.
_____: Saxophone Quartet No. 1. Prem. 26 Nov. 1984,
Graz, Austria.
_____: Saxophonic (sax, orch.). Prem. 15 June 1981,
Graz, Austria.
_____: Solo (sax, tape). Prem. 9 July 1982, Nurem-
berg.
Victor Fenigstein (b. 1924): Memento et Epitaphe.
Kunzelmann, 1980. Prem. 9 July 1982, Nuremberg.
Karl Haidmayer (b. 1927): Concerto No. 1 (sax, winds).
Prem. 24 June 1980, Graz, Austria.
_____: Concerto No. 2 (sax, orch.). Prem. Nov.,
1981, Varna, Bulgaria.
_____: Duet (sax-sp., sax-bs.).
_____: Impromptu (sax solo). Prem. Nov., 1980, Graz,
Austria.
_____: Romaneasca 8 (sax-s., pf.). Prem. 9 July
1982, Nuremberg.
_____: Saxophone Quartet.
_____: Saxophonie 10 (sax septet). Prem. 1982,
Austria.
_____: Sonata No. 1 (sax-s., pf.).
David Johnston (b. 1931): Ballade (sax, wind). Prem.
24 Nov. 1984, Kufstein, Austria.
_____: Duo. Prem. 4 Oct. 1980, Graz, Austria.
_____: Konzert (sax, orch.). Prem. 23 May 1982,
Graz, Austria.
_____: Tut Suite (sax septet). Prem. 1983, Graz,
Austria.
Hannes Kuergel (b. 1906): Konzert (sax, winds, male
choir).
Ladislav Lesko (b. 1932): Intrada (sax septet).
Prem. Oct. 1982, Eisenstaad, Austria.
Gerhard Präsent (b. 1957): Solo für Saxophon (4').
Prem. 3 June 1980, Graz, Austria.


WUILLE, HENRI
b. Antwerp, Belgium          d. Baden, Germany
   1822                         1871


The son of a German instrument maker, Wuille studied
clarinet with Valentin Bender, a bandmaster of the "Guides"
in Brussels, who also taught Adolphe Sax. Before leaving
his native country, Wuille played in the Guides' Band.
Later he became a soloist in the private band of the king
of Belgium. He presented a series of successful recitals
in England and, according to Weston, featured an obligado
(on 2 June 1852) for bass clarinet in a song by Frank Mori

and "a Fantasia of his own composition upon the saxophone, one of the most remarkable instruments of M. Sax's invention, with which the audience was particularly pleased."[9]

The following year, he was engaged as a soloist by Jullien and continued to play concerts and tours with him until 1856. (For information about Wuille's debut on saxophone in the United States, see chapter 3.)

Wuille left England and his engagements with Jullien and, after a short sojourn in Paris, settled in Strasbourg, where he taught clarinet at the Conservatoire. The library of that city has programs of his recitals from 1856 to 1863. Hemke quotes a letter from Georges Kastner to the editor of the Revue et Gazette Musicale of a concert in Baden on 6 July 1858, which featured a solo for saxophone played by Wuille:

> Mr. Wuille, moreover, produced marvelous effects on the saxophone and possesses the true sound of that instrument, an advantage often denied to clarinetists . . . he does not deprive himself of useful innovations, but he has become one of the most ardent propagators of the saxophone. . . . I should not forget to add that the piece which I heard played was perfectly chosen for the instrument as well as the performer. This was a Fantasy, especially composed for Baden, on the themes from Martha.[11]

Composition dedicated to H. Wuille:

Jules Demerssemann (1833-1866): Fantaisie sur un thème original (c. 1860), opus Posth. Cos. (OP).

# 8.

# Annotated Bibliography of Saxophone Soloists in Japan and Australia

AMADIO, CLIVE
b. Australia               d. Australia
   Unknown                    21 October 1983

     Born into a family of woodwind players, Amadio first studied the flute, and after a short time, switched to the clarinet.  When the Australian Broadcasting Commission formed its first Symphony Orchestra, Amadio became Principal Clarinet.  After World War II, he formed his own Light Musical Ensemble with four other performers, who also doubled, and began broadcasting a series of weekly programs which lasted for twenty years--the longest-running light music ensemble in the history of the Australian Broadcasting Co.  In November, 1946, he performed Debussy's Rapsodie; this was the first time a saxophone was featured with an Australian symphony orchestra.  Later he gave the first performances of many other standard saxophone works. Amadio recorded programs for the B.B.C. in London, Radio Madrid, Rot-Weiss-Rot in Vienna, and the Radiodiffusion in Paris. In 1941, he was invited to become Professor of Clarinet and Saxophone at the Sydney Conservatory of Music, and in 1980, he was awarded the Order of Australia by Queen Elizabeth.

## Compositions dedicated to C. Amadio:

     Dulcie Holland (b. 1926):  Aria (1952, sax, strs., 5').  Composer.
       _____: Sax-Happy (1958, sax solo, 3').  Composer.
       _____: Shy One (1956).
       _____: Sonata (1953, 12').  Composer.

CLINCH, PETER G.
b. Geraldton, Western Australia
   26 June 1930

     Clinch began his musical studies at the age of nine.
He completed his professional training at the University of
Western Australia in Perth, where he received the B.M. in
1970 and the M.M. in 1974.  He was awarded the Ph.D. in
Musical Acoustics (1980) at Monash University.  His multiple talents include classical and jazz performance in both
saxophone and clarinet and compositional skills.  A featured performer at WSC conferences in France, England,
Germany, and the United States, he is well known for his
clinics and solo presentations.  He is a Senior Lecturer
at the Conservatory at Melbourne State University and performs with Australia Felix, an avant-garde ensemble.

Publications:

     Clarinet Tutor (Allans, 1976); several arrangements
     and transcriptions for clarinet and saxophone (pub-
     lished in Australia).

Compositions dedicated to P. Clinch:

     Geoffrey D'Ombrain:  Introspections (1975, sax, tape).
     Eric Gross (b. 1926):  Three Bagatelles, opus 96
          (sax solo).  Leeds, 1976.
     John Hawker:  Checkmate (1976).
     Dulcie Howland (b. 1926):  Saturday Stroll.  Allans.
     William Lovelock (b. 1899):  Saxophone Quartet (1977).
          :  Sonata (1974, 18').  Albert.  Prem. 4 July
          1974, WSC, Bordeaux.
     James Penberthy (b. 1917):  Concerto (1970, 10').
     Larry Sitsky:  Amenia: a suite (sax solo).  Prem.
          28 June 1985, WSC, U. of Maryland.
     Margaret Sutherland:  Quartet (1965, sax, str. trio).
     Felix Werder (b. 1922):  Dramaturgy (sax, orch.).
          :  Saxtronic, opus 135 (1973, sax, ch. orch., 18').

Recordings:

     Australian Festival of Music Vol. 9 (Festival 27019,
     music by Penberthy); Music by Felix Werder, Vol. 3
     (Readings GYS 004, 1980); Australian Saxophone Music
     (W & G, 1976, music by Lovelock).


FRASER, PETER
b. Adelaide, South Australia
   15 December 1927

     A pioneer of classical saxophone, Peter Fraser has
done much to promote the saxophone as a serious instrument
in Australia.  In 1935, he started taking piano lessons,
and after hearing someone play semi-classical music on the

saxophone, he borrowed an instrument and a book, and set about teaching himself. An avid listener of saxophone playing, he was enthralled when Marcel Mule's records became available. During World War II, he played in army camps and hospitals, and although there was not much music available in Australia for his instrument, he transcribed many pieces from existing flute, violin, and piano repertoire.

In 1948, Fraser was the first saxophonist to play in the Australian State Final Concerto Competition organized by the Australian Broadcasting Commission. He gave many recitals for the A.B.C., and in the 1950s was busy with commercial radio work. Also active in choir, opera, and oratorio, he was Deputy Conductor of the Adelaide Choral Society. In 1957, he formed the Adelaide Saxophone Quartet, which became the first ensemble in Australia to play the quartet repertoire. Although the quartet is not as active today, the personnel has remained nearly the same; other members of the quartet are Kenneth Wooldridge, Wallis Mac Kinnon, and Maurice Le Doeuff. In 1960, Fraser began a long association with the Adelaide Symphony Orchestra, where he appears as a soloist and plays saxophone parts when required. The high point of his career has been the Australian premiere of Jindrich Feld's Concerto with the Adelaide Symphony, followed by a performance of the same work at the Sydney Opera House with the Sydney Symphony.

In 1983, Fraser became the saxophone teacher at the Collegiate School of St. Peter, and in 1985, he was appointed as a saxophone tutor for the National Music Camp, the training ground for the Australian Youth Orchestra.

ICHIKAWA, YUTAKA
b. Tokyo, Japan
   20 July 1955
     After studies with Yushi Ishiwata at the Kunitachi Music College in Tokyo (1974-78), and the CNRM, Bordeaux, with J. M. Londeix (1978-80), Ichikawa gave his first recital in Tokyo in 1981. A member of the Tokyo Saxophone ensemble, he has taught at the Musashino Music Academy in Tokyo since 1983.

Compositions dedicated to Y. Ichikawa:

   Ryuichi Suenaga (b. 1949): Concerto (sax, band).
        Prem. 10 Oct. 1982.
   _____: Romance (sax solo). Prem. 20 April, 1981, Tokyo.

MUNESADA, KEIJI
b. Fukui, Japan
   18 April 1949
     Munesada studied with Yuichi Omuro at the Kunitachi Music College in Tokyo from 1971 to 1975, and became a

professor of saxophone at the Showa Music College in Atsugi
in 1975. From 1976 to 1978, he studied additionally with
J. M. Londeix at the CNRM in Bordeaux. Munesada was heard
at the WSC in Evanston and he performed Tomasi's Concerto
with the Munich Radio Orchestra at the WSC in Nuremberg on
9 July 1982. He has premiered compositions by Chatman,
Creston, Denisov, and Sauguet in Japan, and performs with
the Tokyo Saxophone Ensemble.

Compositions dedicated to K. Munesada:

> Taduoki Ishihara (b. 1939): Succession (sax, 6 per.).
>     Prem. Oct., 1980.
> Toru Nakamura (b. 1958): Spiritual Song from Small
>     Island (SATB). Prem. 10 July 1982, WSC, Nuremberg.
> Junich Nihashi (b. 1950): 3rd Adagio. Prem. 21
>     Feb. 1984.
> Toshiyuki Ogata (b. 1955): Bleu (sax solo). Prem.
>     21 Feb. 1984.
> Tadashi Yamanouchi: Correlation (mar., sax, db.).
>     Prem. 1 July 1979, WSC, Evanston.


MUTO, KEN-ICHIRO
b. Japan
    16 April 1952

A student of Daniel Deffayet, Muto was awarded a first
prize at the CNSM in 1977. He was one of the Laureate
winners at the Concours International de Saxophone at Gap,
France, in 1979, and a soloist at the WSC held in Evanston
in June of the same year.

Composition dedicated to K. Muto:

> Ichiro Nodaira: Arabesque II (sax solo, 10'). Lem.
>     1983.

Recording:

> Ken-ichiro Muto (FONC 5042, music by Maurice and
> others).


NODA, RYO
b. Amagasaki, Japan
    17 October 1948

From 1968 to 1972, Noda attended the Osaka College of
Music and studied with Arata Sakaguchi. Subsequent studies
took him to Northwestern University, as a pupil of Frederick Hemke (1973-75), and the CNRM at Bordeaux, with J.
M. Londeix. While his repertoire includes literature from
baroque, classic, and romantic periods, he is particularly
brilliant in his avant-garde improvisations and inventive

techniques for the saxophone.  He has been soloist at festivals and concerts in France, Belgium, Holland, Sweden,
Norway, England, Canada, Japan, and The United States.
He won the SACEM Prize for Composition in 1973; his works
for wind instruments are noted for their successful blend
of Japanese and Western art forms.  Many of these compositions have already achieved a permanent position in the
standard repertoire of concert saxophonists.

Compositions:

> Improvisation 1, 2, 3 (1972, 1973, 1974, sax solo,
> Leduc); Maï (1975, sax solo, 7', Leduc); Guernica
> (1973, sax, voice, per.); TORI (1977, sax-sp.,
> oriental flute, 12'); Phoenix (1983); Sketch for Sax-
> ophone Quartet (1973, rev. 1980, 10'); Murasakino No
> Fichu I (1981, AA, 8', Leduc); Shin-En (1979, sax-t.
> solo, 10'); Symphonic Rhapsody Maï 2 (1974, rev. 1979,
> sax, strs., 4 per., pf., cel.); HANA (1980, sax-s.
> solo); Pulse 72± (1982, sax solo, 12', Leduc, 1984);
> Sextet (1980, SATTBB, 12'); Sushigi No Bacho (1985,
> AA, prem. 29 June 1985, WSC, U. of Maryland).

Compositions dedicated to R. Noda:

> Toshi Ichiyanagi:  Trichotomy (1978, sax, pf., per.).
> Maki Ishii:  Black Intention (1978, sax solo, 8').
> Jo Kondo:  A Crow (1978, fl., sax-sp., 10').
> Yori-aki Matsudaira (b. 1931):  Gestaphony (1979, sax
>     solo).
> Isao Matsushita:  Atoll No. 2 (1983).
> Hinoharu Matsumoto:  Archipose IV (1979, sax solo).
> Danielle Henriette Sevrette (b. 1932):  In Diesem
>     Brauss (1975, sax solo).
> Akira Tamba:  Elemental II (1978, sax per.).
> Joji Yuasa:  Not I, but the wind (1976, amplified sax,
>     12').

OMURO, YUICHI
b. Omiya-Shi, Saitama-Ken, Japan
   30 October 1940

     A student of Arata Sakaguchi, Omuro graduated from
the Tokyo National University of Fine Arts and Music with
the B.A. and the M.A. degrees in 1963 and 1965 respectively.  He studied additionally at Eastman (1965-67) with
William Osseck and at Northwestern University with Frederick Hemke in the summers of 1966 and 1967.  He made his
debut in Kilbourn Hall with the Eastman-Rochester Symphony
Orchestra in December, 1966.  He performed the Concertino
by Hiroaki Minami with the Tokyo Symphonic Band in Hibiya,
Japan, in December, 1978.  Since April, 1977, he has been
Professor of Saxophone at the Tokyo National University of
Fine Arts and Music, where he replaced his first teacher.

Publications translated by Y. Omuro:

> Larry Teal:  The Art of Saxophone Playing. AEN-ON
>    Music, 1980.
>    _____: The Saxophonist's Workbook.  Pipers Group,
>    1976.


SAKAGUCHI, ARATA
b. Tokyo, Japan
   2 January 1910

   A student of the cello in Tokyo from 1927 to 1931,
Sakaguchi taught himself the saxophone by studying the
recordings and letters he received from Marcel Mule.  From
1958 to 1973, he gave the first performances in Japan of
works by Creston, Debussy, Glazunov, Ibert, Tomasi, and
several Japanese composers.  In 1951, a class of saxophone
was especially created for him at the Tokyo National University of Fine Arts and Music.

Compositions and edited works:

> Saxophone Method (1955, Zen-On Music Co., Ltd);
> Scales for Saxophone (1979, Selmer-Japan Co.).  He
> also arranged quartets from the works of Albeniz,
> Debussy, Dvorak, Granados, Mendelssohn, and Schumann,
> which have been published from 1978 to 1980 in Japan.

Compositions dedicated to A. Sakaguchi:

> Hido Kobayashi (b. 1931):  Three Pieces for Solo
>    Saxophone (1970).
> Abe Komei:  Divertimento (sax, orch.).  Prem. 19 April
>    1963, Kyoto, Japan.
> Hidetake Konoe (b. 1931):  Quintet (1968, sax, vn.,
>    vla., vcl., db.).
> Roh Matsudaira (b. 1938):  Quintet (1968, sax, strs.)
> Kazuto Osawa (b. 1926):  Sen (1973).
> Takanobu Saito (b. 1926):  Saxophone Quartet No. 2
>    (1968).
> Yuzo Toyama (b. 1930):  Serenade (1968).
> Tadashi Yamanouchi (b. 1940):  Epistoraphé (1968,
>    sax, vcl., mar., vib.).

Recordings:

> Sakaguchi recorded several small pieces for Japan
> Columbia.


SASAKI, YUJI
b. Yokohama-shi, Japan
   29 September 1950

   A student of Arata Sakaguchi at the Tokyo National
University of Fine Arts and Music from 1969 to 1975, Sasaki

studied additionally with Jean-Marie Londeix at the CNRM in
Bordeaux from 1977 to 1979.  He gave his first recital in
Tokyo in November, 1980, and is a member of the Tokyo Saxophone Ensemble.  He is an instructor of Saxophone at Musa-
shino Music Academy in Tokyo.

Compositions dedicated to Y. Sasaki:

    Tetgo Kawakami (b. 1950):  Arabesque.
    Keniro Urata (b. 1941):  Sonata.


SHIMOJI, KEIJI
b. Okinawa, Japan
   8 February 1953

    Shimoji studied at the Kunitache Music College in
Tokyo (1972-76) with Yuichi Omuro and Yushi Ishiwata, and
at the CNRM in Bordeaux with Jean-Marie Londeix (1976-78).
He gave recitals in Okinawa and Tokyo in 1979 and 1980, and
became a member of the Tokyo Kosei Wind Orchestra.  He was
a soloist at the 1979 WSC, Evanston, and was also heard
with the Ensemble International de Saxophones de Bordeaux
at the 1982 WSC, Nuremberg.

Compositions dedicated to and premiered by K. Shimoji:

    Kozo Masuda (b. 1936):  Pièce Brève (1978, sax solo,
       5').
    Toyu Nakamura (b. 1958):  HIDA (1980, sax, strs.).
    _____:  Spiritual Song from Small Island (SATB).
       Prem. 10 July 1982, WSC, Nuremberg.
    Tsuneya Tanaba:  Intermezzo '79. Prem. 28 June 1979,
       WSC, Evanston, Ill.


SMITH, COLIN
b. London, England
   16 March 1944

    After studying at the London College of Music, Smith
received the ALCM and the LLCM degrees in 1969 and 1971,
respectively.  His saxophone teacher was Charles Chapman;
he also studied flute with Richard Taylor.  Smith did
studio sessions and had a broad musical experience in London theaters before settling in Australia, where he works
as a free-lance musician with the Australian Broadcasting
Co. and performs with the Sydney Symphony and Elizabethan
Trust Orchestras.  He is the leader of the Australian Saxophone Quartet (formerly the Contemporary Saxophone Quartet),
which made its debut in Sydney Town Hall on 14 August 1977.
The quartet performed at the WSC in 1979 and has made a
tour of universities in Washington, D.C., and New York.

Compositions dedicated to C. Smith and the Australian
     Saxophone Quartet:

     James Penberthy (b. 1917):  Scherzo & Lamentoso.
          Prem. 23 May 1982, Sydney.
     Graham Powning:  3 Pieces for Saxophone Quartet.
          Prem. 3 May 1982.
          ____ :  Sonata (c. 1984).
     Jeffrey Raheb:  Saxophone Quartet No. 1.  Prem. 23
          October 1980, Sydney.
     John Sullivan (b. 1940):  Aspects of a Landcaspe
          (1983).
          ____ :  Six Sax Songs (1979, SATB).

Recording:

     Australian Saxophone Quartet (R.C.A., music by
     J. Serebrier).


UEDA, KEIJI
b. Yamaguchi, Japan
   27 December 1953

     A graduate of Hiroshima University, where he studied
from 1972 to 1978, Ueda studied saxophone with Kéizo Inoué
and Arata Sakaguchi.  From 1979 to 1982, he studied with
Jean-Marie Londeix at the CNRM at Bordeaux and was a member
of the Ensemble International de Saxophones de Bordeaux.
His Japanese debut was in Hiroshima on 12 May 1983, and
since 1985, he has been Professor of Saxophone at Toku-
shiema bunri University.

Composition:

     Ohanashi (sax solo).

Compositions dedicated to K. Ueda:

     Toshio Horiuchi (b. 1953):  Fantasy (2 saxes, pf.).
          Prem. 27 November 1975.
     Akira Kai (b. 1947):  5 Pieces (1982, SATB).
     Mio Minamikawa (b. 1958):  Objet Shop (2 saxes).
          Prem. 12 May 1983.
     Keiji Kiyoshi (b. 1933):  Sonatina (SAA).  Prem. 14
          Nov. 1977.

# NOTES

CHAPTER 1: A BRIEF HISTORICAL BACKGROUND

1.  Wally Horwood, Adolphe Sax 1814-1894 (Bramley, Hampshire, England: Bramley Books, 1979), p. 19.

2. Albert Remy, quoted in Leon Kochnitzky, Adolphe Sax and his Saxophone (New York: The World Saxophone Congress, 1972), p. 8.

3.  Edwin Fridorich, The Saxophone: A Study of Its Use in Symphonic and Operatic Literature (Ann Arbor: University Microfilms International, 1975), p. 16.

4.  Fred Hemke, The Early History of the Saxophone (Ann Arbor: University Microfilms International, 1975), pp. 306-409.

5.  Ibid., p. 268.

6.  Ibid., p. 267.

7.  Ibid., p. 255.

CHAPTER 2: PARIS CONSERVATOIRE AND OTHER NINETEENTH-CENTURY SOLOS

1.  Fred Hemke, The Early History of the Saxophone (Ann Arbor: University Microfilms International, 1975), p. 348.

2.  Jean-Marie Londeix, 125 Ans de Musique pour Saxophone (Paris: Leduc, 1971), p. 222.

3.  Ibid., p. 66.

4.  Albert Lavignac and Lionel de la Laurence, Ency-

clopédie de la Musique et Dictionaire du Conservatoire
(Paris:  Librairie Delagrave, 1931), Part 2, Vol. 3,
pp. 1660-64.

    5.  Cecil Leeson, The Saxophone Comes of Age (Chicago:
Booklet published by the National School Band Association,
no date), p. 4.


CHAPTER 3:  EARLY SAXOPHONISTS IN ENGLAND AND THE UNITED
    STATES

    1. Fred Hemke, The Early History of the Saxophone
(Ann Arbor:  University Microfilms International, 1975),
p. 373.

    2.  Henry Farmer, Handel's Kettledrums and Other
Papers on Military Music (London:  Hinrichsen Edition,
Ltd., 1965), p. 26.

    3.  Hemke, p. 410.

    4.  Ibid., p. 413.

    5.  Ibid., pp. 410-11.

    6. Wally Horwood, Adolphe Sax 1814-1894 (Bramley:
Hampshire, England:  Bramley Books, 1979), p. 151.

    7.  Hemke, p. 418.

    8.  Letter to the author from Paul E. Bierley (3 De-
cember 1983).

    9.  H. W. Schwartz, Bands of America (Garden City:
Doubleday & Co., 1957), p. 280.

    10.  Hemke, p. 421.

    11.  Schwartz, p. 252.

    12.  Letter to the author from Anne Sebastian, Librar-
ian, The Curtis Institute of Music (17 November 1982).

    13.  Sigurd Rascher, "Once More--the Saxophone," The
Etude, 60 (February, 1942), p. 132.

    14.  Hemke, p. 447.


CHAPTER 4:  VAUDEVILLE AND POPULAR AWARENESS

    1.  Wally Horwood, Adolphe Sax 1814-1894 (Bramley,
Hampshire, England:  Bramley Books, 1979), p. 154.

2. Advertisements, The Etude, 44 (January, March, 1926):   77; 231; 233.

3. Fred Hemke, The Early History of the Saxophone (Ann Arbor:   University Microfilms International, 1975), p. 108.

4. Arthur Hegvik, "The Years of Mike Guerra," The Instrumentalist, 25 (September, 1971):   29.

5. Rudy Vallee, My Time Is Your Time (New York: Ivan Obolensky, Inc., 1962),  p. 28.

6. Ross Russell, Jazz Style in Kansas City and the Southwest (Berkeley:   University of California Press, 1971), p. 233.

7. George Simon, The Big Bands (New York:   MacMillan Co., 1968), p. 12.

8. Russell, p. 2.

9. Ibid., p. 240.

10. Leroy Ostransky, Jazz City (Englewood Cliffs, N. J.:   Prentice-Hall, Inc., 1978), p. 166.

11. Russell, p. 3.

12. Ibid., p. 240.

13. Ibid., p. 30.

14. Simon, p. 27.

15. Ibid., p. 32.

16. Edwin Fridorich, The Saxophone:   A Study of Its Use in Symphonic and Operatic Literature (Ann Arbor: University Microfilms International, 1975), p. 60.

CHAPTER 5:   ANNOTATED BIBLIOGRAPHY OF SELECTED JAZZ
           SAXOPHONE SOLOISTS

1. Rudi Blesh, COMBO:   USA (Philadelphia:   Chilton Book Co., 1971), p. 46.

2. Ibid., p. 43.

3. Ibid., p. 46.

4. Bob Wilber, "Sidney Bechet:   Artist of Genius," The Clarinet, 10, 1 (Fall, 1982:   14.

5. Leonard Feather and Ira Gitler, The Encyclopedia of Jazz in the Seventies (New York: Horizon Press, 1976), p. 87.

6. Ibid., p. 151.

7. Ibid., p. 170.

8. Ibid., p. 177.

9. Rudy Vallee, My Time Is Your Time (New York: Ivan Obolensky, Inc., 1962), p. 51.

10. Feather and Gitler, p. 252.

11. Ross Russell, Jazz Style in Kansas City and the Southwest (Berkeley: University of California Press, 1971), p. 183.

12. Don Heckman, "The Development of Jazz Alto," Down Beat, 30 (23 May 1963): 21.

13. Russell, p. 205.

14. Brian Rust, The Dance Bands (London: Ian Allan, 1972), p. 46.


CHAPTER 6: ANNOTATED BIBLIOGRAPHY OF SAXOPHONE SOLOISTS
        IN THE AMERICAN HEMISPHERE

1. H. W. Schwartz, Bands of America (Garden City: Doubleday & Co., 1957), p. 252.

2. Jim Walsh, "Rudy Wiedoeft and other Saxophone Players," Hobbies (November, 1933): 122.

3. B. J. Cragun, The Business Saxophonist (Chicago: Finder & Urbanek, 1923).

4. Paul Cohen, "Percy Grainger and the Intimate Saxophone," The Saxophone Symposium, Vol. IX, 1 (Winter, 1984), p. 14.

5. Arthur Hegvik, "The Years of Mike Guerra," The Instrumentalist, 26 (Oct., 1971): 40.

6. Fred Hemke, The Early History of the Saxophone, (Ann Arbor: University Microfilms International, 1975), pp. 420-21.

7. Larry Teal, interview with author, 30 July 1983.

8. James Stoltie, "Potsdam: A Great Saxophone Peda-

gogue's Roots," The Saxophone Symposium," Vol. 4, 2
(Spring, 1979):  25.

9.  Wally Horwood, Adolphe Sax 1814-1894 (Bramley,
Hampshire, England:  Bramley Books, 1979), p. 162.

10.  Paul Creston, program for the dedication of the
C. Leeson Archival Saxophone Collection, Bracken Library,
Ball State University, 21 March 1977.

11.  Sigurd Rascher, letter of recommendation (25
November 1980).

12.  Lee Patrick, "Towards the Future with SMR," The
Saxophone Symposium, Vol. VII, 2 (Spring, 1982):  29.

13.  Larry Teal, interview.

14.  Hemke, p. 453.

15.  Letter to the author from Carl Waxman (22 October
1983).

16.  Jim Walsh, "The Wiedoefts:  Further Glimpses into
Their Musical Lives," The Saxophone Symposium, Vol. VI, 3
(Summer, 1981):  12.

17.  Ibid., Vol. VI, 1 (Winter, 1981):  22.


CHAPTER 7:  ANNOTATED BIBLIOGRAPHY OF SAXOPHONE SOLOISTS
            IN EUROPE

1.  Eugene Rousseau, Marcel Mule:  His Life and the
Saxophone (Shell Lake, Wisconsin:  Etoile, 1982), p. 17.

2.  Ibid., p. 46.

3.  Jean-Marie Londeix, 125 Ans de Musique pour
Saxophone (Paris:  Leduc, 1971), p. 77.

4.  Nils Grinde, trans. S. Hamilton, Contemporary
Norwegian Music 1920-1980 (Oslo, Hestholms Boktrykkeri,
1981), p. 63.

5.  Rousseau, p. 10.

6.  Fred Hemke, The Early History of the Saxophone
(Ann Arbor:  University Microfilms International), p. 285.

7.  Colin McCarraher, "Anatoly Vapirov:  A Saxophonist
in Leningrad," Clarinet and Saxophone 7/3 (July, 1982):  5.

8.  Ibid., p. 5.

9.   Rousseau, p. 58

10.   Pamela Weston, <u>More Clarinet Virtuosi of the Past</u>
(Bucks, England:   Halstan & Co., 1977), p. 277.

11.   Hemke, pp. 346-47.

# BIBLIOGRAPHY

Books

Anderson, E. Ruth. Contemporary American Composers.
    Boston:  G. K. Hall & Co., 1982.

ASCAP Biographical Dictionary.  4th ed.  New York: R. R.
    Bowker Co., 1908.

Baines, Anthony.  Musical Instruments Through the Ages.
    Baltimore:  Penguin Books, 1963.

Barzun, Jacques.  Berlioz and His Century.  New York:
    Meridian Books, 1956.

Bate, Philip.  "Saxophone," in The New Grove Dictionary of
    Music and Musicians.  6th ed.  Ed. Stanley Sadie.
    London:  MacMillan, 1980.

Berger, Morroe, Edward D. Berger and Patrick Jones.
    Benny Carter:  A Life in American Music.  Metuchen,
    N.J.:  The Scarecrow Press and the Institute of Jazz
    Studies, Rutgers University, 1982.

Blesh, Rudi.  Combo:  U.S.A.  Philadelphia:  Chilton Book
    Co., 1971.

_____.  Shining Trumpets.  New York:  Da Capo Press, 1958.

Budds, Michael.  Jazz in the Sixties.  Iowa City:  Univer-
    sity of Iowa Press, 1978.

Canadian Chamber Music.  Toronto:  Canadian Music Centre,
    1980.

Chilton, John.  Who's Who of Jazz.  Philadelphia:  Clifton
    Book Co., 1972.

Dawson, James. _Music for Saxophone by British Composers_.
    Needham, Maine:  Dorn Publications, 1981.

_Directory and Instrumentation_.  New York:  American Fede-
    ration of Musicians, Local 802, 1982.

Dorigne, Michel.  _Jazz, culture et société_.  Paris:  Les
    Editions Ouvrières, 1967.

Farish, Margaret.  _Orchestral Music in Print_.  Philadel-
    phia:  Musicolata, Inc., 1979.

Farmer, Henry.  _Handel's Kettledrums and Other Papers on
    Military Music_.  London:  Hinrichsen Edition, Ltd.,
    1965.

Feather, Leonard and Ira Gitler.  _The Encyclopedia of
    Jazz in the Seventies_.  New York:  Horizon Press,
    1976.

Gee, Harry R.  _Clarinet Solos de Concours, 1897-1980_.
    Bloomington, Indiana:  Indiana University Press, 1981.

_General Catalogue of Dutch Contemporary Orchestral Music,
    Chamber Music, and Music on Record_.  Amsterdam:
    Donemus, 1982.

Gourdet, Georges.  "Saxophone," in _Encyclopédie de la
    Musique_, Vol. III.  Ed. François Michel.  Paris:
    Fasquelle, 1961.

Grinde, Nils.  _Contemporary Norwegian Music, 1920-1980_.
    Oslo:  Hestholms Boktrykkeri A. S., 1981.

Harvey, Paul.  _The Saxophonist's Bedside Book_.  London:
    Fentone Music Ltd., 1981.

Hentoff, Nat and Albert McCarthy.  _Jazz_.  New York:
    Rinehard & Co., 1958.

Horwood, Wally.  _Adolphe Sax, 1814-1894_.  Bramley:  Bramley
    Books, 1980.

Howe, Mark Antony de Wolfe.  _The Boston Symphony Orchestra,
    1881-1931_.  Rev. John N. Burk.  Boston and New York:
    Houghton Mifflin Co., 1931.

Hucher, Yves.  _Florent Schmitt_.  Paris:  Editions Le Bon
    Plaisir, 1953.

_International Who's Who in Music and Musicians Direc-
    tory_.  8th ed.  Ed. Adrian Gaster.  Cambridge:
    Melrose Press, 1977.

Kinkle, Roger.  _The Complete Encyclopedia of Popular Music_

and jazz, 1900-1950. New Rochelle, New York:
Arlington House, 1974.

Kochnitzky, Leon. Adolphe Sax and His Saxophone, 3rd ed.
New York: The World Saxophone Congress, 1972.

Kroll, Oskar. The Clarinet. New York: Taplinger Publishing Co., 1968.

Lavignac, Albert and Lionel de la Laurence. Encyclopédie
de la Musique et Dictionaire du Conservatoire, Vol.
3. Paris: Librairie Delagrave, 1931.

Londeix, Jean-Marie. 125 Ans de Musique pour Saxophone.
Paris: Alphonse Leduc, 1971.

_____. Supplement, 1969-1984 to 125 Ans de Musique pour
Saxophone. Cherry Hill, New Jersey: Roncorp, 1985.

Musik in Geschichte und Gegenwart, Die. Ed. Friederich
Blume. Kassel: Barenreiter Verlag, 1953.

Musique Pour Saxophone. Paris: Alphonse Leduc, 1956.

Ostransky, Leroy. The Anatomy of Jazz. Seattle: University of Washington Press, 1960.

_____: Jazz City. Englewood Cliffs, N.J.: Prentice Hall,
Inc., 1978.

Perrin, Marcel. Le Saxophone, 2nd ed. Plan de la Tour,
Var, France: Editions d'Aujourd'hui, 1979.

Rousseau, Eugene. Marcel Mule: His Life and the Saxophone. Shell Lake, Wisconsin: Etoile, 1982.

Russell, Ross. Jazz Style in Kansas City and the Southwest. Berkeley: University of California Press, 1971.

Rust, Brian. The Dance Bands. London: Ian Allan, 1972.

Schwartz, H. W. Bands of America. Garden City, New York:
Doubleday & Company, Inc., 1957

_____. The Story of Musical Instruments. Garden City,
New York: Doubleday & Company, Inc., 1938.

Simon, George. The Big Bands. New York: Macmillan Co.,
1968.

Slonimsky, Nicolas, ed. Baker's Biographical Dictionary of
Musicians. 7th ed. New York: G. Schirmer, 1984.

Teal, Larry. The Art of Saxophone Playing. Evanston,
Illinois: Summy-Birchard, 1963.

Thiels, Victor. "Le Saxophone," in Encyclopédie de la
    Musique et Dictionaire du Conservatoire, Vol. 3.
    Paris: Librairie Delagrave, 1931.

Thomas, J. C. Chasin' the Trane. Garden City, New York:
    Doubleday & Company, Inc., 1975.

Vallee, Rudy. My Time Is Your Time. New York: Ivan
    Obolensky, Inc., 1962.

Voxman, Himmie and Lyle Merriman. Woodwind Solo and Study
    Material. Evanston, Illinois: Instrumentalist, 1975.

White, William. A History of Military Music in America.
    Westport, Connecticut: Greenwood Press, 1944.

Wilkins, Wayne. The Index of Saxophone Music. Magnolia,
    Arkansas: Music Register, 1979.


Periodicals

As. Sa. Fra. Bulletin. Paris: Association des Saxophon-
    istes de France. No. 1 (October, 1972) - No. 24
    (April, 1985).

Black, Robert. "The Saxophone in Perspective--Retrospec-
    tive and Prospective." Instrumentalist, 26 (June,
    1979): 18.

Brenta, Gaston. "Adolphe Sax et la facture instrumentale."
    Bulletin de la classe des Beaux-Arts, 49 (1967):
    54-88.

Burnau, John. "Adolphe Sax--Inventor, Part I." Instru-
    mentalist, 21 (November, 1966): 21; "Part II." 21
    (January, 1967): 42, 44, 46.

Douse, Kenneth. "The Saxophone." Instrumentalist, 2
    (November, 1947): 14-15.

Gallodoro, A. "Singing on a Sax." Woodwind World, 3
    (January-February, 1959): 7.

Grainger, Percy. "The Saxophone's Business in the Band."
    Instrumentalist, 4 (September-October, 1949): 6-7.

Heckman, D. "The Development of Jazz Alto." Down Beat,
    30 (23 May 1963): 20-21.

_____. "The Saxophone-Instrument of Jazz Innovation."
    Down Beat, 31 (21 May 1964): 17-19.

Hegvik, Arthur. "The Years of Mike Guerra, Part I."
    Instrumentalist, 25 (June, 1971): 34-36; August,

1971:   31-32; "Part II," 26 (September, 1971):   28-30;
"Part III--The Genius," 26 (October, 1971):   39-41.

Houlik, James.  "The Bray of the Saxophone."  Instrumentalist, 22 (June, 1968):   58-60.

Lysing, Mervin.  "Development of the Saxophone."  The
School Musician, 37 (April, 1966):   37, 74.

Mule, Marcel.  "The Saxophone."  Symphony, 4 (November,
1950):   7.

_____:  "The Saxophone."  Instrumentalist, 12 (April,
1958):   30.

Patrick, Lee.  "The Saxophone."  Instrumentalist, 22
(November, 1967):   70.

Quayle, Nolbert Hunt.  "Stars and Stripes Forever:  Mem-
ories of Sousa and His Men."  Instrumentalist 9
(September, 1954):   33-35, 45-46; 9 (October, 1954):
44-47, 52; 9 (November, 1954):   16-17, 46-48; 9 (December, 1954):   18-20, 40; 9 (January, 1955):   33-36;
9 (February, 1955):   40-43; 9 (March, 1955):   30-32;
9 (April, 1955):   16-18.

Rascher, Sigurd.  "A Dedicated and Devoted Sax Disciple."
Woodwind World, 4 (February, 1963):   10.

_____:  "A Master Lesson on the Ibert Concertino da Camera."
Instrumentalist, 22 (April, 1968):   36-38.

_____:  "Once More--The Saxophone."  The Etude, 60 (Feb-
ruary, 1942):   95, 131.

_____:  "The Rational Saxophone."  Woodwind Magazine, 2
(May, 1950):   4.

_____:  "The Saxophone."  Instrumentalist, 6 (October,
1951):   14-15.

Saxophone Journal.  Needham, Massachusetts:  No. 24 (Winter, 1980) - Vol. 9, No. 2 (May, 1982); Medfield, Massachusetts:  Vol. 10, No. 3 (Fall, 1985).

The North American Saxophone Alliance.  The Saxophone
Symposium.  Fulton, New York:  Vol. 1 (Winter, 1976) -
Vol. 9:  3 (Summer, 1984); Gainesville, Florida:  Vol.
9:  4 (Fall, 1984) - Vol. 10:  3 (Summer, 1985).

The World Saxophone Congress Newsletter.  Vol. I (June,
1970) - Vol. IV (1974).

## Pamphlets

Gallodoro, A. Saxophone-Clarinet Notebook. Elkart,
    Indiana: H. & A. Selmer, Inc., 1956.

Hemke, Frederick and Walker Smith. The Orchestral Saxo-
    phone. Elkart: The Selmer Co., 1975.

Leeson, Cecil. The Saxophone Comes of Age. Chicago:
    National School Band Association, no date.

Petiot, André. Catalogue de Buffet-Crampon. Paris:
    Draeger Frères, 1962.


## Dissertations and Documents

Fridorich, Edwin. "The Saxophone: A Study of Its Use in
    Symphonic and Operatic Literature." Ed. D. disser-
    tation, Columbia University, 1975.

Hemke, Fred L. "The Early History of the Saxophone."
    Dissertation, The University of Wisconsin, 1975.

Kaiser, James E. "The Saxophone in Chamber Music: An
    Annotated Bibliography of Original Published Works."
    D. Mus. document, Indiana University, 1980.

Leeson, Cecil. "The Basis of Saxophone Tone Production:
    A Critical and Analytical Study." Doc. F.A. disser-
    tation, Chicago Musical College, 1955.


## Other Sources

Beers, Thomas. Woodwind Literature Study Guide. Dallas:
    Thomas Beers, 1983.

The Edwin A. Fleisher Music Collection in the Free Library
    of Philadelphia. 2 vols. Philadelphia: 1933, 1945.

Hamel, Maurice. Notes Complémentaires sur Adolphe Sax.
    Paris: Archives of H. & A. Selmer, 1940.

Mauk, Steven. The History of the Saxophone: A Selected
    Annotated Bibliography. Ithaca, New York: Steven
    Mauk, no date.

## Programs of the World Saxophone Congress

    Bordeaux: 3-6 July 1974.
    London: 28-31 July 1976.
    Evanston, Illinois: 28 June-1 July 1979.
    Nuremberg: 7-11 July 1982.
    College Park, Maryland: 25-29 June 1985.

Letters to the Author

Bierley, Paul E., 3 December 1983.
Bogaard, Ed., 23 May 1983.
Daneels, François, 23 April and 22 November 1984.
Deakin, Gerald E., 4 January and 4 August 1983.
Deffayet, Daniel, 27 September 1981.
Douse, Kenneth, 24 January and 20 February 1983.
Fragioni, Mariano, 22 October 1984.
Gould, Bert, 11 August and 26 August 1983.
Krein, Millicent, 12 September 1983.
Lavalle, Paul, 3 October 1983.
Levin, Irving, 20 December 1982, 14 January and 28
    August 1983, 19 July 1984, 9 July and 19 September
    1985.
Londeix, Jean-Marie, 9 April and 18 December 1984,
    22 March 1985.
Lunde, Lawson, 11 August 1985.
Nozy, Norbert, 27 June 1983.
Patrick, Lee, 19 October 1984.
Rascher, Sigurd M., 15 August 1983.
Richmond, Eero, 23 July 1984.
Ripper, Peter, 18 August 1983.
Savoie, Bernard, 15 November 1984.
Sebastian, Anne, 17 November 1982 and 6 January 1984.
Taggart, Mark A., 9 October 1984.
Teal, Larry, 1 December 1982, 1 July, 14 August, 22
    August, and 21 September 1983.
Trier, Stephen, 9 September 1983.
Trisko, E. H., 23 October 1984.
Tygiel, Martha, 3 December 1981.
Van Steenberger, Anna, 28 August 1983 and 11 Sep-
    tember 1984.
Waxman, Carl, 22 October 1983 and 9 May 1984.

# APPENDIX

## Key to Publishers, Agents, and Selected Recording Companies

AA
: Agencja Autorska
Rybek Starego Miasta 27
00-272 Warsaw, Poland

ACA
: American Composers Alliance
170 W. 74th St.
New York, N.Y. 10023

Adagio-Belgica
: Adagio-Belgica
79, rue des Eperonniers
1000 Brussels, Belgium

Aebersold
: Jamey Aebersold Publ.
1211 Aebersold Drive
New Albany, IN 47150

ALF
: Alfred Music Co., Inc.
15335 Morrison St.
Sherman Oaks, CA 91403

Allans
: Allans Music
(see Australia)

Allard
: Joseph Allard, Composer
134 Downey Drive
Tenafly, NJ 07670

AMC
: American Music Center
250 W. 54th St.
New York, NY 10019

AMP
: Associated Music Publ.
(see G. Schirmer Inc.)

Andel                          Edition Andel (Elkan, U.S. Agent)
                               Madeliefjeslaan 26
                               B-8400 Oostende, Belgium

Andrieu                        (See ALF or Presser)

Arbeitsgruppe                  Arbeitsgruppe Saxophon e.V.
   Saxophon                    Günter Priesner
                               Rötenäckerstrasse 2
                               8500 Nuremberg 90, Germany

Ars Nova                       Ars Nova
                               322 Swain Ave.
                               Bloomington, IN 47401

Artisan                        Artisan Press (see PHIL)

ASCAP                          American Society of Composers,
                                  Authors, and Publishers
                               One Lincoln Plaza
                               New York, NY 10023

As.Sa.Fra.                     Association des Saxophonistes de
                                  France
                               c/o Jacques Charles
                               29, rue Miollis
                               75015 Paris, France

Australian Music               Australian Music Information
                                  Center, Ltd.
                               P.O. Box N9, Grosvenor St.
                               Sydney, NSW 2000, Australia

Ayscue                         Brian Ayscue, Composer
                               1217 Sylvan Drive
                               Haddon Heights, NJ 08035

Balamp                         Balamp Publisher
                               7340 Second Blvd.
                               Detroit, MI 48202

Bar.                           Barenreiter Verlag
                               (MMB or EAM, U.S. Agents)
                               Heinrich-Schuetz Allee 35
                               D-3500 Kassel, Germany

Barn.                          C. L. Barnhouse, Inc.
                               100 B Avenue East
                               Oskaloosa, Iowa 52577

Baron                          Baron Music Co.
                               P.O. Box 149
                               Oyster Bay, L.I., NY 11771

| | |
|---|---|
| Bauzin | Pierre Bauzin, Composer<br>51 Allée des Micocouliers<br>Hameau de Puissanton<br>06220 Vallauris, France |
| Bay | Mel Bay Publications, Inc.<br>4 Industrial Dr.<br>Pacific, MO 63069 |
| BB | Bote und Bock K. G. (AMP, U.S. Agent)<br>Hardenbergstrasse 9a<br>1 Berlin 12, Germany |
| Bel. | Belwin-Mills Publishing Corp.<br>15800 N.W. 48th Ave.<br>P.O. Box 4340<br>Miami, FL 33014 |
| Bela. | Belaieff (see B.H. or Peters) |
| Benjamin | Anton J. Benjamin (see AMP) |
| Berandol | Berandol Music, Ltd.<br>11 St. Joseph St.<br>Toronto M4Y 1J8, Canada |
| Berklee | Berklee Press<br>1265 Boylston St.<br>Boston, MA 02115 |
| BH | Boosey and Hawkes, Inc.<br>200 Smith St.<br>Farmingdale, NY 11735 |
| Bil. | Editions Billaudot<br>(Presser, U.S. Agent)<br>14, rue de l'Echiquier<br>75010 Paris, France |
| Bilik | Jerry Bilik Music, Inc.<br>Suite 500, 9107 Wilshire Blvd.<br>Beverly Hills, CA 90210 |
| Black Swan | Black Swan Publications<br>P.O. Box 7702<br>Rochester, NY 14622 |
| BMIC | British Music Information Center<br>10 Stratford Place<br>London, WIN 9AE, England |
| Bourne | The Bourne Co.<br>437 5th Ave.<br>New York, NY 10016 |

| | |
|---|---|
| Brandon | Cy Brandon, Composer<br>120 Maple St.<br>Wrightsville, PA 17368 |
| Braun | Editions Braun (see Bil.) |
| Brewster | Brewster Records<br>1822 Monroe St.<br>Evanston, IL 60202 |
| Br. H. | Breitkopf and Härtel<br>(AMP, U.S. Agent)<br>Walkmühlstrasse 52<br>D-6200 Wiesbaden, Germany |
| Brosh | Thomas D. Brosh, Composer<br>Box 440396<br>Aurora, CO 80044 |
| Broude | Alexander Broude, Inc.<br>575 Eighth Avenue<br>New York, NY 10018 |
| Brussels | Brussels Saxophone Quartet<br>(unpubl. music)<br>Av. des Cèpes, 4<br>1050 Brussels, Belgium |
| BTM | Big Three Music Corp<br>1350 Avenue of the Americas<br>New York, NY 10019 |
| CANF | Centre d'Art National Français<br>B. P. 44<br>31012 Toulouse, France |
| CBDM | Belgian Centre for Music Documentation<br>Rue d'Arlon 75-77<br>B-1040 Brussels, Belgium |
| CBS | Columbia Records, Inc.<br>51 W. 52nd St.<br>New York, NY 10019 |
| CF | Carl Fischer, Inc.<br>62 Cooper Square<br>New York, NY 10003 |
| C.G. | A. B. Carl Gehrmans Musikförlag<br>(Hemer, U.S. Agent)<br>Vasagatan 46<br>Stockholm, Sweden |
| Chandler | Erwin Chandler, Composer<br>P. O. Box 183<br>Mohnton, PA 19540 |

| | |
|---|---|
| Chang | Li-Ly Chang, Composer<br>c/o Music Dept.<br>Towson State University<br>Towson, MD 21204 |
| Chappell | Chappell and Company, Ltd.<br>(Presser, U.S. Agent)<br>50 New Bond St.<br>London W14 2BR, England |
| Chester | (See MMB) |
| Chou | Editions Choudens<br>(Peters, U.S. Agent)<br>38, rue Jean-Mermoz<br>75008 Paris, France |
| CMC | Canadian Music Center<br>1263 Bay St.<br>Toronto, Ontario M5R 1C1, Canada |
| CMIC | Czechoslovak Music Information Center<br>Besedni 3<br>Prague 1, Czechoslovakia |
| Colin | Charles Colin Music Publ.<br>315 W. 53rd St.<br>New York, NY 10019 |
| Colombo | Franco Colombo (see Bel.) |
| Colosseum | Colosseum Records<br>Case postale 112, Ch-4024<br>Bâle, Switzerland |
| Combre | Editions Combre<br>24, boulevard Poissonière<br>75009 Paris, France |
| Contemporaines | Editions Contemporaines<br>23, rue Pierre-Sémard<br>75009 Paris, France |
| Cor | Cor Publishing Co.<br>67, Bell Place<br>Massapequa, NY 11758 |
| Coronet | Coronet Recording Co.<br>4971 N. High St.<br>Columbus, Ohio |
| Costallat | (See Bil., Presser) |
| CPP | Columbia Pictures Publ.<br>P.O. Box 4340<br>Miami, FL 33014 |

| | |
|---|---|
| Crawford | Jerry Crawford, Composer<br>Sam Houston State University<br>Huntsville, TX 77340 |
| Crescendo | (See FEMA) |
| Crest | Crest Records, Inc.<br>220 Broadway<br>Huntington Station, NY 11746 |
| CRI | Composers Recording, Inc.<br>170 W. 74th St.<br>New York, NY 10023 |
| Crystal | Crystal Records, Inc.<br>2235 Willida Lane<br>Sedro Woolley, WA 98284 |
| Cumberland | Cumberland Records<br>321 Bowwood Drive<br>Nashville, TN 37217 |
| Curci | Edizioni Curci<br>(BTM, U.S. Agent)<br>Galleria del Corso 4<br>20122 Milan, Italy |
| CV | Composers Voice Records<br>(see Don., C. F. Peters) |
| Da Capo | Da Capo Press<br>227 W. 17th St.<br>New York, NY 10011 |
| Dansk | Danish Music Information Center<br>Skoubogade 2<br>DK-1158 København K, Denmark |
| Delamarre | Pierre Delamarre<br>Composer/Saxophonist<br>7, rue de Toutes-Aides<br>44600 St. Nazaire, France |
| Delrieu | Georges Delrieu<br>(Galaxy, U.S. Agent)<br>Palais Bellecour b - 14, rue Trachel<br>06 Nice, France |
| Dinant | Dinant Records<br>P.O. Box 135<br>Harned, KY 40144 |
| DiPasquale | James A. DiPasquale, Composer<br>4058 Woodman Ave.<br>Sherman Oaks, CA 91423 |

Doblinger            (See AMP)

Don.                 Donemus, Paulus
                     (Peters, U.S. Agent)
                     Potterstraat 14
                     1071 CZ Amsterdam, Holland

Dorn                 Dorn Publications
                     Needham Publishing Co.
                     P.O. Box 106
                     Medfield, MA 02052

Duckworth            William Duckworth, Composer
                     Bucknell University
                     Lewisburg, PA 17837

Dur.                 Durand et Cie
                     (Presser, U.S. Agent)
                     21, rue Charles Vernet
                     75008 Paris, France

EAM                  European American Music
                     P.O. Box 850
                     Valley Forge, PA 19482

EFM                  Editions Françaises de Musique
                     115, rue du Bac
                     75007 Paris, France

Elkan                Henri Elkan
                     1316 Walnut St.
                     Philadelphia, PA 19107

Elkan-Vogel          Elkan-Vogel (see Presser)

Emerson              June Emerson Wind Music
                     Ampleforth, Yorkshire
                     YO6 4DD, England

E.M.Tr.              Editions Musicales Transatlantiques
                     (Presser, U.S. Agent)
                     50, rue Joseph de Maistre
                     75018 Paris, France

Enchanté             Enchanté Recordings
                     14, Brenda Lane, R.R. 11
                     Muncie, IN 47302

Enoch                Enoch et Cie (see AMP)
                     27, Boulevard des Italiens
                     75009 Paris, France

Esc.                 Editions Max Eschig
                     (AMP, U.S. Agent)
                     48, rue de Rome
                     75008 Paris, France

| | |
|---|---|
| Ethos | Ethos Publications<br>P.O. Box 2043<br>Oswego, NY 13126 |
| Etoile | Etoile Music, Inc.<br>Shell Lake, WI 54871 |
| Eul. | Edition Eulenberg<br>(EAM, U.S. Agent)<br>Postfach 8134<br>Aoliswill, Germany |
| FEMA | FEMA Music Publications<br>P.O. Box 395<br>Naperville, IL 60540 |
| F. Fox | Frederick Fox, Composer<br>School of Music<br>Indiana University<br>Bloomington, IN 47401 |
| Finnish | Finnish Music Information Center<br>Runeberginkatu 15 A<br>SF-00100 Helsinki 10, Finland |
| Five Studios | Five Studios Records<br>(see Trutone) |
| Fleisher | Fleisher Collection<br>Philadelphia Free Library<br>Logan Square<br>Philadelphia, PA 19103 |
| Foley | Charles Foley Co.<br>(see Bel., CF) |
| Fox | Sam Fox Publ. Co.<br>(see CF) |
| Galaxy | Galaxy Music Co.<br>131 W. 86th St.<br>New York, NY 10024 |
| Gallet | Gallet et Fils<br>(see Elkan) |
| G.C. | (See Crest) |
| Gee | Harry R. Gee, Composer/Author<br>419 S. 32nd St.<br>Terre Haute, IN 47803 |
| General | General Music Publishing, Inc.<br>P.O. Box 267<br>Hastings-on-Hudson, NY 10706 |

| | |
|---|---|
| Ger | Gervan<br>50, Chemin de Veurglat<br>Brussels, Belgium |
| GIA | GIA Publications<br>7404 S. Mason Ave.<br>Chicago, IL 60638 |
| Gornston | David Gornston Publ.<br>(see Fox, Presser) |
| Gunmar | (See Margun) |
| Hamelle | J. Hamelle, Editeur<br>(see Presser) |
| Hansen | Wilhelm Hansen<br>(MMB, U.S. Agent)<br>Gothersgade 9-11<br>DK-1123 København, Denmark |
| Harris | Frederich Harris Music<br>Oakville, Ontario, Canada |
| Hartley | Walter S. Hartley, Composer<br>27 Lowell Place<br>Fredonia, NY 14063 |
| Harvey | Paul Harvey<br>Saxophonist/Composer<br>36 Alton Gardens<br>Twickenham, TW 27 PD, England |
| Heilner | Irwin Heilner, Composer<br>101 Dawson Ave.<br>Clifton, NJ 07012 |
| Hemer | Al. Hemer Music Corp.<br>4190 N. Buffalo St.<br>Orchard Park, NY 14127 |
| Heu. | Heugel et Cie<br>(see Leduc, Presser) |
| Highgate | Highgate Press<br>(see Galaxy) |
| Hill | William Hill<br>1125 So. 5th Ave.<br>Arcadia, CA 91006 |
| HL | Hal Leonard Publ. Co.<br>P.O. Box 13819<br>Milwaukee, WI 53213 |

| | |
|---|---|
| HMC | Horspfal Music Concern<br>1611 W. Thirty Second St.<br>Minneapolis, MN 55408 |
| Hof. | Musikverlag Friedrich Hofmeister<br>(Broude, U.S. Agent)<br>6238 Hofmein/Leipzig, Germany |
| Holland | Dulcie Holland, Composer<br>67 Kameruka Road<br>Northbridge, NSW 2063, Australia |
| Howland | Russ Howland, Composer<br>(see Hill) |
| HS | Henri Selmer<br>(see Bil.) |
| Instrumentalist | The Instrumentalist<br>1418 Lake St.<br>Evanston, Il 60201 |
| IMC | International Music Co.<br>545 Fifth Ave.<br>New York, NY 10017 |
| Intersong | (See Chappell, Presser) |
| Jecklin | Jecklin Records<br>(see Colosseum) |
| JFC | Japan Federation of Composers<br>Ohrinato Bldg. 14<br>Suga-Cho Shinsuku-ku<br>Tokyo, Japan |
| Jobert | Editions Jobert<br>(see Presser)<br>76, rue Quincampoix<br>75003 Paris, France |
| Kendor | Kendor Music, Inc.<br>P.O. Box 178<br>Delevan, NY 14042 |
| Kjos | Neil A. Kjos Music Co.<br>4382 Jutland Dr.<br>San Diego, CA 92117 |
| Kunzelmann | Edition Kunzelmann<br>305 Bloomfield Ave.<br>Nutley, NY 07110 |
| Lamb | John David Lamb, Composer<br>1907 E. Blaine<br>Seattle, WA 98112 |

| | |
|---|---|
| Lang | Lang Music Publ.<br>Box 11021<br>Indianapolis, IN 46201 |
| Leduc | Alphonse Leduc & Cie<br>175, rue St. Honoré<br>75040 Paris, France |
| Leeds | (See Bel.) |
| Lem. | Henri Lemoine & Cie<br>(Presser, U.S. Agent)<br>17, rue Pigalle<br>75009 Paris, France |
| Lienau | (See Peters) |
| Litolff | (See Peters) |
| Lombardo | Robert Lombardo, Composer<br>1040 W. Wellington<br>Chicago, IL 60657 |
| Lud. | Ludwig Music Publ. Co.<br>557 East 140 St.<br>Cleveland, OH 44110 |
| Lunde | Lawson Lunde, Composer<br>1420 S. Busse<br>Mt. Prospect, IL 60056 |
| Ly | Harald Lyche & Co.<br>Post bosk 2171 Strømsø<br>3000 Drammen, Norway |
| Marbot | Marbot Edition<br>(see Peer) |
| Marg. | Margaritat<br>(see Bil.) |
| Margun | Margun Music, Inc.<br>167 Dudley Road<br>Newton Center, MA 02159 |
| Marks | (See Bel.) |
| Martin | Robert Martin Editions Musicales<br>Boite Postale 502<br>71009 Mâcon, France |
| Mason | Lucas Mason, Composer<br>234 W. 13th St.<br>New York, NY 10011 |

Maurer                    Maurer, Editions Musicales
                          7, avenue du Verseau
                          B-1150 Brussels, Belgium

MCA                       MCA Music
                          445 Park Avenue
                          New York, NY 10022

MHS                       Musical Heritage Society
                          14 Park Road
                          Tinton Falls, NJ 07724

Milestone                 Milestone Records
                          10th and Parke
                          Berkeley, CA 94710

MM                        McGinnis & Marx
                          133 Seventh Avenue
                          New York, NY 10014

MMB                       Magnamusic-Baton, Inc.
                          10370 Page Industrial Blvd
                          St. Louis, MO 63132

MMO                       Music Minus One
                          (see Bel.)

Modern                    Edition Modern
                          Elizabethstrasse 38
                          D-8000 München 40, Germany

Mol.                      Molenaar's Muziekcentrale N.V.
                          Industrieweg 23, Postbus 19
                          1520 AA Wormerveer, Holland
                          or:
                          G & M International Music Dealers, Inc.
                          (U.S. Agent)
                          Box 2098
                          Northbrook, IL 60062

NASA                      North American Saxophone Alliance
                          The Saxophone Symposium
                          Thomas L. Liley, Editor
                          University of Kansas
                          Lawrence, KS 66045

NMIC                      Norwegian Music Information Center
                          Tordenskjoldsgate 6 B
                          N-Oslo 1, Norway

Noël                      Pierre Noël
                          (see Presser)

Norsk                     Norsk Musikforlag
                          (see MMB)

| | |
|---|---|
| Nov. | Novello & Co., Ltd.<br>(Presser, U.S. Agent)<br>Borough Green, Seven Oaks<br>Kent, England |
| Otama | Otama Music<br>Box 18445<br>Cleveland, OH 44118 |
| Oxford | Oxford University Press, Inc.<br>200 Madison Ave.<br>New York, N.Y. 10016 |
| Pan | Edition Pan<br>Pl 144<br>00101 Helsinki, Finland |
| PAS | Paul Schmitt Publications<br>110 N. 5th St.<br>Minneapolis, MN 55403 |
| PBN | Bibliothèque Nationale<br>Dept. de la Musique<br>2, rue Louvois<br>75002 Paris, France |
| Peer | Peer-Southern-Organisation<br>(see SMPC) |
| Penberthy | James Penberthy, Composer<br>1 O'Connell St.<br>Kangaroo Point<br>Old 4169, Australia |
| Percussion Plus | Percussion Plus<br>P.O. Box 307<br>Winchester, VA 22601 |
| Peters | C. F. Peters Corp.<br>373 Park Ave. S.<br>New York, NY 10016 |
| Phil. | Philharmusica Corp.<br>(Autograph Editions)<br>110 W. Crooked Hill Rd.<br>Pearl River, NY 10965 |
| Philippo | Edition Philippo<br>(see Combre) |
| Polish | Polish Music Center<br>(see AA for address) |
| Presser | Theodore Presser Co.<br>Bryn Mawr, PA 19010 |

| | |
|---|---|
| Price | Paul Price Publications<br>477 Kipp St.<br>Teaneck, NJ 07666 |
| Pro Art | (See Bel.) |
| PWM | Polskie Wydawnictwo Muzyczne<br>(Belwin, U. S. Agent)<br>Krakowskie Przedmiescie 7<br>Warszawa, Poland |
| RE | Ries & Erler, Berlin<br>(see Peters, U.S. Agent) |
| Ricordi | (See Bel.) |
| Richardson | Louis Richardson, Composer<br>School of Music, SUNY<br>Fredonia, NY 14063 |
| Robbins | Robbins Music Corp.<br>(see BTM) |
| Roncorp | Roncorp<br>P.O. Box 724<br>Cherry Hills, NJ 08003 |
| RR | Editions Rideau Rouge<br>(see Presser) |
| Rubank | Rubank, Inc.<br>16215 N.W. 15th Ave.<br>Miami, FL 33169 |
| Runyon | Runyon Products, Inc.<br>P.P. Box 1018<br>Opelousas, LA 70570 |
| Sal. | Editions Salabert<br>(G. Schirmer, U.S. Agent)<br>22, rue Chauchat<br>75009 Paris, France |
| Sch. F. | Schott Frères<br>(Elkan and EAM, U.S. Agents)<br>30, rue Saint-Jean<br>1000 Bruxelles, Belgium |
| Schilling | Hans Schilling, Composer<br>Norikerstrasse 1933<br>8500 Nuremberg, W. Germany |
| Schirmer | G. Schirmer, Inc.<br>866 Third Ave.<br>New York, NY 10022 |

| | |
|---|---|
| Schott | Schott & Co., Ltd.<br>(see MAG, Bel.) |
| Seesaw | Seesaw Music Corp<br>2067 Broadway<br>New York, NY 10023 |
| Sha. | Shawnee Press<br>Delaware Water Gap, PA 18237 |
| Sik. | Editions Sikorski<br>(see Bel.) |
| Ska. | Skandinavisk Musikforlag<br>Borgerdage 2<br>Kǿbenhavn, Denmark |
| SMC | Southern Music Co.<br>Box 329<br>San Antonio, TX 78292 |
| SMPC | Peer Southern Organization<br>1740 Broadway<br>New York, NY 10019 |
| Spratt | Spratt Music Publishers<br>170 N.E. 33rd St.<br>Ft. Lauderdale, FL 33334 |
| Smithsonian | Smithsonian Collection Recordings<br>(see CBS) |
| STIM | Swedish Music Information Center<br>Box 5091<br>S-102 Stockholm, Sweden |
| Studio | Studio P/R<br>(see CPP) |
| Swiss | Schweizerlishes Musik Archiv<br>Bellariastrasse 82<br>CH-8038, Zurich, Switzerland |
| Tenuto | Tenuto<br>(see Presser) |
| Tritone | Tritone Press<br>(see Presser) |
| Trutone | Trutone Records<br>163 Terrace St.<br>Haworth, NJ 07641 |
| UME | Union Musical Espanolo<br>(AMP, U.S. Agent) |

| | |
|---|---|
| Uni. | Universal Edition<br>(EAM, U.S. Agent)<br>Postfach 130<br>A-1015 Wien, Austria |
| University Micro-<br>films | University Microfilms International<br>P.O. Box 1764<br>Ann Arbor, MI 48106 |
| University Press | University Press<br>P.O. Box 1267<br>Ann Arbor, MI 48106 |
| Wa | Waterloo Music Co., Ltd.<br>Waterloo, Ontario, Canada |
| Wahr | George Wahr<br>316 State St.<br>Ann Arbor, MI 48108 |
| Warner Bros. | Warner Bros. Publ.<br>265 Secaucus Rd.<br>Secaucus, NJ 07094 |
| Werder | Felix Werder, Composer<br>3/374 Auburn Road<br>Hawthorn, VIC 3122, Australia |
| Wilder | (See Margun) |
| WIM | Western International Music<br>2859 Holt Ave.<br>Los Angeles, CA 90034 |
| Wingert | Wingert-Jones Music, Inc.<br>Box 1878<br>Kansas City, MO 64141 |
| Witmark | (See Warner Bros.) |
| Worley | John Worley, Composer<br>64 Woodside Ave.<br>Oneonta, NY 13820 |
| Wyman | Laurence Wyman, Composer/Saxophonist<br>School of Music, SUNY<br>Fredonia, NY 14063 |
| Ybarra | Ybarra Music<br>P.O. Box 665<br>Lemon Grove, CA 92045 |
| Yoshioka | Emmett Yoshioka, Composer<br>3364 Hardesty St.<br>Honolulu, HA 96816 |

Zimmermann                Zimmermann
                          (Peters, U.S. Agent)
                          Postfach 4293
                          6 Frankfurt/Am Main, Germany

Zalo                      Zalo Publications
                          P.O. Box 913
                          Bloomington, IN 47402

# INDEX